204979

D1758700

A Historical Guide to NGOs in Britain

Also by the authors:

Matthew Hilton, James McKay, Nick Crowson & Jean-François Mouhot, *The Politics of Expertise: How NGOs Shaped Modern Britain* (Oxford: Oxford University Press, 2012)

Matthew Hilton & James McKay (eds), *The Ages of Voluntarism: How We Got to the Big Society* (Oxford: British Academy/Oxford University Press, 2011)

Nick Crowson, Matthew Hilton & James McKay (eds), *NGOs in Modern Britain: Non-State Actors in Society and Politics since 1945* (Basingstoke: Palgrave, 2009)

Matthew Hilton, *Choice & Justice: Forty Years of the Malaysian Consumer Movement* (Penang: Universiti Sains Malaysia Press, 2009)

Matthew Hilton, *Prosperity for All: Consumer Activism in an Era of Globalization* (Ithaca, NY, 2009)

Marie-Emmanuelle Chessel, Alain Chatriot & Matthew Hilton, (eds), *Au nom du consommateur: la consommation entre mobilisation sociale et politique publique dans les pays occidentaux au XX siécle* (Paris: La Decouverte, 2004)

Matthew Hilton, *Consumerism in Twentieth-Century Britain: The Search for a Historical Movement* (Cambridge, 2003)

Martin Daunton & Matthew Hilton, (eds), *The Politics of Consumption: Material Culture and Citizenship in Europe and America* (Oxford: Berg, 2001)

Matthew Hilton, *Smoking in British Popular Culture, 1800–2000* (Manchester, 2000)

Nick Crowson, *Britain and Europe: A Political History since 1918* (Abingdon: Routledge, 2010)

Nick Crowson, *The Conservative Party and European Integration since 1945: At the Heart of Europe?* (Abingdon: Routledge, 2006)

Nick Crowson, *The Longman Companion to the Conservative Party since 1830* (Harlow: Longman, 2001)

Nick Crowson (ed.), *Fleet Street, Press Barons and Politics: The Journals of Collin Brooks, 1932–1940* (Cambridge University Press/Royal Historical Society, 1998)

Nick Crowson, *Facing Fascism: The Conservative Party and the European Dictators 1935–40* (London: Routledge, 1997)

Jean-François Mouhot, *Des Esclaves Energétiques: Réflexions sur le changement climatique* (Seysel, Champ Vallon, 2011)

Jean-François Mouhot, *Les Réfugiés acadiens en France (1758-1785): l'impossible réintégration?* (Québec: Septentrion, 2009; second edition, Rennes: Presses Universitaires de Rennes, 2012)

Charles-François Mathis and Jean-François Mouhot, ed., *Une Protection de l'Environnement à la Française (XIXe-XXe siècles)* (Seysel: Champ Vallon, forthcoming)

A Historical Guide to NGOs in Britain

Charities, Civil Society and the Voluntary Sector since 1945

Matthew Hilton
Professor of Social History, University of Birmingham

Nick Crowson
Reader in Contemporary British History, University of Birmingham

Jean-François Mouhot
Marie Curie Research Fellow, Georgetown University & Ecole des Hautes Etudes en Sciences Social, Paris

James McKay
Postdoctoral Research Fellow, University of Birmingham

UCB

204979

© Matthew Hilton, Nicholas Crowson, Jean-François Mouhot & James McKay 2012

All rights reserved. No reproduction, copy or transmission of this publication may be made without written permission.

No portion of this publication may be reproduced, copied or transmitted save with written permission or in accordance with the provisions of the Copyright, Designs and Patents Act 1988, or under the terms of any licence permitting limited copying issued by the Copyright Licensing Agency, Saffron House, 6-10 Kirby Street, London EC1N 8TS.

Any person who does any unauthorized act in relation to this publication may be liable to criminal prosecution and civil claims for damages.

The authors have asserted their right to be identified as the authors of this work in accordance with the Copyright, Designs and Patents Act 1988.

First published 2012 by
PALGRAVE MACMILLAN

Palgrave Macmillan in the UK is an imprint of Macmillan Publishers Limited, registered in England, company number 785998, of Houndmills, Basingstoke, Hampshire RG21 6XS.

Palgrave Macmillan in the US is a division of St Martin's Press LLC, 175 Fifth Avenue, New York, NY 10010.

Palgrave Macmillan is the global academic imprint of the above companies and has companies and representatives throughout the world.

Palgrave® and Macmillan® are registered trademarks in the United States, the United Kingdom, Europe and other countries

ISBN: 978-0-230-30444-4

This book is printed on paper suitable for recycling and made from fully managed and sustained forest sources. Logging, pulping and manufacturing processes are expected to conform to the environmental regulations of the country of origin.

A catalogue record for this book is available from the British Library.

A catalog record for this book is available from the Library of Congress.

10   9   8   7   6   5   4   3   2   1
21   20   19   18   17   16   15   14   13   12

Printed and bound in Great Britain by
CPI Antony Rowe, Chippenham and Eastbourne

Contents

List of Abbreviations and Sources

The publications, websites or databases listed below have been used to source many of the figures presented in this volume. For the sake of brevity and clarity, instead of providing bibliographical information each time for these, we have used the following abbreviations:

Annual reports and accounts, organisations concerned: these have been consulted in one or more of the following places: (a) (in the case of companies) in the form of hard files, microfiches or electronic copies supplied by Companies House (www.companieshouse.gov.uk); (b) in other places such as the archives of the organisation concerned, or libraries or repositories such as the British Library, the Wellcome Library or other university libraries.

Beveridge 1949: William Henry Beveridge, *The Evidence for Voluntary Action: Being Memoranda by Organisations and Individuals and Other Material Relevant to Voluntary Action* (London, 1949).

CAF: Charities Aid Foundation.

Charity Commission: The Charity Commission website provides figures and information both for individual charities and for the whole sector. See: www.charity-commission.gov.uk.

Charity Statistics: Refers to an annual report published by CAF between 1977 and 2007, under slightly different titles: *Charity Statistics* (1977/78–1985/86); *Charity Trends* (1987–93); *Dimensions of the Voluntary Sector* (1995–99); *Dimensions* (2000 and 2002); *Charity Trends* (2003–07).

DANGO: Database of Archives of UK Non-Governmental Organisations since 1945, available at: www.ngo.bham.ac.uk.

Guardian Directory of Pressure Groups: Chris Bazlinton, Anne Cowen and Peter Shipley, *The 'Guardian' Directory of Pressure Groups & Representative Associations* (London, 1976).

Guardian* & *The Times: Unless otherwise indicated, figures showing the total number of mentions of particular NGOs in the *Guardian* have been compiled using ProQuest Historical Newspapers *The Guardian* and *The Observer* (1945–2003) and Nexis (2003–07). For *The Times*, the *Official Index to The Times* (formerly known as *Palmer's Index to The Times Newspaper*) has been used.

NCVO: National Council for Voluntary Organisations.

NCVO Almanac: Refers to a report that has been published by the NCVO since 1996, initially every two years, and more recently yearly, under slightly different titles: *The UK Voluntary Sector Statistical Almanac* (1996); *The UK Voluntary Sector*

Almanac (1998–2007); *The UK Civil Society Almanac* (2008–). Some of these reports are available free on the NCVO website at: www.ncvo-vol.org.uk/almanac.

Social Trends: Published annually by the Office for National Statistics (ONS) since 1970. The most recent reports are available at: www.statistics.gov.uk/statbase/Product.asp?vlnk=5748.

Top 3000 Charities: Refers to a guide published annually by CaritasData since 1993, under slightly different titles: *Henderson Top 1000 charities* (1993); *Henderson Top 2000 charities* (1994–96); *Baring Asset Management Top 3000 Charities* (1997–99); *Top 3000 Charities* (2000–) (under slightly different titles: *Dresdner RCM Global Investors Top 3000 charities*; *Allianz Dresdner Asset Management Top 3000 charities*; *RCM Allianz Dresdner Asset Management Top 3000 charities*).

UK Giving: Annual report published jointly by CAF and the NCVO since 2004. The reports are available at: www.cafonline.org/default.aspx?page=17922.

Wells Collection: Wells International donors advisory service, *1973 Supplemental Edition of the 1971 Wells Collection of U.K. Charitable Giving Reports* (London, 1975).

Wolfenden 1978: John Wolfenden, *The Future of Voluntary Organisations: Report of the Wolfenden Committee* (London, 1978).

World Values Survey: Data from the World Values Survey has been downloaded from their website: www.worldvaluessurvey.org.

Yearbook of International Organizations: Union of International Associations, *Yearbook of International Organizations* (published annually since 1948). See: www.uia.be/yearbook.

All URLs were confirmed active on 12 April 2011.

List of Tables, Figures and Boxes

The datasets for the figures in this volume can be seen at www.ngo.bham.ac.uk

Tables

Figures

Boxes

Preface

The 'Big Society', announced by the new Conservative-Liberal Democrat coalition government in 2010, has certainly changed the way we talk about the voluntary sector, charities, non-governmental organisations (NGOs), civil society or, as the previous Labour government put it, the third sector. The name might be different, but the accompanying debate remains the same. Essentially, it revolves around a series of questions that have concerned policy makers, activists, sociologists and political scientists for decades: what is the relationship between the governmental and non-governmental sectors? What is the overall contribution of voluntarism to society? How has this changed over time? Have citizens become more apathetic, and are they less likely to 'join in'? What motivates citizens to unite and work together in organisations?

So many of these questions are historical. That is, they are predicated on assumptions about the past that are constructed as norms, often from which we are supposed to have deviated. Usually, the evidence presented for these contemporary historical claims is rather shaky, and compiling the data for this book has made this even clearer. The claims often rest on studies that are not easily comparable across time, or opinion polls where the answer given by respondents vary widely depending on the question being asked. Similarly, gathering historical data on organisational income can be a treacherous task. As a result, claims of growth or decline of the sector (including those presented in the following pages) should be treated with due caution. Notwithstanding this general disclaimer, this book is designed to provide a solid base of historical evidence. As well as being a starting point for all historians interested in NGOs, charities and voluntary organisations, the volume is also intended as a resource for academics and policy makers today. If claims are to be made about the deviations of society and politics from some given point in the past, then it is at least to be hoped that the data presented in this volume give policy making a greater and more informed historical consciousness.

This book is one outcome of a Leverhulme Trust-funded project on 'Non-Governmental Organisations in Britain since 1945' (Grant number F00094AV) on which Matthew Hilton and Nicholas Crowson were the principal and co-investigators, and James McKay and Jean-François Mouhot were the two research fellows. A companion volume, *The Politics of Expertise*, will be published subsequently in which we offer our own interpretations of the data presented here. Some of the preliminary work was undertaken during an earlier project, on which the four authors collaborated: the Database of Archives of UK Non-Governmental Organisations since 1945 (www.dango.bham.ac.uk), funded by the Arts and Humanities Research Council (Grant Number 112181), and for which the assistance of Sarah Davies and Caroline Mullen must be acknowledged.

We are especially grateful to Michael Strang, formerly of Palgrave, who commissioned this work and guided us through various production issues. Thanks are also due to Ruth Ireland, editor at Palgrave, and Yvonne Taylor, at Companies House in Cardiff, who went out of her way to help locate and access records of various organisations. We also would like to thank authors and editors who have allowed us to reproduce some of their work (the source for all material appears under each individual figure or table). Every reasonable effort was made to get permissions for all material reproduced in the volume.

The final completion of the manuscript would not have been possible without the really quite excellent work of Jamie Perry. He was specially commissioned to undertake some targeted data collection, but his own reports and interpretations of the data actually feed through into any number of the following chapters. We are grateful to Chris Moores, a colleague at Birmingham, whose own research on civil liberties has addressed many of the concerns of this book and who kindly agreed to write the entry on Martin Ennals in Chapter 5. We would also like to thank Mathew Cooke for his research assistance during the summer of 2010, and Michael Bichard, Nicholas Deakin and Pat Thane for their helpful advice about the shape of the project.

The actual amount of work necessary to collect and compile all the material was seriously underestimated. We are therefore especially grateful to our project administrator, Herjeet Marway, who has kept us all organised these last three years and who, at times, became a researcher herself in a field far removed from her own interests in global ethics and philosophy.

The datasets for the figures in this volume can be seen at www.ngo.bham.ac.uk. Additional figures with datasets that could not be included in this volume due to space considerations are also located there.

1
Definitions

People have always gathered together to try and influence the world around them. That, thankfully, is a constant. What changes is how we as a society think of them, what we call them, and how we analyse, regulate and classify them. The varied terminology can be bewildering to a newcomer – charities, voluntary groups, pressure groups, new social movements, non-governmental organisations, the third sector, civil society, the Big Society – the list goes on and on. Providing precise definitions for what sorts of organisations these labels embrace (and exclude) has, moreover, been recognised by many as a hopeless task. But despite that, definitions are still worth bothering with. Each label carries with it a distinct set of connotations, denoting particular ways of looking at society, different conceptions of the role of social action and, often, the precise historical contexts from which these terms emerged. These can tell us a lot about changing assumptions about social activism and its role in society.

Charities

The only term actually defined by law is 'charity'. Until the law was updated in 2006, the definition came from the preamble to a seventeenth-century law, the 1601 Statute of Uses (see Box 1.1).

Although the 1601 Act was repealed in 1888, the preamble was retained, and was summarised by the judge, Lord Macnaghten, in the Pemsel case shortly afterwards. Macnaghten rationalised the long lists of the preamble into four 'heads of charity', and it was this definition that passed into common usage: '"Charity" in its legal sense comprises four principal divisions: trusts for the relief of poverty; trusts for the advancement of education; trusts for the advancement of religion; and trusts for other purposes beneficial to the community, not falling under one of the previous heads.'

The task of policing this definition, and compliance with the law more generally, fell in England and Wales to the Charity Commissioners. The Commissioners were established in the mid nineteenth century; their role was revised and expanded

---

Box 1.1: What is a charity? (I)

Preamble to the Elizabethan Statute of Charitable Uses, 1601:

'Whereas Lands, Tenements, Rents, Annuities, Profits, Hereditaments, Goods, Chattels, Money and Stocks of Money have been heretofore given, limited, appointed and assigned as well by the Queen's most Excellent Majesty, and Her most noble Progenitors, as by sundry other well disposed Persons, for some Relief of aged, impotent and poor People; some for the Maintenance of Sick and Maimed Soldiers and Mariners, Schools of Learning, free Schools and Scholars in Universities, some for the Repair of Bridges, Ports, Havens, Causeways, Churches, Sea-Banks, and Highways; some for the Education and Preferment of Orphans; some for or toward the Relief, Stock or Maintenance for Houses of Correction; some for Marriages of Poor Maids; some for Supportation, Aid and Help of young Tradesmen, Handicraftsmen, and Persons decayed, and others for Relief or Redemption of Prisoners or Captives; and for Aid or Ease of any poor Inhabitants concerning payment of Fifteens, setting out of Soldiers or other Taxes ...'

Report of the Committee on the Law and Practice Relating to Charitable Trusts, Cmd. 8710 (London, 1952), p. 31.

---

by the 1960 Charities Act, thereby inaugurating the current system of oversight. The Commissioners therefore became the key arbiters in the lives of charities. This was true in general terms of regulatory oversight, but particularly so for those who sought to move beyond providing support or services, and actually influence the society around them. Seeking to generate or influence social change could be a perilous thing for charities to do, as their status (and the reputational and financial benefits it brought with it) was in part dependent on them not being 'political'.

The definition of what constituted being overly 'political' became a running source of contention. Although, as we will see, the term can encompass a broad range of activities, here it was principally taken to mean 'party political', seeking to influence the legislature and change the law. At least until restrictions were progressively eased from the 1990s, if was felt that while a charity could properly respond to government consultations, or provide members of parliament with briefing materials, anything that led the Commissioners to believe that a charity was seeking to actually change the law could result in the charity's trustees being found in breach of trust, and legal proceedings to recoup funds improperly spent. The international development sector in particular came under the Commissioners' scrutiny. Oxfam, for example, was investigated in the 1970s and the 1990s. War on Want, meanwhile, was under scrutiny throughout the 1980s, both for activities deemed political, and more general failures of administration. A damning report was published by the Commissioners in 1991, detailing the charity's failings, while the charity, chastened by a series of organisational crises, resolved to work closely with the Commission going forward.

The unforgiving nature of charity law in this respect was such that many campaigning groups formed in the 1960s and 1970s deliberately chose not to register as charities, so as not to incur these restrictions. The environmental groups Greenpeace and Friends of the Earth followed this route (albeit also setting up ancillary charitable arms for their purely educational and research work). So did the World Development Movement, established by international development charities as a specifically campaigning group at the end of the 1960s, following the failure of a previous (charitable) collaborative effort, Action for World Development, to pass muster with the Commissioners. Amnesty provides a counter-example. Over a number of years the organisation attempted to establish either a charitable arm, or reconstitute itself fully as a charity. Following an unsuccessful appeal to the High Court in the early 1980s, a charitable arm was finally established in April 1986.

In recent years, however, governments have taken a more permissive view of political and campaigning activities by charities. Furthermore, in 2006, the 1601 definition of what constituted charitable purposes was finally disposed of, and a new definition became law (see Box 1.2).

Box 1.2: What is a charity? (II)

Under the 2006 Charities Act, charities are those institutions established for charitable purposes only, for the public benefit and working for:

- the prevention or relief of poverty
- the advancement of education
- the advancement of religion
- the advancement of health or the saving of lives
- the advancement of citizenship or community development
- the advancement of the arts, culture, heritage or science
- the advancement of amateur sport
- the advancement of human rights, conflict resolution or reconciliation or the promotion of religious or racial harmony or equality and diversity
- the advancement of environmental protection or improvement
- the relief of those in need by reason of youth, age, ill-health, disability, financial hardship or other disadvantage
- the advancement of animal welfare
- the promotion of the efficiency of the armed forces of the Crown, or of the efficiency of the police, fire and rescue services or ambulance services
- any other purposes either recognised under existing charity law, or within the spirit of or analogous to any purposes falling within any of the preceding criteria.

Adapted from Charities Act 2006, available at: www.legislation.gov.uk/ukpga/2006/50.

Voluntary sector

Critics of activist charities will often assert that these groups should busy themselves looking after the less fortunate, rather than meddling in political matters. In doing so, they invoke an idea of selfless and supposedly apolitical voluntarism – people coming together of their own free will, to work for the common good. Sometimes the idea of voluntarism has been ridiculed, with participants being portrayed as middle-class do-gooders, or patronising Lady Bountifuls. At other times, it has been celebrated as the grassroots source of democracy and social engagement – a tradition that goes back to the nineteenth century work of Alexis de Tocqueville. And whether laughed at or lionised, the terminology of voluntarism, voluntary organisations, and the voluntary sector remains relevant today. Witness, for example, the names of prominent umbrella groups for the sector: the National Council for Voluntary Organisations, or the Association of Chief Executives of Voluntary Organisations. Precisely what it means, however, is a long-running problem.

William Beveridge, father of Britain's welfare state, made one of the many attempts to define voluntary action in his report of the same name in 1948 (see Box 1.3).

Box 1.3: What is a voluntary organisation? (I)

'The term "Voluntary Action", as used here, means private action, that is to say action not under the direction of any authority wielding the power of the State ... The distinctively "voluntary" character of [voluntary organisations] is the product, not of the kind of workers they employ, but of their mode of birth and method of government. A voluntary organization properly speaking is an organization which, whether its workers are paid or unpaid, is initiated and governed by its own members without external control ... [Furthermore] the term Voluntary Action does imply that the agency undertaking it has a will and life of its own.'

William Beveridge, *Voluntary Action* (London, 1948), p. 8.

That Beveridge stepped into this territory at all carries with it a certain irony, for the terminology of voluntarism, and in particular its supposed heyday in Victorian England, has long been used by critics of Beveridge's welfare state to provide an alternative vision of society, where the role of taxation and state provision is dramatically curtailed. And the language of voluntarism was not without political connotations for Beveridge, either. He saw the freedom to gather together and pursue common aims as a hallmark of the British way of life. In doing so, he explicitly drew reference to the European totalitarianism so recently defeated. In seeing it as a national characteristic, rather than a particular set of institutions or organisations, Beveridge also sidestepped the need to define his field in precise terms. He was concerned in his report specifically with the voluntary social services, and in particular what their ongoing role was in the new welfare state he had done so much to design. Beyond the social services, however, the field of voluntarism was simply acknowledged as infinitely wide and varied, with no need for further delineation.

Others have attempted more encompassing definitions, for example classifying organisations in terms of their shared characteristics. One influential report by Barry Knight recognised seven criteria for voluntary groups: independent beginnings; self-governing structures; independence from other agencies; independent financing; the use of volunteers; the distribution of surpluses not for profit; and a worthwhile purpose.[1]

Any such attempts are bound to be contentious. Compare, for example, Beveridge and Knight on whether or not volunteers are a necessary part of the voluntary

---

1   Barry Knight, *Voluntary Action* (London, 1993), pp. 73–4.

sector. For Beveridge, the term voluntarism refers to the fact that these groups have constituted freely, without state direction, and implies nothing about the tenure of those who work within them. For Knight, on the other hand, volunteers are one of his seven criteria (although he also, like Beveridge, stresses the significance of independence). Also worth noting is Knight's final criteria: worthwhile purpose. The assumption that the voluntary sector is something that does 'good' things is endemic – while Sunday League football teams would be included, organised groups of football hooligans would not. Subjective value judgements are implicit in the process of constructing definitions, however scientific and objective they may appear.

Another approach to defining the sector is to consider the different areas it works in (see Box 1.4).

Box 1.4: What is a voluntary organisation? (II)

Salamon and Anheier's International Classification of Non-Profit Organisations (ICNPO) provides twelve broad headings:

1. Culture and recreation
2. Education and research
3. Health
4. Social services
5. Environment
6. Development and housing
7. Law, advocacy and politics
8. Philanthropic intermediaries and voluntarism promotion
9. International activities
10. Religion
11. Business and professional associations, unions
12. Other groups not classified elsewhere.

Lester Salamon and Helmut Anheier, *Defining the Non-Profit Sector* (Manchester, 1997), pp. 70–4.

This definition comes from a US-based research project, and therefore uses the terminology of non-profits, rather than voluntarism. In doing so, it is not so much an alternative to Knight's internal characteristics approach (it is first necessary to define what non-profits are), but rather an extension of it – looking at the fields where they work. But what both approaches allow, through the classifications, is quantification: just how big is this sector? Such questions are not of merely academic interest – they have a political dimension. If umbrella bodies are able to point to a particular number of organisations in their sector – and the bigger the better – they are in a stronger position to lobby policy makers and politicians for consideration, whether in the form of funding, recognition, or favourable structural change.

Pressure groups

In doing so, the sector's advocates are acting as pressure groups, in itself a further term that litters the field. Pressure groups have been classified as 'organized entities that have characteristics such as defined membership, stated objectives in relation to public policy and, often, a paid staff working to attain those objectives'.[1]

Whereas the voluntary sector theoretically extends from major organisations like housing associations and household names like Save the Children, all the way down to reading clubs and flower arranging societies, those who study pressure groups have a much more focused subject. They are acknowledged to be that which charities were for a long time forbidden from being – actors in the policy process. What's more, like voluntarism, the term 'pressure group' also has particular historical connotations. The apotheosis of the pressure group system, in Britain at least, came with the post-war planning consensus, when business and the unions were the acknowledged second and third elements of a tripartite conception of policy making. While this was always something of a simplification, with the advent of Thatcherism and its disdain for consensus, it became a positive anachronism. However, even the Thatcher governments saw the need to consult with relevant groups when framing policy, and the terminology has developed to discriminate between those groups embedded within and recognised by that process (insider groups) and those without such recognition, be it by choice or exclusion (outsider groups). Given that the whole conception of pressure groups is the exertion of influence, insider status is therefore the goal (see Box 1.5).

Box 1.5: What is an insider group?

Three elements to an insider group:

1. Recognised by government as being legitimate representative of a given interest or cause
2. Engaging in formal and informal consultation with government, by virtue of that recognition
3. Agreeing to respect the rules and norms of the above engagement.

Adapted from Wyn Grant, 'Pressure Politics: The Changing World of Pressure Groups', *Parliamentary Affairs*, 57:2 (2004), p. 408.

New social movements

In many ways the antithesis of the insider/pressure group is the new social movement. Where pressure groups seek to discuss policy with governments and civil servants, new social movements have an entirely different concept of power – for them, it is found not in the corridors of power, but out on the street, in the mobilisation of ordinary people. That said, the term is once again a child of the post-war years. As the trauma of war faded, citizens began to feel the benefits of a long period of economic growth – better public services, including access to education, and increased levels of affluence. By the 1960s, with the huge expansion of further education, a generation of young people were free of the constraints and

---

1   Wyn Grant, *Pressure Groups and British Politics* (Basingstoke, 2000).

deprivations their parents had suffered, less willing to defer to the monolithic and class-based politics of Labour and the Conservatives, and enabled to explore their views and politics in more self-expressive ways. This was the era of the students' movement, the women's movement, gay rights, the peace movement, and radical environmentalism. Collectively, these are seen as the classic institutions of the so-called 'new' social movements, typically distinguished from political parties, for example, by the fact 'that their adherents are motivated by *expressive* as well as *instrumental* considerations'.[1]

Clearly then, new social movement is a term that can only capture some elements of social action, with its focus not only on particular fields, but also on particular ways of doing things. Many of today's most familiar campaigning names emerged out of this period, such as CND, Greenpeace and Shelter. Often, although not exclusively, these groups rapidly develop from their informal and youthful beginnings to become highly professionalised, not to mention wealthy, organisations. Furthermore, in locating power among citizens, the theory also implies a degree of struggle against other centres of power (see Box 1.6), something relatively rare, at least in the British context.

Box 1.6: What is a social movement?

Three characteristics of social movements:

1. They are involved in conflictual relations with clearly defined opponents
2. They are linked by dense informal networks
3. They share a distinct collective identity.

Adapted from Donatella Della Porta and Mario Diani, *Social Movements*, 2nd edn (Oxford, 2006), pp. 20–1.

Third sector versus Big Society

All of the above terms are in common usage. However, often one phrase emerges as particularly favoured by politicians, policy makers and academics, and therefore enjoys a special moment in the sun. Over recent years in Britain, this process of linguistic preferment has been seen not once, but twice.

Under New Labour, the 'third sector' emerged as the favoured term, designed to go beyond classic definitions of the voluntary sector to embrace old and new forms such as mutuals and social enterprises. It came as part of the Blair/Brown governments' prioritisation of the role such groups could have in the delivery of public services. In 2006, an Office of the Third Sector was established in the Cabinet Office. It rationalised previous institutional reforms, such as the Active Community Unit, the Civil Renewal Unit and the Social Enterprise Unit; it also complemented the significant funding and capacity-building programmes delivered by that government, as well as other legal and institutional changes such as the

---

1   Paul Byrne, *Social Movements in Britain* (Abingdon, 1997), p. 13.

2006 Charities Act, and the introduction of the Compact. Indeed, so embedded was the term within the government's wider social programme, that it has been suggested that it should be understood as a strategic concept, rather than a precise definition (see Box 1.7).

Box 1.7: What is the third sector?

As with other labels (non-governmental organisation, voluntary sector, and so on), there have been varied attempts to define the third sector. Some of these are exogenous, attempting to define the sector by what it is not; while others are endogenous, seeking to find commonalities with which to define the sector from within. Such attempts are unlikely to be uncontested. A more fruitful approach is to see the third sector as an essentially discursive creation, emerging from the socio-political realities of the day. Influential actors both within and outside the sector have identified a shared – and probably temporary – interest in defining it in a particular way. There, the composition and unity of the third sector is best understood as strategic, rather than intrinsic.

Adapted from P. Alcock, 'A Strategic Unity: Defining the Third Sector in the UK', *Voluntary Sector Review*, 1:1 (2010), pp. 5–24.

Such was the term's association with New Labour that it was inevitable that a new government – particularly one equally committed to expanding the role of charities under the Big Society project – would in turn seek another label. And in doing so, the Conservative-Liberal Democrat coalition reached for an extremely old one – 'civil society'. Yet again, it is a term that carries with it ambiguities. Perhaps more than any other, it is culturally specific, carrying baggage accumulated from ancient Greek and Roman thought onwards. At times it has indicated everything but the state; at others, the state has been perceived as civil society's crucial guarantor. Currently, it normally indicates an intermediate space between private life, the state, and the market, with an implicit understanding that these boundaries are hard to draw (see Box 1.8).

Box 1.8: What is civil society?

'Civil society refers to the arena of un-coerced collective action around shared interests, purposes and values. In theory, its institutional forms are distinct from those of the state, family and market, though in practice, the boundaries between state, civil society, family and market are often complex, blurred and negotiated. Civil society commonly embraces a diversity of spaces, actors and institutional forms, varying in their degree of formality, autonomy and power. Civil societies are often populated by organizations such as registered charities, development non-governmental organizations, community groups, women's organizations, faith-based organizations, professional associations, trades unions, self-help groups, social movements, business associations, coalitions and advocacy groups.'

Centre for Civil Society, *Report on Activities, 2002–05* (London, 2005).

Non-governmental organisations

The principal term favoured in this volume is 'non-governmental organisation', falling somewhere between the cosiness of the pressure group and the energy of the new social movement. It was an expression originally coined for those groups with consultative status at the United Nations, and for much of its life, the term has retained this international connotation, being particularly associated with international development agencies which work in partnership with, but are independent from, government. Despite this longevity, there has never been a solid consensus about how NGOs should precisely be defined. The United Nations has adopted a detailed definition, with an understandable focus on humanitarian work and developing civil society (see Box 1.9).

Box 1.9: What is an NGO? (I)

'A non-governmental organization (NGO) is a not-for-profit, voluntary citizens' group, which is organized on a local, national or international level to address issues in support of the public good. Task-oriented and made up of people with common interests, NGOs perform a variety of services and humanitarian functions, bring citizens' concerns to governments, monitor policy and programme implementation, and encourage participation of civil society stakeholders at the community level. They provide analysis and expertise, serve as early warning mechanisms, and help monitor and implement international agreements. Some are organized around specific issues, such as human rights, the environment or health.'

United Nations' definition, available at: www.un.org/dpi/ngosection/criteria.asp.

Others have taken more minimal approaches, arguing that 'any organisation that is not established by an agreement among governments is an international non-governmental organisation', or seeing an NGO as 'an independent voluntary association of people acting together on a continuous basis, for some common purpose, other than achieving government office, making money or illegal activities'.[1] Perhaps because of this relative uncertainty about the term, its usage in the domestic arena is still relatively uncommon. Nevertheless, its prominence has increased over recent decades, for example amongst the environmental movement, but also building momentum more generally. Here it is adopted by groups keen to stress both their professional competence and their independent credentials. Implicit within the phrase is also the idea of influence and action – an organisation that seeks, in some sense, to shape society around it. It is in this sense, of a voluntary group seeking a wider influence, that the term is used in this volume (see Box 1.10).

Over the course of the twentieth century, associational life in Britain has undergone dramatic changes. As societies have become richer, better educated,

---

1   Akira Iriye, *Global Community: The Role of International Organizations in the Making of the Contemporary World* (Berkeley, 2002) p. 2; Peter Willets, 'What is an NGO?', www.staff.city.ac.uk/p.willetts/CS-NTWKS/NGO-ART.HTM, pp. 4–5, 17–19.

> **Box 1.10: What is an NGO? (II)**
>
> 'An NGO is non-violent organisation that is both independent of government and not serving an immediate economic interest, with at least some interest in having socio-political influence.'
>
> Database of Archives of UK Non-Governmental Organisations since 1945 (DANGO), available at: www.ngo.bham.ac.uk/Defining.htm.

and more diverse, different organisational forms have developed and emerged in response. NGO is the term that best captures the dominant and most interesting groups of our current time – assertive, independent, modern, professional, and essentially non-ideological organisations, championing between them a dizzying number of causes and concerns.

As we have seen, the precise label chosen – be it charity, voluntary group, pressure group, social movement, or NGO – can be deeply embedded within historical, social and political contexts. Also, labels can say just as much about the assumptions of the labeller, as they do about the characteristics of what is labelled. In themselves, the various names we have used to describe these groups over the years, tell their own story. But however informative they may be, names can only take the student of social action so far. Actions count for more than words. It is to what these groups actually do, rather than what they are called, that we now turn.

Further reading

Inquiries, official and otherwise, into the British voluntary sector are an excellent source of information. See particularly William Beveridge, *Voluntary Action* (London, 1948); *Report of the Committee on the Law and Practice Relating to Charitable Trusts*, Cmd. 8710 (London, 1952); Lord Goodman, *Charity Law and Voluntary Organisations* (London, 1976); Committee on Voluntary Organisations, *The Future of Voluntary Organisations* (London, 1978); Barry Knight, *Voluntary Action* (London, 1993), and Commission on the Future of the Voluntary Sector, *Meeting the Challenge of Change* (London, 1996).

For pre-Second World War voluntarism, see Frank Prochaska, *The Voluntary Impulse: Philanthropy in Modern Britain* (London, 1988), or Justin Davis-Smith, 'The Voluntary Tradition: Philanthropy and Self-Help in Britain 1500–1945', in Justin Davis Smith, Colin Rochester and Rodney Hedley (eds), *An Introduction to the Voluntary Sector* (London, 1995). For a more in-depth introduction, see Geoffrey Finlayson, *Citizen, State and Social Welfare in Britain 1830–1990* (Oxford, 1994).

Definitions and classifications are explored in Jeremy Kendall and Martin Knapp, 'A Loose and Baggy Monster: Boundaries, Definitions and Typologies', in Justin Davis Smith, Colin Rochester and Rodney Hedley (eds), *An Introduction to the Voluntary Sector* (London, 1995), and Lester Salamon and Helmut Anheier, *Defining the Non-Profit Sector* (Manchester, 1997).

Those wishing to explore the pressure group/interest group literature should begin with Wyn Grant, *Pressure Groups and British Politics* (Basingstoke, 2000).

For an introduction to (new) social movements, see Jeff Goodwin and James Jasper (eds), *The Social Movements Reader* (Oxford, 2003), and Nicola Montagna and Vincenzo Ruggiero (eds), *Social Movements: A Reader* (Abingdon, 2008). A good narrative introduction can be found in Holger Nehring, 'The Growth of Social Movements', in Paul Addison and Harriet Jones (eds), *A Companion to Contemporary Britain* (Oxford, 2005).

For NGOs internationally, see Peter Willetts (ed.), *The 'Conscience of the World': The Influence of Non-Governmental Organisations in the UN System* (London, 1996). In the British context, see Matthew Hilton et al., *The Politics of Expertise: How NGOs Shaped Modern Britain* (Oxford, 2013).

For an introduction to the third sector, see Pete Alcock, 'Voluntary Action, New Labour and the "Third Sector"', in Matthew Hilton and James McKay (eds), *The Ages of Voluntarism* (London, 2011).

On civil society, see Jose Harris (ed.), *Civil Society in British History* (Oxford, 2003), and Nicholas Deakin, *In Search of Civil Society* (Basingstoke, 2001).

2
The Scale and Growth of NGOs, Charities and Voluntary Organisations

Origins

NGOs are by no means a recent phenomenon. They have their antecedents in the eighteenth century, if not before. Indeed, the Society for the Promotion of Christian Knowledge has published religious propaganda from 1698 up until the present. But it was in the eighteenth century that missionary work, as an organised activity, really expanded. Some continued to aim to spread faith in Britain, such as the Religious Tract Society (established in 1799) but others turned their attention abroad, following in the wake of the imperialist project. For instance, Methodists established their first missionary organisation in 1786 while the Church Mission Society, the wing of the Anglican Church, was created in 1799.

What is remarkable is that many of today's organisations can trace their history directly back to this time. The Church Mission Society still operates under the same name, as does the Board of Deputies of British Jews, established in 1760 to assist the Jewish communities of London. Others offer a more complicated history, though institutional connections can be made over two centuries.

Most frequently cited is the example of Anti-Slavery International. This NGO has only gone under this name since 1995. Prior to that it was known as Anti-Slavery International for the Protection of Human Rights (1990–95), the Anti-Slavery Society for the Protection of Human Rights (1956–90) and the Anti-Slavery Society (1947–56). This latter body had been the result of an amalgamation in 1909 between the British and Foreign Anti-Slavery Society and the Aborigines Protection Society which operated as the British and Foreign Anti-Slavery and Aborigines Protection Society until 1947. The British and Foreign Anti-Slavery Society was founded in 1839, yet even this emerged out of previous anti-slavery groups that successfully campaigned for the abolition of the slave trade in 1807 and the ban on slavery in the British empire in 1833. Indeed, if we are to be wholly accurate then Anti-Slavery International first began as an organisation with the 1787 founding of the Society for the Effecting the Abolition of the Slave Trade by several Quakers and the Anglicans

Thomas Clarkson, Granville Sharp and Philip Sansom (joined shortly after by William Wilberforce).

NGOs ought therefore not to be regarded as the product of just the last two to three decades or developments since 1945. Although there are obvious problems over the terminology, socio-political organisations, whether referred to as NGOs, civil society organisations, voluntary associations or, in many cases, charities, have existed in one form or another for decades if not centuries. Table 2.1 provides a much longer list of NGOs currently operating in Britain which can trace their origins back to the eighteenth or nineteenth centuries.

Table 2.1: Some key NGOs today with their origins in the eighteenth and nineteenth centuries

NGO	Year of origin
Society for the Promotion of Christian Knowledge	1698
Board of Deputies of British Jews	1760
Anti-Slavery International	1787
BMS World Mission (Baptist Missionary Society)	1792
Church Mission Society	1799
Bible Society (British and Foreign Bible Society)	1804
Royal National Lifeboat Institution	1824
Royal Society for the Prevention of Cruelty to Animals	1824
Zoological Society of London	1826
Royal London Society for the Blind	1838
Society of St Vincent de Paul	1844
YMCA (Young Men's Christian Association) England	1844
Vegetarian Society of the United Kingdom	1847
Salvation Army	1864
Fawcett Society	1866
Barnardo's	1867
Royal National Institute of the Blind	1868
Action for Children (National Children's Homes, NCH)	1869
Charity Organisation Society (Family Action)	1869
British Red Cross Society	1870
Co-operative Union	1870
National Anti-Vivisection Society (NAVS)	1875
Mothers' Union	1876
St John Ambulance (Order of St John)	1877
Children's Society (Church of England Children's Society)	1881
Church Army	1882
Fabian Society	1884
National Society for the Prevention of Cruelty to Children	1884
Toynbee Hall	1884
Royal Society for the Protection of Birds	1889
British Deaf Association	1890
National Council of Women	1895
National Trust	1895

Source: DANGO, www.dango.bham.ac.uk.

Voluntary associations in Victorian Britain

The real stimulus to the growth in organisations came in the nineteenth century. Indeed, much of the literature on the history of voluntary associations and charities is concerned with a debate as to whether the Victorian era represents a 'golden age' for philanthropic activity. Such forms of participation owe their origins to the forms of civic culture that emerged at the local and provincial level. Rapid industrialisation created an expanding middle class that sought out new forms of associational life that in many ways consolidated its new position in society.

All of the major provincial cities created a thriving 'public sphere' of recreational and educational associations. Although somewhat distinct in being a port city rather than an industrial conurbation such as Manchester, Birmingham or Leeds, Liverpool was fairly typical in the early nineteenth century in having a large number of civic bodies populated by social elites. As elsewhere, in the first two decades of the nineteenth century, Liverpool acquired a Philosophical and Literary Society, an Athenaeum, a Lyceum, an Academy of Art, a Royal Institution, a Museum of National History, an Art Gallery, as well as all the donated emblems of the modern city: squares, walkways, open spaces, prominent statues, public parks and botanical gardens.

Such forms of civic participation became the basis for further voluntary initiative and philanthropic activity during the Victorian period. Public subscriptions paid for social housing, education, hospitals and even relief during times of industrial unrest. In 1871, voluntary day schools were responsible for more than half the total number of elementary school places in England and Wales. Even after public hospitals were rapidly built in the late nineteenth century, subscription hospitals were still responsible for 20 per cent of all hospital beds in England and Wales in 1911. The leading exponent of the 'golden age' thesis, Frank Prochaska, has estimated that the middle classes spent a larger amount of their income on charity than on any item in their budget except food.

'Joining in', though, was not just a middle-class activity. Studies of working-class life in towns such as Reading have found similar vibrant forms of associational life. Some of this might well derive from middle-class reforming initiatives, such as the Mechanics' Institutes, though often working-class members soon appropriated such organisations to their own needs, such as the Club and Institute Unions. But working-class initiative also provided the forms of mutual assistance then lacking from local or central government. The growth of trade unions is well known, but the consumer's co-operative movement had become Britain's largest food retailer by the outbreak of the First World War. Most startling, however, is the growth in the number of friendly societies: that is, those mutual support organisations that provided insurance, pensions, savings and loans. Table 2.2 shows – accepting much double counting – that the total membership of all forms of friendly society grew from around 1 million at the end of the 1810s to over 15 million by the outbreak of the First World War. By the time of the introduction of the welfare state in 1945, the cumulative total was over 40 million.

Table 2.2: Membership of Friendly Societies in the United Kingdom, 1801–1914

Date	Membership
1801	648,000
1803	704,350
1813	821,319
1814	833,728
1815	925,429
1872	2,254,881
1875	3,404,187
1876	4,364,772
1889-91	7,415,971
1899	11,750,130
1902	13,344,494
1905	14,606,969
1910	14,507,963
1911	14,940,103
1912	15,681,013
1913	15,398,682
1914	15,189,960
1915	15,852,645
1916	16,301,969
1922	22,265,277
1924	22,933,317
1926	24,335,806
1928	25,309,438
1930	26,947,550
1931	27,698,517
1932	28,407,319
1933	29,376,678
1934	30,655,883
1935	31,963,637
1936	33,118,719
1937	34,208,871
1945	40,145,847

Source: Bernard Harris, *The Origins of the British Welfare State: Social Welfare in England and Wales, 1800–1945* (London, 2004), pp. 82, 194.

If we turn our attention to the national level, the specific focus of this book, we nevertheless find a thriving and expanding number of socio-political actors. Much of the impetus initially came from the great moral reforms of the Victorian era. This had begun with organisations aiming to promote religious life, such as the Religious Tract Society (1799) and the Society for the Diffusions of Useful Knowledge (1827) but it soon incorporated a whole range of single-issue pressure groups that aimed to reform individual behaviour or else provoke state intervention in the regulation of a particular vice. Older, more violent forms of popular culture were attacked through organisations such as the Royal Society for the Prevention of Cruelty to Animals (1824), though each of the minor vices associated with new forms of urban life – drinking, gambling, smoking, swearing – would come to have at least one pressure group organised to promote its eradication.

The Charity Organisation Society (COS), established in 1869, came to embody the spirit of philanthropy that marked out the Victorian period's preference for non-state solutions. The COS, headed by Helen Bosanquet, may have left a popular legacy that spoke bitterly of having 'washed the charity' out of a second-hand garment, but it also rationalised much voluntary action in London and created a professional, expert institution ready to advise governments on aspects of social welfare. It meant that charity would continue to play a crucial role in British social policy. In 1911 the gross annual receipts of registered charities exceeded public expenditure on the Poor Law. If we add the funds held in mutual aid societies, as well as unregistered charities, then the figure would be much higher still.

The twentieth century

As political enfranchisement led to more statist solutions to social problems and as political parties reoriented themselves to an era of mass politics (see Table 2.3), so other socio-political actors also sought a mass following. The early twentieth century witnessed the emergence of large-scale associations which often served a recreational function but which increasingly came to have a say on a range of issues affecting their members.

Table 2.3: Individual party membership, 1928–48 (000s)

Year	Conservative	Labour
1928		215
1929		228
1930		277
1931		297
1932		372
1933		366
1934		381
1935		419
1936		431
1937		447
1938		429
1939		409
1940		304
1941		227
1942		219
1943		236
1944		266
1945		487
1946	911	645
1947	1,200	608
1948	2,200	629

Note: All figures for the Conservative Party are estimates because until 1998 central membership records were not kept, and there were similar difficulties with the Labour Party.

Sources: John Marshall, 'Membership of UK Political Parties', updated 17 August 2009, available at: www.parliament.uk/commons/lib/research/briefings/snsg-05125.pdf; Nick Crowson, *The Longman Companion to the Conservative Party since 1830* (London, 2001), p. 130.

Middle-class, non-feminist and often socially conservative women's associations thrived in the first half of the twentieth century. As Table 2.4 shows, both the Mothers' Union and the Women's Institutes could claim around half a million members by mid century, with the National Union of Townswomen's Guilds providing another quarter of a million members. Again, though, and as in the nineteenth century, associational life was not confined to the middle classes. Although the consumers' co-operative movement is primarily an organisation serving the economic interests of its members, and is thus not included for analysis in this volume, its social wing, the Women's Co-operative Guild, operated much like the Women's Institute, albeit for working-class women. Table 2.5 shows that it too saw large increases in its membership.

Table 2.4: Membership of selected women's organisations, 1900–50 (000s)

Organisation	1900	1929	1930s	1942	1945	1947	1950
Mothers' Union (1876)	169		538				500
National Federation of Women's Institutes (1915)		271	238	295		349	500
National Union of Townswomen's Guilds (1929)			54			87	250
Church of Scotland Women's Guild (1887)							160
Women's Unionist Association			940				
Women's Voluntary Services					970		

Sources: Cordelia Moyse, *A History of the Mothers Union: Women, Anglicanism and Globalisation, 1876–2008* (London, 2009); Caitriona Beaumont, 'The Women's Movement, Politics and Citizenship, 1918–1950s', in Ina Zweiniger-Bargielowska (ed.), *Women in Twentieth Century Britain* (Harlow, 2001), pp. 262–77; Samantha Ruth Clements, 'Feminism, Citizenship and Social Activity: The Role and Importance of Local Women's Organisations, Nottingham 1918–1969', unpublished PhD thesis, University of Nottingham, 2008, available at: http://etheses.nottingham.ac.uk/474/; Anne. F.C. Bourdillon, *Voluntary Social Services: Their Place in the Modern State* (Methuen, 1945), p. 213; William Beveridge and Alan Frank Wells, *The Evidence for Voluntary Action* (London, 1949); Caitriona Beaumont, 'Housewives, Workers and Citizens: Voluntary Women's Organisations and the Campaign for Women's Rights in England and Wales during the Postwar Period', in Nick Crowson, Matthew Hilton and James McKay (eds), *NGOs in Contemporary Britain: Non-State Actors in Society and Politics since 1945* (Basingstoke, 2009), p. 64.

Table 2.5: Information about the Women's Co-operative Guild, 1885–1951

Year	Membership	Branches
1885	376	10
1890	1,640	54
1900	12,809	273
1910	25,897	520
1914	32,182	600
1917	27,060	580
1921	50,600	905
1925	53,664	1,139
1930	66,566	1,395
1935	77,807	1,615
1939	87,246	1,819
1940	65,174	1,805

continued

Table 2.5: continued

Year	Membership	Branches
1941	49,222	1,529
1945	51,392	1,671
1950	59,666	1,729
1951	58,785	1,692

Source: Gillian Scott, *Feminism and the Politics of Working Women: The Women's Co-operative Guild, 1880s to the Second World War* (London, 1998), p. xii.

Data are not so readily available for other types of organisation, although it is clear that by the middle of the twentieth century a number of organisations had obtained extremely impressive memberships (see Tables 2.6 and 2.7 for membership of youth and outdoor organisations). Yet other forms of organisation were also emerging which appeared more like today's modern NGOs. As Table 2.8 demonstrates, the diversity that marked socio-political action in the nineteenth century only served to continue and expand.

Table 2.6: Membership of youth organisations, 1951 (000s)

Youth organisation	No. members
Cub Scouts	192
Brownies	184
Scouts	237
Girl Guides	221
Sea Cadet Corps	19
Army Cadet Corps	64
Air Training Corps	38
Combined Cadet Force	58
Boys' Brigade	142
Methodist Association of Youth Clubs	101
Boys' Youth Club (continuous)	58
Girls' Youth Clubs (continuous)	78
Total	1,392

Sources: *Social Trends* (various years); Peter Hall 'Social Capital in Britain', *British Journal of Political Science*, 29 (1999), pp. 417–61.

Table 2.7: Membership of outdoor recreational bodies, 1939, 1947, 1951 (000s)

Outdoor body	1939	1947	1951
Camping Club of GB and Ireland	10	11.5	14
Caravan Club			11
Youth Hostel Association	83.5	187	237
Ramblers' Association			9
British Horse Society			4
The Pony Club			20

continued

Table 2.7: continued

Outdoor body	1939	1947	1951
British Canoe Union			1
Royal Yachting Association			1
British Sub-Aqua Club			2
British Cycling Federation			67
Cyclists' Touring Club	36.5		54
British Field Sports Society			27

Source: *Social Trends* (various years); Peter Hall, 'Social Capital in Britain', *British Journal of Political Science*, 29 (1999), pp. 417–61; Anne F.C. Bourdillon, *Voluntary Social Services: Their Place in the Modern State* (London, 1945), p. 213; Beveridge 1949.

Table 2.8: Some key NGOs today with their origins in the early twentieth century

NGO	Year of origin
Fauna and Flora International	1903
Workers' Educational Association	1903
Scout Association	1907
Royal National Institute for Deaf People	1911
Royal Society of Wildlife Trusts (The Wildlife Trusts)	1912
Rotary International in Great Britain and Ireland	1913
Fellowship of Reconciliation, England	1914
National Federation of Women's Institutes	1915
One Parent Families (National Council for One Parent Families)	1918
Women's Unionist Association	1918
National Council for Voluntary Organisations	1919
Chatham House (The Royal Institute of International Affairs)	1920
Howard League for Penal Reform	1921
Royal British Legion	1921
Campaign to Protect Rural England	1926
BBC Children in Need Appeal	1927
Townswomen's Guilds	1929
Youth Hostels Association (YHA) England and Wales	1930
British Council	1934
Liberty	1934
Ramblers' Association (aka The Ramblers)	1935
Relate	1938
Women's Royal Voluntary Service	1938
Citizens Advice	1939
Progressio	1940
RoSPA (Royal Society for the Prevention of Accidents)	1941
Oxfam	1942

Source: DANGO, www.dango.bham.ac.uk.

In particular, a new type of organisation, associated more with professional expertise rather than amateur voluntarism, began to appear. Think tanks connected to the political parties, such as the Labour movement's Fabian Society, had existed since 1884, but they would be joined by a range of independent bodies, such as Chatham House (1920), as well as pressure groups such as the Howard League for Penal Reform (1921) and the National Council for Civil Liberties (1934, now Liberty). Many were associated with social and economic planning, such as the Next Five Years group and Political and Economic Planning (1931, now Policy Studies Institute). They sought a voice and legitimacy not through a mass membership or political affiliation but through an independent and professional voice. If they were a product of the interwar years, their emphasis on expertise, technocratic solution and independence from any one of the mainstream political parties meant they were important pioneers of the sort of NGO that would emerge after the Second World War.

Box 2.1: Key dates in the early history of NGOs

1818	Establishment of Charity Commission
1834	Poor Law Amendment Act direct poor relief principally through the workhouse
1846	Friendly societies were allowed to register with the Registrar of Friendly Societies
1853	Permanent Board of Commissioners was set up at the Charity Commission
1869	Establishment of Charity Organisation Society
1870	Goschen Minute of the Relief of the Poor in the Metropolis set out the relationship between charity and the state: charities were to deal with those on the verge of destitution, while the state was a provider of last resort
1875	Friendly Societies Act established the post of Chief Registrar
1889	First volume of Charles' Booth's *Life and Labour of the People* published
1901	Seebohm Rowntree's *Poverty: A Study of Town life* published, setting out important concept of 'primary poverty'
1905–09	Royal Commission on the Poor Laws
1906	Election of Liberal government that introduced many early welfare reforms, including National Insurance Act of 1911
1919	National Council for Social Service was established to provide better coordination and discourage overlap within a vibrant and diverse sector.
1934	Elizabeth Macadam publishes *The New Philanthropy* helping to redefine the relationship between the state and the voluntary social services
1946	National Insurance Act effectively ends Poor Law system.

Expansion since 1945

In this sense, there is nothing that is distinct about the post-1945 period in the history of NGOs, civil society and the voluntary sector. Their rise has been long and gradual. But if there is one thing that distinguishes the latter half of the twentieth century (and through to the present), it is the relationship these organisations have had with other forms of associational and political life. For if, in the period prior to 1945, NGOs, voluntary associations and charities grew alongside political parties and trade unions, in the period since, the analysis has tended to focus on them as alternative forms of political action.

It is not difficult to understand why. The mid twentieth century was the high point of a certain form of political action. Both party memberships and voter turnouts peaked and the trade unions, if not yet at a numerical peak, seemed at the height of their political powers. Figure 2.1 shows that voter turnout at general elections has declined from a peak of over 80 per cent in 1950 and 1951. Similar patterns can be discerned for local elections (see Figure 2.2). This reflects an overall loss of interest in formal party political affiliation, no better reflected than in the dramatic, long-term falls in membership of both the Labour and the Conservative Parties (Figure 2.3).

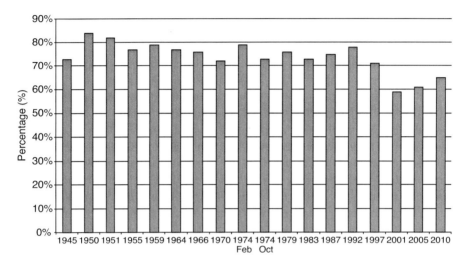

Figure 2.1: Post-war turnout for general elections, 1945–2010 (number of votes cast as a percentage of the number of people on the electoral registers in force at the time of the elections)

Sources: *Social Trends*, 33 (2003), p. 20; International Institute for Democracy and Electoral Assistance; data for 2005 and 2010 from UK political info, available at: www.ukpolitical.info/Turnout45.htm.

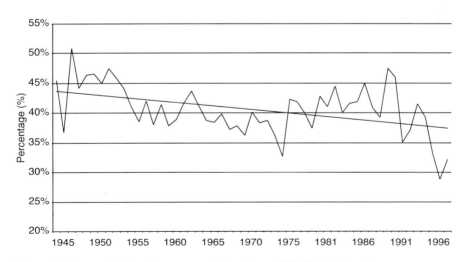

Figure 2.2: Turnout at local government elections, 1945–97 (England)

Source: Colin Rallings and Michael Thrasher, *British Electoral Facts 1832–1999* (Aldershot, 2000), pp. 235–6.

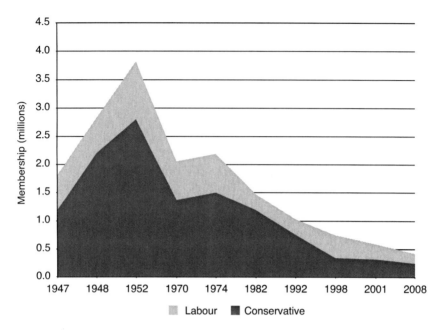

Figure 2.3: Labour and Conservative Party membership, 1947–2008

Note: The figures for the Conservative Party are estimates because no central membership records were kept.

Sources: Nick Crowson, *The Longman Companion to the Conservative Party since 1830* (London, 2001), p. 149; John Marshall, *Membership of UK Political Parties* (London, 2009), available at: www.parliament.uk/documents/commons/lib/research/briefings/snsg-05125.pdf.

Such trends are related to more general declines in the forms of associational life that had formed the bedrock of civic participation in the nineteenth and early twentieth centuries. Crucial here has been the fall in Church membership (Figure 2.4), which may be related to the similar reductions in the membership of traditional women's groups (Figure 2.5) and service organisations (Figure 2.6). Although membership of trade unions continued to rise after 1945, from the end of the 1970s it has fallen sharply (Figure 2.7).

However, decline has been matched by growth elsewhere. The most obvious overall trend is one of the massive expansion in the number of NGOs, charities and voluntary associations since the end of the Second World War. Figure 2.8 shows the growth in the number of registered charities. Today, there are around 180,000. Similar trends are noticeable whether we use a crude selection of NGOs judged to have a national profile (Figure 2.9) or the number of organisations that have chosen to affiliate with the National Council of Voluntary Organisations (NCVO) (Figure 2.10). The latter body estimates that if one were to take a wide definition of associational life, such that it included the local as well as the national, the recreational, sporting and cultural as well as the activist-based and the political, then there may well have been up to 900,000 organisations in the UK in 2010. Such a multitude of organisations goes beyond the scope of this book, but it is nevertheless clear that there has been a persistent growth in the number of socio-political actors. Table 2.9 builds on others covering previous periods to show that some of the commonly known NGOs today were established in every decade since the 1940s.

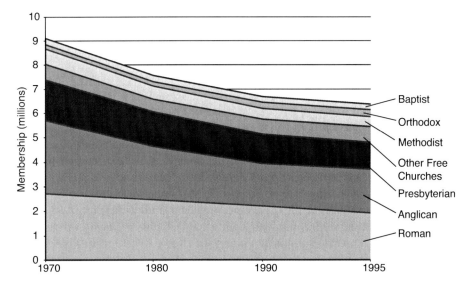

Figure 2.4: Church membership, 1970–95 (active adult members, UK)

Source: *Social Trends*, 29 (1999), p. 220, Table 13.23, 'Church Membership' (data from Christian Research).

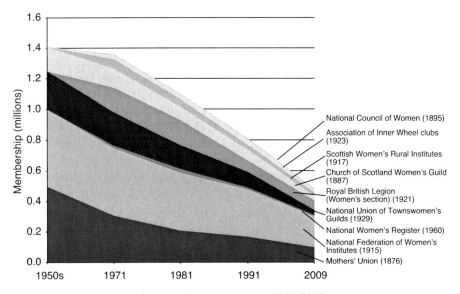

Figure 2.5: Membership of women's organisations, 1950–2009

Sources: *Social Trends* (various years); Annual reports and accounts, organisations concerned.

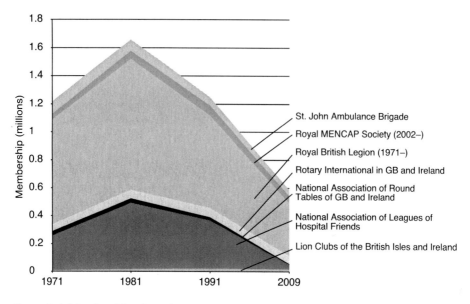

Figure 2.6: Membership of service organisations, 1971–2009

Note: The figures for 2009 are often based on a different method of counting that is often not consistent with previous figures.

Sources: *Social Trends* (various years); Annual reports and accounts, organisations concerned.

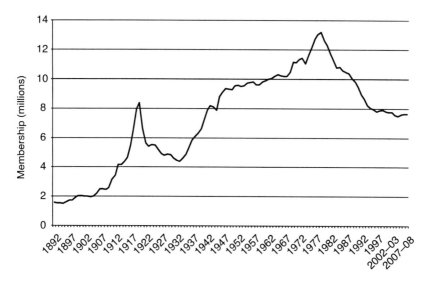

Figure 2.7: Trade union membership, 1892–2008

Source: James Achur, *Trade Union Membership 2009* (London, 2010), p. 10. This publication is available only from the internet and can be downloaded from www.bis.gov.uk/policies/employment-matters/research/trade-union-stats. Sources originally from Labour Force Survey, Office for National Statistics; Department for Employment (1892–1974); Certification Office (1974, 2007/08).

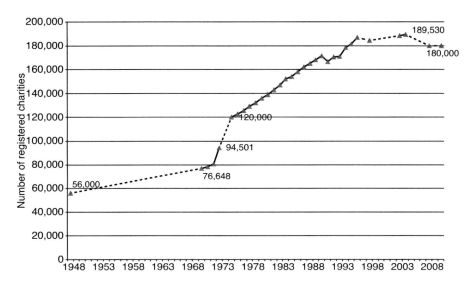

Figure 2.8: Number of registered charities, 1948–2010

Sources: Anne F.C. Bourdillon, *Voluntary Social Services: Their Place in the Modern State* (London, 1945), p. 213; William H. Beveridge. *Voluntary Action: A Report on Methods of Social Advance* (London, 1948), p. 212; Jeremy Kendall and Martin Knapp, *The Voluntary Sector in the United Kingdom, Johns Hopkins Nonprofit Sector Series* (Manchester, 1996), p. 5; Wolfenden 1978, p. 34; Charity Statistics (various years); NCVO Almanac (various years); *Charity Commission Annual Report 2009/10*, p. 22, available at: www.charity-commission. gov.uk/Library/about_us/Charity_Commission_Annual_Report_09_10.pdf; Charity Commission, www. charity-commission.gov.uk/About_us/About_charities/factfigures.aspx.

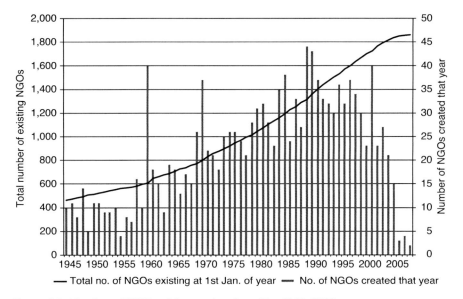

Figure 2.9: Number of NGOs with a national profile, 1945–2008

Source: DANGO, www.dango.bham.ac.uk.

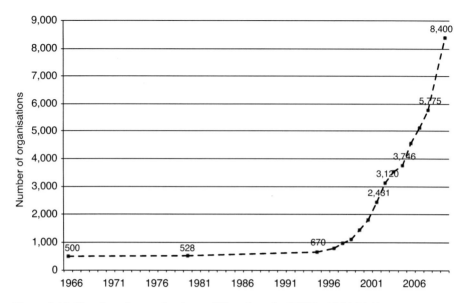

Figure 2.10: Number of organisations affiliated to the NCVO, 1966–2010

Sources: NCVO website, www.ncvo-vol.org.uk/about/NCVO-from-1919-to-1993, and www.ncvo-vol.org.uk/ membership/meet-our-members; Commission on the Future of the Voluntary Sector and Nicholas Deakin, *Meeting the Challenge of Change: Voluntary Action into the 21st Century – The Report of the Commission on the Future of the Voluntary Sector* (London, 1996), p. 57; and personal communication from David Kane, NCVO.

Table 2.9: Prominent NGOs, with year of formation

NGO	Year of formation
MIND	1946
MENCAP	1946
Soil Association	1946
Alcoholics Anonymous	1947
European Movement	1948
Cruse Bereavement Care	1950
Samaritans	1953
Spastics Society	1953
Indian Workers' Association	1954
Institute of Economic Affairs	1955
Consumers' Association	1957
Homosexual Law Reform Society	1958
Campaign for Nuclear Disarmament	1958
Institute of Race Relations	1958
Amnesty International	1961
British Heart Foundation	1961
World Wildlife Fund	1961
Help the Aged	1961
National Viewers' and Listeners' Association	1964
Child Poverty Action Group	1965

continued

Table 2.9: continued

NGO	Year of formation
Shelter	1966
Society for the Protection of Unborn Children	1966
Joint Council for the Welfare of Immigrants	1967
Campaign for Homosexual Equality	1969
Festival of Light	1971
Friends of the Earth	1971
Campaign for Better Transport (Transport 2000)	1973
Life Style Movement	1974
Low Pay Unit	1974
Centre for Policy Studies	1974
Campaign Against the Arms Trade	1974
Advisory Service for Squatters	1975
International Fund for Animal Welfare	1976
Peace People	1976
Greenpeace	1977
Sustrans	1977
Adam Smith Institute	1977
Muslim Aid	1981
Neighbourhood Watch	1982
Terrence Higgins Trust	1982
Afghan Aid	1983
Re-Solv, Society for the Prevention of Solvent Abuse	1984
Islamic Relief	1984
Pesticides Action Network	1986
Rainforest Foundation	1989
Earth First!	1991
Fairtrade Foundation	1992
Big Issue	1995
Reclaim the Streets	1995
Countryside Alliance	1997
Muslim Council of Britain	1997

In many ways, the decline experienced in certain sectors has been matched by expansion in others (Figure 2.11). The environmental movement, as we will see in subsequent chapters, has seen particularly impressive growth in membership. The total cumulative membership of environmental and conservation groups in 2008 (and accepting much double counting) was nearly 7 million (see Figure 2.12). Likewise, reflecting a society that spends more on leisure and personal consumption, membership of many outdoor and recreational groups has continued to expand (Figure 2.13).

But of greater significance is the changing nature of the sector. What has become increasingly apparent is that the model of civic participation provided by, for instance, the Women's Institute, has been replaced by one in which large-scale NGOs have emerged that rely less on the face-to-face interaction of members. The issues surrounding such a change will be explored in later chapters. For now it is sufficient to note that whatever the implications of the emergence of new forms of organisation, it has at least created a massively expanded sector. The total income

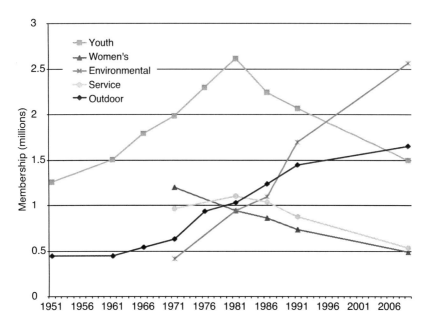

Figure 2.11: Total membership of various organisations arranged by category, 1951–2009

Sources: Aggregate data based on *Social Trends* (various years), the organisations concerned, and many other sources.

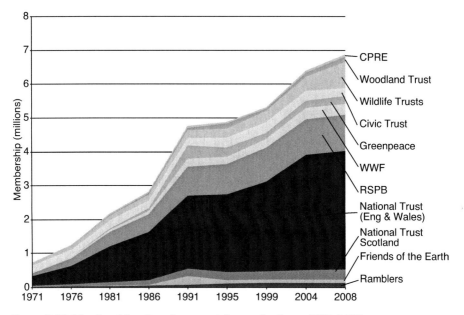

Figure 2.12: Membership of environmental organisations, 1971–2008

Sources: *Social Trends* (various years); Annual reports and accounts, organisations concerned; Neil Carter, *The Politics of the Environment: Ideas, Activism, Policy* (Cambridge, 2007).

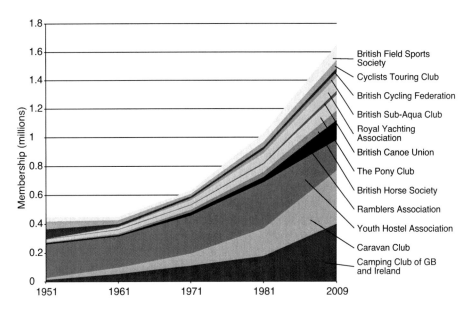

Figure 2.13: **Membership of outdoor/recreational organisations, 1951–2009**

Sources: *Social Trends* (various years); Peter Hall, 'Social Capital in Britain', *British Journal of Political Science*, 29 (1999), pp. 417–61; Annual reports and accounts, organisations concerned.

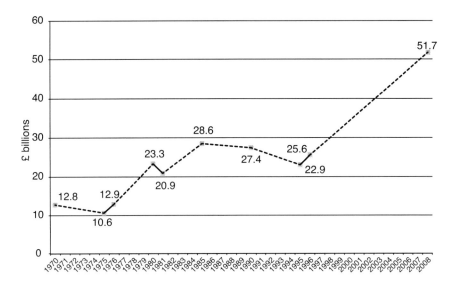

Figure 2.14: **Total income of all registered charities, 1970–2008 (adjusted for inflation, 2009)**

Sources: Wolfenden 1978; Charity Statistics (various years); *Charity Commission Annual Report 2009/10*, www.charity-commission.gov.uk/Library/about_us/Charity_Commission_Annual_Report_09_10.pdf.

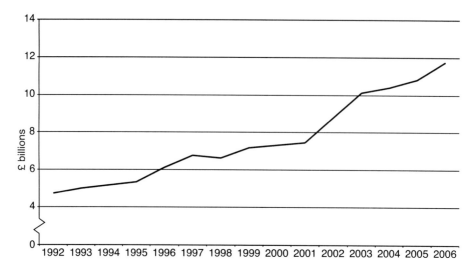

Figure 2.15: Income of top 500 charities, 1992–2006 (adjusted for inflation, 2009)

Source: Charity Statistics (various years).

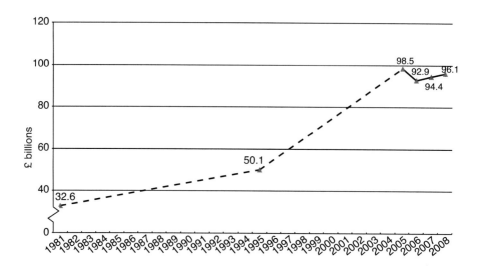

Figure 2.16: Total assets, 'general charities', 1981–2008 (adjusted for inflation, 2009)

Note: The figure for 1981 relates to all registered charities, not just general charities, but is used as a proxy for general charities. The general charities definition is used by various bodies, including the NCVO. It comprises most general charities, but excludes schools, excepted charities, government charities, universities, housing associations, places of worship, and so on. A full definition of the term can be found, for example, in *NCVO Almanac 1996*, p. 11.

Sources: *Charity Statistics*, 4 (1984), p. 57; NCVO Almanac (various years).

of all charities has risen from around £12 billion in 1970 to over £50 billion today (Figure 2.14). Within this, it is obvious that many of the larger charities predominate, with much of this income being enjoyed by what is relatively just a handful of NGOs (Figure 2.15). The sector has become a formidable presence in British society and politics and an economic powerhouse in its own right. As Figure 2.16 shows, the total assets held by 'general charities' has tripled over the last 30 years, from a figure of just over £30 billion in 1980 to one of around £100 billion today.

Further reading

No works exist which cover the history of all forms of socio-political organisation – be they NGOs, charities or voluntary associations – over such a long period. Instead, the literature tends to be divided into particular subsections. Historians have tended to focus on civic culture and voluntary association. For some excellent work on associational life in British provincial towns in the nineteenth century, see Robert J. Morris, *Class, Sect and Party: The Making of the British Middle Class, Leeds 1820–50* (Manchester, 1990); Simon Gunn, *The Public Culture of the Victorian Middle Class* (Manchester, 2000); Alan Kidd and David Nicholls (eds), *Gender, Civic Culture and Consumerism: Middle-Class Identity in Britain, 1800–1940* (Manchester, 1999), and Alan Kidd and David Nicholls (eds), *The Making of the British Middle Class? Studies of Regional and Cultural Diversity since the Eighteenth Century* (Stroud, 1998).

For the campaigns promoting 'rational recreation', see Peter Bailey, *Leisure and Class in Victorian England: Rational Recreation and the Contest for Control, 1830–1885* (London, 1978); Francis M.L. Thompson, 'Social control in Victorian Britain', *Economic History Review*, 34 (1981), pp. 189–208; Brian Harrison, *Peaceable Kingdom: Stability and Change in Modern Britain* (Oxford, 1982); Hugh Cunningham, *Leisure in the Industrial Revolution c.1780–c.1880* (London, 1980); John M. Golby and Arthur W. Purdue, *The Civilisation of the Crowd: Popular Culture in England 1750–1900* (London, 1984), and James Walvin, *Leisure and Society 1830–1950* (London, 1978). For specific organisations committed to particular commodities, see Brian Harrison, *Drink and the Victorians: The Temperance Question in England, 1815–1872*, 2nd edn (Keele, 1994); Matthew Hilton, *Smoking in British Popular Culture, 1800–2000* (Manchester, 2000); Carl Chinn, *Better Betting with a Decent Feller: Bookmaking, Betting and the British Working Class, 1750–1990* (London, 1991); Mark Clapson, *A Bit of a Flutter: Popular Gambling and English Society, c. 1823–1961* (Manchester, 1992), and David Dixon, *From Prohibition to Regulation: Bookmaking, Anti-Gambling, and the Law* (Oxford, 1991).

The case that the Victorian era represented a 'golden age' for philanthropy and volunteering has been most strongly put by Frank Prochaska. See his *The Voluntary Impulse: Philanthropy in Modern Britain* (London, 1988), and *Women and Philanthropy in Nineteenth-Century England* (Oxford, 1980). For alternative approaches to the subject, see Martin Daunton (ed.), *Charity, Self-Interest and Welfare in the English Past* (London, 1996); Jane Lewis, *The Voluntary Sector, the State and Social Work in Britain: The Charity Organisation Society/Family Welfare Association since 1869* (Aldershot, 1995). In particular, to see how working-class organisations fit into this literature, see Stephen Yeo, *Religion and Voluntary Organisations in Crisis* (London, 1976); Peter Gurney, *Co-operative Culture and the Politics of Consumption in England, c. 1870–1930* (Manchester, 1996), and Gillian Scott, *Feminism and the Politics of Working Women: The Women's Co-operative Guild, 1880s to the Second World War* (London, 1998).

For how this sector adapted to an expanding welfare state, see Geoffrey Finlayson, 'A Moving Frontier: Voluntarism and the State in British Social Welfare', *Twentieth-Century British History*, 1 (1990), pp. 183–206; Derek Fraser, *The Evolution of the British Welfare State: A History of Social Policy since the Industrial Revolution* (London, 1973); Pat Thane, *The Foundations of the Welfare State*, 2nd edn (London, 1996); Bernard Harris, *The Origins of the British Welfare State: Society,*

State and Social Welfare in England and Wales, 1800–1945 (Basingstoke, 2004), and Geoffrey Finlayson, *Citizen, State and Social Welfare in Britain, 1830–1990* (Oxford, 1994).

And for how new forms of organisation emerged in the interwar decades, see Helen McCarthy, 'Parties, Voluntary Associations and Democratic Politics in Interwar Britain', *Historical Journal*, 50:4 (2007), pp. 891–912; Ross McKibbin, *Classes and Cultures: England 1918–1951* (Oxford, 2000), and Arthur Marwick, 'Middle Opinion in the Thirties: Planning, Progress and Political "Agreement"', *English Historical Review*, 79 (1964), pp. 285–98.

3
Key Sectors' Profiles since 1945

1. Medicine and health

Charity and voluntarism have played a leading role in the medicine and health field throughout history. Indeed, it was only in the mid twentieth century that they experienced a relative decline. However the rise of the state, as in so many fields, did not mark the end of voluntary provision; it remains a vitally important element of the overall picture. Instead, the nature of non-state provision has changed, and continues to do so to this day.

Voluntary providers of medical care often have long and venerable histories. St John Ambulance, for example, is today a leading provider of first-aid training and support. The organisation can trace its roots to eleventh-century crusading knights and the Order of St John. Dissolved by Henry VIII, it was revived in the nineteenth century, with the current body formed in 1877.

Up until the mid twentieth century, many of the country's major (and minor) hospitals were the products of the voluntary sector, including famous London institutions such as Guy's, St Bartholomew's and St Thomas's, and provincial centres such as Addenbrookes in Cambridge and the Manchester Royal Infirmary. However, the vision of a universal, state-funded service gained ground in the 1930s and 1940s, as part of the post-war vision of a welfare state laid out by William Beveridge. It fell to the Labour government elected in 1945 to fulfil this vision (see Box 3.1.1) and it was the launch of the National Health Service (NHS) in 1948 which finally took the voluntary hospitals into public ownership.

Of course, the 1940s did not mark the eclipse of voluntarism in the medicine and health fields. Indeed, there was a significant element of continuity. Voluntary income could remain an important factor for particular hospitals, as witnessed by the success of the Great Ormond Street Hospital Children's Charity. Charitable trusts, such as Nuffield, also provided ongoing, non-statutory resources. Meanwhile, voluntary providers continued to be significant, albeit in a more ancillary manner. Macmillan Cancer Support, for example, is a major provider of both care and advocacy. Macmillan's direct relief work began in the 1920s, but it was not until

---

Box 3.1.1: Extract from *Let Us Face the Future*, the Labour Party's 1945 general election manifesto

'By good food and good homes, much avoidable ill-health can be prevented. In addition the best health services should be available free for all. Money must no longer be the passport to the best treatment.

In the new National Health Service there should be health centres where the people may get the best that modern science can offer, more and better hospitals, and proper conditions for our doctors and nurses. More research is required into the causes of disease and the ways to prevent and cure it.

Labour will work specially for the care of Britain's mothers and their children – children's allowances and school medical and feeding services, better maternity and child welfare services. A healthy family life must be fully ensured and parenthood must not be penalised if the population of Britain is to be prevented from dwindling.'

---

the 1970s that it began to fund its now-familiar nursing service. Marie Curie Cancer Care is another example of a charity acting as a major provider of care and support. In this instance, the organisation was triggered, rather than sidelined, by the NHS, beginning in 1948 as a project to keep the Marie Curie name alive, after the Marie Curie Hospital in Hampstead had been absorbed into the newly formed NHS.

Research institutions both continued in existence and continued to be formed, at times reshaping themselves to accommodate the new reality of living alongside the NHS. As medical knowledge advanced through the nineteenth and twentieth centuries, so too did the costs and specialised knowledge necessary to continue the work. In this way, the expanding medical field naturally created a constant need for organisational champions, each promoting and protecting their specific area of research. The Imperial Cancer Research Fund (1902) and the Cancer Research Campaign (1923) were early, and prominent, examples: the latter funded the groundbreaking work of Sir Richard Doll on the link between smoking and lung cancer. These two bodies came together in 2002 to form Cancer Research UK, one of Britain's leading charities in any field. Doll's insights, meanwhile, gave rise in turn to anti-smoking groups, the most prominent of which is Action on Smoking and Health (ASH) (1971).

Other leading examples include the British Heart Foundation (1961) and the British Lung Foundation (1985). Today, there is a dizzying array of such NGOs. Large and small, well-known or obscure, from the Multiple Sclerosis Society (1953) and the Alzheimer's Society (1979), to the Cavernoma Alliance (2005), typically these groups will seek to promote research and sponsor their chosen field, as well as championing the cause of sufferers. In other contexts, the changing health landscape has altered the mission of voluntary groups, without necessarily diminishing their significance. The King Edward's Hospital Fund for London was established to raise funds for the capital's voluntary hospitals. Post-1948, when such a need no longer existed, it turned its attention to policy and research. Today, as the King's Fund, it is widely recognised as a leading voice in health policy debates.

For all this continuity, change was a significant feature, too, as NGOs emerged to reflect the developing social understanding and context around questions of medicine and health. One such example is in sexual and reproductive health. Groups such as Brook (1964), the Family Planning Association (1966) and the British Pregnancy Advisory Service (1968) were all in their own way expressions of the permissive society, seeking both to provide services in their own right, and to ensure that the assumptions and priorities behind statutory provision kept up with changing social norms. Of course, not all the groups generated at this time were marching in the same direction. Growing concern about illegal drug use gave rise to bodies which sought to treat addiction and misuse, such as Addaction (1967), as well as those conceived to assist illegal drug users in their brushes with the law, as was the case with Release (1967).

End of life is another morally charged field where NGOs have been prominent in contributing to ongoing, and contentious, debates that see Dignity in Dying (1935) ranged against a plethora of opposing groups, including the Pro-Life Alliance (1996), Right to Life (2003), and the Care Not Killing Alliance (2005). Meanwhile, the prominence of voluntary counselling groups dealing with bereavement, such as Cruse (1959) and Compassionate Friends (1969), has mirrored the rise of generalist counselling organisations, as NGOs like Mind (1946) and the Samaritans (1953) have become household names.

Just as health and medical provision, like its social context, has developed over the years, so too has the subject of all this activity: the patient. The passing of the age of deference, and the rise of the consumer, can be clearly seen here.

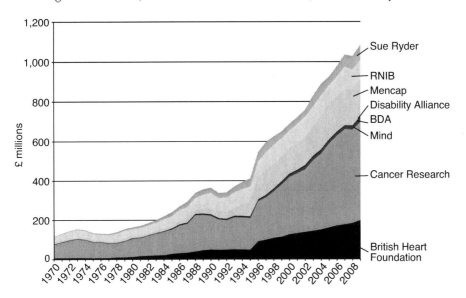

Figure 3.1.1: Income of selected medicine and health NGOs, 1970–2009 (adjusted for inflation, 2009)

Source: Annual reports and accounts, organisations concerned; Charity Statistics (various years).

The Patients Association (1963), for example, was deliberately established as a consumer organisation for the British healthcare system, providing service users with advice and information, and campaigning for improvements. In a related vein came Action against Medical Accidents (1982), founded by Peter Ransley, and set up in the wake of his television play, *Minor Complications*. The assertiveness and self-confidence of the patient/consumer is reflected in the growing incidence of user-led groups more generally, a development particularly seen in the disability field over recent decades.

As has been seen, although one could be forgiven for assuming that the rise of the state over the twentieth century crowded out other providers, there has in fact always been something of a mixed economy in this field, a mix that has never stopped changing and developing. Arguably, the period from the 1970s and 1980s onwards has been something of a golden age for voluntarism. On the one hand, the ability of these groups to attract funding to pursue their independent work has flourished (see Figure 3.1.1). At the same time, voluntary organisations have increasingly been recognised as potential providers of services, as successive governments have fallen out of love with the idea of a monolithic public sector, and the 'contracting culture' has maintained the momentum it originally got under the Thatcher administrations. Over the last century, state provision has changed the shape and role of the sector in this field, but it has never removed the basic need for it.

Table 3.1.1: Some prominent NGOs, with formation dates (NGOs profiled in this book are shown in bold)

NGO	Year of formation
British Red Cross Society	1870
King's Fund	1897
Macmillan Cancer Support	1911
Dignity in Dying (Voluntary Euthanasia Society)	1935
Nuffield Foundation	1943
Mind: National Association for Mental Health	1946
Marie Curie Cancer Care	1948
Samaritans	1953
National Childbirth Trust	1956
British Heart Foundation	1961
Patients Association	1963
Brook	1964
Family Planning Association	1966
Addaction	1967
Release	1967
British Pregnancy Advisory Service	1968
ASH (Action on Smoking and Health)	1971
Alzheimer's Society	1979
Action against Medical Accidents	1982
British Lung Foundation	1985
Cancer Research UK	2002

Source: DANGO, www.dango.bham.ac.uk.

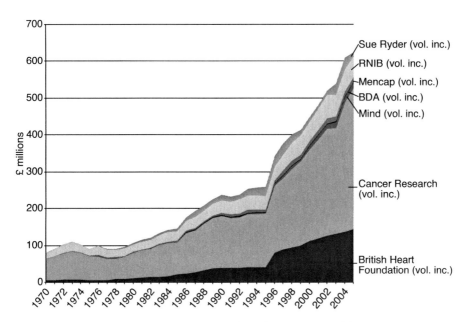

Figure 3.1.2: Voluntary income of selected medicine and health NGOs, 1970–2005 (adjusted for inflation)

Source: Charity Statistics (various years).

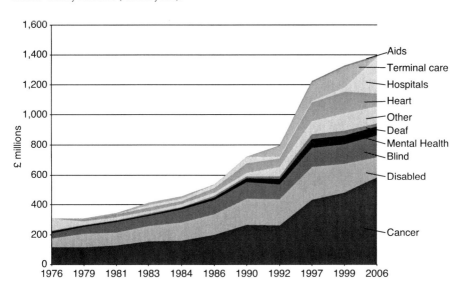

Figure 3.1.3: Breakdown per subsector of the voluntary income of medicine and health charities among the top 200/500 charities, 1976–2006 (adjusted for inflation)

Note: Data have been adjusted to reflect inflation and a change in the sample from top 200 to top 500 charities.

Source: Charity Statistics (various years).

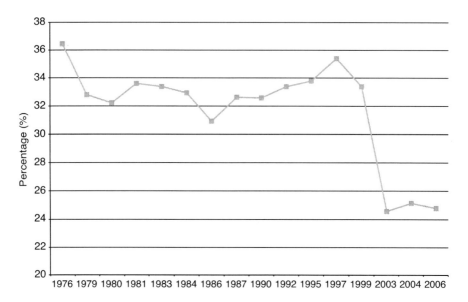

Figure 3.1.4: Income of medicine and health charities as a proportion of the total income of top 200/500 charities, 1976–2006

Note: This figure shows that the share of income of medicine and health charities, while it has increased in real terms over the period 1976–2006, has declined compared to the other sectors analysed in Charity Statistics: general welfare, international aid, the young, animals, environment, religious groups and mission work, arts and educational research, and others.

Source: Charity Statistics (various years).

Further reading

Useful histories of the welfare state include Nicholas Timmins, *The Five Giants: A Biography of the Welfare State*, 2nd edn (London, 2001), and Rodney Lowe, *The Welfare State in Britain since 1945*, 3rd edn (Basingstoke, 2005). On health policy specifically, see Christopher Ham, *Health Policy in Britain*, 6th edn (Basingstoke, 2009).

For the earlier twentieth century, see Pat Thane, *The Foundations of the Welfare State*, 2nd edn (London, 1996), and Derek Fraser, *The Evolution of the British Welfare State: A History of Social Policy since the Industrial Revolution*, 4th edn (Basingstoke, 2009). See also Jose Harris, *William Beveridge: A Biography* (Oxford, 1977).

2. General/social welfare

This diverse sector is broadly unified by a concern for the well-being of those less fortunate in society who encounter their position through birth, circumstance or accident. Many organisations in this arena trace their origins back into the nineteenth century, drawing upon a philanthropic/charitable heritage that has seen the active citizen engage in social action in the form of service provision, mutual aid, campaigning and advocacy: for example, the Royal National Lifeboat Institution (RNLI) (1824), the Children's Society (1881), the National Society for the

Prevention of Cruelty to Children (1884) and the National Children's Home (1898). Prochaska has characterised this heritage as the history of kindness, whilst others drawing upon a Marxist inspiration imply that it was a means of consolidating the power of the rich and dividing the poor – although such an observation overlooks the not inconsiderable role of charitable support within the working classes for the working class.

British social policy had been dominated by the Poor Laws, first passed in 1598 and continuing till 1948. The 1834 Poor Law Commission emphasised two principles: less eligibility (meaning the position of the pauper must be worse than that of a labourer) and the workhouse test (no relief outside the workhouse). The hatred of the Poor Law informed much of the development of the early twentieth-century social services – including national insurance, means tests and healthcare – being framed to avoid having to rely on them. Although the state expanded its safety net, the opportunities for social action to assist in the relief of those less fortunate persisted and expanded alongside the state. This is the area most commonly associated with popular notions of charity, not least because the legal definition of charity included reference to relief of poverty. As Chapter 8 will show, when the public are asked what constitutes charitable work, they equate it with 'caring' and helping the needy in society. Consequently, many of the NGOs in this sector are those most frequently cited as leading charities by the public.

Since 1945 this sector has continued to expand, despite the creation of the welfare state in 1948 and the acceptance by the state that it was responsible for its citizens from the cradle to the grave. Explaining this growth rests with a number of factors. The impact of the Second World War as well as the legacy of the 1930s depression may explain early developments: evacuation had highlighted the divisions within society, whilst the sacrifice made in the service of one's country and the need to provide for the returning service men and women played its part too. The foundation of organisations such as Mind (1946), Mencap (1946) and the Samaritans (1953) tells a story in which service provision and care were key features of the two decades following the Second World War.

Expansion in the sector again occurred in the 1960s. There was a proliferation of organisations as poverty was 'rediscovered': Help the Aged (1961), Child Poverty Action Group (CPAG) (1965) and Shelter (1966). The Disability Income Group was initiated in 1965 by two housewives suffering from multiple sclerosis, and the organisation's launch was announced in the *Observer* (see Box 3.2.1). By the end of the 1970s there were 42 groups in existence which could be defined as belonging to the poverty lobby. This growth, it has been suggested, was due to those on the political left losing patience with the Labour Party. They looked instead to the voluntary and charitable sectors to seek to ameliorate the conditions of the worst off. Socialist, or left-wing, political persuasions were clearly evident amongst many who chose professional work in the sector. However, there are dangers in overstating that generalisation. For instance, the foundation of the Crisis at Christmas homeless appeal shows that politically active Conservatives, including Iain Macleod, could be the leading motivators.

> **Box 3.2.1: Disablement Income Group's launch**
>
> 'A married woman, working full-time in her home, is at present not eligible for any form of compensation for chronic sickness or disability, and may not even draw National Assistance – no matter how sadly her health and circumstances decline or how poorly paid her husband may be. One of the main objectives of the recently formed Disablement Income Group (its founders are themselves disabled by incurable disease) is to press for legislation to remedy this injustice ... Membership of D.I.G. is open to all sympathisers.'
>
> Hugh Sampson, chairman DIG, to editor of the *Observer*, 26 September 1965, p. 10.

Religious persuasion may also explain the reinvigoration or creation of many organisations. For example, CPAG owes much to individuals from the Quaker's Social and Economic Affairs Committee. Many organisations concerned with homelessness have their origins in Christian values, and often in their early incarnations had explicit religious underpinnings: Shelter was initially a fundraising alliance of Church-based housing groups and considered itself to be a Christian charity, whilst St Anne's Shelter in Leeds was founded by local Catholic priest Father Bill Kilgallon. Many of them have since become secular organisations, as the demands of professionalisation and charitable law have dictated.

The rediscovery of poverty was the latest in a long intellectual tradition, dating back to Adam Smith, at the end of the eighteenth century, of social research being conducted that leads to formulation of policy actions. Charles Booth and Seebohm Rowntree were studying the 'condition of England' and outlining policy answers for government in the late nineteenth century, and in the first half of the twentieth century Sidney and Beatrice Webb and many others were similarly engaged. These individuals became embedded into wider networks that combined intellectuals and scholars with practitioners, all committed to the improvement of their society.

In the 1950s and 1960s, British universities began to reflect more widely these concerns and the growth of sociology, and the creation of departments concerned with social administration further transformed matters. The Beveridge Report and its 'four giants' had created the impression that social inequality and poverty would be eradicated. Yet from the 1950s it became apparent that despite the claims of the third Rowntree study into poverty in York, it had not been banished and was an issue that that was prevalent amongst not just the elderly but also children, and was growing as a problem. Peter Townsend and Brian Abel Smith's pioneering work on the 'poverty trap' at the London School of Economics (LSE) probably represents the most well-known example but, collectively alongside other studies, significantly undermined the notion that the welfare state was an unqualified success.

These academics and intellectuals have often combined together in campaigning alliances. During the twentieth century, different coalitions and places of association combined to help write the story of social reform campaigning. The Fabian Society, Toynbee Hall and the LSE worked together in the first half of the century. During the Wilson years the LSE and the Institute of Community Studies led by Michael Young were particularly influential, as was London University's Institute for Education, the National Children's Bureau and the Nuffield Foundation.

From the 1970s the sector saw increasing numbers of graduates with professional qualifications securing paid jobs with these organisations. Although the volunteer remained vitally important, these NGOs were being staffed and run by full-time professionals. This reflected a trend that had been developing since 1945 whereby many of these organisations offering service delivery developed professional training qualifications and standards that became nationwide benchmarks in their particular field of specialism. Similarly, the creation of professional standards bodies, such as the Standing Conference of Organisations of Social Workers (SCOSW), created in 1962, and the expansion of the academic social sciences from the late 1960s, meant that universities began to offer postgraduate training, such as PORTVAC (Programme for Research and Training in Voluntary Action) created at Brunel in 1978.

With the rise of the graduate professional new innovations in fundraising, lobbying, casework and media relations began to be applied. The growth in revenue streams and media profiles is apparent from Figures 3.2.1–3.2.4. But, as ever, the generalisation needs some caveats. Certain organisations were better than others at revenue generation (as shown in Figure 3.2.1), such that by the early 1970s Shelter had a turnover of several million whilst CPAG operated on very meagre resources. During the 1960s and 1970s many NGOs in this sector, through their casework, service provision and research briefings, had a significant impact upon the perceptions held of the less well-off in society amongst decision makers and the media. Their discursive impact was probably more significant than their ability to secure legislative change. The era witnessed changing perceptions of the reasons for homelessness, for example, and there was a general sense that structural rather than personal factors explained the circumstances of the disadvantaged. During the 1980s this would come under challenge from the political establishment as the NGO sector strove unsuccessfully to overcome beliefs about the intentional underclass. Only from the late 1990s would structural explanations become acceptable once more. At the same time, from the 1980s, despite many in the sector having concerns over the ideological climate, they found themselves being co-opted into service provision as the state looked to reduce public expenditure and lured organisations with grants from government bodies such as the Manpower Services Commission and the Voluntary Services Unit.

Innovations in this sector were also drawn from across the Atlantic. This was particularly noticeable in the manner in which a number of groups from the late 1960s began a reorientation whereby they no longer dispensed charity to their clients but instead offered them advice about their rights. For instance, Frank Field created the Low Pay Unit, there was a growth in Citizens Advice Bureaux, and the Family Law and Legal Advice Centre was established in 1976. Another development from the 1970s was a gradual move toward democratisation as NGOs in this sector decided to give their clients a greater voice and to make them less elitist and metropolitan. The contrasts are clear: St Anne's Shelter in Leeds was innovative in 1970 for including the views of the homeless in its needs survey, whereas Shelter, which made much of its claim to know the views of the homeless in its publicity, actually had no place for them to be consulted.

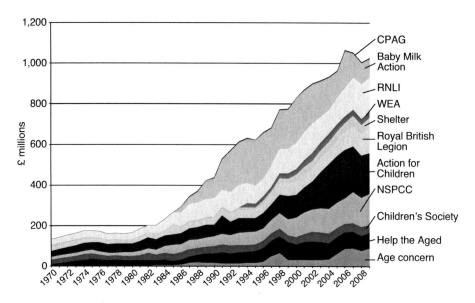

Figure 3.2.1: Total income of selected organisations from the top 65 NGOs in the general/social welfare sector, 1970–2009 (Age Concern, Help the Aged, Children's Society, NSPCC, NCH/Action for Children, Royal British Legion, Shelter, WEA, RNLI, Baby Milk Action, CPAG) (adjusted for inflation, 2009)

Sources: Charity Statistics (various years) Annual reports and accounts, organisations concerned; Charity Commission.

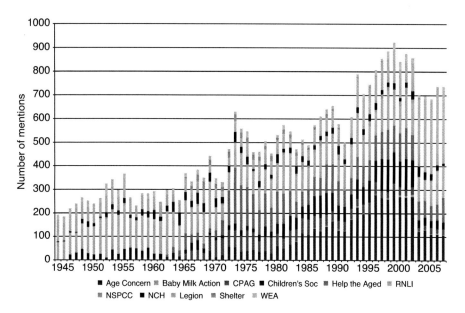

Figure 3.2.2: Number of mentions of general welfare NGOs in the *Guardian*, 1945–2008

Source: *Guardian* (various years). This image can be viewed in colour at www.ngo.bham.ac.uk

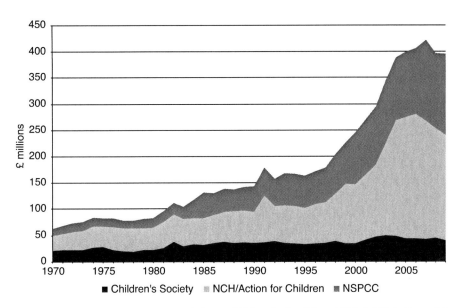

Figure 3.2.3: Cumulated income of three children's charities, 1970–2009 (adjusted for inflation, 2009)

Sources: Charity Statistics (various years) Annual reports and accounts, organisations concerned; Charity Commission.

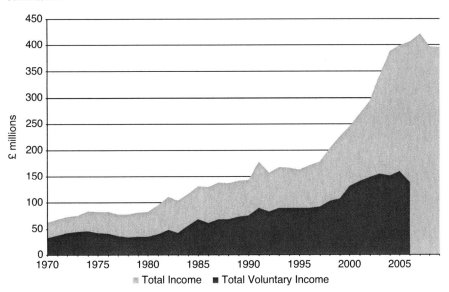

Figure 3.2.4: Income (voluntary and total) of three children's charities, 1970–2009 (NCH/ Action for Children, Children's Society, NSPCC) (adjusted for inflation, 2009)

Note: Voluntary income data is missing after 2006.

Sources: Charity Statistics (various years) Annual reports and accounts, organisations concerned; Charity Commission.

As was earlier observed, many of the organisations in this sector are the most widely recognised and respected by the public. However, as Figure 3.2.5 illustrates, they are faced with declining voluntary revenues and also greater public scrutiny. They have found that their management is being placed under ever greater scrutiny, not solely by the bureaucratic demands of government and the Charity Commission, but also by a less compliant media that has provoked considerable controversy – as the National Society for the Prevention of Cruelty to Children (NSPCC), amongst others, has discovered – over the percentage of donations being used for administrative and campaigning costs rather than being used for good causes.

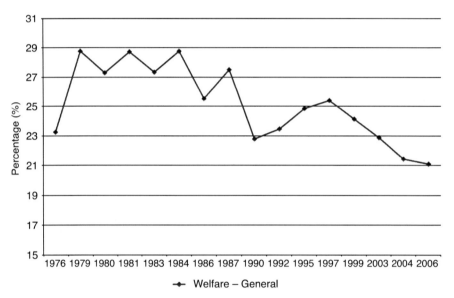

Figure 3.2.5: Income share of general welfare charities as a percentage of the wider income of the largest 200/500 charities in the UK, 1976–2006

Source: Charity Statistics (various years).

Further reading

For an introductory overview of the problems of equality in society, particularly in terms of old age and disability, see the essays in Pat Thane (ed.), *Unequal Britain: Equalities in Britain since 1945* (London, 2010). Frank Prochaska has written widely on the subject of philanthropy and charity in the nineteenth and twentieth centuries including *Christianity and Social Service in Modern Britain: The Disinherited Spirit* (Oxford, 2008). Geoffrey Finlayson, *Citizen, State and Social Welfare in Britain 1830–1990* (Oxford, 1994) provides the historical context for social policy and charts the moving frontier of the relationship between the state and the voluntary sector. A number of the organisations in this sector feature in Paul Whiteley and Stephen Winyard, *Pressure for the Poor: The Poverty Lobby and Policy Making* (London, 1987).

3. International aid and development

International aid and development NGOs have their origins in missionary activity, and their history arguably stretches back to the eighteenth century. The Methodist Missionary Society (established 1786) and the Church Missionary Society (1799) may have been primarily concerned with evangelism, but they engaged in projects that provided more material assistance to local communities around the world. However, an important impetus came with the foundation of the International Committee of the Red Cross (ICRC) in 1863, after Henry Dunant had assisted both warring sides at the Battle of Solferino in 1859. The British Red Cross Society began soon after the outbreak of the Franco-Prussian War in 1870 and was known as the British National Society for Aid to the Sick and Wounded in War. It adopted the Red Cross emblem and became formally known as the British Red Cross in 1905. By this time it had been joined by other faith-based humanitarian groups such as Quakers' Friends War Victims Relief Committee (1870) and the Salvation Army (1864).

World wars and totalitarianism provided the immediate context for the growth of emergency relief organisations in the twentieth century. Fight the Famine Council was set up in 1919 to help young victims of the First World War and it soon became Save the Children. It was followed by various Anglo-Jewish organisations in the 1930s that dealt with the specific refugee crisis resulting from Nazi persecution. The most prominent was the Central British Fund for World Jewish Relief (1933), which later became World Jewish Relief, the main Jewish organisation dealing with overseas aid.

In the Second World War further faith-based initiatives came in the form of Oxfam which began as the Quaker-inspired Oxford Committee for Famine Relief in 1942. Christian Aid was created in 1945 as Christian Reconstruction in Europe (and later the Inter-Church Aid and Refugee Service) to deal with the immediate refugee crisis at the end of the war. However, the desire to avoid the horrors of conflict also provoked a wider spirit of internationalism. In 1945, the socialist publisher, Victor Gollancz, established Save Europe Now which became very active in providing relief to central Europe. In 1951, he established the Association for World Peace to campaign for peace and development and, with the support of many prominent Labour MPs, especially Harold Wilson, this became War on Want in 1952.

If religion, mission, empire and war had provided the principal contexts for the early history of humanitarian intervention, world government and the more technical goal of 'development' were keys to international aid after 1945. The United States embarked upon an aid programme inspired by President Truman's Four Point Speech of 1949 which heralded 'a bold new program for making the benefits of our scientific advances and industrial progress available for the improvement and growth of underdeveloped areas'. This was to be carried through by the various United Nations' agencies and given momentum by the exigencies of the Cold War, which saw the US especially link its aid to a foreign policy geared around preventing states falling into communist hands. Indeed, a key text of this new era of development, W.W. Rostow's *The Stages of Economic Growth* (1960), was subtitled 'a non-communist manifesto'.

British NGOs closely followed UN initiatives. The UN World Refugee Year 1959 was an opportunity for Oxfam and War on Want to raise their profiles, as was the Freedom From Hunger Campaign launched by the Food and Agriculture Organisation in 1960 and which led to the formation of over 1,000 groups around the country. Other initiatives that would become associated with the UN Development Decade also impacted on NGO thinking as they came to realise the importance of long-term development rather than relief. And key publications in the history of development, such as the Pearson Report, *Partners in Development* (1969), and the Brandt Commission's *North–South: A Programme for Survival* (1980), have had a profound impact on the language and operations of NGOs.

The limited scale of NGOs in the 1960s meant they could only engage in small-scale projects, often relying on old imperial, Church-based contacts to maintain links with impoverished rural communities. Their basic work was still dominated by emergency relief, not least because their frequency only ever seemed to increase (see Box 3.3.1). From 1963, the British Red Cross, Christian Aid, Oxfam, Save the Children Fund and War on Want began working together through the Disasters Emergency Committee (DEC), which continues to operate today (and which now includes ActionAid, Catholic Agency for Overseas Development (CAFOD), Care International UK, Concern Worldwide, Help the Aged, Islamic Relief, Merlin, Tearfund and World Vision).

Box 3.3.1: Some key emergencies involving British NGOs and public appeals coordinated by DEC

Year	Place	Type
1960	Agadir	Earthquake
1961	Congo	Famine
1963	Skopje	Earthquake
1966	Varto, Turkey	Earthquake
1966	Bihar	Famine
1969	Biafra	Civil War
1970	Bangladesh	Cyclone
1974	Bangladesh	Famine
1979	Cambodia	Famine
1984	Ethiopia	Famine
1988	Bangladesh	Floods
1988	Sudan	Famine/civil war
1994	Rwanda	Genocide/refugees
1998	Sudan	Famine/civil war
1998	Central America	Hurricane
2001	India	Earthquake
2004	Indonesia	Tsunami
2004	Sudan	Conflict/famine
2005	Pakistan/India	Earthquake
2010	Haiti	Earthquake

The huge amount of funds directed to NGOs for emergencies has been dual-edged. It has certainly enabled them to grow, and many have become enormous, highly professional organisations seemingly a far cry from their voluntarist roots. But it has also trapped them into the sort of short-term relief work which their professional, expert staff believes does not lead to long-term development.

And development, as advocated by NGOs, has been able to promote itself as an alternative model to the massive aid programmes favoured by many official donors. In the 1960s, initiatives such as the Gramdam land reform movement initiated by the Gandhian, J.P. Narayan, convinced many NGOs of the benefits of small-scale projects in which local communities are full participants. Their thinking was further bolstered by figures such as Ivan Illich and E.F. Schumacher (*Small is Beautiful*, 1973) as well as liberation theology and notions of 'conscientisation' associated with the Marxist-influenced Brazilian writer, Paulo Freire, and his *Pedagogy of the Oppressed* (1968) that urged an active role for the poor themselves in their own development.

As official aid came under pressure from financial constraints and the changing tempo of Cold War tensions, the alternative model provided by NGOs came to be looked upon more favourably by donor governments. In Britain, the state began to fund NGOs because of their supposed 'comparative advantage' in reaching the very poorest members of society. As early as 1966, the then Ministry of Overseas Development supported the establishment of a Voluntary Committee on Overseas Aid and Development so that it could engage with the NGO community. In 1975, the Labour government initiated the Joint Funding Scheme to fund half the costs of specific projects. Such initiatives have expanded, especially under the Conservatives in the 1980s, as it cut back on official funding and sought out non-state mechanisms for promoting development. By the end of the decade, block grants were being given to the principal NGOs and around 100 NGOs were eligible for project funding.

Closer relations with the state have undoubtedly created opportunities for longer-term development work, but it has also meant that NGOs have become accountable to donors, with much of their work and efforts being directed by donor priorities rather than autonomous policy. Ultimately, the alternative nature of NGO approaches to development begins to disappear. Moreover, the state has policed NGO activity in other ways. The Charity Commissioners have often investigated NGOs when they have been seen to be too political, most notably in 1990 when, following pressure from right-wing groups such as Western Goals, the three NGOs War on Want, Christian Aid and Oxfam were investigated by the Charity Commissioners for their links with left-wing groups in countries such as South Africa and Nicaragua. But this has been a longstanding problem. Indeed, in 1969 the World Development Movement was established as a non-charitable body to take on many more overtly political topics, and in 1973, Christian Aid and Oxfam helped launch *New Internationalist*.

By the 1990s, the international aid and development NGOs were among the leading players of the NGO world (see Figures 3.3.1–3.3.4). They have continued to enjoy considerable public support as well as funding from the state, locking themselves into a relationship which seems as much geared towards securing future contracts as it does to genuine grassroots development. Yet NGOs have increasingly argued for a whole new approach to development, one that tackles structural inequities in the system of global economic governance. Accordingly, NGOs have become increasingly networked in global coalitions, lobbying and campaigning against the policies of the World Bank, the International Monetary Fund and the World Trade Organisation. Since 1988, over 40 NGOs had been involved in the Debt Crisis Network. These moved the debate forward in 1997 with the launch of Jubilee 2000, a truly global campaign but which involved around 110 NGOs in the UK Coalition. Similar mobilisations have continued with Make Poverty History, the Trade Justice Movement and Live 8.

Table 3.3.1: Prominent NGOs in the international aid and development sector (NGOs profiled in this book are shown in bold)

NGO	Year of formation
Action Aid	1972
Anti-Slavery International	1909
Band Aid	1984
British Red Cross Society	1870
Care International UK	1985
CAFOD	1962
Christian Aid	1945
Comic Relief	1984
Disasters Emergency Committee	1963
Fairtrade Foundation	1992
Islamic Relief	1984
Make Poverty History	2005
One World Trust	1951
Overseas Development Institute	1965
Oxfam	1942
Plan UK	1937
Save the Children Fund	1919
Tearfund	1968
Trade Justice Movement	2000
Voluntary Services Overseas	1961
War on Want	1952
World Development Movement	1969
World Vision UK	1982

Source: DANGO, www.dango.bham.ac.uk.

As NGOs have assumed a more central role in the development industry, they have also come under more fierce criticism. There exist longstanding critiques of development from the left (that it is used to promote capitalism and neo-colonialism) and the right (that it encourages dependency), but NGOs have usually been excluded. More recent commentary has pointed to how poverty has not been alleviated and that the principal beneficiaries of aid have been the administrators of aid themselves. As the lines between official and unofficial aid have been blurred in the contracting culture, NGOs have become the objects of scorn too. At worst, as in Biafra in 1969, Ethiopia in the 1980s and Sudan in the 1990s, their aid has been said to have prolonged war and misery as aid packages have reached military as much as civilian populations. At best, the competition between NGOs in securing government contracts must certainly lead to inefficiencies and uncoordinated operations that local elites are able to exploit to their own advantage. Certainly, more measures of NGO effectiveness have often been requested, though of the few detailed investigations into NGO projects around the world, their work has been shown to have some impact on the poor.

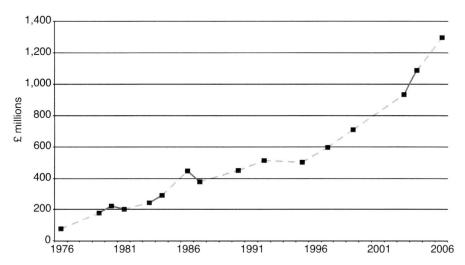

Figure 3.3.1: Cumulative voluntary income of international aid and development charities listed in the top 200 (1976–90) and top 500 charities (1992–2005) (adjusted for inflation)

Note: Data have been adjusted to reflect inflation and a change in the sample from top 200 to top 500 charities.

Source: Charity Statistics (various years).

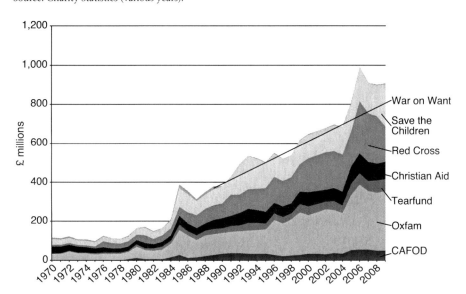

Figure 3.3.2: Income of selected international aid and development organisations, 1945–2009 (adjusted for inflation, 2009)

Source: Annual reports and accounts, organisations concerned; Charity Statistics (various years).

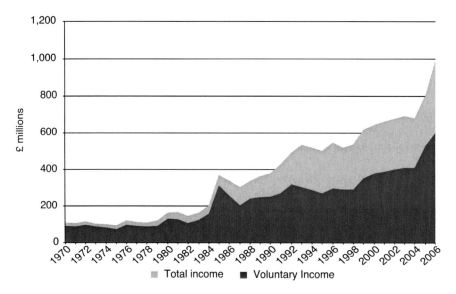

Figure 3.3.3: Voluntary versus total income of selected top international aid and development charities (CAFOD, Christian Aid, Oxfam, Save the Children, Tearfund, War on Want, Red Cross), 1970–2006 (cumulative totals, adjusted for inflation, 2009)

Source: Annual reports and accounts, organisations concerned; Charity Statistics (various years).

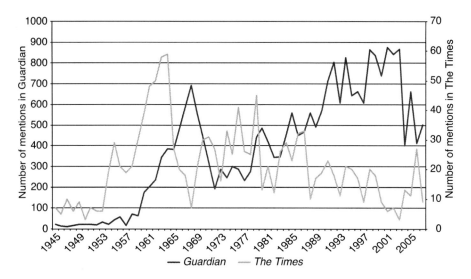

Figure 3.3.4: Number of mentions of CAFOD, Christian Aid, Oxfam, Save the Children, Tearfund, War on Want and the World Development Movement in the *Guardian* and *The Times*, 1945–2007

Note: The drop in the number of occurrences in the *Guardian* after 2003 is due to a change in the databases used, from ProQuest to Nexis. It does not necessarily reflect a drop in the number of mentions of NGOs.

Source: *Guardian* & *The Times*.

Further reading

On the history of development most generally, see Gilbert Rist, *The History of Development: From Western Origins to Global Faith*, 3rd edn (London, 2008). For overviews of British aid and NGOs, see Clare Saunders, 'British Humanitarian, Aid and Development NGOs, 1949–Present', in Nick Crowson, Matthew Hilton and James McKay (eds), *NGOs in Contemporary Britain: Non-state Actors in Society and Politics since 1945* (London, 2009), pp. 38–58; Ian Smillie, *The Alms Bazaar: Altruism Under Fire – Non-Profit Organizations and International Development* (London, 1995); Anuradha Bose and Peter Burnell (eds), *Britain's Overseas Aid since 1979: Between Idealism and Self-Interest* (Manchester, 1991), and Peter Burnell, *Foreign Aid in a Changing World* (Buckingham, 1997). See also the specific case studies of NGOs listed in Chapter 4.

4. Environment, heritage and conservation

Britain, in the nineteenth century, was one of the first countries in the world to give birth to organisations devoted to the protection of the natural world. The first prominent groups were the Commons Preservation Society (1865), the National Trust (1895) and the Royal Society for Wildlife Trusts (1912). The rise of these groups closely corresponds to the development of industry, the growth of cities (and the resource wars between cities and their peripheries that accompanied it, as in the famous example of Manchester's struggle for the waters of Thirlmere), and romantic sensibilities towards the preservation of cherished landscapes. These groups lobbied for the introduction of pieces of legislation protecting the countryside or facilitating access (for example, the 'Freedom to Roam' bill introduced in parliament in 1884).

While these earlier groups were predominantly made up of social elites, other groups were born during the interwar period, often with a different social makeup. The Campaign to Protect Rural England (CPRE), for example, was mostly made up of middle-class professionals. Its role was to coordinate the efforts of and facilitate communication between local and regional organisations who aimed to protect the English landscape and countryside, as well as access it (for example, the mass trespasses on Kinder Scout in 1932). In 1936, the CPRE allied with groups of outdoor enthusiasts such as the Ramblers Association and the Youth Hostels Association (YHA) – predominantly made up of middle- and working-class recreational users of the countryside – to form a Standing Committee on National Parks (SCNP) which pressed the case for national parks (enshrined in law in 1949).

However, environmental ideas and conservation groups remained marginal until the 1960s and 1970s. After the end of the Second World War, the impact of new technologies such as nuclear power, the 'Green Revolution' and the appearance of many new synthetic materials triggered a sense of awe amongst the general population. Yet nuclear energy, the boom in motor vehicles, the enormous expansion of the world's population and urbanisation also raised new levels of anxieties amongst some and awareness about environmental issues: the murderous Great Smog of London in 1952, for example, encouraged the first large-scale environmental legislation (Clean Air Act, 1956). Meanwhile, conservationists became concerned by the threats posed to endangered fauna and unspoiled landscapes around the world, which led to the creation in 1961 of the World Wildlife Fund (now the World Wide

Fund for Nature) (WWF), founded by four Britons: Sir Julian Huxley, Sir Peter Scott, Max Nicholson and Guy Mountfort.

Environmental matters really started to come under the spotlight during the next decade. Starting with the publications of Rachel Carson's *Silent Spring* in 1962, Paul Ehrlich's *Population Bomb* (1968) or the Club of Rome's *Limits to Growth* report (1972), a 'second wave' of environmental agitation spread rapidly across the US and Europe. Several new campaigning groups were created in the wake of these publications, which met with exceptional success in Britain: Friends of the Earth (1971) and Greenpeace (1977), both independent branches of North American-based organisations, immediately captured the imagination of the public with their media stunts. The first of these high-profile events was organised by Friends of the Earth in 1972, when the environmental group decided to drop thousands of non-returnable bottles to a manufacturer of soda drinks. The media coverage immediately brought the environmental body to the attention of the general public and drew in thousands of supporters and donors.

Throughout the 1970s and 1980s, these new NGOs, as well as more traditional groups such as the National Trust, grew at a very fast pace, both in terms of the number of supporters, as well as their income and staff levels (see Figures 3.4.1–3.4.4). Beside the publications mentioned above and the perceived spread and intensification of pollution, this phenomenal growth was also fuelled by the energy crises of the 1970s. Growth was also linked to the growing mediatisation of environmental issues: the risks associated with new technologies were further hammered home by various disasters which made international news during the period, such as *Torrey Canyon* (1967), Seveso (1976), Three Mile Island (1979), Bhopal (1984) (8,000–30,000 dead), Chernobyl (1986), and the *Exxon Valdez* black tide in Alaska (March 1989). The latter took place only a few months before the European elections of June 1989, which saw the biggest score ever recorded in the UK by the Green Party at any elections (14.5 per cent). This high score might also perhaps be attributed in part to the success of the Montreal agreement banning CFCs which entered into force in January 1989 and was followed by the first meeting of the signatory countries in May 1989 and to remarks made by the then British prime minister, Margaret Thatcher, about global warming, which became an important topic for environmental groups around that time. The success of the UK Green Party at the European elections was partially matched by higher-than-normal results in many other European countries, such as France and Germany (see Box 3.4.1).

The 1990s, however, was a period of relative stagnation for most 'second'- or 'third'-wave environmental NGOs in Britain, as Figures 3.4.1–3.4.4 clearly show.

Box 3.4.1: 1989 European elections: surge in the green vote

The Green Party in the UK obtained 15 per cent of the vote (its highest score ever). In France, two green lists obtained over 11.5 per cent of the vote (the highest score for the green vote in France, until the 2009 European elections). In Germany and in Italy, the green vote gathered 10 per cent and 6 per cent of the vote respectively, the highest score so far in both countries.

Most of these groups saw the number of their supporters, as well as their income in real terms, stand still or even decline. Part of the reason was that the large environmental NGOs such as Greenpeace, Friends of the Earth and WWF were criticised by their more radical members for becoming too 'institutionalised' and losing their cutting edge. As a consequence, the 1990s also saw the emergence and increasing competition from self-labelled 'disorganisations', such as Earth First! These were involved in some of the most high-profile campaigns of the 1990s, such as the demonstrations against the construction of a highway at Twyford Down. NGOs such as Friends of the Earth refused to take the risk of facing legal action against them and were replaced in the frontline by individual 'tree-huggers' who adopted non-violent direct action to try (unsuccessfully) to stop the construction of the highway.

To some extent these groups appeared to many environmental campaigners as more participative and modern than the ageing NGOs created in the 1970s. However, the latter groups were continuing their lobbying, and managed to grab the media's attention on a number of occasions, including the occupation by Greenpeace of the Brent Spar oil platform in the North Sea (1995). While these new groups continued to remain the focus of most of the media's attention, however, the older, more institutionalised preservationist groups, such as the National Trust or the Royal Society

Table 3.4.1: Prominent or representative environment, heritage and conservation NGOs, with year of formation (NGOs profiled in this book are shown in bold)

NGO	Year of formation
Commons Preservation Society	1865
Selborne Society	1885
Royal Society for the Protection of Birds (RSPB)	1889
National Trust	**1895**
Royal Society for Wildlife Trusts	1912
Campaign to Protect Rural England (CPRE)	1926
Ramblers	**1935**
Soil Association	**1946**
World Wide Fund for Nature (WWF)	**1961**
Conservation Society (ConSoc)	1966
Intermediate Technology Development Group/Practical Action	1966
Friends of the Earth (initially imported from the US)	**1971**
Campaign for Better Transport (Transport 2000)	1973
Life Style Movement	1974
Greenpeace	**1977**
Sustrans	1977
Pesticide Action Network UK (PAN UK) (formerly Pesticides Trust)	1986
Rainforest Foundation	1989
Earth First	1991
Reclaim the Streets (RtS)	1995
GM Freeze	1995
Campaign Against Climate Change	2001
Stop Climate Chaos Coalition	2005

Source: DANGO, www.dango.bham.ac.uk.

for the Protection of Birds, continued to undergo a steady growth, which puts into perspective the stagnation of some organisations highlighted above.

More recently, in the 2000s, due to the return to the forefront of environmental concerns about climate change, many environmental groups have joined forces in large coalitions such as Stop Climate Chaos – including groups from the first, second and third waves such as the National Trust, the CPRE and Friends of the Earth – to campaign against climate change. Indeed, this now acts as an umbrella term that covers older environmental notions too (as well as broader ideas about social justice), and several core themes dear to preservationists have resurfaced through what is now called the defence of 'biodiversity', forming a coherent link between the late nineteenth- and early twenty-first century organisations. The media often attributes the Climate Change Act (which became law in November 2008) to the relentless lobbying of environmental groups in 2007 and 2008 (in particular, the 'Big Ask' campaign coordinated by Friends of the Earth).

Key statistics for the environment, heritage and conservation sector

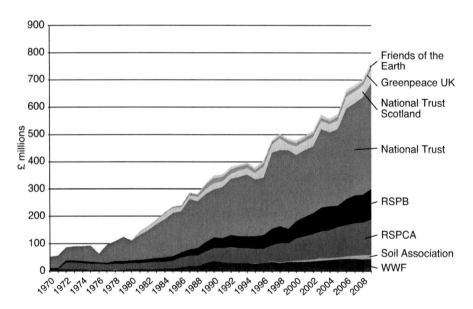

Figure 3.4.1: Cumulated income of selected environmental organisations in the UK, 1970–2009 (adjusted for inflation, 2009)

Sources: Charity Statistics (various years); Annual reports and accounts, organisations concerned; Charity Commission.

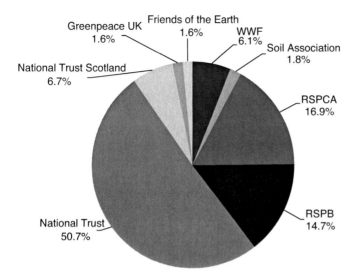

Figure 3.4.2: Income size of environmental organisations in 2009 relative to the income of all environmental organisations in sample

Source: Annual reports and accounts, organisations concerned; Charity Statistics; Charity Commission.

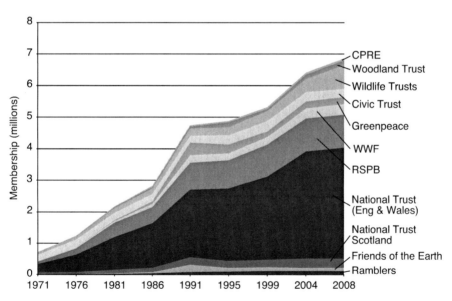

Figure 3.4.3: Membership of selected environmental organisations, 1971–2008

Sources: Estimations based on sometimes conflicting sources: Annual reports and accounts, organisations concerned; *Social Trends* (various years); Neil Carter, *The Politics of the Environment: Ideas, Activism, Policy* (Cambridge, 2007); Francis Sandbach, *Environment, Ideology and Policy* (Oxford, 1980); Paul Byrne, *Social Movements in Britain* (London, 1997); Robert Lamb, *Promising the Earth* (London, 1996); Joe Weston, *The F.O.E. Experience: The Development of an Environmental Pressure Group* (Oxford, 1989); Peter Rawcliffe, *Environmental Pressure Groups in Transition* (Manchester, 1998).

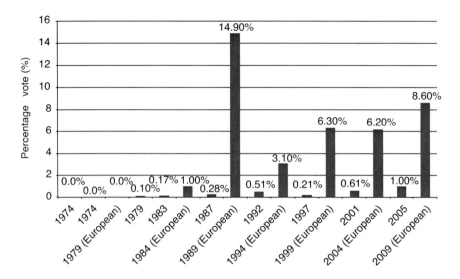

Figure 3.4.4: Score of the Green Party at elections (UK)

Sources: David Boothroyd, United Kingdom Election Results, www.election.demon.co.uk; UK Parliament website, www.parliament.uk.

Further reading

For an introduction to the history and key concepts of the environmental movement in Britain, see Neil Carter, *The Politics of the Environment: Ideas, Activism, Policy*, 2nd edn (Cambridge, 2007). For a shorter introduction, see Christopher Rootes, 'Environmental NGOs and the Environmental Movement in England', in Nick Crowson, James McKay and Matthew Hilton, *NGOs in Contemporary Britain: Non-State Actors in Society and Politics Since 1945* (Basingstoke, 2009). For the organisational development of the sector, see Grant Jordan and William Maloney, *The Protest Business? Mobilizing Campaign Groups* (Manchester, 1997); Peter Rawcliffe, *Environmental Pressure Groups in Transition* (Manchester, 1998), and Christopher John Bosso, *Environment, Inc: From Grassroots to Beltway* (Lawrence, 2005).

5. Think tanks

During the 1980s a significant amount of media attention was devoted to New Right organisations, like the Institute for Economic Affairs (IEA) and the Centre for Policy Studies (CPS). An impression arose that 'think tanks' in Britain were a relatively new creature that had emerged during the late 1960s and were largely of the political right. In fact, these represented only the latest incarnation of think tanks in a process that can be traced back to the mid nineteenth century, and which cover a range of public policy interests from defence and diplomatic matters to the social to economic, bound together by a sense that ideas are important. These many organisations occupy a middle ground between government and the informed public and, by engaging in research and advocacy, have sought to influence both the direction of policy and the terms of public debate.

Legitimate questions may be asked about the extent of their influence. Critics suggest that they skew debate in their competition for the attention of elected officials and that their apparent 'expert analysis' is a threat to democratic structures. At the same time it is possible to argue that they themselves are a prism through which to recognise evolving policy concerns. For example, think tanks concerned with foreign policy research have extended their agendas over the twentieth century away from the high political concerns about diplomatic strategy towards wider low-policy anxieties about international economic and environmental issues conducted within the framework of globalisation.

There is a long lineage of groups in Britain coming together out of concern for specific matters in society which they believe can be enhanced by an alteration of the contemporary intellectual standpoints. The growing complexities of government that emerged from the early part of the nineteenth century provided opportunities for such interested parties, and sometimes, due to their expertise, gave them influence disproportionate to their numerical strengths. Thus the Philosophic Radicals, via their journal, *The Westminster Review*, carried considerable influence over social legislation, not least the 1834 Poor Law. The Royal United Services Institute for Defence Studies (RUSI), established in 1831 as the Naval and Military Museum, with patronage from the Duke of Wellington, aimed to bring together the youngest and brightest officers so that military policy and developments could be discussed and questioned amongst professionals regardless of rank or title. The influence of the English Positivists has been identified in the transformation of trade union law during the nineteenth century. Essentially these groupings were a combination of political ginger groups and philosophical debating forums, and the Fabians (founded in 1884) very much drew upon these historical antecedents.

The interwar years marked the next phase of think tank evolution. Concerns with international affairs and policy planning very much dominated the agendas, but these organisations were often a shadowing operation to a government department, fostering close links between Whitehall and the think tank sector, and also enjoying links with the US. Thus the Royal Institute of International Affairs (founded in 1920 and receiving its royal charter in 1926) operated in tandem with its New York-based sister organisation, the Council on Foreign Relations, and worked closely with the Foreign Office.

The 1930s witnessed the foundation of Political and Economic Planning (PEP), and the National Institute of Economic and Social Research (NIESR) in 1938 which had links with the Treasury. Both these organisations have been credited with creating the conditions that were necessary for post-war planning. NIESR was the first organisation to produce and publish economic forecasts and to seek to identify likely world economic trends. Its influence spilt over not only into Whitehall and the broadsheet media, but also into the academic discipline of economics as taught in British universities. Similarly, PEP's 1937 report on welfare reforms is credited with having influenced the creation of the NHS in 1948.

The post-1945 years saw the emergence of more specialised think tanks such as the International Institute for Strategic Services (IISS) (1958), as well as more ideologically partisan bodies such as the Institute of Economic Affairs (1957), the Centre for Policy Studies (1974) and the Adam Smith Institute (1977). These right-leaning partisan organisations explicitly rejected the notion of offering policy based upon detached scholarly analysis. Instead they conceived themselves as political actors: the CPS as an insider moulding the Conservative Thatcherite revolution; the Adam Smith Institute as an outrider championing the neo-liberal cause and driving a wider conservative movement. There was certainly a growing critique emerging that suggested the older established think tanks like Chatham House were detached from policy and too interested in academia.

The late 1980s and 1990s saw an expansion in the range of British think tanks that rejected modes of academic policy research in favour of more polemical and advocacy driven work. There was also a deliberate attempt from the other political parties to seek to create counter think tanks to the Conservative sympathisers. Labour modernisers during the mid-1980s increasingly recognised the need for a modernising left-wing intellectual community that could fashion policy advice for Labour leaders. The answer was the Institute for Public Policy Research (IPPR) (established 1988) directed by James Cornford who used his experiences at the Outer Circle Policy Unit in the 1970s to model the IPPR operations using limited funds and staffing levels to mobilise external resources.

The Social Democrat Party did so similarly with the Social Market Foundation (SMF) (1989). However, by 1992 it was relaunched as a more Conservative-oriented organisation interested in public service reform, with Danny Finkelstein as director, and having secured charitable status and financial support from David Salisbury. In the post-Thatcher age the SMF occupied a fertile territory and its pamphlets contributed to evolving Conservative thought and attracted the attention of ministers and civil servants, especially David Willetts. The SMF was broadly sympathetic to John Major's administration on matters relating to domestic and public sector reform – having a preference for internal market reforms rather than privatisation.

The term 'think tank' is problematic, being both misused and misunderstood by commentators, participants and the wider public alike. The term itself has a military background, having been used during the Second World War to refer to a secure room where strategy and plans could be discussed. In the aftermath of war it gained currency in American circles to delineate research organisations contracted to the US military, such as the RAND Corporation. The term only began being used in Britain from the late 1960s, and usually in connection with American military/ foreign policy research organisations with close links to government. Both *The Times* and the *Guardian* first used the term in the summer of 1967 in articles from their American correspondents. Thereafter the term gained wider use and currency and was applied to a much broader group of organisations that were engaged in a wider range of public policy research and advocacy.

During the 1970s there was evidently an assumption that 'think tanks' ought to be associated with, if not of, government, as the application of the nickname of 'the Think Tank' to the Central Policy Review Staff suggests. This was a research policy unit established by Edward Heath in 1970 within Number 10, and for much of that decade the notion of 'think tank' in Britain became synonymous with one particular policy planning research unit until Thatcher abolished it in 1983.

Within the umbrella of think tanks, three subcategories are apparent: those engaged in academic research but without the burden of students (for example, the Royal Institute of International Affairs (RIIA), commonly known as Chatham House); those that contract their research services out either to government or to private client groups (such as the Policy Studies Institute); and a final category that adopts a partisan position and engages in advocacy, and often adopts campaigning or pressure group tactics (like Demos). What distinguishes this last subcategory from pressure groups is the likelihood that they will be interested in a wider range of subject matters rather than single issues. But the boundaries are being blurred not least because pressure groups are increasingly reliant on detailed research to justify and quantify their campaign position.

Ultimately, whatever the label applied, the reality is that these organisations share broadly similar objectives and engage in broadly similar activities. The differences ultimately come down to the scale of emphasis. They are concerned with setting the parameters of elite opinion and debate, and they are seeking access to the process of public policy decision making. The academic and policy thinkers assigned to these organisations ought to be conceived as an alternative civil service. But they share an important distinction from the civil servants of Whitehall in that they are not tied by the oversight of ministerial responsibility and, because they are concerned with the presentation of potential policy rather than its implementation, they can adopt more utopian standpoints.

Table 3.5.1: Foundation dates of key think tanks (NGOs profiled in this book are shown in bold)

Think tank	Year of formation
Fabians	1884
Round Table	1909
Royal Institute of International Affairs	1920
Howard League	1921
PEP	1931
National Institute for Economic and Social Research	1938
Institute for Race Relations	1952
Institute for Economic Affairs	1957
Overseas Development Institute	1965
Institute for Fiscal Studies	1969
Centre for Policy Studies	1974
Adam Smith Institute	1978
New Economics Foundation	1986
Institute for Public Policy Research	1988
Social Democratic Foundation	1989
Demos	1993
Young Foundation	2005
Open Europe	2005
Institute for Government	2009

Source: DANGO, www.dango.bham.ac.uk.

Although the notion that these think tanks are independent is questionable, their potential value to policy makers and politicians is the deniability of their ideas. Because they have acquired credibility with the media, it means that they also form a shield for policy makers. With a media that is willing to give credence and publicity to even the most controversial of think thank ideas, it has been recognised that the public appears more willing to accept (or at least consider) policies than if they had first come direct from a government minister. The closeness of the relationship is also evident in the revolving doors of personnel between the think tanks, the civil service and political parties. The career trajectories of David Willetts and John Redwood from think tanks to government serve as just two such examples.

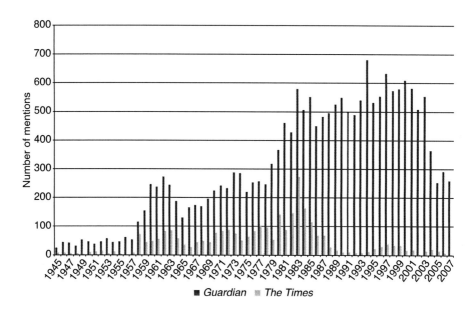

■ *Guardian*   ▨ *The Times*

Figure 3.5.1: Number of mentions of key think tanks and political organisations (Centre for Policy Studies, Fabian Society, Howard League for Penal Reform, Institute for Fiscal Studies, Liberty; Policy Studies Institute, Vegetarian Society, Which?, Victim Support) in the *Guardian* and *The Times*, 1945–2007

Source: *Guardian* & *The Times*.

Further reading

For insider accounts of think tanks, see John Hoskyns, *Just In Time: Inside the Thatcher Revolution* (London, 2000). For the Centre for Policy Studies and for a view on working within 'the Think Tank', the CPRS, see Tessa Blackstone and William Plowden, *Inside the Think Tank: Advising Cabinet 1971–1983* (London, 1988).

For some historical perspective on the impact of planning in the interwar years, see Arthur Marwick, 'Middle Opinion in the Thirties: Planning, Progress and Political "Agreement"', *English Historical Review*, 79:311 (1964), pp. 285–98. For a controversial analysis of impact of the New Right think tanks, see Richard Cockett, *Thinking the Unthinkable: Think Tanks and the Economic Counter-Revolution 1931–83* (London, 1995). More measured evaluations can be found in Michael Kandiah and Anthony Seldon (eds), *Ideas and Think Tanks in Contemporary Britain, vols 1–2* (Newbury, 1996–97).

On defining think tanks, see Simon James, 'The Idea Brokers: The Impact of think Tanks on British Government', *Public Administration*, 71 (1993), pp. 491–506; Diane Stone and Andrew Denham (eds), *Think Tank Traditions: Policy Research and the Politics of Ideas* (Manchester, 2004), and Richard Higgott and Diane Stone, 'The Limits of Influence: Foreign Policy Think Tanks in Britain and the USA', *Review of International Studies*, 20:1 (1994), pp. 15–34.

6. Human rights

'Human rights' activism is actually a relatively recent phenomenon in the UK, as in much of the Western world. Groups that have campaigned on what we today perceive to be human rights have more frequently associated their work with 'civil liberties'. The confusion arises because of the ascendancy of rights talk at the end of the Second World War, the creation of the United Nations and the signing of the Universal Declaration of Human Rights (UDHR) in 1948. There is a tendency to see these as benchmarks from which human rights organisations have taken their cue, leading to the slow, inexorable rise of rights through to their dominance over the last two to three decades. Yet the events of the 1940s did not trigger widespread discussion of human rights. The United Nations Association observed the international human rights day (10 December, the date when the General Assembly adopted the UDHR) with barely a murmur. And, indeed, even at Amnesty International, there was little talk of human rights work in the 1960s.

If human rights as the basis for socio-political action do not find a rich tradition in the UK, organisations committed to the defence of civil liberties do. If we adopt a loose definition, it is possible to find roots in the eighteenth century from the anti-slavery movement, though it was not until 1957 that the forerunner to Anti-Slavery International proclaimed itself actually for human rights. Likewise, the rights of specific cohorts of the population have been defended by, for example, suffragettes and trade unions. One example of early international success by a British NGO was the adoption, by the League of Nations, of the Declaration of the Rights of the Child in 1924. This had been written by Eglantyne Jebb, the founder of Save the Children which had pushed for a rights-based approach since its foundation in 1919. In 1921, PEN International, the association of writers, was formed in London. While it has worked to promote intellectual cooperation, it has also sought to protect literature and writers from various threats and accordingly sees itself as a human rights body.

The most direct origins of a human rights 'movement', though, lie with the formation of the National Council of Civil Liberties (NCCL) in 1934. Frustrated at police tactics in dealing with hunger marchers, the journalist Ronald Kidd founded the organisation to ensure the civil liberties of those engaged in lawful protest were not being infringed. As a 'watchdog' body, its profile was helped by the recruitment of some leading public figures: E.M. Forster served as its president, with Clement Attlee, Aneurin Bevan, Aldous Huxley, J.B. Priestley and Bertrand Russell all included in the impressive list of vice-presidents.

However, the organisation soon struggled, not least because it came to be associated with the Communist Party, a perhaps unfair accusation against an organisation which genuinely tried to be non-party political but which increasingly drifted to the left as its campaigns brought it into conflict with the government. It did attempt to engage to a degree with ideas of human rights. Many of the figures associated with the NCCL also had links to an organisation called For Intellectual Liberty, a body set up in 1936 by intellectuals defending international peace, liberty and culture. During the war, other sympathisers, such as H.G. Wells, attempted to mobilise support behind an international bill of rights, but the NCCL itself had fallen into something of a decline. Afterwards, its international collaborations in developing human rights saw it fall foul of Cold War divisions and no sustained global agenda of rights or liberties was put forward.

With the UDHR also failing to capture the public imagination, human rights re-emerged in a more legalistic manner and more concerned with the imprisonment of political activists under authoritarian regimes. The British wing of the International Commission of Jurists (formed in 1952), JUSTICE, was set up in 1957 by, among others, Peter Benenson, who would go on to found Amnesty in 1961. Such internationalism was part of a wider concern for social justice that saw issues being increasingly understood in terms of the abuse of civil and political rights. In this sense, Amnesty's foundation needs to be situated alongside the creation of other social movements, especially the Movement for Colonial Freedom in 1954 and the Anti-Apartheid Movement, founded in 1959.

Once created, Amnesty's rise and domination of the human rights field was remarkable, both domestically and internationally. Just three years after its formation, in 1964, it was granted consultative status at the UN, and by 1966 it claimed to have instigated the release of 1,000 prisoners of conscience. With its rapidly expanding membership and branch organisation structure, Amnesty made human rights a social movement rather than the preserve of legal experts. Yet with its prominent branding, savvy marketing initiatives and celebrity endorsement, it also featured all the hallmarks of the modern NGO. Moreover, by the 1970s it was operating in an environment in which human rights had been placed on the global diplomatic agenda. It served a purpose for governments to be seen to be supporting Amnesty, a trend consolidated with its award of the Nobel Peace Prize in 1977.

This is not to say that civil liberties activism was not also undergoing something of a revival at the same time. NCCL was revitalised by the social movements of the 1960s, acting as something of a friendly uncle-figure to a new generation of protester. Yet such engagement also expanded the repertoire of NCCL's work, and the resources it committed to issues such as women's rights, race, gay liberation and civil rights in Northern Ireland increased rapidly. However, this was done at a time when the language of human rights was capturing the imagination much more so than that of civil liberties. It is therefore of little surprise that, in 1989, NCCL changed its name to Liberty and declared itself to be working to defend human rights.

Nevertheless, the nature of human rights activism was highly circumscribed for long periods. The original UDHR had set out not only civil and political rights but economic and social rights too. Rights to a decent standard of living, to shelter,

Box 3.6.1: Key international instruments in human rights protocols since the Second World War

1948	Universal Declaration of Human Rights
1951	Convention Relating to the Status of Refugees
1952	Convention on the Political Rights of Women
1955	Standard Minimum Rules for the Treatment of Prisoners
1965	International Convention on the Elimination of All Forms of Racial Discrimination
1966	International Covenant on Civil and Political Rights
1966	International Covenant on Economic, Social and Cultural Rights
1975	Helsinki Accords
1981	Convention on the Elimination of all Forms of Discrimination Against Women
1984	Convention Against Torture
1989	Convention on the Rights of the Child
1990	International Convention on the Protection of the Rights of All Migrant Workers and Members of their Families
1993	Vienna Declaration and Program of Action
2002	Rome Statute of the International Criminal Court

Box 3.6.2: Preamble to the Universal Declaration of Human Rights

'Whereas recognition of the inherent dignity and of the equal and inalienable rights of all members of the human family is the foundation of freedom, justice and peace in the world,

Whereas disregard and contempt for human rights have resulted in barbarous acts which have outraged the conscience of mankind, and the advent of a world in which human beings shall enjoy freedom of speech and belief and freedom from fear and want has been proclaimed as the highest aspiration of the common people,

Whereas it is essential, if man is not to be compelled to have recourse, as a last resort, to rebellion against tyranny and oppression, that human rights should be protected by the rule of law,

Whereas it is essential to promote the development of friendly relations between nations,

Whereas the peoples of the United Nations have in the Charter reaffirmed their faith in fundamental human rights, in the dignity and worth of the human person and in the equal rights of men and women and have determined to promote social progress and better standards of life in larger freedom,

Whereas Member States have pledged themselves to achieve, in co-operation with the United Nations, the promotion of universal respect for and observance of human rights and fundamental freedoms,

Whereas a common understanding of these rights and freedoms is of the greatest importance for the full realization of this pledge,

Now, Therefore THE GENERAL ASSEMBLY proclaims THIS UNIVERSAL DECLARATION OF HUMAN RIGHTS as a common standard of achievement for all peoples and all nations, to the end that every individual and every organ of society, keeping this Declaration constantly in mind, shall strive by teaching and education to promote respect for these rights and freedoms and by progressive measures, national and international, to secure their universal and effective recognition and observance, both among the peoples of Member States themselves and among the peoples of territories under their jurisdiction.'

food, and so on, have been eschewed by human rights bodies such as Amnesty and have been left to the sphere of international aid and development NGOs. However, bodies such as Oxfam and War on Want did not seriously engage with the language of rights until the 1980s, when the 'right to development' began to take off in various UN agencies. Thereafter, but particular following the Vienna Declaration and Programme of Action, as adopted at the 1993 World Conference on Human Rights, most international aid and development NGOs have adopted a rights-based approach to development which assumes that securing access to basic human rights is a precondition for poverty alleviation. And at the same time, human rights NGOs have travelled in the same direction, increasingly arguing that civil and political rights are indivisible from economic and social rights.

If rights-talk now seems all-pervasive, the influence of NGOs is by no means assured. The more aspirational economic and social rights might prompt more high-sounding rhetoric than concrete action, and it is not always clear how far political and civil rights must bend to the interests of government and diplomacy. The election of the Labour government in 1997 seemed to bring many former human rights activists into power and certainly resulted in the passing of the Human Rights Act of 1998 as well as the 2000 Freedom of Information Act. But Liberty, Amnesty and other human rights organisations still find themselves frequently in conflict with the state. In particular, the new security agenda which has emerged after 2001 has resulted in a situation whereby many human rights NGOs perceive rights to be in retreat. Not only are new measures associated with the 'war on terror' threatening hard-won civil liberties, but the practical realisation of declared human rights is as much the product of *realpolitik* as it was in the 1940s or 1970s.

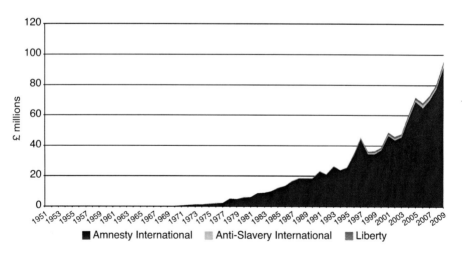

Figure 3.6.1: Cumulated income of three human rights organisations, 1951–2009 (adjusted for inflation, 2009)

Source: Annual report and accounts, organisations concerned; Charity Statistics (various years); Charity Commission.

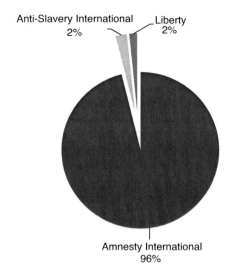

Figure 3.6.2: Income size of human rights organisations in 2009 relative to the total income of all organisations in sample

Sources: Annual report and accounts, organisations concerned; Charity Statistics (various years); Charity Commission.

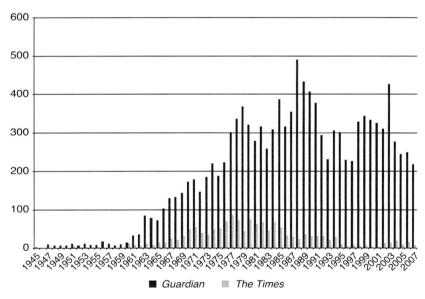

Figure 3.6.3: Number of mentions of human rights organisations (Anti-Apartheid Movement/ACTSA (Action for Southern Africa), Amnesty International, Anti-Slavery International, Liberty) in the *Guardian* and *The Times*, 1945–2007

Note: The drop in the number of occurrences in the *Guardian* after 2003 is due to a change in the databases used, from ProQuest to Nexis. It does not necessarily reflect a drop in the number of mentions of NGOs.

Source: *Guardian* & *The Times*.

Further reading

For international accounts of the modern history of rights, see William Korey, *NGOs and the Universal Declaration of Human Rights: 'A Curious Grapevine'* (Basingstoke, 1998), and Samuel Moyn, *The Last Utopia: Human Rights in History* (Cambridge, 2010).

On the UK specifically, see Tom Buchanan, 'Human Rights Campaigns in Modern Britain', in Nick Crowson, Matthew Hilton and James McKay (eds), *NGOs in Contemporary Britain: Non-State Actors in Society and Politics since 1945* (Basingstoke, 2009), and Chris Moores, 'The Progressive Professionals: The National Council for Civil Liberties and the Politics of Activism in the 1960s', *Twentieth Century British History*, 20:4 (2009), pp. 538–60.

For case studies of Amnesty, see Anne-Marie Clarke, *Diplomacy of Conscience: Amnesty International and Changing Human Rights Norms* (Princeton, 2001); Stephen Hopgood, *Keepers of the Flame: Understanding Amnesty International* (Ithaca, NY, 2006), and Jonathan Power, *Like Water on Stone: The Story of Amnesty International* (London, 2001).

7. Gender, sex and sexuality

The gender and sexuality field has seen enormous advances over the twentieth century and beyond, from the extension of the franchise after the First World War, to the passage of the Equalities Act in 2006. Yet the story is not one of straightforward, steady progress. Different agendas have ebbed, flowed and intertwined over the period. Principal among these have been formal, legal equality between the sexes, identity politics, the regulation of sexuality, and the financial security of children and families. While each of these themes has been championed by a diverse and growing campaigning sector, the progress made towards gender and sexual equality over the century should not blind one either to major setbacks along the way, or to significant issues that remain unresolved.

The winning of the vote in the interwar period was the triumphant culmination of many decades of feminist campaigning. Although there were major tactical differences – notably between the constitutionalist suffragists and the radical suffragettes – up until 1928, winning the vote provided a unifying goal for the women's movement. Following that victory, underlying class and political differences fractured the movement into different strands: while those who became known as the egalitarian feminists sought to maintain a focus on formal legal equality, the new feminism was concerned more with the day-to-day lives of ordinary women. Part of this was the growing politics centring on women's bodies, signified by the formation of the Abortion Law Reform Association (ALRA).

Meanwhile, women's associational groups grew dramatically. Organisations such as the Women's Institute, the Mothers' Union, the Townswomen's Guild and the Women's Co-operative Guild were often not overtly feminist, and yet did much to formulate and promote progressive notions of female citizenship during the mid twentieth century. Despite pressures to the contrary, this work continued in the post-war years, and met with important successes in both the home and the workplace. Domestically, the introduction of the Family Allowance in 1945 gave mothers of two or more children direct financial support, as part of the wider introduction of Beveridge's welfare state. The lifting of the marriage bar for certain professions also enabled middle-class women to participate fully in the workforce, while in 1955, equal pay for women was won by women in the non-industrial civil service.

The respectable reformism of the mid twentieth-century women's movement was by necessity replicated by those who sought to alleviate the plight of homosexual men (lesbians being formally unrecognised, and therefore unregulated, by the law). While anal intercourse between men had long been the subject of harsh punishment (carrying the death penalty until the early nineteenth century), it was the infamous Labouchere amendment to the 1885 Criminal Law Amendment Act which fully exposed homosexual men to state repression and the danger of blackmail, through the blanket prohibition of any act deemed a gross indecency.

Despite this repressive framework, pressure for reform did grow in the post-war years. The American sexologist Alfred Kinsey's *Sexual Behaviour in the Human Male* (1948) gained widespread coverage and revealed the sheer extent of homosexual activity, and the Church of England Moral Welfare Council argued for the decriminalisation of homosexual behaviour in the early 1950s. In this context, and amidst high-profile scandals and prosecutions, the Wolfenden Committee was established in 1954, and in 1957 recommended the decriminalisation of private and consenting homosexual activity for adults over the age of 21. In doing so, Wolfenden endorsed the Moral Welfare Council's position that the law should not be used to enforce morality, but rather should be concerned with public protection. Following Wolfenden, the Homosexual Law Reform Society (HLRS) was established, which focused on the quiet lobbying of politicians.

During the 1960s, three distinctly different strands can be identified in the politics of gender and sexuality. In the first, the quiet and effective lobbying of groups such as ALRA and the HLRS bore fruit in the so-called permissive society legislation. In 1967 the Sexual Offences Act decriminalised homosexuality, while the Abortion Act provided legal access to abortion for all women for the first time. Other reforms, such as the introduction of no-blame divorces, heightened the sense that Victorian morality was finally crumbling. Nevertheless, the reforms were still cautious and limited, for all their relative radicalism: women's access to abortion would be regulated by the necessary approval of GPs, while homosexual men still faced far more legal restrictions on their sexual behaviour than their heterosexual peers.

The second strand, in many ways enabled by the political space created by the permissive society reforms, was the rise of identity politics. Fuelled by rising levels of affluence and education, and given intellectual ballast by writers as diverse as Betty Frieden, Germaine Greer and Kate Millett, a more radical and assertive second-wave feminism emerged in Britain at the end of the decade. Key here was the Women's Liberation Movement which, although relatively short-lived, played an important role in articulating and formulating the demands of a new generation of feminists (see Box 3.7.1).

In the third strand, meanwhile, the 'rediscovery of poverty', initially driven by social policy academics and later championed by a new cohort of campaign groups, brought to light the failure of the welfare state to eliminate poverty in Britain. In the context of gender and family life, new groups emerged such as the Child Poverty Action Group, and Gingerbread, run by and for single parents, and demonstrated

Box 3.7.1: The seven demands of Women's Liberation (finalised in Birmingham, 1978)

'The women's liberation movement asserts a woman's right to define her own sexuality, and demands:

1. Equal pay for equal work
2. Equal education and job opportunities
3. Free contraception
4. Free 24-hour community-controlled childcare
5. Legal and financial independence for women
6. An end to discrimination against lesbians
7. Freedom for all women from intimidation by the threat or use of male violence. An end to the laws, assumptions and institutions which perpetuate male dominance and men's aggression towards women.'

that the rise of identity politics did not mean that society had progressed beyond material concerns. High-profile strike action, such as that at Ford Dagenham in the 1960s, and the Grunwick dispute in the 1970s, also underlined the fact that much remained to be won in the workplace.

In many ways, the 1970s were a golden age of activism and advance for the politics of gender and sexuality. Women's Lib, through its loose networks of activism, conferences and publication, asserted the right to a far broader concept of sexual equality than had hitherto been considered by the mainstream women's movement, while also placing emphasis on raising the awareness of individual women of the prejudices and restrictions they faced in their everyday lives. Echoing this, and encouraged by the receding threat of legal repression, gay liberation completely recast the politics of homosexuality, turning quiet apology into assertive pride in just a couple of years. Meanwhile, women also won legislative victories over equal pay and sexual discrimination, although how effective these laws were at combating the evils they identified remained an open question.

The sense of advance, which had built up during the activism and reforms of the previous years, came to a juddering halt in the 1980s. In part, this was down to the harsh economics of the age, as unemployment, inflation and fiscal retrenchment undermined the scope for progressive change. However, the hegemony of the New Right's profound social conservatism also played an important part. In Britain, this phenomenon was both led and symbolised by Margaret Thatcher, the country's first female premier, who famously felt she owed nothing to Women's Lib. Much of the New Right's challenge to progressive morality came within the context of Thatcher's assault on local government – the label 'loony-left council' was to the 1980s what 'political correctness gone mad' would be to the 1990s and beyond. And here, gay men were the particular targets. As the gay community reeled from the advent of HIV/AIDS, itself used as a stick with which to beat them, a concocted media storm over sex education in the school curriculum led to the introduction of Section 28 of the 1988 Local Government Act. This specifically forbade the promotion of homosexuality in state schools, or teaching that presented homosexuality 'as a pretended family relationship'. In response to increased levels of hostility and challenge, new organisations formed, such as Stonewall and OutRage! for gay rights, and the Terrence Higgins Trust to combat HIV/AIDS.

Box 3.7.2: Gender, sex and sexuality: key legislation

1918	Partial extension of suffrage, to women aged over 30
1928	Universal women's suffrage
1955	Equal pay for women in public sector
1967	Sexual Offences Act
1967	Abortion Act
1969	Divorce law reform
1970	Equal Pay Act
1975	Sex Discrimination Act
1988	Section 28 (repealed 2003)
1993	Labour Party adopts all-women shortlists
1994	Age of consent for gay men lowered to 18
2001	Age of consent for gay men lowered to 16
2004	Civil Partnership Act
2006	Equality Act

Table 3.7.1: Some prominent NGOs (with formation dates) (NGOs profiled in this book are shown in bold)

NGO	Year of formation
Fawcett Society	1866
Mothers' Union	1876
Co-operative Women's Guild	1883
Women's Institute	1915
National Council for the Unmarried Mother and Her Child (later One Parent Families)	1918
Townswomen's Guild	1929
Abortion Law Reform Association (later Abortion Rights)	1936
Marriage Guidance Council (later Relate)	1938
Equal Pay Campaign Committee	1943
Homosexual Law Reform Society	1958
Minorities Research Group	1963
North West Committee of Homosexual Law Reform Society (later Campaign for Homosexual Equality)	1964
Child Poverty Action Group	1965
Women's Liberation Front	1969
Gay Liberation Front	1970
Women's Aid	1971
Terrence Higgins Trust	1982
Stonewall	1989
OutRage!	1990

Source: DANGO, www.dango.bham.ac.uk.

The 1997–2001 New Labour administration came into office seeking to address the unequal treatment of women and minority groups and, in a limited sense, succeeded in doing so. The gay rights agenda saw particular gains, with the equalisation of the age of consent, the repeal of Section 28, and the introduction of civil partnerships, amongst other things. More generally, the 2006 Equality Act enshrined the notion that discrimination on the grounds of gender, sexuality, disability, faith, colour or age was no longer permissible. However, such advances should not be overemphasised. As the experience of the 1970s legislation demonstrated, changing the law only goes so far, and while attitudes have shifted, discrimination remains in many areas, such as the ongoing pay gap between men and women. Other promises also remained unfulfilled: over the lifetime of the government, it became increasingly obvious that a striking pledge to abolish child poverty by 2020 would never be achieved, adding yet another failure to decades of government attempts to address this issue.

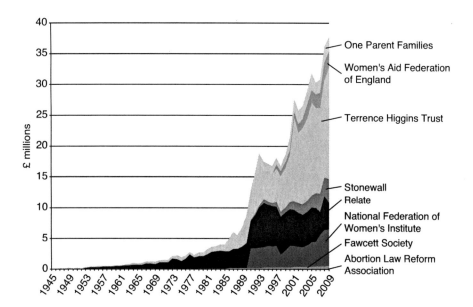

Figure 3.7.1: Cumulated income of eight gender and sexuality organisations, 1945–2009 (adjusted for inflation, 2009)

Note: Data for ALRA cover only the years 1945–69, and data between 1975 and 2003 for the Fawcett Society are missing.

Sources: Annual report and accounts, organisations concerned; Charity Statistics (various years); Charity Commission.

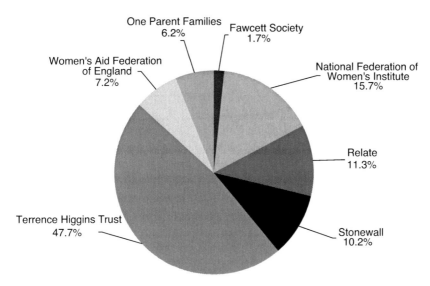

Figure 3.7.2: Income size of gender and sexuality organisations in 2009 relative to the income of all organisations in sample

Sources: Annual reports and accounts, organisations concerned; Charity Commission.

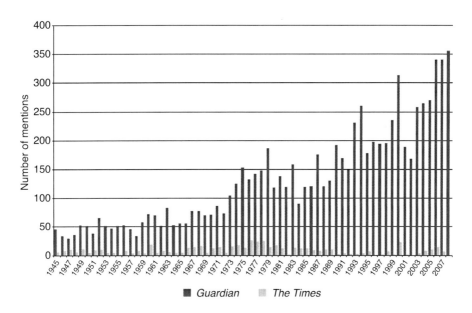

Figure 3.7.3: Number of mentions of gender and sexuality organisations (Abortion Rights, Fawcett Society, National Federation of Women's Institute, Relate, Stonewall, Terrence Higgins Trust, Women's Aid Federation, Society for the Protection of Unborn Children, One Parent Families) in the *Guardian* and *The Times*, 1945–2007

Source: *Guardian* & *The Times*.

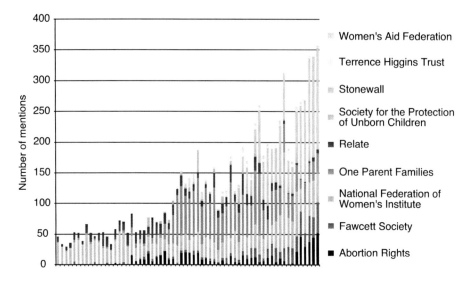

Figure 3.7.4: Number of mentions of the same organisations in the *Guardian*, with a breakdown per organisation

Source: *Guardian*.

Further reading

For a general overview, see the relevant chapters in Pat Thane (ed.), *Unequal Britain: Equalities in Britain Since 1945* (London, 2010).

Excellent surveys of the women's movement can be found in Martin Pugh, *Women and the Women's Movement in Britain, 1914–1999* (Basingstoke, 2000); Ina Zweiniger-Bargielowska, *Women in Twentieth-Century Britain: Social, Cultural and Political Change* (Harlow, 2001), and S. Bruley, *Women in Britain since 1900* (Basingstoke, 1999). On female sexuality, see Hera Cook, *The Long Sexual Revolution: English Women, Sex, and Contraception, 1800–1975* (Oxford, 2004). For second-wave feminism particularly, see Anna Coote and Beatrix Campbell, *Sweet Freedom: The Struggle for Women's Liberation*, 2nd edn (Oxford, 1987), or Sheila Rowbotham, *Women in Movement: Feminism and Social Action* (London, 1992).

For issues around family poverty and single parenthood, see Tanya Evans, 'Stopping the Poor Getting Poorer: The Establishment and Professionalisation of Poverty NGOs, 1945–95', in Nick Crowson, Matthew Hilton and James McKay (eds), *NGOs in Contemporary Britain: Non-State Actors in Society and Politics since 1945* (Basingstoke, 2009).

Introductions to the LGB movement over the twentieth century can be found in Jeffrey Weeks, *Coming Out: Homosexual Politics in Britain from the Nineteenth Century to the Present* (London, 1977), and Matthew Waites, 'Lesbian, Gay and Bisexual NGOs in Britain: Past, Present and Future' in Nick Crowson, Matthew Hilton and James McKay (eds), *NGOs in Contemporary Britain: Non-State Actors in Society and Politics since 1945* (Basingstoke, 2009). For gay liberation more specifically, see Lisa Power, *No Bath but Plenty of Bubbles: An Oral History of the Gay Liberation Front, 1970–73* (London, 1995), and Lucy Robinson, *Gay Men and the Left in Post-war Britain: How the Personal Got Political* (Manchester, 2007).

8. Race and ethnic minority groups

Organisations based on race have a long history. So long as people of different ethnic groups have settled in modern Britain, institutional structures have arisen to support such communities. For instance, in 1779, the Jewish Bread, Meat and Coal Society was formed as the Society for Distributing Bread, Meat and Coal Amongst the Jewish Poor During the Winter Season (Meshebat Naphesh). Even earlier, in 1760, the Board of Deputies of British Jews was established and has continued to represent Britain's Jewish community ever since.

Undoubtedly, though, it is the legacy of empire which marks out the history of race and ethnic minority groups in Britain. Even in this regard, though, we are not dealing with simply a post-Second World War phenomenon. In 1887 the West Indian barrister Henry Sylvester-Williams formed the African Association in London to encourage pan-African unity, an initiative that would eventually feed into the Pan-African Congress organised in Manchester in 1945 by the Trinidadian, George Padmore, and Ghana's Kwame Nkrumah. Likewise, immigrants from the sub-continent formed their own support groups. For instance, prior to the creation of the Indian Workers' Association (IWA) in the 1950s, earlier groups operating under the same name had appeared in London in the 1930s and in Coventry in 1938.

However, with the arrival of mass immigration after 1945, new organisations proliferated. Many of these existed at the local level and worked to serve the needs of their communities. Collaboration between such groups at the national level was often prevented through political differences. For this reason the Joint Council for the Welfare of Immigrants (JCWI) was set up in 1967 specifically to focus on the relief of hardship and poverty faced by many immigrants arriving in Britain. This deliberately distanced itself from the political issues being addressed by other organisations, and within a few years 115 immigrant organisations had affiliated.

The political role of black and ethnic groups was shaped by the experience and threat of racism. Again, such a trend was not specific to the post-war period. Jewish organisations were set up to deal with the consequences of continental fascism, such as the Jewish Refugee Committee (1938) and the Association of Jewish Refugees (1941). But the threats were not only from abroad. The League of Coloured Peoples began campaigning against racial discrimination in Britain in 1931. And in 1936, the Board of Deputies established the Jewish Defence Committee, to meet the threat of the British Union of Fascists. After the war, the think tank, the Institute of Race Relations (IRR), was created by the Royal Institute of International Affairs (Chatham House) in 1952, but became an independent charity in 1958 in the aftermath of the Notting Hill riots.

The storm created by Enoch Powell's 'rivers of blood' speech triggered a more general upsurge in black organisations. The Campaign Against Racial Discrimination had existed since 1964, but it would be eclipsed by new groups such as the Black People's Alliance which emerged from an IWA initiative in 1968 and the Runnymede Trust, formed in the same year. This latter body deliberately set out to be a think tank and has worked to fight racism targeting all minority groups in the UK.

The revival of the far right created new challenges for the thinking behind black and ethnic minority activism. Much of the intellectual input was predicated on the assumption that race was inextricably linked with class. This was no more clearly demonstrated than in the very title of the journal of the IRR, *Race and Class*, but it could also be seen in the efforts and difficulties faced by groups such as the IWA as they sought to align their activism within the broader labour and trade union movement. The more ethnic minorities experienced racism as a reality, however, the more race itself seemed the primary motivation. And because racism was a common experience for Afro-Caribbean and sub-continent immigrants as a whole, then the whole meaning of race began to be challenged.

The Black People's Alliance was just one example of an attempt to politically unify different ethnic groups under one banner. In the early 1970s, the IRR became more radicalised and adapted itself into an anti-racist think tank that increasingly invoked the term 'black' to signify all immigrant groups. Important cross-currents intertwined between NGOs and the universities, though it is questionable whether the political concept of 'black' ever truly unified, at the practical level, many diverse communities with very different cultures and traditions.

Around the same time, the rise to prominence of the National Front triggered the creation of various anti-fascist groups that likewise sought broad-ranging alliances between black groups and anti-racist sympathisers. The Campaign Against Racism and Fascism was set up in the mid 1970s and worked with bodies such as the IRR to tackle racism in all its forms. Moreover, a second generation of immigrants were beginning to emerge that would alter the face of anti-racist politics. A key event was the murder of 18-year-old Gurdip Singh Chaggar in Southall. The IWA supported the resulting protests, but a younger generation sought its own voice, principally through the Asian Youth Movement. These lent their support to the Social Workers' Party Anti-Nazi League which played a key role in defeating fascism, particularly through the energy and support of the Rock Against Racism concerts in 1978.

The establishment of the Commission for Racial Equality in 1976 created something of a centre of gravity for black and ethnic minority groups, as well as further stimulating their growth and activities. Yet rather than creating a more unified movement, it is arguable that the politics of race has become increasingly fragmented. This is not only because of the decline in popularity of the far right, which removed an immediate common enemy, but because of the support for community groups which, arguably, has seen different ethnic minorities retreat into the specific issues affecting their communities rather than the wider problems of racism as a whole.

Since the 1980s, the politics of racial unity as expressed by initiatives such as the Asian Youth Movement have given way to the emergence of robust, national organisations which only serve a particular ethnic group. For instance, the Muslim Council of Britain was set up in 1997 to serve as the national umbrella body for Muslim organisations. Similar organisations have emerged for other groups, such as the Hindu Council. This has triggered ongoing discussions about the nature of multiculturalism in Britain, particularly prominent being the Runnymede Trust. In 1997, it set up the Commission on the Future of Multi-Ethnic Britain, chaired by Bhikhu Parekh, which reported in 1997. Many of its recommendations were taken up by the government and were based on what it regarded as three central concepts: 'cohesion, equality and difference'. That is, it captured the desire of black and ethnic minority groups to promote equality whilst also respecting the very real differences between communities.

Yet despite such differences, the day-to-day work of such organisations continues to be on the practical issues facing immigrants in adapting to a new environment. The JCWI has continued to lobby parliament during all subsequent passing of legislation relating to immigrants and refugees. Most recently, in 2010, it launched the 'I Love Migrants' campaign to help emphasise the positive impacts migration has had on the UK. The increased numbers of asylum seekers and economic migrants from new areas of the world has also seen the flourishing of new race and ethnic minority groups that tackle similar sorts of issues to those faced by bodies such as IWA in the 1950s. Likewise, the perceived rise in anti-Muslim prejudice revives issues about fragmentation or unity within ethnic minority organisations.

Box 3.8.1: Some fundamental principles of the report of the Commission on the Future of Multi-Ethnic Britain

'1. All individuals have equal worth irrespective of their colour, gender, ethnicity, religion, age or sexual orientation, and have equal claims to the opportunities they need to realise their potential and contribute to collective wellbeing.
2. Citizens are both individuals and members of particular religious, ethnic, cultural and regional communities. Britain is both a community of citizens and a community of communities, both a liberal and a multicultural society, and needs to reconcile their sometimes conflicting requirements.
3. Since citizens have differing needs, equal treatment requires full account to be taken of their differences. When equality ignores relevant differences and insists on uniformity of treatment, it leads to injustice and inequality; when differences ignore the demands of equality, they result in discrimination. Equality must be defined in a culturally sensitive way and applied in a discriminating but not discriminatory manner.
4. Every society needs to be cohesive as well as respectful of diversity, and must find ways of nurturing diversity while fostering a common sense of belonging and a shared identity among its constituent members.
5. While such values as tolerance, mutual respect, dialogue and peaceful resolution of differences are paramount, as are such basic ethical norms as respect for human dignity, equal worth of all, equal opportunity for self-development and equal life chances, society must also respect deep moral differences and find ways of resolving inescapable conflicts. Human rights principles provide a sound framework for handling differences, and a body of values around which society can unite.
6. Racism, understood either as division of humankind into fixed, closed and unalterable groups or as systematic domination of some groups by others, is an empirically false, logically incoherent and morally unacceptable doctrine. Whatever its subtle disguises and forms, it is deeply divisive, intolerant of differences, a source of much human suffering, and inimical to the common sense of belonging lying at the basis of every stable civilisation. It can have no place in a decent society.'

Taken from Bhikhu Parekh, 'Introduction', *Report of the Commission on the Future of Multi-Ethnic Britain* (2000), available at: www.runnymedetrust.org/reportIntroduction.html.

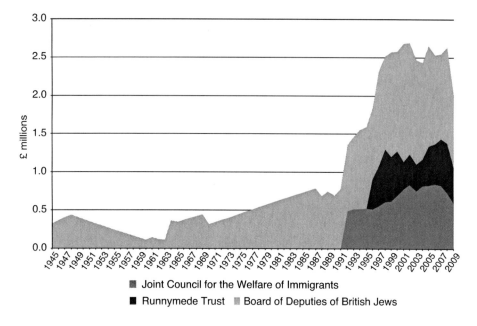

Figure 3.8.1: Income of three race, religion and ethnic minorities groups, 1945–2009 (adjusted for inflation, 2009)

Sources: Annual report and accounts, organisations concerned; Charity Statistics (various years); Charity Commission.

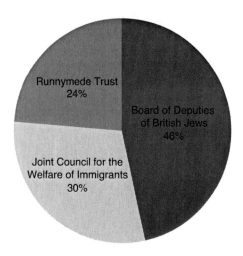

Figure 3.8.2: Income size of the same organisations in 2009 relative to the income of all three organisations in sample

Sources: Annual reports and accounts, organisations concerned; Charity Commission.

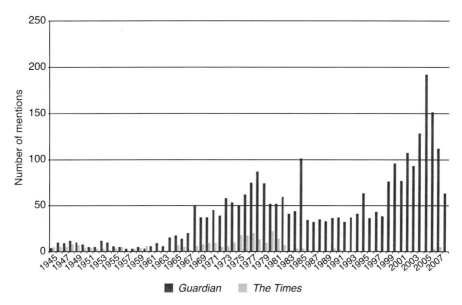

Figure 3.8.3: Number of mentions of race, religion and ethnic minorities groups (Board of Deputies of British Jews, Indian Workers' Association, Joint Council for the Welfare of Immigrants, Muslim Council of Britain, Runnymede Trust) in the *Guardian* and *The Times*, 1945–2007

Source: *Guardian* & *The Times*.

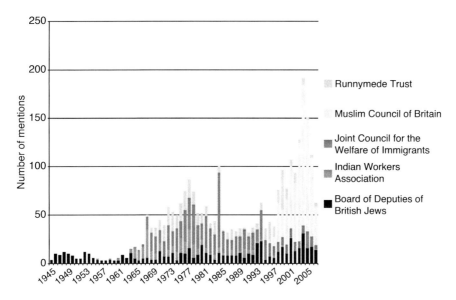

Figure 3.8.4: Number of mentions of the same organisations in the *Guardian*, with a breakdown per organisation

Source: Guardian.

Further reading

Some useful profiles can be found in Peter Barberis, John McHugh and Mike Tyldesley, *Encyclopedia of British and Irish Political Organizations* (London, 1999). Introductory overviews include John Solomos, *Race and Racism in Contemporary Britain*, 2nd edn (London, 1993); *Harry Goulbourne* (ed.), *Black Politics in Britain* (Aldershot, 1990); Terri Sewell, *Black Tribunes: Black Political Participation in Britain* (London, 1993), and Kalbir Shukra, *The Changing Pattern of Black Politics in Britain* (London, 1998).

Two classic works on the politics of race include Paul Gilroy, *'There Ain't No Black in the Union Jack': The Cultural Politics of Race and Nation* (London, 1987), and Ambalavaner Sivanandan, *A Different Hunger: Writings on Black Resistance* (London, 1982). More specific studies of particular moments and ethnic groups can be found in Dave Renton, *When We Touched the Sky: The Anti-Nazi league, 1977–1981* (Cheltenham, 2006), and Gurharpal Singh and Darshan Singh Tatla, *Sikhs in Britain: The Making of a Community* (London, 2006), which covers the IWA.

4
Leading Campaign Groups and NGOs in the UK

Introduction

This chapter introduces 63 NGOs. These are not the 'top' 63 in the sense of being the largest or the wealthiest or the most prominent. Rather, they are a range of NGOs that represent the diversity of the sector. They have been chosen to help illustrate the range of activities and modes of operation that NGOs are engaged in.

General note

This chapter presents historical data on selected NGOs. All datasets can be found at www.ngo.bham.ac.uk – the data come from many sources, including annual reports and specialised publications such as Charity Statistics. It is important to note, however, that statistics are not always fully consistent year on year. Accounting techniques have changed since 1945, for example, and therefore the figures reported below might not always be fully comparable. Similar problems arise with membership levels: the definition of what constitutes a member or a supporter can (and does) change over time. Norms for reporting the number of staff have also evolved, from simple headcounts to 'full-time equivalent' (FTE) figures. Every effort has been made to correct such 'artificial' changes in the data that follow.

Abortion Rights (merged Abortion Law Reform Association and National Abortion Campaign)

Abortion Rights was formed in 2003 from the merger of the Abortion Law Reform Association (ALRA; formed 1936) and the National Abortion Campaign (NAC; formed 1975). The campaign for abortion reform can be a prism through which to see visions of femininity and sexuality. Whilst the 1967 Abortion Act might be the most obvious legacy of Abortion Rights, the discursive impact of the NGOs in terms of challenging notions of family, motherhood and domesticity is equally important.

The ALRA's moderate and middle-class nature has been emphasised, and criticism made of its failure to achieve radical ends. This criticism overlooks the difficulties of conducting an abortion debate in the public sphere before the 1970s and the limited channels available to the ALRA: namely, the medical and legal professions, Whitehall and Westminster, and women's organisations. Many doctors, family planners and teachers were sympathetic to the cause, and the funding it began receiving in the 1960s from the American Hopkins Funds Board meant it had considerable resources to devote to opinion polling. Only during the 1970s did the debate spill over into wider public protest politics led by the NAC.

The ALRA evolved from a voluntary NGO aiming to foster discussion on abortion with the expectation of reform of the law, to an organisation during the 1950s that was seeking to shape political, medical and legal opinion as well as offering advice for ordinary people, to one during the 1960s that had paid professional staff and was a highly effective lobbyist that wanted a voice, consultation and influence. It was never a mass membership organisation, and from its beginning relied on private channels of funding. In the post-1945 years it succeeded in gaining the support, as patrons, of many figures of the establishment which gave it legitimacy and invitations to present evidence to committees of inquiry. During the 1950s its contacts with the Labour Party resulted in a series of private members' bills which, although unsuccessful, reinvigorated the organisation. The arguments for abortions also began to change during the 1960s, with a downplaying of the working-class concerns for reproduction towards a framing around health concerns for the mother and the foetus.

The NAC was formed in 1975 after a 1974 private member's bill had tried to revoke the 1967 Act. Its approach was three pronged: to defend, implement and revise the 1967 Act in a manner acceptable to feminists. The NAC widened, and radicalised, the debate, as the influence of second-wave feminism took hold, and placed greater emphasis on abortion being the right of individuals, rather than simply mothers or wives. It was particularly effective at forging links with Labour MPs and the trade union movement. It led the campaign against the 1979 Corrie private member's bill, including a mass lobby of parliament in February 1980. There was a gradual sidelining of its feminist political aims, although not total abandonment, as it sought to balance the demands of the radicals with those of its establishment collaborators. This led to a split in 1983 as those who wanted to address the broad range of women's reproductive rights formed a new campaign.

Abortion became an election issue for the first time in 1997 due to the NAC's 'Abortion on Request' campaign and the ALRA's drafting of a new private member's bill.

Box 4.1: Classified advertisement

'Commitment to Choice: National Abortion Campaign seeks volunteers. Experience or interest in campaign/press work, research, fundraising, computers or office work especially welcome. Must be pro-choice.'

Guardian, 10 September 1997, p. B67.

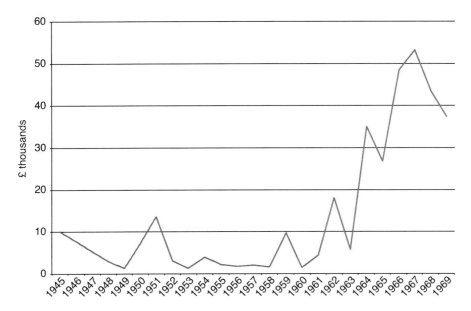

Figure 4.1: Income of the Abortion Law Reform Association, 1945–1969 (adjusted for inflation, 2009)

Note: No further information about the income of ALRA was available after 1969. As for the NAC, their archives (at the Wellcome Library in London) are currently waiting to be catalogued and are therefore unavailable to researchers.

Source: Annual reports and accounts, ALRA.

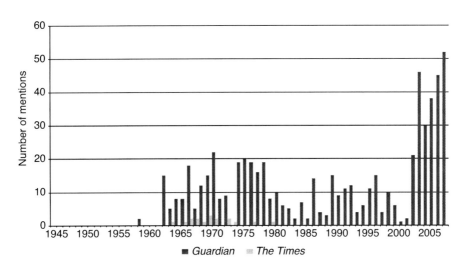

Figure 4.2: Number of mentions of abortion rights in the *Guardian* and *The Times*, 1945–2007

Source: *Guardian* & *The Times*.

Further reading

Lesley Hall, *The Life and Times of Stella Browne: Feminist and Free Spirit* (London, 2011); Stephen Brooke, 'The Sphere of Sexual Politics: The Abortion Law Reform Association, 1930s to 1960s', in Nick Crowson, Matthew Hilton and James McKay (eds), *NGOs in Contemporary Britain: Non-state Actors in Society and Politics since 1945* (Basingstoke, 2009), pp. 77–94; Lesley Hoggart, *Feminist Campaigns for Birth Control and Abortion Rights in Britain* (Lampeter, 2002).

Action for Children (formerly National Children's Home 1898–2000; the Children's Charity 2000–08)

Action for Children is one of the UK's leading children's charities, providing services throughout the UK to vulnerable and socially-excluded children. Since 1969 the charity has also promoted child protection policy and safeguarding practices outside of the UK. It has assisted in the provision of child and youth services and community projects in the Caribbean, Central America (Belize), Russia and Southern Africa. In 2004–08 it partnered the UK government (Department for International Development) in implementing a Child Protection Programme for the British Overseas Territories. It campaigns on child welfare, having in the past been a leading advocate of adoption, and a major provider of residential care facilities for a significant period of its existence.

The charity was established by Thomas Stephenson, with the assistance of fellow Methodists Alfred Mager and Frances Horner, opening a Children's Home for boys living on the streets of Lambeth in 1869, at 8 Church Street, Waterloo (now Exton Street). It admitted girls from 1871 when it moved to Bonner Road in Bethnal Green. A second home was opened at Edgworth Farm on the Lancashire Moors in 1872, and eventually the organisation was operating 150 establishments nationwide. Many of its homes sought to provide the residents with skills that would help them find work as adults. Its first home had 29 residents, expanding by 1900 to 1,100, and to almost 4,000 by 1946. Former residents include the Tottenham Hotspur footballer Walter Tull (1888–1918), comedian and writer Stanley Unwin (1911–2002) and actress Shirley Anne Field (1938–).

The majority of homes have closed since the 1970s and the charity has reoriented itself towards preventative interventions supporting parents via family aid schemes, day nurseries and family centres. Some critics believe that by turning to campaigning on behalf of children and to contracting 'new' non-residential services with local authorities, former residential care charities such as Action for Children are attempting to disassociate themselves from a long history of poor management and abusive services.

It is clear that by the 1930s, organisations such as this had lost the founder impetus that marked out their early years, and when combined with financial resource issues, it is evident that many of the voluntary childrens' home bodies had lost their reputation as reforming innovators. The National Children's Home (NCH) was one of the early campaigners for adoption and became an adoption agency in 1926. During the mid 1960s it began helping with the placement of children with disabilities or histories of abuse, thus extending the boundaries of childcare practice beyond what was once thought possible.

Currently it employs 6,500 people and runs 420 projects across the UK, working with 156,000 children, young people and families. In line with its current preference for early pre-emptive intervention, the charity published research in July 2010 which claimed that interventions in issues of child neglect could save the public purse £486 billion over 20 years as they impact on crime, mental health and family breakdowns. The organisation has secularised but still remains a charity of the Methodist Church. It has also undergone several name changes in the past decade, the latest in 2008 after research suggested that only 1 per cent of the public were aware of its work and thought the name was holding the organisation back.

Key dates

1926   Adoption Act – enables NCH to become an adoption agency
1948   Children's Act
1969   Extends its interests overseas
1989   Children's Act – enshrines principle that child welfare should take priority
       over parental interests and needs
2000   Name changes to the Children's Charity
2006   Market research shows that the public are unaware of its activities
2008   Renamed Action for Children

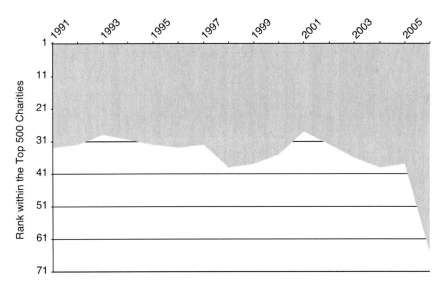

Figure 4.3: Action for Children's charitable ranking by voluntary income, 1991–2006

Source: Charity Statistics.

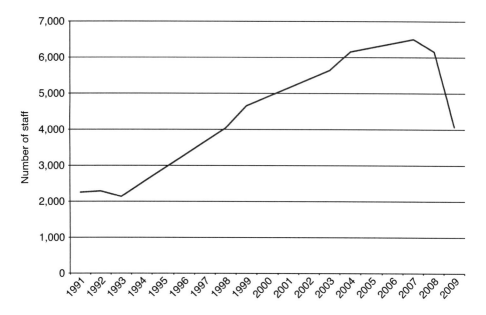

Figure 4.4: Number of staff working for Action for Children

Sources: Top 3000 Charities; Charity Commission.

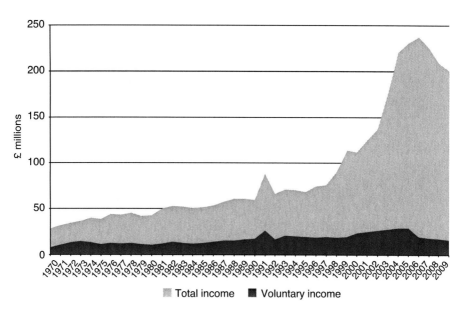

Figure 4.5: Total and voluntary income of Action for Children, 1970–2009 (adjusted for inflation, 2009)

Sources: Wolfenden 1978; Wells collection; Charity Statistics; Charity Commission.

Further reading

Jon Lawrence and Pat Starkey (eds), *Child Welfare and Social Action in the 19th and 20th centuries: International Perspectives* (Liverpool, 2001); James Walvin, *A Child's World: A Social History of English Childhood 1800–1914* (London, 1982); Philip J. Howard, *Philip: A Strange Child* (Bournemouth, 2007).

Action for Southern Africa (formerly South African Boycott Movement and Anti-Apartheid Movement)

Emerging in 1959 as a consumer-based protest against apartheid, with roots in the anti-colonial establishment and nineteenth-century humanitarian networks, the anti-apartheid movement was strongly influenced by Christian activists. Then in 1960, following the declaration of a state of emergency, the Sharpeville massacre and the banning of the African National Congress (ANC), the boycott movement became the Anti-Apartheid Movement (AAM).

Using a mixture of consumer boycotts, sanctions and disinvestment campaigns alongside more traditional forms of political protest and political lobbying, the AAM aimed to persuade state and civil society institutions, as well as individuals, that the racially driven ideology of the South African government was unacceptable. Broader campaigns developed with the aim of isolating South Africa economically, diplomatically, culturally and in sporting terms. Campaigns against the 1969 winter Springbok rugby tour of Britain and the 1970 cricket tour, led by Peter Hain, and including a clash between 7,000 protesters and police in Manchester, successfully targeted South African sporting links.

South African exiles, such as Trevor Huddleston and Michael Scott, formed links with the AAM, giving the organisation a transnational character, but it was also a membership organisation with branches across the country, with 189 in existence by 1986. Relations were sometimes fraught between the local activists and the national leadership, and consequently they were at times two interrelated, but distinct, movements.

During the 1980s the AAM was unsuccessful at persuading the Thatcher government to sever links with South Africa, but this only served to increase domestic support for sanctions as it became a marker of broader dissatisfaction with 'Thatcherism'. Business involvement in South Africa was also targeted, whether the banking sector (for example, Midland Bank in 1974, and Barclays during the 1980s) or the arms industry companies, which flouted the 1977 UN arms embargo. Popular support for the AAM peaked during the mid 1980s as the township violence reignited, illustrating the inevitably close connection between the movement's actions with those occurring in South Africa. The AAM forged alliances, both at the local and national level, with a range of other groups, local authorities and political figures, especially on the political left. There were also links with the anti-apartheid groups overseas and with the ANC.

An iconography of anti-apartheid emerged alongside the movement, and the image of the imprisoned ANC activist Nelson Mandela (see Box 4.2) became universally recognised and promoted on T-shirts, in street and building names, and in popular music.

In 1994, with the collapse of apartheid, and democratic elections in South Africa, the AAM became Action for Southern Africa (ACTSA). The organisation now focuses on international development, the aftermath of conflict, and the challenge of HIV/AIDS.

Box 4.2: Advertisement, text with an image of Nelson Mandela's face

'What hope does Christmas bring for him? On Sunday Nelson Mandela will spend his 27th consecutive Christmas in prison. No friends. No freedom ...

This Christmas Archbishop Trevor Huddleston CR, President of the Anti-Apartheid Movement, is appealing for funds to help launch the "Boycott Apartheid '89" Campaign. And you can show your support for the Campaign now by signing the "Boycott Apartheid '89" pledge on the coupon below. We hope to collect tens of thousands of pledges throughout 1989.'

Guardian, 23 December 1988, p. 9.

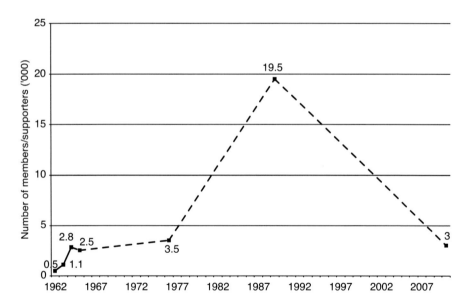

Figure 4.6: Number of members and supporters of the Anti-Apartheid Movement/ACTSA, 1962–2010

Sources: Roger Fieldhouse, *Anti-Apartheid: The History of the Movement in Britain* (London, 2005); Guardian Directory of Pressure Groups; BOND website, www.bond.org.uk/membership-directory3. php/0014000000Hvk9aAAB/action-for-southern-africa.

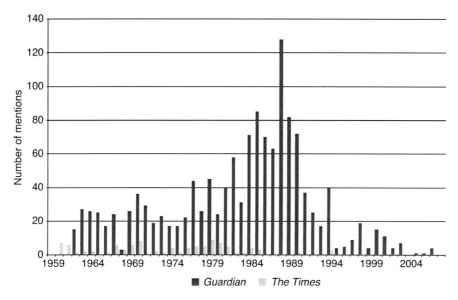

Figure 4.7: Number of mentions of the Anti-Apartheid Movement/ACTSA in the *Guardian* and *The Times*, 1945–2007

Source: *Guardian* & *The Times*.

Further reading

Rob Skinner, 'The Anti-Apartheid Movement, Pressure Group Politics, International Solidarity and Transnational Activism', in Nick Crowson, Matthew Hilton and James McKay (eds), *NGOs in Contemporary Britain: Non-State Actors in Society and Politics since 1945* (Basingstoke, 2009), pp. 129–46; Roger Fieldhouse, *Anti-Apartheid: The History of the Movement in Britain* (London, 2005).

Age UK (formerly Age Concern and Help the Aged)

Age UK was formed in 2009 as a merger between Age Concern and Help the Aged, adopting its current name in 2010. Age Concern England was a charity registered as the National Council on Ageing, and is the federal umbrella body of local Age Concern organisations that offer direct services to local people, such as day centres, lunch clubs and contracts with local authority social services and NHS Trusts. They exploit the nationally recognised brand name of Age Concern and seek to conform to nationally determined standards of operation. It emerged from a conference convened in October 1940 by the National Council of Social Services which formed a committee comprising of representatives from voluntary organisations and three government departments. In 1944 it became the National Old People's Welfare Committee. Age Concern as a title was introduced in the early 1970s, by which point it had become the most prominent organisation aiming to improve the economic and social welfare conditions of the elderly. It has a large professional staff and is sustained by a significant body of volunteers around the country.

Help the Aged was originally founded in 1961 to raise emergency aid for the elderly overseas, but quickly added a UK focus. It was formed by Cecil Jackson-Cole. Early initiatives such as the minibus campaign to provide transport to the day centres arose out of spontaneous need rather than intentional forethought. Pioneers in the arena of press advertising, they appointed their first professional fundraiser, the Wells organisation, in 1973. High-profile campaigns included the 1975 'Adopt a Granny', and the 1998 'Heating or Eating?' campaign, which is credited with persuading the government to introduce winter fuel payments for pensioners. Although its first permanent gift shop opened in Bexhill in 1963, Cole's association with Oxfam meant that he was reluctant for Help the Aged to enter the charity shop market, and so its expansion into this area did not occur until the mid 1980s – it now has around 400 shops. In 1977 Help the Aged (Trading) Ltd was launched and this developed a warehouse-based mail order trading operation as an additional line of revenue.

Political observers of the late 1980s considered that despite the scale of the pensioner vote Whitehall did not look upon either the National Federation of Old Age Pensions Associations or Age Concern as 'truly negotiating bodies' and a sense emerges that the elderly lobby has been 'influential' but not 'powerful'. Yet the Department of Health still viewed the organisational accountability of Age Concern favourably and unsuccessfully tried to merge the Alzheimer's Disease Society into it in 1987. Organisationally, Age Concern's accountability rests with the National Council as well as a more informal responsibility to the affiliated organisations. Senior management, the chief executive and trustees' relationship is akin to that between a minister and his departmental civil servants.

Since the mid 1990s there have been a succession of name changes for Age Concern's National Council. By 1995 it had become known as the National Old People's Welfare Council and then the National Council on Ageing.

Key figures

John Pearson (1928–): director's deputy, Help the Aged, late 1960s and 1970s
Cecil Jackson-Cole (1901–1979): founder and director, Help the Aged
Jack Jones (1913–2009): trade unionist and pensioner campaigner, Age Concern, 1978–2009, European Federation of Retired and Elderly Persons, 1991–2009
Sally Greengross (1935–): joined Age Concern 1977, director 1987–2000, vice-president 2002–09, Help the Aged International 2000–07, created life peer 2000

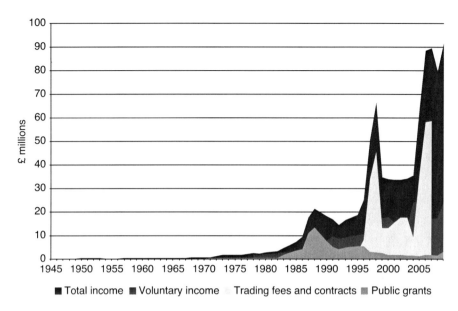

Figure 4.8: Income of Age Concern, 1945–2009 (adjusted for inflation, 2009)

Sources: Annual reports and accounts, Age Concern; Charity Statistics; Charity Commission.

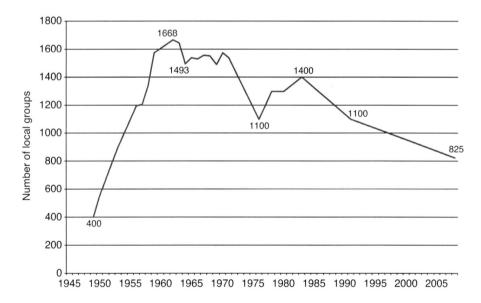

Figure 4.9: Number of Age Concern local groups, 1949–2008

Sources: Annual reports and accounts, Age Concern; Charity Statistics; *Social Trends*, 15 (1985), p. 159; *Social Trends*, 23 (1993), p. 155; Charity Commission.

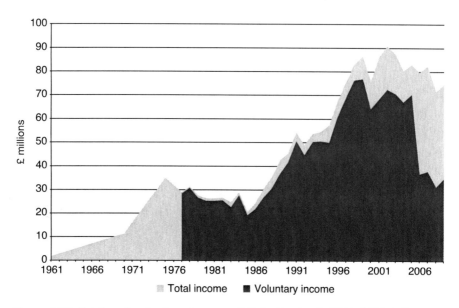

Figure 4.10: Total and voluntary income of Help the Aged, 1961–2009 (adjusted for inflation, 2009)

Note: The sharp fall in voluntary income is 2006 is due to change in reporting methods by Charity Statistics.

Sources: Annual report and accounts, Help the Aged; Wolfenden 1978; Wells Collection; Charity Statistics.

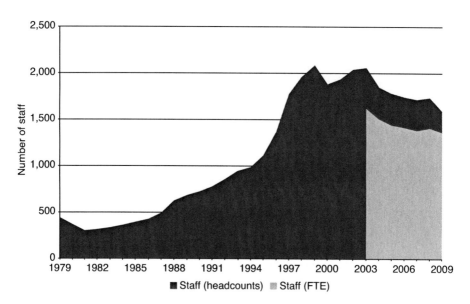

Figure 4.11: Number of staff working for Help the Aged, 1979–2009

Note: Full-time equivalent ('FTE') not available before 2003; 'headcounts' includes both full-time and part-time staff.

Source: Annual reports and accounts, Help the Aged.

Further reading

Kenneth Hudson, *Help the Age: Twenty-One Years of Experience and Achievement* (Oxford, 1982); Pat Thane, *Old Age in English History* (Oxford, 2000); John Macnicol and Andrew Blaikie, 'The Politics of Retirement, 1908–48', in Margot Jeffreys (ed.), *Growing Old in the Twentieth Century* (Abingdon, 1989).

Amnesty International

Amnesty International was established in 1961 following the publication of an article, 'The Forgotten Prisoners', by labour lawyer Peter Benenson in the *Observer*. Up until this point, the language of civil liberties had been preferred in Britain. But Amnesty International helped promote the notion of human rights, becoming a powerful social movement by the 1970s that championed the abuses of the rights to freedom of conscience contained in Articles 18 and 19 of the Universal Declaration of Human Rights (UDHR). Its global influence was recognised as early as 1977 when it was awarded the Nobel Peace Prize.

Amnesty operated from the start by mobilising campaigns in defence of 'prisoners of conscience'. By 1966 it could claim that 1,000 of these had been released since the organisation was formed. It also rapidly established an international secretariat and an international presence: in 1964 it was granted consultative status at the United Nations. In the late 1960s, Martin Ennals took over from Benenson and placed the organisation on a more secure and professional footing.

In the 1970s, the language of human rights in the international arena expanded, not least because of the systematic abuses committed by assorted military juntas and the deployment of rights as a tool of diplomacy during the US presidency of Jimmy Carter. Amnesty took full advantage, capturing the public imagination not only through high-profile cases such as that of the arrested Brazilian academic, Luiz Basilio Rossi, in 1973, but through popular culture events such as the Secret Policeman's Ball begun in 1976. Amnesty had started the decade with less than 20 staff. It finished with around 150, together with a global membership of around 200,000 individuals and about 2,000 local groups in 38 countries.

Amnesty has tried to appear politically neutral. Local groups have deliberately focused on prisoners from communist, capitalist and developing-world countries. Yet accusations of bias have been levelled, especially because of the high proportion of Amnesty investigations into prisoners in Israel and the United States. But another criticism has stemmed from Amnesty's focus on political and civil rights at the expense of social and economic rights. Although it has advocated women's rights since 1994, the full embrace of all the rights contained in the UDHR was not made until the turn of the twenty-first century.

Nevertheless, its popularity has continued to grow. It has pioneered new forms of activism, from text messaging campaigns to innovative uses of social networking media. In 2010 its global membership approached 3 million.

Key figures

Eric Baker: founder and secretary-general, 1966–68

Peter Benenson: founder and secretary-general, 1961–66
Martin Ennals: secretary-general, 1968–80
Sean MacBride: chairman of executive, 1961–75
Pierre Sané: secretary-general, 1992–2001

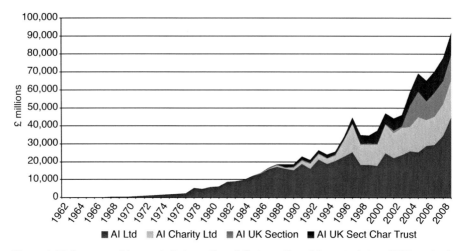

Figure 4.12: Income of Amnesty International (International Secretariat and UK section), 1962–2009 (adjusted for inflation, 2009)

Note: Amnesty International in the UK is made up of two different entities: the International Secretariat and the UK section of AI. Both of these entities have two different arms, one charitable and one non-charitable. AI Charity Ltd is the charitable arm of AI Ltd and AI UK Section Charitable Trust is the charitable arm of AI UK section.

Sources (for all): Annual reports and accounts, Amnesty International; AI Charity and AI UK section Charitable Trust: Charity Commission; Charity Statistics.

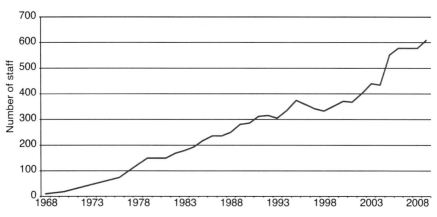

Figure 4.13: Number of staff working for Amnesty International (International Secretariat and UK Section), 1968–2009

Note: AI Charity Ltd has no employees.

Sources: Annual reports and accounts, Amnesty International; Guardian Directory of Pressure Groups.

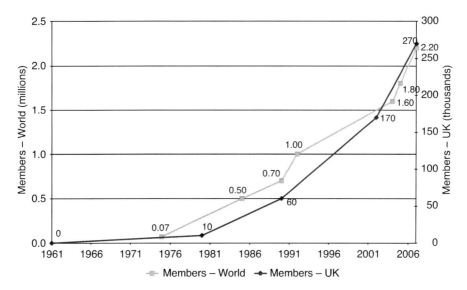

Figure 4.14: Amnesty International membership (world and UK section), 1961–2007

Sources: www.amnesty.org/en/who-we-are/history; www.amnesty.org.uk/timeline.asp.

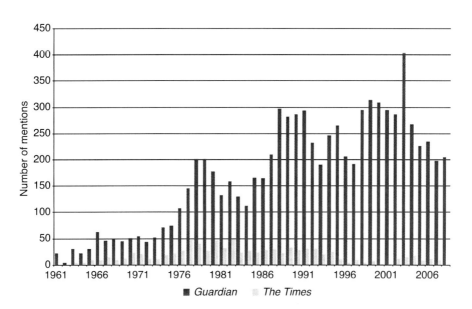

Figure 4.15: Number of mentions of Amnesty International in the *Guardian* and *The Times*, 1945–2007

Source: *Guardian* & *The Times*.

Further reading

Jonathan Power, *Like Water on Stone: The Story of Amnesty International* (London, 2001); Anne-Marie Clarke, *Diplomacy of Conscience: Amnesty International and Changing Human Rights Norms* (Princeton, 2001); Stephen Hopgood, *Keepers of the Flame: Understanding Amnesty International* (Ithaca, NY, 2006); Tom Buchanan, 'Human Rights Campaigns in Modern Britain', in Nick Crowson, Matthew Hilton and James McKay (eds), *NGOs in Contemporary Britain: Non-State Actors in Society and Politics since 1945* (Basingstoke, 2009); Tom Buchanan, '"The Truth Will Set You Free": The Making of Amnesty International', *Journal of Contemporary History*, 37:4 (2002), pp. 575–97.

Animal Aid

Animal Aid is Britain's largest animal rights group. The group was established in 1977, and as such formed part of the wider animal rights movement that gathered momentum in that decade. Inspired by the philosophy of writers such as Tom Regan and Peter Singer (see Box 4.3), there was growing activism around the notion that animals were bearers of inalienable rights, which morally could not be compromised for human advantage. This activism was therefore differentiated from older animal welfare groups such as the Royal Society for the Prevention of Cruelty to Animals (RSPCA), and had far more in common philosophically with turn of the century anti-vivisectionist bodies such as the British Union for the Abolition of Vivisection (BUAV) and the National Anti-Vivisection Society (NAVS). However, the activism was also differentiated by its tendency towards radicalism in tactics as well as thought – direct action and grassroots organisation were to some extent the hallmarks of the milieu into which Animal Aid was born.

In the group's early years, the focus of activity was principally anti-vivisection activism. Demonstrations at prominent and contentious sites of animal experimentation, such as the Ministry of Defence's Porton Down facility, and the Huntingdon research centre in Cambridgeshire, were launched. Campaigns were also run against the cosmetics company Revlon, and later in the decade the group became involved in a public dispute with the neuroscientist Professor Colin Blakemore, surrounding its role in protests against his work.

Animal Aid was also involved in a high-profile attempt by more radical activists to win control of the BUAV during 1980–81. This initiative was both successful and short-lived – radicals were elected onto the BUAV board in 1980, with Jean Pink becoming president. Following their suspension, they were subsequently re-elected, but Pink then resigned in 1981, in protest at BUAV policies. Other work on vivisection has involved the promotion of the group's Humane Research Donor Card, facilitating the posthumous donation of human tissue to medical science.

Animal Aid's campaigning has not been confined to anti-vivisection, however. The livestock industry is an ongoing focus, and the group has long championed vegetarianism and veganism as part of a broader 'cruelty-free' lifestyle. This work forms part of its 'Living without Cruelty' campaign, embracing fashion, cosmetics and other lifestyle consumption. The group has also been associated with campaigning against horseracing generally, and the Grand National in particular.

Animal Aid was formed by Jean Pink, closely associated with the group for its early years. During much of the 1980s, it was led by Mark Gold, succeeded in the 1990s by Andrew Tyler.

Box 4.3: Speciesism

'Speciesism – the word is not an attractive one, but I can think of no better term – is a prejudice or attitude of bias toward the interest of members of one's own species and against those members of other species. It should be obvious that the fundamental objections to racism and sexism … apply equally to speciesism. If possessing a higher degree of intelligence does not entitle one human to use another for his own ends, how can it entitle humans to exploit nonhumans for the same purpose?'

Peter Singer, *Animal Liberation* (New York, 1975), p. 7.

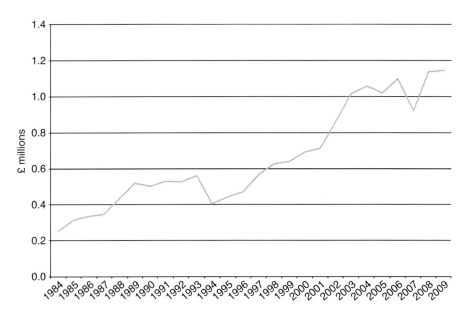

Figure 4.16: Turnover of Animal Aid, 1984–2009 (adjusted for inflation, 2009)

Source: Annual reports and accounts, Animal Aid.

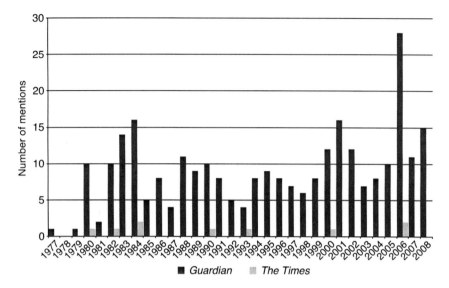

Figure 4.17: Number of mentions of Animal Aid in the *Guardian* and *The Times*, 1977–2008

Source: *Guardian* & *The Times*.

Further reading

Robert Garner, 'The Politics of Animal Rights', *British Politics*, 3:1 (2008), pp. 110–19; Peter Singer, *Animal Liberation: Towards an End to Man's Inhumanity to Animals* (New York, 1975).

Anti-Slavery International

Anti-Slavery International (ASI) is the leading NGO campaigning against all forms of slavery, and can trace its history all the way back to the eighteenth century. In 1787, several Quakers and the Anglicans Thomas Clarkson, Granville Sharp and Philip Sansom (joined shortly after by William Wilberforce) founded the Society for Effecting the Abolition of the Slave Trade. This campaigned for the abolition of the slave trade in 1807 and for the ban on slavery in the British empire in 1833. It was the precursor to the 1839 British and Foreign Anti-Slavery Society, the direct predecessor of ASI.

The British and Foreign Anti-Slavery Society merged in 1909 with Aborigines Protection Society, and they operated as the British and Foreign Anti-Slavery and Aborigines Protection Society until 1947, then the Anti-Slavery Society (1947–56), followed by the Anti-Slavery Society for the Protection of Human Rights (1956–90), Anti-Slavery International for the Protection of Human Rights (1990–95) and eventually ASI in 1995.

ASI's campaign focus has expanded as it has covered all forms of slavery. In the nineteenth century it concentrated on extending the British government's abolition of slavery to all other countries. It then moved on to looking at indentured labour within the British empire in the early twentieth century. Since the Second

World War it has extended this definition so that it came to adopt a human rights perspective (indeed, it likes to claim today that it is the world's oldest human rights organisation). This means that the NGO has extended the definition of slavery to include child labour, debt bondage, forced labour, forced marriage and human trafficking. Indeed, such a definition lay behind its work with others in getting the appointment, in 2007, of a UN Special Rapporteur on contemporary forms of slavery.

Today, it works to investigate instances of slavery all around the world and to lobby governments and international agencies to combat such abuses. Importantly, it also has a strong educational role, promoting awareness of the history of slavery. For instance, in 2008, it was a key organisation in making the transatlantic slave trade part of the UK national curriculum.

Key dates

1839   Formation of Anti-Slavery Society
1840   ASI convenes world's first anti-slavery convention
1890   First comprehensive anti-slavery treaty, the Brussels Act, passed
1920   Ending of indentured labour in British colonies
1926   International Slavery Convention
1984   Human Rights Fund for Indigenous People
1998   Global March Against Child Labour

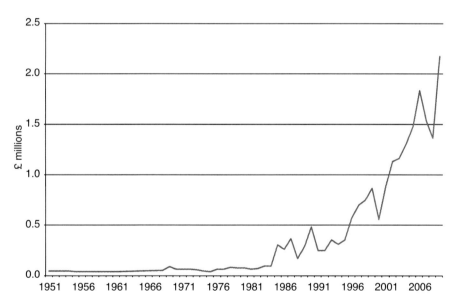

Figure 4.18: Income of Anti-Slavery International, 1951–2009 (adjusted for inflation, 2009)

Sources: Annual reports and accounts, Anti-Slavery International; *Yearbook of International Organisations*; Charity Commission.

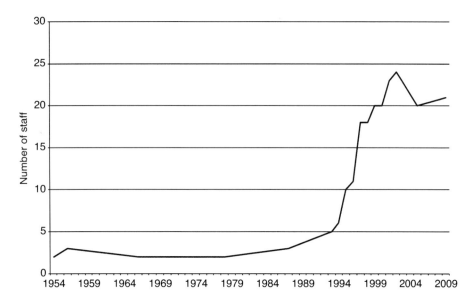

Figure 4.19: Number of staff working for Anti-Slavery International, 1954–2009

Sources: Annual reports and accounts, Anti-Slavery International; *Yearbook of International Organisations*; Charity Commission.

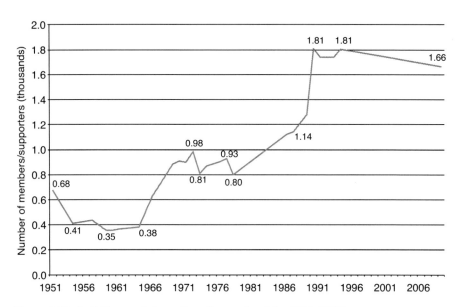

Figure 4.20: Anti-Slavery International's membership, 1951–2009

Note: These figures relate to individual members, but some figures include member organisations (55 in 2009).

Sources: Annual reports and accounts, Anti-Slavery International; *Yearbook of International Organisations*; Charity Commission; contact with Anti-Slavery International (2009).

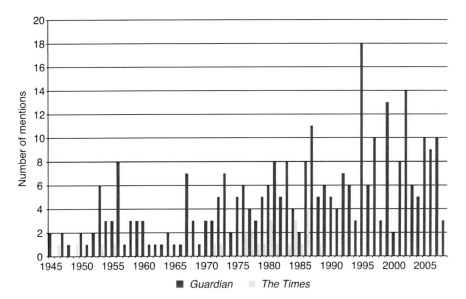

Figure 4.21: Number of mentions of Anti-Slavery International in the *Guardian* and *The Times*, 1945–2007

Source: *Guardian* & *The Times*.

Further reading

Adam Hochschild, *Bury the Chains: The First International Human Rights Movement* (London, 2005); Clare Midgley, *Women Against Slavery: The British Campaigns, 1780–1870* (London, 1992).

Baby Milk Action

Baby Milk Action is the British body associated with the worldwide campaign against the inappropriate marketing of breast-milk substitutes. The problem was identified as early as 1939 when child health pioneer Cicely Williams addressed the Singapore Rotary Club with a lecture entitled 'Milk and Murder'. In 1973, the *New Internationalist* published 'The Baby Food Tragedy', followed the next year by War on Want's *The Baby Killer*. This was translated in Switzerland as *Nestlé Kills Babies*, by the Bern Third World Action Group, leading to a libel suit brought by Nestlé which it eventually won in 1976, though not without bringing about a tremendous amount of bad publicity against itself. In 1977 the Infant Formula Action Coalition was formed in the US, triggering a worldwide boycott of Nestlé products.

The International Baby Food Action Network was formed in 1979 to coordinate the wider campaign, with Baby Milk Action as the British wing. This alliance of NGOs successfully lobbied the World Health Organisation into adopting a Code of Marketing of Breast-milk Substitutes in 1981, which set out basic rules for the sales of infant formula. The nature of the problem, as Baby Milk Action sees it, is associated with the mixing of formula with contaminated water, the insufficient quantities used of the relatively expensive product, and the more general dilemma of marketing a replacement for what is a naturally available and more nutritious form of nourishment.

Since 1981, Baby Milk Action has seen its role as one of monitoring the implementation of the Code, as well as lobbying the UK parliament to bring abuses of it in the developing world to public attention. It has worked with various faith-based, academic and development organisations, such as those connected to the Interagency Group on Breastfeeding Monitoring, to commission research into code violations in various national settings. It has sought to counter Nestlé propaganda in the UK by lobbying parliament and by monitoring the company's public pronouncements, such as in 1999 when the organisation successfully complained to the Advertising Standards Authority after Nestlé claimed that it marketed infant formula 'ethically and responsibly'.

Box 4.4: The International Code of Marketing of Breast-milk Substitutes

Passed in 1981 by the World Health Organisation, the Code 'affirms the right of every child and every pregnant and lactating woman to be adequately nourished'. Its eleven Articles seek to ban various marketing practices such as the giving away of free examples to pregnant women, the use of official healthcare facilities to promote the product, the clear separation of advice from health and commercial bodies, and the labelling of products in misleading language. It promotes instead the use of clear and objective information about the costs and benefits of both breastfeeding and infant formula. Since 1981, 65 countries have enacted legislation implementing all or parts of the Code. Legislation and enforcement, however, have been seen to vary.

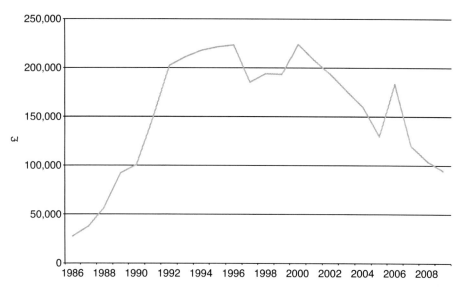

Figure 4.22: Income of Baby Milk Action, 1986–2009 (adjusted for inflation, 2009)

Source: Annual reports and accounts, Baby Milk Action.

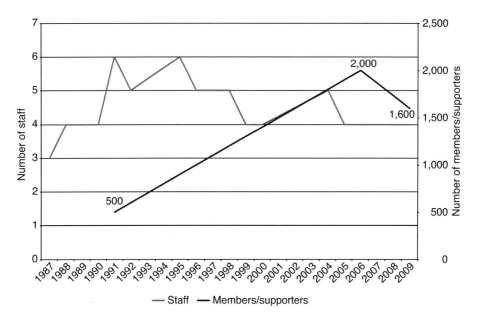

Figure 4.23: Numbers of Baby Milk Action's staff and supporters, 1987–2009

Sources: Annual Reports and accounts, Baby Milk Action; contact with Baby Milk Action (2009).

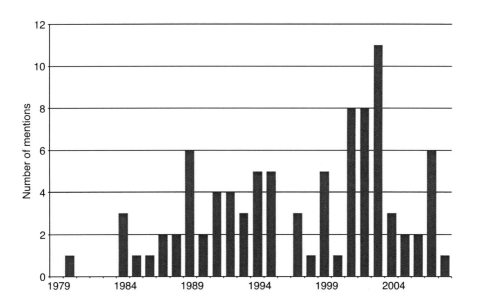

Figure 4.24: Number of mentions of Baby Milk Action in the *Guardian*, 1980–2008

Note: There were no mentions of Baby Milk Action in the *Official Index to The Times*.
Sources: Proquest Historical Newspapers *The Guardian* and *The Observer* (1945–2003) and Nexis (2003–07).

Further reading

Andrew Chetley, *The Baby Killer Scandal: A War on Want Investigation into the Promotion and Sales of Powdered Baby Milks in the Third World* (London, 1979); Matthew Hilton, *Prosperity for All: Consumer Activism in an Era of Globalisation* (Ithaca, NY, 2009).

Board of Deputies of British Jews

Only under the presidency of Moses Montefiore (1784–1885) did the Board establish its credentials as the representative body of British Jewry. Although founded in 1760, and located in Woburn House, Tavistock Square, and then 6 Bloomsbury Square since 2001, its campaigning only really emerged in the twentieth century.

It campaigned unsuccessfully against the 1905 Aliens Act. It worked to improve the British reception of Jewish refugees fleeing Nazi Germany, although significant elements within the organisation were anxious that these new immigrants should assimilate with British society lest they stoke anti-semitism. This was something being encouraged by the British Union of Fascists in the 1930s. Not all sections of the Jewish community understood the Board's apparent conservatism towards the refugees, most notably the left-wing Jewish People's Council.

During the interwar period the Board had representatives from both the non-Zionist and Zionist debates, but as the 1930s progressed, particularly after the Peel Report, the Zionist argument appeared to gain the upper hand, illustrated by the election of the Zionist Selig Brodetsky as president of the Board in 1939. It showed that Zionism, no doubt due to the traumatism of Nazism, had secured the Jewish community's support, but it also marked the ending of the dominance of the old-established families of the nineteenth-century migration.

The claims that the Board is representative of the Jewish community have been challenged. Over half of the Jewish population are located in London, but there are also large communities in Manchester, Leeds and Glasgow, as well as other cities. However, the total population is in decline, down from over 300,000 in 1914 to 267,000 in 2001. Only those Jews who are part of a synagogue that is affiliated to the Board are members, and it was once famously dismissed by Labour MP Ian Mikardo as the 'Board of Dead Bodies'. There are 460 deputies drawn from synagogues and other organisations, who act akin to MPs and meet monthly. The Board itself is smaller and does not consider religious matters – this being the arena of the chief rabbi.

Internal relations within the Board have not always been smooth. During the late 1970s and 1980s, for instance, the leadership of Chief Rabbi Immanuel Jakobovits appeared to associate the Board with the politics of Thatcherism. Controversies about its structures and procedures, disputes between Orthodox and Liberal elements of the community and the debates about Zionism and Israel's position in the Middle East have all caused, and continue to cause, debate.

A positive projection of the image of Jewry has been a key aspect of the Board's mission, whether this was providing advice to new immigrants arriving about assimilation in the 1930s or collaborating in inter-faith forums, such as the Council of Christians and Jews, or providing more general information for non-Jews about

Judaism, Israel and Britain's Jewish community. A representative of the Board attended the first meeting of the United Nations in San Francisco.

It has helped in the rehabilitation of Holocaust survivors and campaigned for compensation. The Board played a key role in the 1983 Holocaust memorial situated in Hyde Park. After the Holocaust the fight against anti-semitism has remained the core theme of the Board. Education is seen as a key means of tackling this problem and it works with education authorities to combat racism and religious discrimination in schools. During the Cold War, a new wave of Eastern European and Russian Jews fled Communism. Collaboration occurred with Russian refugee groups and then became coordinated through the National Council for Soviet Jewry, established in 1975.

Key figures

Neville Laski (1890–1969): president, 1933–39

Selig Brodetsky (1888–1954): mathematician and Zionist; president, Board of Deputies 1939–52

Victor Mishcon (1915–2006): solicitor, and life peer 1978; vice-president, Board of Deputies 1967–73

Greville Janner (1928–): barrister and Labour MP; Board of Deputies 1979–85; chairman, Holocaust Education Trust 1987–

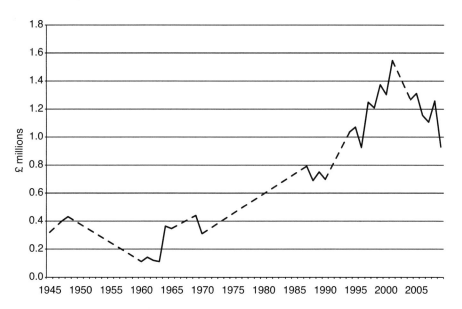

Figure 4.25: Income of the Board of Deputies of British Jews, 1945–2009 (general fund, adjusted for inflation, 2009)

Sources: Annual reports and accounts, Board of Deputies of British Jews; Charity Commission.

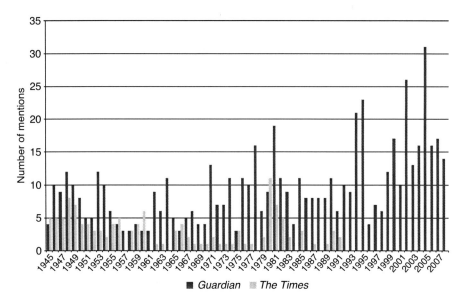

Figure 4.26: Number of mentions of the Board of Deputies of British Jews in the *Guardian* and *The Times*, 1945–2007

Source: *Guardian* & *The Times*.

Further reading

Geoffrey Alderman, *The Jewish Community in British Politics* (Oxford, 1983); Todd M. Endelman, *The Jews of Britain* (Berkeley, 2002).

British Deaf Association

The British Deaf Association (BDA) is the country's leading deaf-led deaf organisation, focused on the promotion and wider acceptance of British Sign Language (BSL), and representing the interests of those who use it.

Given its use both by deaf people themselves and by those who live and work with them, BSL can boast more British users than Welsh or Gaelic. It was officially recognised by the British government in 2003. However, that recognition did not bring with it legal protection, meaning that BSL users do not have full rights to access information and services. The BDA regards this position as discriminatory, and campaigns for its revision, believing that BSL is the most effective route for enabling deaf people to participate equally in society.

The context for the BDA's formation came in 1880, and the decision of the Second International Congress of Education of the Deaf to strongly endorse oral methods of teaching deaf children, and to discourage the use of sign language. Oral methods, which privilege the use of English, thereby became the dominant educational approach for a century, despite ongoing concern and controversy over its efficacy, and the implications of this for the life prospects of deaf people. In order to challenge the primacy of the oral method, and to protect the rights of deaf people, the British Deaf and Dumb Association was formed by Francis Maginn in 1890, adopting the current name in 1971.

From the 1970s, research findings endorsed the richness of BSL as a language, while the 1979 report *The Deaf School Child* found an average reading age of just eight years amongst school-leavers taught with the oral method. The growing recognition of BSL has not, however, resulted in a settled consensus on the best way to teach deaf children. The oral method continues to be used, as does, since the 1980s, the total communication method, which integrates BSL with other forms of communication. Alongside choice and excellence in teaching provision more generally, the BSL wishes to see instituted a right to bilingual education, where BSL and subsequently English are introduced as stand-alone languages.

In the 1990s, the BDA attracted media attention by stipulating that those applying to fill its vacant chief executive position would need to be deaf themselves. This move, seen as a major step in the direction of genuine representation, came after demonstrations outside the Annual General Meeting of another deaf body, the Royal National Institute for Deaf People (RNID), also seeking a new chief executive. In the event, the RNID became the first to make such an appointment, when it appointed Doug Alker to the role in December 1994.

Recent chief executives

E. Wincott (1990s)
J. McWhinney (early 2000s)
Simon Wilkinson-Blake (late 2000s)

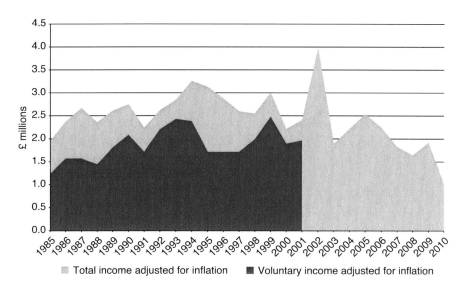

Figure 4.27: Total and voluntary income of the British Deaf Association, 1985–2010 (adjusted for inflation, 2009)

Note: The data for voluntary income after 2001 are missing.

Sources: Annual reports and accounts, BDA; Charity commission; Charity Statistics.

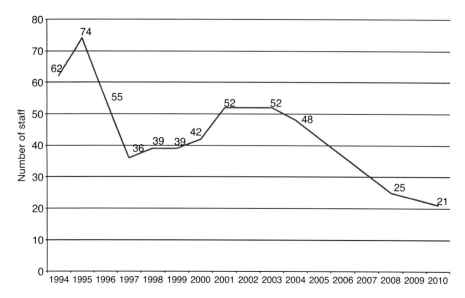

Figure 4.28: Number of staff working for the British Deaf Association, 1994–2010

Sources: Annual reports and accounts, BDA; Charity commission; Charity Statistics.

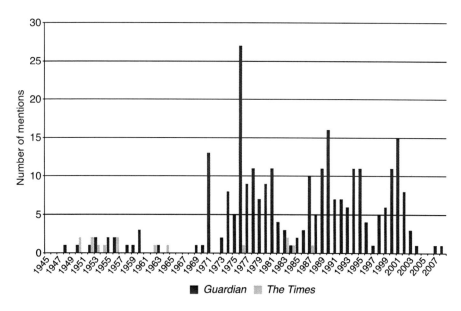

Figure 4.29: Number of mentions of the British Deaf Association in the *Guardian* and *The Times*, 1945–2007

Source: *Guardian* & *The Times*.

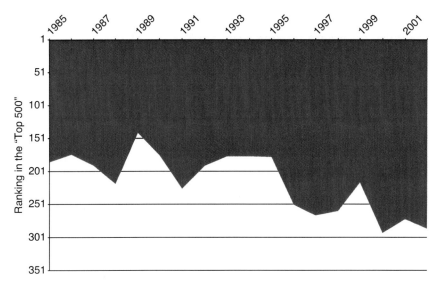

Figure 4.30: The British Deaf Association's charitable ranking by voluntary income, 1975–2006

Note: After 2002, BDA dropped out of the top 500 UK charities by voluntary income.

Source: Charity Statistics.

British Heart Foundation

One of Britain's leading charities, the British Heart Foundation (BHF) is dedicated to eliminating heart and vascular disease as major causes of disability and premature death.

The BHF was established by medical professionals in 1961, with the specific goal of generating public funds for medical research. At the time, when 281,000 annual deaths in England and Wales were attributed to heart disease – more than 50 per cent of all deaths – the Medical Research Council gave only limited support to work in the field. A public appeal was launched with a target of £3.5 million. In a demonstration of the broad support its work attracted, the newly established BHF boasted the Duke of Edinburgh as its patron, and Lord Alexander of Tunis as president.

Since its foundation, the context in which the BHF operates has changed dramatically, as medical research and understanding has surged ahead, in no small part thanks to the BHF itself. The 1960s were a period of particular breakthrough, with the introduction of beta-blockers, the pioneering of open heart surgery and heart transplants, and the introduction of pacemakers. Balloon angioplasty techniques, enabling artery-widening without the need for open heart surgery, were introduced in the 1970s and complemented with the development of stents in the 1990s, over which time the significance of physical activity in cardiac health came to be far better understood, and anti-clotting drugs, such as aspirin, became commonly used.

Given these advances, the BHF diversified into public education, campaigning and rehabilitation work, while still maintaining a research focus. Working with statutory and voluntary sector partners, campaigns against smoking and obesity have been undertaken, the latter in partnership with Diabetes UK and Cancer Research UK under the Change4life banner. The BHF is also a participant, along with 40 other voluntary organisations, in the Cardio & Vascular Coalition (CVC), a lobbying and campaigning umbrella group promoting public health priorities over the coming decade. More specific campaigns are also run, including the successful lobbying of the Scottish government to ban the sale of cigarettes from vending machines, a hitherto major way of children circumventing sales restrictions.

Care for heart patients is another priority, understanding and enhancing provision, representing and responding to patient needs, and driving up nursing standards through initiatives such as the Nurse Excellence awards, and the BHF Heart Nurses. Finally, the BHF undertakes public outreach work in order to tackle health inequalities through the targeting of specific at-risk communities, whether defined through deprivation and social exclusion, or membership of particular ethnic groups.

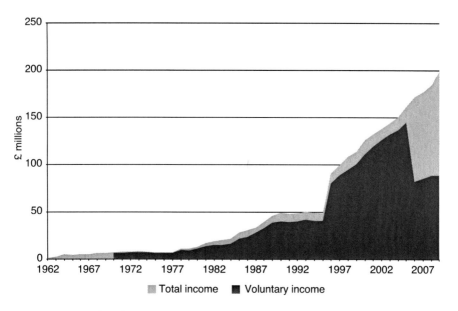

Figure 4.31: Total and voluntary income of the British Heart Foundation, 1970–2009 (adjusted for inflation, 2009)

Note: The drop in voluntary income in 2006–08 is probably due to a change in accounting and reporting methods, rather than an actual drop in income.

Sources: Annual reports and accounts, British Heart Foundation; Charity Commission; Charity Statistics.

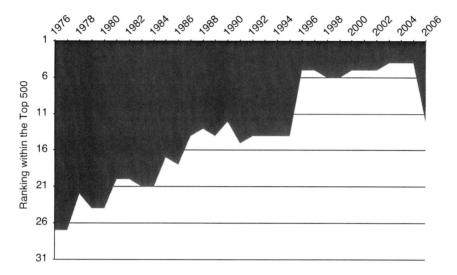

Figure 4.32: The British Heart Foundation's charitable ranking by voluntary income, 1976–2006

Source: Charity Statistics.

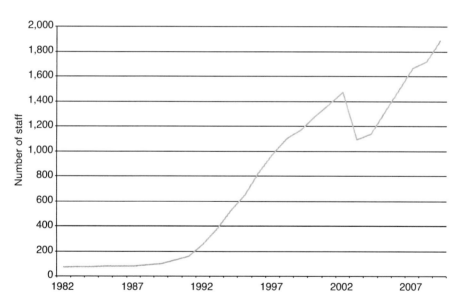

Figure: 4.33: Number of staff working for the British Heart Foundation, 1982–2009

Sources: Charity Statistics; Top 3000 Charities.

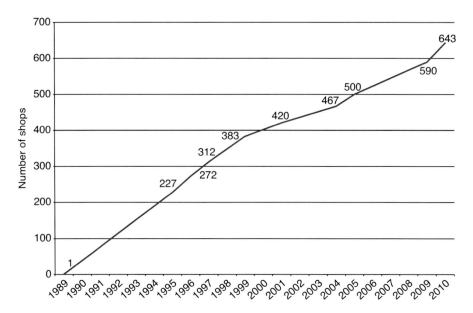

Figure 4.34: Number of shops owned by the British Heart Foundation, 1989–2010

Source: Annual reports and accounts, British Heart Foundation.

Further reading

www.bhf.org.uk
'War Declared on Heart Diseases', *Guardian*, 12 June 1963.

Campaign for Nuclear Disarmament

The Campaign for Nuclear Disarmament (CND) began in 1958 following an initial meeting organised by Canon John Collins, along with a host of prominent public figures associated with the Labour Party, the Churches, the universities and the arts. Formed in response to the growing fears about nuclear war, as well as the attitude of senior Labour figures to unilateral nuclear disarmament, this ostensibly single-issue NGO became one of the leading social movements of the late twentieth century.

CND was always about much more than the nuclear bomb. For members of the New Left it epitomised the expansion of political participation beyond Westminster. Taking politics beyond party, CND was to act as a vanguard for a revitalised left that would align the traditional concerns of the working class with the new, 'expressive' forms of politics associated with a more affluent age. Ordinary people would be brought into politics through organisations such as NGOs, creating a truly mass social movement. That CND ultimately failed to live up to these expectations is a salutary lesson for those who have positioned NGOs as an alternative form of political democracy.

The tensions that have beset so many NGOs were apparent at the very start. Unable to decide whether it was an elite organisation made up of prominent, influential individuals, or a mass membership organisation, CND only reluctantly supported the first march from London to Aldermaston in 1958 that was organised by the Direct Action Committee. Such forms of protest, along with CND's iconic symbol and its slogan 'Ban the Bomb', made the organisation incredibly prominent, so much so that it persuaded the Labour Party to adopt a unilateral policy stance in 1960 (a decision overturned the following year).

Again reflecting a more general issue about radicalism versus reformism, the unity of CND was disturbed in 1960 when Bertrand Russell resigned to form the Committee of 100, which adopted a stance of direct action in potential contradiction of Collins' advocacy of lawful protest. The Committee expanded the remit of CND's protests but it did not reach out beyond its affluent social base. Indeed, in his classic study of the organisation published in 1968, Frank Parkin identified CND supporters as 'middle-class radicals'.

With the waning of Cold War tensions following the 1963 Test Ban Treaty, support for CND declined. It was revived from the late 1970s following growing international tensions. Membership expanded rapidly and the organisation embraced direct action. It drew on new cohorts of the population, particularly Youth CND, and was able to bring crowds of around a quarter of a million to protests held in London in the early 1980s. Most emblematically, it drew on and benefited from the energy of the broader peace movement, particularly that associated with the Greenham Common Women's Peace Camp.

Since the end of the Cold War its fortunes have again declined, though it remains active in campaigns against Trident and in aspects of British foreign policy. In particular, in the early 2000s it collaborated with the broader Stop the War Coalition, and helped organise the enormous protests in 2002 and 2003 using the slogan 'Don't Attack Iraq'.

Key figures

Canon John Collins: chair, 1958–64
Bertrand Russell: first president; founder of Committee of 100
J.B. Priestley: playwright, broadcaster and co-founder
Pat Arrowsmith: co-founder and proponent of direct action
Michael Foot: co-founder, and leader of the Labour Party, 1980–83
E.P. Thompson: author of pamphlet *Protest and Survive* (1980)
Bruce Kent: general secretary, 1979–85; chair, 1987–90
Kate Hudson: chair, 2003–10; general secretary, 2010–

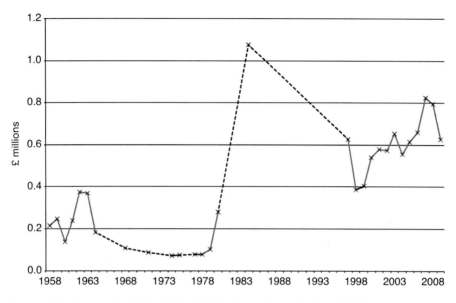

Figure 4.35: Income for CND, 1958–2009 (adjusted for inflation, 2009)

Sources: Annual reports and accounts, CND; minutes of the Executive Committee (consulted through Primary Source Microfilm, *Archives of the Campaign for Nuclear Disarmament* (Left in Britain, Part 5)).

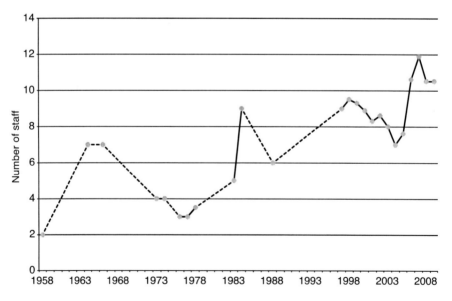

Figure 4.36: Number of staff working for CND, 1958–2009

Sources: Annual reports and accounts, CND; minutes of the Executive Committee (consulted through Primary Source Microfilm, *Archives of the Campaign for Nuclear Disarmament* (Left in Britain, Part 5)); Guardian Directory of Pressure Groups.

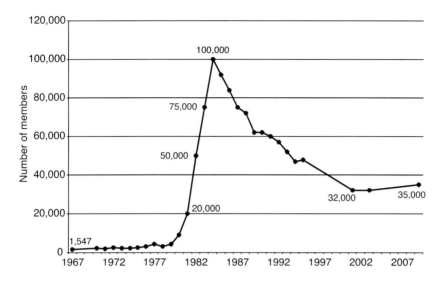

Figure 4.37: CND's membership, 1967–2009

Sources: Annual reports and accounts, CND; minutes of the Executive Committee (consulted through Primary Source Microfilm, *Archives of the Campaign for Nuclear Disarmament* (Left in Britain, Part 5)); CND website; Paul Byrne, *Social Movements in Britain* (London and New York, 1997), p. 91.

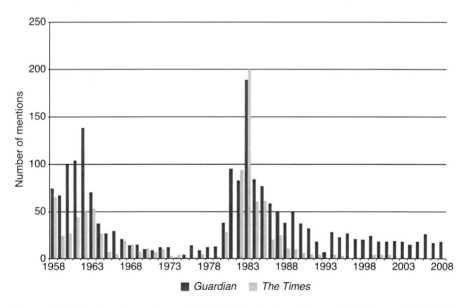

Figure 4.38: Number of mentions of the CND in the *Guardian* and *The Times*, 1958–2008

Source: *Guardian* & *The Times*.

Further reading

There are dozens of histories and studies of CND, but see Paul Byrne, *The Campaign for Nuclear Disarmament* (London, 1988); Frank Parkin, *Middle-Class Radicalism: The Social Bases of the British Campaign for Nuclear Disarmament* (Manchester, 1968); Kate Hudson, *CND – Now More Than Ever: The Story of a Peace Movement* (London, 2005).

Cancer Research UK (formerly The Cancer Research Campaign and Imperial Cancer Research Fund)

Cancer Research is one of the UK's super charities formed from a merger in 2002. Its origins go back to 1902 when doctors from the Royal Colleges of Surgeons and Physicians founded the Imperial Cancer Research Fund (ICRF). A split in approach arose in the 1920s when some doctors and scientists wanted to focus more heavily on clinical research rather than fundamental laboratory research which had been the emphasis of ICRF – so the Cancer Research Campaign was founded.

As early as 1935, these organisations began warning of the dangers of sun exposure and skin cancer. Early chemical breakthroughs pioneered treatments for breast and prostate cancers that would become standard treatments for a number of decades, and during the 1950s they funded work that led to the development of key chemotherapy drugs. The charities were also at the forefront of establishing the links between smoking and cancer. Until the 1960s heart disease was the largest cause of death in England and Wales. However, from 1969 cancer became the leading cause of death in women, and for men from 1995. Childhood cancers were the focus of considerable research efforts in the 1970s, and this decade also saw Cancer Research collaborating with the National Health Service (NHS) to establish the first oncology departments.

During the 1980s, the charities continued to develop new cancer drugs, to pioneer drugs trials and to review longer-term clinical results. They also developed techniques for establishing which genes increased the risks of developing particular cancers. The 1990s saw a growing awareness of the impact of lifestyle on cancer risks, and these featured in the health campaigns and cancer prevention messages of the charities, as well as the enhanced educational information the charities provided. This went in tandem with a developing close relationship between pharmaceutical industry products and public health policy interventions, such as products to help smokers quit and No Smoking Days that the charities sought to promote. The cancer charities formed part of the wider health coalition that included Action Against Smoking (ASH), which ultimately culminated in the banning of smoking in the work place and enclosed public spaces in 2007.

During the 2000s the charity funded the opening of five flagship research institutes in Cambridge, Oxford, London, Manchester and Glasgow, as well as funding some university clinical departments. In May 2007 it launched its ten goals to shape its work over the next decade.

Although there have been moves towards greater cooperation across the entire health sector since the Department of Health's 2007 Cancer Reform Strategy, Cancer Research UK is part of a largely uncoordinated mosaic of activity that comprises government, the NHS and the Medical Research Council, professional associations, the pharmaceutical industry and the charities. It is consistently the most 'trusted' of charities in surveys of the public and generates its revenue entirely from public donations, legacies and fundraising events such as the Race for Life.

Box 4.5: Imperial Cancer Research Fund advertisement

'The fight against cancer – mankind's cruellest enemy – is being intensified. The Imperial Cancer Research Fund seeks your help in building new laboratories in Lincoln's Inn Field. Due to open next year, this will be the most advanced research centre in Europe. But £1,000,000 is needed to complete it.

... To widen its activities and to speed results, the Fund – which received no official grant – makes this *personal* appeal to you. Will you please help – *now?*'

The Times, 15 February 1960, p. 4.

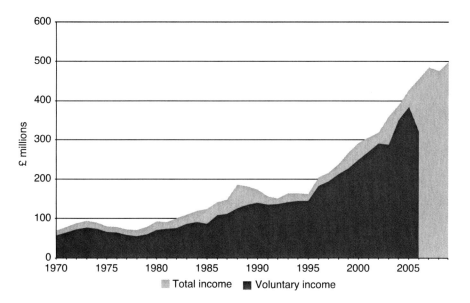

Figure 4.39: Total and voluntary income of Cancer Research UK, 1970–2009 (adjusted for inflation, 2009)

Note: The graph amalgamates the total and voluntary income of both the Cancer Research Campaign and the Imperial Cancer Research Fund before their merger in 2000, and then the income of Cancer Research UK after the two organisations merged. Data for voluntary income after 2006 were not available.

Sources: Charity Statistics; Charity Commission; Wolfenden 1978; Wells Collection.

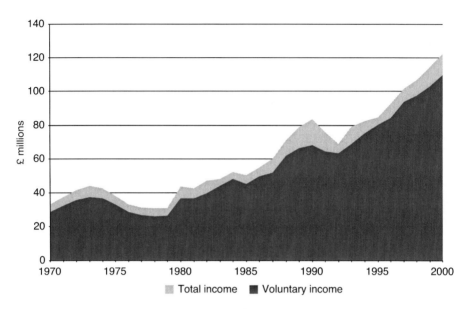

Figure 4.40: Total and voluntary income of Cancer Research Campaign, 1970–2000 (adjusted for inflation, 2009)

Sources: Charity Statistics; Wolfenden 1978; Wells Collection.

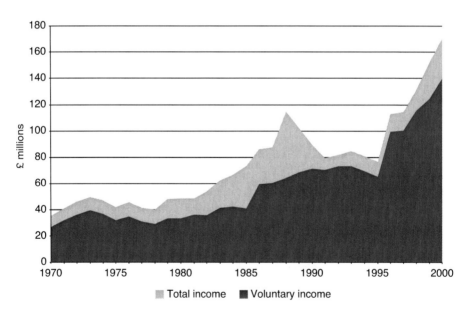

Figure 4.41: Total and voluntary income of Imperial Cancer Research Fund, 1970–2000 (adjusted for inflation, 2009)

Sources: Charity Statistics; Wolfenden 1978; Wells Collection.

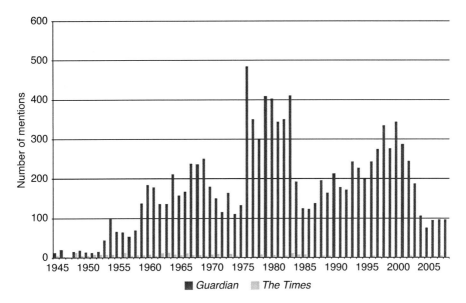

Figure 4.42: Number of mentions of Cancer Research UK (including the Cancer Research Campaign and the Imperial Cancer Research Fund) in the *Guardian* and *The Times*, 1945–2007

Note: The values provided above are an amalgam of the data for Cancer Research UK, the Cancer Research Campaign and the Imperial Cancer Research Fund.

Source: *Guardian* & *The Times*.

Further reading

Virginia Berridge, *Marketing Health: Smoking and the Discourse of Public Health in Britain* (Oxford, 2007); C.E. Dukes, 'The Origin and Early History of the Imperial Cancer Research Fund', *Annals of the Royal College of Surgeons of England* (1965), pp. 1165–9.

Catholic Agency for Overseas Development

The Catholic Agency for Overseas Development (CAFOD) is the British arm of a worldwide Catholic aid and development initiative overseen by the Caritas International Federation. The global movement traces its roots all the way back to 1897 in Freiburg, Germany, although it was not until the 1924 Eucharistic World Congress in Amsterdam that a more established body emerged, the name Caritas Catholica being adopted in 1928. The Second World War badly interrupted its work, though by 1951 the first General Assembly of Caritas Internationalis took place. British Catholics lagged behind their European counterparts, but in 1960 the National Board of Catholic Women held a Family Fast Day. This generated sufficient interest within the Church such that the Catholic Bishops of England and Wales officially established CAFOD in 1962.

British Catholic humanitarianism came some years after Anglican and secular initiatives. In many ways it needed the catalyst of papal legitimacy to encourage further work in social intervention. Pope Paul IV's *Populorum Progressio* of 1967 committed Catholics to the 'development of peoples' as a whole, while in 1971, the Vatican's *A Call to Action* encouraged grassroots action and *Justice in the World* emphasised civic participation. By the end of the 1960s CAFOD had caught up with other development agencies. It joined the Disasters Emergency Committee (DEC) that coordinates British humanitarian fundraising and it cooperated with other Catholic agencies, principally International Co-operation for Development and Solidarity (CIDSE) which is a consortium of 14 European and North American Catholic development agencies founded in 1969.

From the 1970s, CAFOD has consistently worked with other faith-based groups to set out some of the key development initiatives, from making a commitment to spend 0.7 per cent of gross domestic product (GDP) on aid, to setting out policy on trade, debt and poverty reduction. From 1976 it has accepted funding from the UK government, kickstarting an expansion of its operations which has seen it run projects all around the world, especially Latin America. Mission remains central to its work, but its broader commitment to social justice makes many of its practical initiatives indistinguishable from those of Christian Aid and other faith-based NGOs. Indeed, CAFOD has been a central partner in more recent campaigns such as Drop the Debt, Trade Justice and Fair Trade.

Key Catholic texts relating to development

John XXIII, *Mater et Magistra*, 1961
Second Vatican Council, *Gaudium et Spes*, 1965
Paul VI, *Populorum Progressio*, 1967
Synod of Bishops, *Justice in the World*, 1971
John Paul II, *Sollicitudo Rei Socialis*, 1987
Benedict XVI, *Caritas in Veritate*, 2009

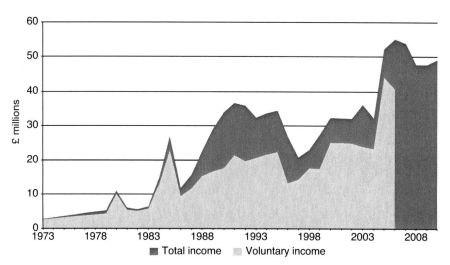

Figure 4.43: Voluntary and total income of CAFOD, 1973–2010 (adjusted for inflation, 2009)

Sources: Wells Collection; Charity Statistics; Charity Commission.

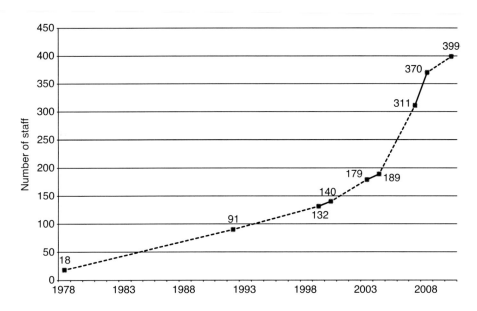

Figure 4.44: Number of staff working for CAFOD, 1978–2010

Sources: *Yearbook of International Organisations*; Top 3000 Charities; Charity Commission.

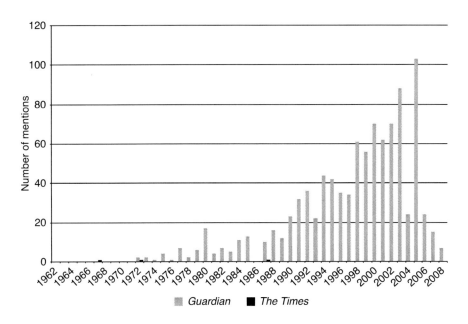

Figure 4.45: Number of mentions of CAFOD in the *Guardian* and *The Times*, 1967–2008

Source: *Guardian* & *The Times*.

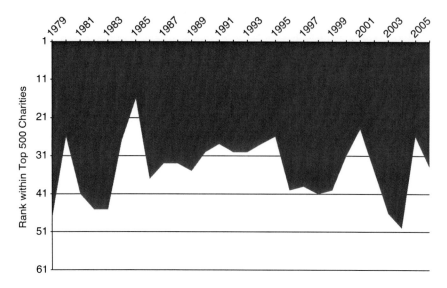

Figure 4.46: CAFOD's charitable ranking by voluntary income, 1979–2005

Source: Charity Statistics.

Further reading

Peter J. Burnell, *Charity, Politics and the Third World* (London, 1991); Clare Saunders, 'British Humanitarian, Aid and Development NGOs, 1949–Present', in Nick Crowson, Matthew Hilton and James McKay (eds), *NGOs in Contemporary Britain: Non-State Actors in Society and Politics since 1945* (Basingstoke, 2009), pp. 38–58.

Centre for Policy Studies

The Centre for Policy Studies (CPS) was formed in 1974 by Sir Keith Joseph and Alfred Sherman with the dual purpose of research and lobbying. Located in a basement room at 8 Wilfred Street, near Westminster, it sought to promote free enterprise and was responsible for the political growth of monetarism. It was sponsored by private business funds with donations from 17 Confederation of British Industry (CBI) member firms and was independent of Conservative Party funding.

The think tank acted as speechwriter and policy developer for Joseph, including his June 1974 Upminster speech. It succeeded in converting a sceptical shadow cabinet to previously unpopular polices that would prove electoral assets in future years, such as trade union reform. It promoted alternatives to what Joseph saw as the 'six poisons' crippling Britain: excessive government expenditure, high taxation, egalitarianism, nationalisation, trade unions and the anti-enterprise culture. It proved the training ground for a succession of Thatcherite policy advisors: Ralph Harris, Alfred Sherman, Hugh Thomas, John Hoskyns, David Young, Norman Strauss and Alan Walters. Many of its leading figures were initially unfamiliar in Conservative circles. But Joseph soon drew Thatcher to them as a vice-chairman.

Jews were prominent, and this was symptomatic of the shift of many Jewish businessmen from Labour to the Conservatives.

Overall, in the 1970s the CPS was anxious that the British economy had been overly politicised and was being subjected, and consequently damaged, by the political necessity of short-term policies that carried electoral appeal. It strongly supported the monetarist policies of Thatcher's first administration, but found its influence declining in the late 1980s as their source of ideological patronage dissipated – for example, Joseph's retirement, Geoffrey Howe's move to the Foreign Office and Thatcher's resignation.

Its relationship with the formal Conservative Party, especially the Research Department (CRD, a rival for policy initiatives) was often fraught. This tension arose not least because the CRD's remit was to devise policy (usually short term) to gain electoral victory, whereas the CPS' aim was to widen and enhance public discussion, thus giving the Conservatives a freer hand. It was a tussle which the CPS ultimately won when the CRD's role was downgraded by Thatcher and its independence of operation reigned in. It also sought to influence through books, pamphlets and organised debates, focusing on topics such as health and education, defence and nationalisation of industry. Personal rifts amongst key individuals sometimes diminished its influence: Hugh Thomas and Alfred Sherman fell out in 1981 and Thomas resigned, and in 1982 Norman Strauss left the organisation. Tensions also existed as the CPS began to criticise the Conservative government of John Major for not being Thatcherite enough. Foreign policy has traditionally not been of great interest to this think tank, but the growth of European integration, especially after the Single European Act (1986) and the ending of the Cold War, has led to a greater interest in foreign policy concerns.

Key figures

Alan Walters (1926–2009): economist; chief economic advisor to Thatcher, 1981–84
Keith Joseph (1918–1994): Conservative politician and CPS founder
Alfred Sherman (1919–2006): journalist and political activist; first director of the CPS, 1974–84

Box 4.6: Keith Joseph's Upminster speech announcing the CPS's launch, 22 June 1974

'Thirty years of increasing state ownership and control have so weakened the economy that its socialist critics can use the very weaknesses created as justification for still further collectivism. The only conceivable basis for prosperity rests on a healthy competitive private sector, a market economy within a framework of humane laws and institutions.'

The Times, 24 June 1974, p. 2.

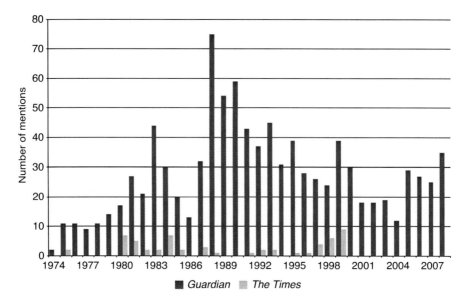

Figure 4.47: Number of mentions of the Centre for Policy Studies in the *Guardian* and *The Times*, 1974–2008

Source: *Guardian* & *The Times*.

Further reading

Michael J. Todd, *The Centre for Policy Studies: Its Birth and Early Days*, Essex Papers in Politics and Government, 81 (1991); Michael Kandiah and Anthony Seldon (eds), *Ideas and Think Tanks in Contemporary Britain, vols 1–2* (Newbury, 1996–97); Richard Cockett, *Thinking the Unthinkable: Think Tanks and the Economic Counter-Revolution, 1931–83* (London, 1995).

Child Poverty Action Group

Formed in 1965 due to a synergy of interest in child poverty from Quakers, London School of Economics (LSE) academics and social service managers, the Child Poverty Action Group (CPAG) (supported with seed-funding from Joseph Rowntree Trust, and then the Home Office's Voluntary Services Unit) established a reputation for detailed policy research. Initially campaigning for increased child benefits, its critics have accused it of being too middle class and piecemeal in its policy responses.

Seen as part of the phenomenon of cause groups that emerged in the 1960s with the 'rediscovery' of poverty, its impact has been contested. It was certainly influential on academic debate, but it has proved less successful at changing popular attitudes and practical policy. This failing stemmed from its ideological egalitarian agenda – aiming for equality of income – which governments consistently dismissed as impractical. Consistently unpopular with government (and especially Thatcher's 1980s administrations) due to its research role, it was deemed by Nigel Lawson a 'deeply sinister body'. Its campaign against the Social Services review in 1984-86 fell largely on deaf ears, with it succeeding only in securing two small concessions during the passage of the parliament bill.

It has been better received by the civil service who looked favourably upon its research. Ultimately it is influential due to its detailed policy research, with good media links (particularly in the broadsheet media), but not powerful.

During the 1970s, tensions persisted within CPAG over whether it should be a membership or a lobby organisation. Today it boasts 3,500 members and subscribers – fees for which account for 9 per cent of its annual income. CPAG has moved from being a shoestring group to a modern professional (if still radical) organisation located in White Lion Street, London, currently employing 40 staff split between the London organisation and its sister Scottish organisation based in Glasgow. This professionalisation has not been without difficulties, and in 1992 staff took industrial action over changes to their terms and conditions.

It publishes frequent policy books with the intention of providing campaigners, opinion formers and the public with accessible information and argument, and these account for 50 per cent of its income stream. It also produced the *Poverty* magazine. It has a citizens' rights office which provides telephone and letter advice on welfare issues and takes on 'test cases' to challenge the interpretation of Social Security or Tax Credit laws. It also provides a training course in welfare rights (which accounts for 11 per cent of its annual income).

Key figures

Harriett Wilson (1916–2002): sociologist; co-author of *Parents and Children in the Inner City* (1978); founder and CPAG vice-chair, 1965–81

Peter Townsend (1928–2009): sociologist and academic; research officer with PEP (Political and Economic Planning), 1952–54; author, including, with Brian Abel-Smith, *The Poor and the Poorest* (1965); Fabian Society chairman, 1965–66; CPAG chairman, 1969–89

Garry Runciman, third Viscount (1934–): sociologist and academic; CPAG treasurer, 1972–97, who launched the Endowment Fund campaign in 1976

Frank Field (1942–): CPAG director, 1969–79; Low Pay Unit, 1974–80; Labour MP, 1979–, and minister for welfare reform, 1997–98; chairman, Review on Poverty and Life Chances, 2010

Ruth Lister (1949–): CPAG from 1971; assistant director 1975–79; director, 1979–87; professor of social policy, Loughborough University, 1994–

Sally Witcher (1960–): campaign worker, Disability Alliance, 1989–93, CPAG director, 1993–98

Key campaigns

1968–69   Child Benefits and increases in Family Allowances, including Child Benefits Now campaign, 1977–79

1980–81   Against the Social Security Acts

1984–86   Social Security review

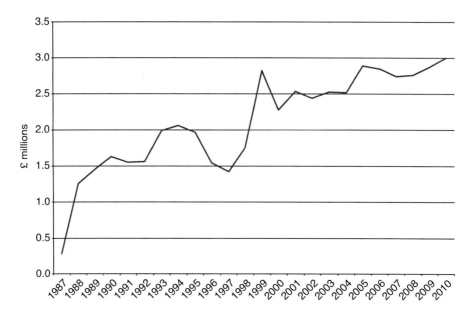

Figure 4.48: Income of CPAG, 1987–2010 (adjusted for inflation, 2009)

Sources: Annual reports and accounts, CPAG; Charity Commission; Top 3000 Charities.

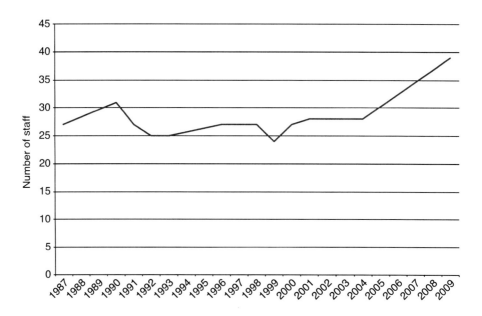

Figure 4.49: Number of staff working for CPAG, 1987–2009

Sources: Annual reports and accounts, CPAG; Charity Commission; Top 3000 Charities.

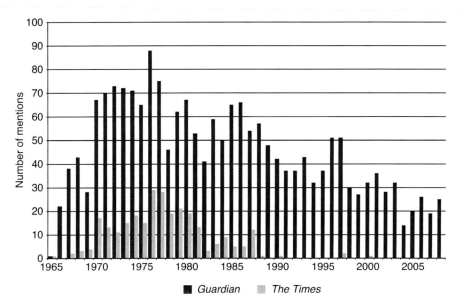

Figure 4.50: Number of mentions of CPAG in the *Guardian* and *The Times*, 1965–2008

Source: *Guardian* & *The Times*.

Further reading

Michael McCarthy, *Campaigning for the Poor: CPAG and the Politics of Welfare* (London, 1986); Frank Field, *Poverty and Politics: The Inside Story of the CPAG Campaigns in the 1970s* (London, 1982); Rodney Lowe (ed.), 'Introduction' and Witness Seminar on founding of CPAG, *Contemporary British History*, 9:3 (1995), pp. 612–37; Patrick Seyd, 'The Child Poverty Action Group', *Political Quarterly*, 24:2 (1976), pp. 189–202.

Children's Society

Originally known as the Waifs and Strays Society, the Children's Society was founded in 1881 by evangelical Christian brothers Edward and Robert de Montjoie Rudolf in South Lambeth, London. Motivated by a belief that the Church of England should be providing free residential support for destitute children, the brothers set about fundraising and forming a committee of clergy and interested lay people. In August 1881 the Archbishop of Canterbury, Archibald Tait, agreed to become president, with the organisation securing official Church of England recognition. By 1890 it was running 35 homes with 1,600 children under its care, and was arranging the foster care of children. By 1905 this had expanded to 93 homes with 3,410 children in its care, and 175 homes by 1918.

Underpinning the homes was a redemptive 'saving of souls' ethos and a sense of 'care through order'. Boys were prepared for trades and girls for domestic service. In 1946 the 'Waifs and Strays' title was dropped due to the stigmatism it attracted. During these immediate post-war decades the organisation's Victorian ancestry was still apparent but it is clear that it was opening up to new ways of thinking.

Fostering grew in popularity and the organisation began rethinking the primacy of residential care. In 1936 it introduced a grant scheme designed to help parents facing money problems to keep their child at home, and during the 1950s this was helping around 700 children a year.

During the late 1950s it established 33 residential nurseries. Its nursery nurse training scheme became the template for training adopted by the Ministry of Education's National Nursery Examination Board (NNEB). During the 1950s it moved to mixed homes run by married couples and was increasingly influenced by child guidance thinking, development psychology and the rise of the social worker. The 1946 Curtis Report was seen as laying the foundation for the new age of 'modern' childcare, but equally, if not more, important was the work of John Bowlby on secure attachment theory.

With the moral panic over child abuse in the 1970s, the Society began moving away from residential care, but it has become widely recognised that the failings of this residential care system (not just within the Society, but across the voluntary and state sector) are long and systematic, in what was one of the most unregulated and most exploited environments. It also moved away from adoption and fostering. In 1969 it opened its first day-care centre in South London; others around the country followed. The Society marked its centenary with twelve purpose-built family centres, situated on deprived housing estates. In 1986 the Society and Church established the Community and Diocesan Development Teams to help local communities identify solutions to their needs.

The evangelical founding zeal has become secularised, but the association with the Church of England remains, and Christian values are prominent in its vision and mission, even if the ambitions of the Society are now based on broad policy, advocacy and outreach.

Box 4.7: The Children's Society, *A Manifesto for a Good Childhood*, July 2009

'Society owes it to children and young people to make a commitment to make their lives better now and to improve childhood for future generations. The Children's Society is therefore calling on all political parties to make a new commitment to childhood in any new administration they form. This manifesto identifies three key areas where political change and leadership are needed to realise such a commitment.

To put children's well-being at the heart of UK public policy.
To prioritise the interests of children who face the greatest disadvantage.
To include children as valued citizens in reforms for democratic renewal.'

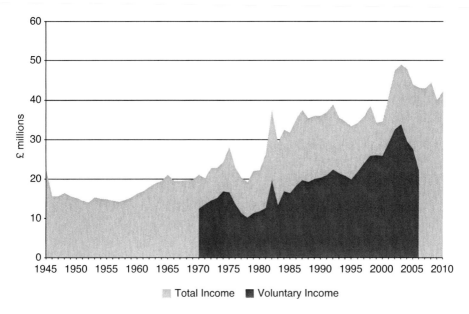

Figure 4.51: Voluntary and Total Income for The Children's Society, 1945–2010 (adjusted for inflation, 2009)

Note: Figures for voluntary income before 1970 or after 2006 are unavailable.

Sources: Annual reports and accounts, Children's Society; Wolfenden 1978; Wells Collection; Charity Statistics; Charity Commission.

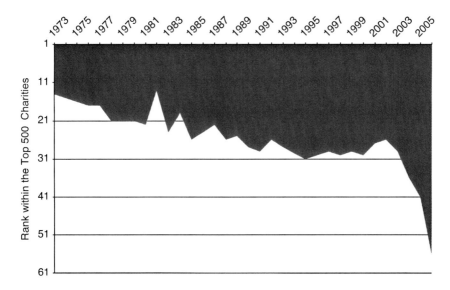

Figure 4.52: The Children's Society charitable ranking by voluntary income, 1973–2005

Sources: Wells Collection; Charity Statistics.

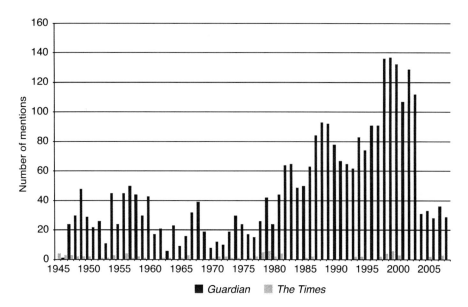

Figure 4.53: Number of mentions of the Children's Society in the *Guardian* and *The Times*, 1945–2007

Source: *Guardian* & *The Times*.

Further reading

Shuna Kennedy, 'The Power of Positioning: A Case History of the Children's Society', *International Journal of Nonprofit and Voluntary Sector Marketing*, 3 (1998), pp. 224–30; John Stroud, *Thirteen Penny Stamps: The Story of the Church of England Children's Society (Waifs and Strays) from 1881 to the 1970s* (London, 1971); Alyson Brown and David Barrett, *Knowledge of Evil: Child Prostitution and Child Sexual Abuse in Twentieth Century England* (Cullompton, 2002); David Webb, 'A Certain Moment: Some Personal Reflections on Aspects of Residential Childcare in the 1950s', *British Journal of Social Work* (2009), pp. 1–15.

Christian Aid

Christian Aid has its origins in the World Council of Churches (WCC), a body set up in 1937 that built on ecumenical movements such as the Young Men's Christian Association (YMCA), the Young Women's Christian Association (YWCA), the Student Christian Movement and the International Missionary Council. In 1945, one of the WCC's many bodies, the Department of Reconstruction, merged with the European Central Bureau for Inter-Church Aid (established in 1921) to become the Department of Reconstruction and Inter-Church Aid (alternatively termed Christian Reconstruction in Europe). This became a department of the British Council of Churches, changing its name to the Inter-Church Aid and Refugee Service in 1949 and later to Christian Aid in 1964 as it identified itself with the increasingly prominent 'Christian Aid week' begun in 1957.

The organisation still remains associated with this fundraising event, taking place in the second week of May every year. By 2007 it called upon 300,000 volunteer collectors. Mission has been central to its work. Its first director, Janet Lacey, constantly reiterated the point that mission and aid go hand in hand. Writing in 1961, she claimed 'We are commanded to take the good news to all nations. To do that means harnessing the total resources of trained man-power, using all the variety of gifts given to man.'

Yet at the same time Christian Aid has also become a mainstream aid organisation working alongside the likes of War on Want: 'Oxfam with hymns', as it has often been put. It has collaborated with the Disasters Emergency Committee (DEC) from its formation in 1963. It joined the Voluntary Committee on Overseas Aid and Development in 1965, and in 1968 it published the Haslemere Declaration with Oxfam and other NGOs that set the tone for much NGO development thereafter. In the 1970s it supported alternative, grassroots development projects and it increasingly politicised development policy. It worked with Oxfam and War on Want to launch the World Development Movement in 1969 and it helped launch the *New Internationalist* in 1973.

It became an early recipient of government funding and, with Oxfam, received the first block grants in 1977 that enabled considerable freedom in its disbursement. Such contracts also facilitated a massive expansion from the 1980s which, tied with the institutional support base provided by its Church membership, means it has continued to be a leading player in development campaigns: Drop the Debt, the Trade Justice Movement, Make Poverty History and Jubilee 2000. Faith therefore remains a crucial motivation for many development activists, though in a manner which enables Christian Aid policies to mirror those of its secular counterparts.

Key figure

Janet Lacey was the guiding figure behind Christian Aid as she led the organisation from 1952 to 1968. As well as an effective director, she also wrote many of its key pamphlets, constantly reiterating the interconnections between faith and development. As she put it in 1970, 'Christian Aid is not just another charity but should be a reconciling factor in the Church and the world, between nationality, classes and between Christian and non-Christian.' If Christian Aid's campaigns appear to owe little to theology and more to politics, Lacey's writings explain why many Anglicans are motivated to support international aid and development charities.

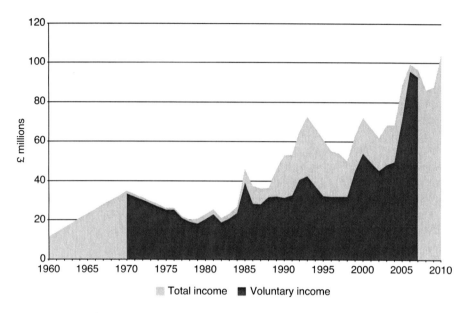

Figure 4.54: Voluntary and total income of Christian Aid, 1960–2010 (adjusted for inflation, 2009)

Note: Total income between 1960 and 1970 is inferred. There are no data on voluntary income after 2007.

Sources: *Social Trends*, 7 (1976), p. 197; Wolfenden 1978; Charity Statistics; Charity Commission.

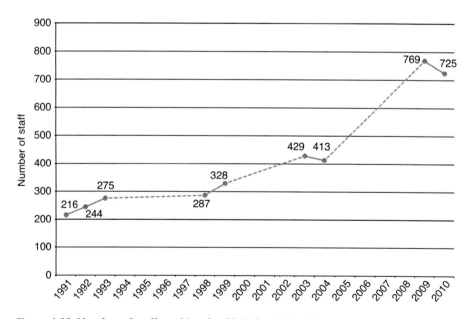

Figure 4.55: Number of staff working for Christian Aid, 1991–2010

Sources: Top 3000 Charities; Charity Commission.

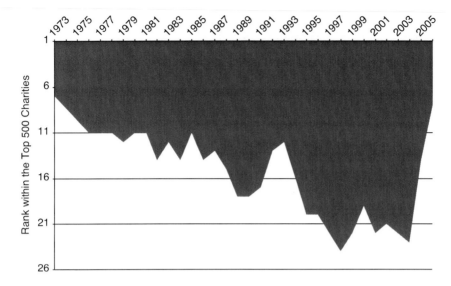

Figure 4.56: Christian Aid's charitable ranking by voluntary income, 1973–2005

Source: Charity Statistics.

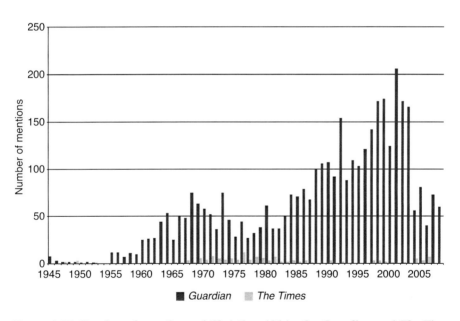

Figure 4.57: Number of mentions of Christian Aid in the *Guardian* and *The Times*, 1945–2007

Source: *Guardian* & *The Times*.

Further reading

Janet Lacey, *A Cup of Water: The Story of Christian Aid* (London, 1970); Michael Taylor, *Not Angels but Agencies: The Ecumenical Response to Poverty – A Primer* (London, 1995); Matthew Hilton, 'International Aid and Development NGOs in Britain and Human Rights since 1945', *Humanity*, forthcoming 2013.

Disability Alliance

Disability Alliance was formed in 1974 by Peter Townsend as an umbrella group for 50 voluntary organisations concerned with disability (by 2011 this had increased to 250 members). Its purpose has been, like the Disablement Income Group (DIG; created 1965), to campaign for a national disability income and against the broader issue of disability poverty. The disabled had secured piecemeal gains due to the Chronically Sick and Disabled Persons' Act (1970) and an expansion in disability and attendance allowances. An invalid care allowance was introduced in 1976 and extended in 1981 to non-relatives with caring responsibilities and finally to married women caring for spouses in 1987.

The distinction between the Disability Alliance and DIG was that the Alliance wanted a separate, independent benefit for those who cared for disabled persons, whilst DIG argued that if disabled people are given a proper, adequate income, it would be unnecessary to pay carers separately. The challenge that the Disability Alliance has faced with its campaign is the rigidity of charity law that prevents it from campaigning in an overtly political manner. In making its case for a disability allowance it sought to produce evidence of the chronic financial circumstances of the disabled, whilst seeking to produce data that showed such an income would not place a disproportionate burden on the public purse.

However the Disability Alliance's emphasis on the symptoms of disablement poverty produced critical responses from some elements of the radical disabled community (such as the Union of the Physically Impaired Against Segregation) who consider that the system discriminates against disabled people. They consider groups like the Disability Alliance to be failing to represent disabled people and believe that they are instead constructing an 'expert' view of the problem. This argument is representative of a wider disability debate about whether organisations are *for* or *of* the disabled.

As a single issue cause group, the Disability Alliance's foundation was symptomatic of a reaction against the perceived failure of the traditional disability voluntary organisations to overcome the inappropriate manner which the disabled are treated. But in turn the failure of Disability Alliance to achieve its goal has led to the emergence of self-help (for example, the Spinal Injuries Association) and populist groups (such as Sisters Against Disablement) for the disabled.

The eradication of disability poverty remains the Alliance's primary goal, but the constant revamping of the benefits systems and the economic retrenchment since 2010 means that gains accrued since 1997 are under threat. For example, the Cameron coalition government intends to replace the Disability Living Allowance with a Personal Independence Payment in 2013–14 which will be based on mobility and daily living needs. Aside from campaigning, the Disability Alliance also offers advice on disability rights, publishing the *Disability Rights Handbook* which offers legal advice and legal case histories on matters relating to disability.

Box 4.8: *Disability Alliance Strategic Plan 2010–2013*, p. 8

'Our vision
We want to see a society in which disabled people and those with long term illness or injury, are able to live free of poverty in order to enjoy the same independence, access to life chances, human rights and opportunities as other citizens.

Our Mission
Our mission is to promote, lobby and campaign for and support public policy and legislation that:

Reduces the number of disabled people living in poverty
Reduces the level of poverty experienced by disabled people
Better tackles disability poverty, increases independence and improves the life chances and opportunities available to disabled people.'

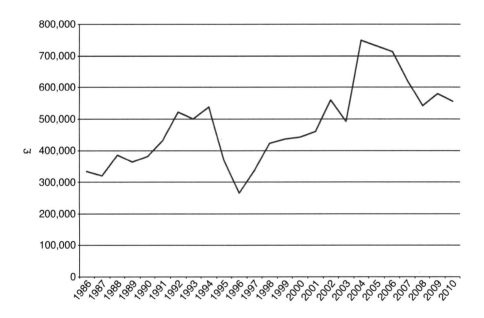

Figure 4.58: Total income of the Disability Alliance, 1986–2010 (adjusted for inflation, 2009)

Sources: Annual reports and accounts, Disability Alliance; Charity Commission.

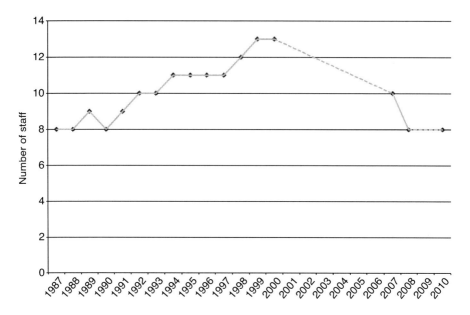

Figure 4.59: Number of staff working for the Disability Alliance, 1987–2010

Sources: Annual reports and accounts, Disability Alliance; Charity Commission.

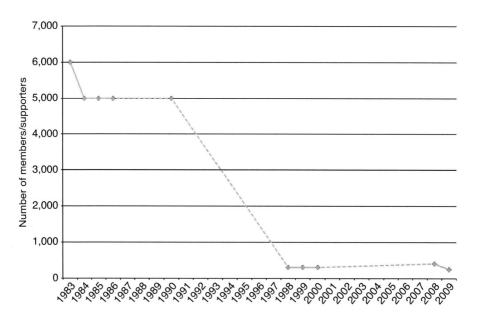

Figure 4.60: The Disability Alliance's members and supporters, 1983–2009

Sources: *Social Trends*; Annual reports and accounts, Disability Alliance; Disability Alliance website.

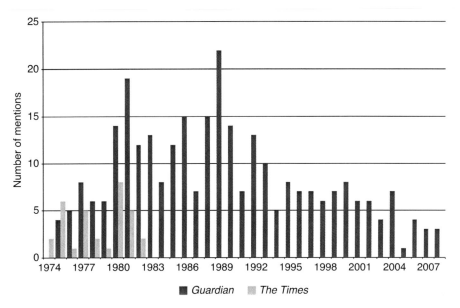

Figure 4.61: Number of mentions of the Disability Alliance in the *Guardian* and *The Times*, 1974–2008

Source: *Guardian* & *The Times*.

Further reading

Michael Oliver, *The Politics of Disablement* (Basingstoke, 1990); Jane Campbell and Michael Oliver, *Disability Politics: Understanding Our Past, Changing our Future* (Abingdon, 1997); Mike Bury, 'Defining and Researching Disability: Challenges and Responses', in Colin Barnes and Geoff Mercer (eds), *Exploring the Divide* (Leeds, 1996), pp. 18–38; Vic Finkelstein, 'A Personal Journey into Disability Politics' (2001), www.independentliving.org/docs3/finkelstein01a.pdf; Mike Oliver, 'The Disability Movement is a New Social Movement!', *Community Development Journal*, 32:3 (1997), pp. 244–51.

Fabian Society

The Fabian Society has been a leading presence on the British left for more than a century. A rarity among think tanks for its nationwide, democratic membership structure, and perhaps best known for its publications, the Society was founded in 1884 and has long provided a prominent platform for gradualist socialism.

The Society can be understood as an attempt to make socialism safe for liberal democracy by encasing it within mainstream ideological norms. Emerging around the same time as the Social Democratic Federation and the Socialist League, the Fabians eschewed the radicalism of their peers. Marxism was set aside in favour of W.S. Jevons' theory of marginal utility, far more compatible with a path of parliamentary reformism. Meanwhile, the 1886 formation of the Fabian Parliamentary League, which quickly became synonymous with the Society as a whole, formalised the constitutional approach, and confirmed their belief in the essential neutrality of the state. The advent of the Second Boer War (1899–1902) forced the Society to consider its approach to imperialism. The result was George Bernard Shaw's pamphlet *Fabianism and the Empire* (1900), which endorsed the supposedly responsible imperialism of the British state as a necessary staging post to world federation. Finally, politics – and perhaps even more importantly, administration – was conceptualised as the task of well-trained and benign experts, rather than anything that could emerge from a more participative democratic model. This overall tone of moderation and paternalism was exemplified by Sidney Webb's comment to the 1923 Labour Party conference on 'the inevitability of gradualness'.

The Society was a founder member of what became the Labour Party, in 1900. For several years, however, the focus remained on other channels – trying to make an independent impact, and working through other political parties. It was not until the First World War that the Labour Party came to be perceived as the central forum for Fabian work. In 1918, the Society played a key part in providing the party with both a constitution and a policy programme, *Labour and the New Social Order*.

A proud record of influential publications was achieved from the outset, with Webb's *Facts for Socialists* (1887) and *Fabian Essays in Socialism* (1889). The latter title was a major seller, demonstrating an intellectual heterogeneity, largely encased within gradualism and Whiggish optimism. The Fabian Tracts series, still publishing but now renamed Fabian Ideas, has been the vehicle for much of this output: the first Tract, *Why are the Many Poor?*, came in 1884. But the Society's history has not been smooth. A low period in the 1920s and 1930s lead to the emergence of a separate New Fabian Research Bureau in 1931, which merged with the Society in 1939, keeping the older body's name. The Social Democratic Party split in the early 1980s also hit the Society hard, losing key figures like Shirley Williams. More recently, straightforward competition has also taken its toll. As the general secretary commented at the end of the twentieth century, the Society was once 'the intellectual heart of the Left', but progressive think tanks (such as Demos and the Institute for Public Policy Research, IPPR), were by that point in far greater supply. Nevertheless, it remains an important forum for progressive debate.

Key dates

1884   Formation
1889   *Fabian Essays in Socialism* published
1918   Increased engagement with the Labour Party marked by a Fabian-inspired constitution, and the adoption of *Labour and the New Social Order*
1931   Formation of the rival New Fabian Research Bureau

Key figures

George Bernard Shaw
Sidney and Beatrice Webb
Margaret and G.D.H. Cole

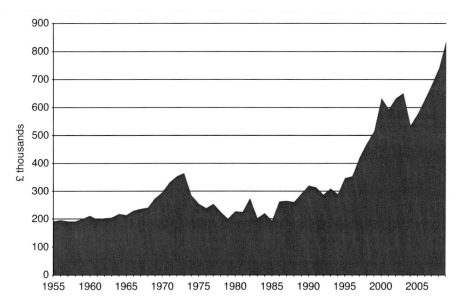

Figure 4.62: Total income of the Fabian Society, 1955–2009

Source: Annual reports and accounts, Fabian Society.

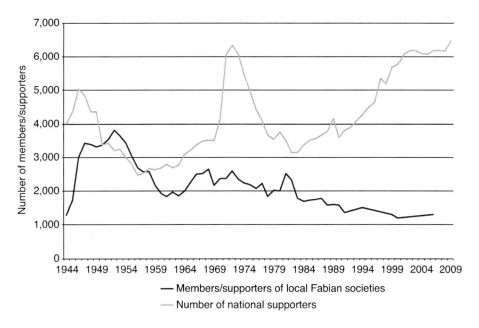

— Members/supporters of local Fabian societies

— Number of national supporters

Figure 4.63: Number of members and supporters of local and national Fabian societies, 1944–2009

Source: Annual reports and accounts, Fabian Society.

Table 4.1: Royal Commissions in which the Fabian Society has given evidence

Royal Commission
Equal Pay
Population
Taxation of Profits and Income
East Africa
Marriage and Divorce
Local Government in London
The Press
Trade Unions
Local Government in Scotland
Local Government in England
The Constitution
NHS
Criminal Procedure

Note: The Fabian Society is the organisation which has given most evidence to Royal Commissions in the period between 1946 and 1993.

Source: Royal Commissions.

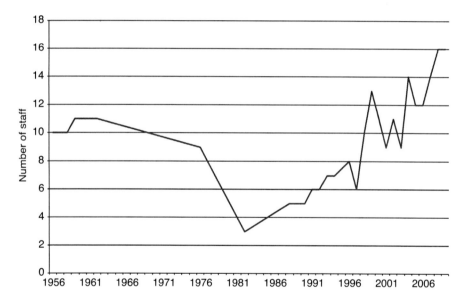

Figure 4.64: Number of staff working for the Fabian Society, 1956–2006

Note: The figures are headcounts only and do not include part-timers.

Source: Annual reports and accounts, Fabian Society.

Further reading

Margaret Cole, *The Story of Fabian Socialism* (London, 1961); Edward R. Pease, *The History of the Fabian Society* (London, 1916); Patricia Pugh, *Educate, Agitate, Organize: 100 Years of Fabian Socialism* (London, 1984).

Fawcett Society

The Fawcett Society is a moderate feminist campaign group, named in honour of the constitutionalist suffrage campaigner Millicent Fawcett.

The Society traces its roots back to the 1860s, when Fawcett was a founder member of the London National Society for Women's Suffrage. A prominent suffrage campaigner in the latter part of the nineteenth century, Fawcett subsequently led the formation of the National Union of Women's Suffrage Societies (NUWSS). This became the leading body of the more moderate campaigners, when the distinction between suffragists and suffragettes emerged at the start of the twentieth century.

A more heterogeneous feminist politics followed the extensions of the franchise in 1918 and 1928. Fawcett was president of the NUWSS until after the First World War, when she was succeeded by Eleanor Rathbone. With this move, the NUWSS, now renamed the National Union of Societies for Equal Citizenship (NUSEC), began to lean towards the new feminism, emphasising the need for improvements in women's everyday lives as wives and mothers. New feminists were thereby distinguished from egalitarian feminists, such as Fawcett, who continued to focus upon formal, legal equality between the sexes. The debate over new feminism led to a split in the NUSEC in 1927, as egalitarians abandoned it for other groups.

The interwar period was an unhappy one for the NUSEC. The organisation, noting the growth of the Women's Institute movement, established what became the Townswomen's Guild during the 1930s. While its progeny met with modest success, the NUSEC continued to decline, losing many of its affiliated organisational members. Indeed, it was through an affiliate that the story eventually continued. The London Society for Women's Service, descendent of the group, Fawcett helped establish in the 1860s; it remained in existence, and took on the Fawcett name in the 1950s.

For much of the later twentieth century, the Society eked out a very modest existence. While it had important input into the sexual equality legislation of the 1970s, it was largely overshadowed by the Women's Liberation Movement. The 1970s were a point of particular crisis, which saw the separation of the Fawcett Library from its parent body (becoming in due course the Women's Library, now part of London Metropolitan University). Nevertheless, a dramatic revival took place at the end of the century, marked by professionalisation, expansion, and rising membership.

Key dates

1866   Formation of London National Society for Woman (later Women's) Suffrage
1897   Formation of the NUWSS, under Millicent Fawcett's leadership
1920s   Extension of franchise leads to more heterogeneous feminist politics
1953   Fawcett Society name adopted

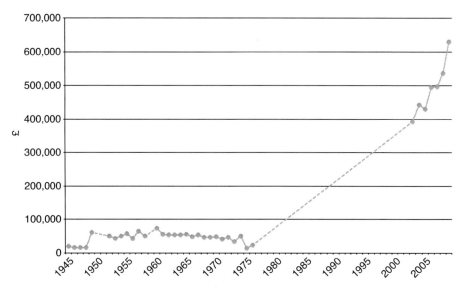

Figure 4.65: Income of the Fawcett Society, 1945–2009 (adjusted for inflation, 2009)

Sources: Annual reports and accounts, Fawcett Society; Charity Commission.

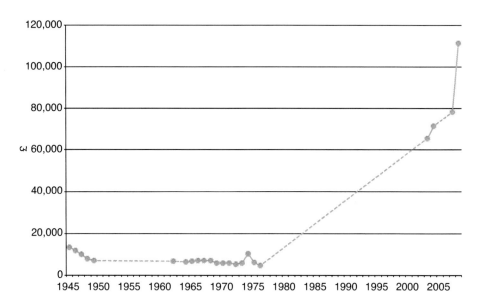

Figure 4.66: Subscriptions from supporters, 1945–2008 (adjusted for inflation, 2009)

Sources: Annual reports and accounts, Fawcett Society; Charity Commission.

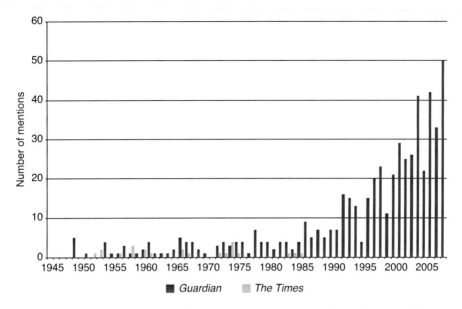

Figure 4.67: Number of mentions of the Fawcett Society in the *Guardian* and *The Times*, 1945–2007

Source: *Guardian* & *The Times*.

Further reading

Jane Grant, 'The Fawcett Society: An Old Organization for the New Woman?', *Women: A Cultural Review*, 10:1 (1999), pp. 67–77; Janet Howarth, 'Fawcett, Dame Millicent Garrett (1847–1929)', in *Oxford Dictionary of National Biography* (Oxford, 2004); Martin Pugh, *Women and the Women's Movement in Britain, 1914–1959* (Basingstoke, 1992); Ina Zweiniger-Bargielowska (ed.), *Women in Twentieth-Century Britain* (Harlow, 2001).

Friends of the Earth

Friends of the Earth (England, Wales and Northern Ireland) is a major environmental campaign group, active on a wide range of issues from waste and recycling to global trade and climate change, all with the goal of seeing humankind living in an environmentally sustainable way. The national organisation is affiliated to Friends of the Earth International, and is further complemented by more than 200 largely autonomous local groups, campaigning on environmental issues in their area.

Friends of the Earth began in the US in 1969, at a time of growing concern for environmental degradation and the apparently unsustainable impact of human activity. Key publications such as Rachel Carson's *Silent Spring* (1962) and the Club of Rome's *Limits to Growth* (1972) brought these concerns to a wider audience, and helped to shift the priorities of the environment movement away from more established notions of conservation and preservation. Indeed, in some ways Friends of the Earth itself typifies this shift. It was formed by Dave Brower, former leader of the venerable American conservation group the Sierra Club. Brower left the

Sierra Club following a series of disagreements over politicised campaigning and nuclear power, and established Friends of the Earth as a deliberately unconventional alternative. Seeking to encourage grassroots activism for radical ends, Brower is commonly credited with coining the slogan 'Think global, act local.'

Friends of the Earth came to the UK in 1971, following a visit by Brower. Originally, the plan was to establish an offshoot body, closely controlled by its US parent. However, Brower was persuaded to give a large degree of independence to the student activists he recruited to lead the new group, including Graham Searle and Richard Sandbrook. The fledgling organisation rapidly made a name for itself with its slick, direct action campaign against the drinks manufacturer Schweppes, dumping thousands of bottles at its headquarters following Schweppes' decision to make its bottles non-returnable.

During the 1980s, like many of its counterparts in the environmental movement, Friends of the Earth enjoyed a dramatic period of expansion. This was in part driven by growing environmental concern in the public at large, but also by the sophisticated marketing techniques increasingly adopted by the NGO world. This expansion went into reverse with the recession of the early 1990s, with real-term income not recovering its previous levels until the early 2000s.

It was during the 2000s that the NGO enjoyed what was arguably its greatest success to date, leading a broad-based civil society coalition in the 'Big Ask' campaign for reductions in UK greenhouse gas emissions. The campaign reached fruition in the 2008 Climate Change Act, requiring 80 per cent cuts in UK emissions by 2050.

Key campaigns

1971	Recycling and packaging: Friends of the Earth dumps 1,500 non-returnable bottles outside Schweppes' headquarters
1972–75	'Save the Whale'; nuclear energy
Late 1970s	Energy conservation
Mid 1980s	Acid rain; pesticides; rainforests; protection of endangered areas
End of 1980s	Ozone depletion; global warming; waste
1990s	Energy; road building; genetically modified crops
2000s	'Big Ask' climate change campaign

Key leaders

In addition to Dave Brower, the founder of the international organisation, there have been key figures leading the national group. These include:

Graham Searle (early 1970s)
Tom Burke (1975–79)
Jonathon Porritt (1984–90)
Charles Secret (1993–2003)
Tony Juniper (2003–08)
Andy Atkins (since 2008)

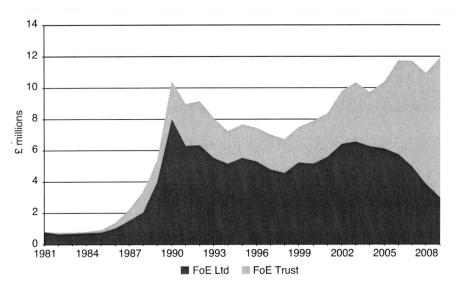

Figure 4.68: Income of Friends of the Earth Limited and Friends of the Earth Trust, 1981–2009 (adjusted for inflation, 2009)

Sources: Annual reports and accounts, Friends of the Earth; Charity Commission.

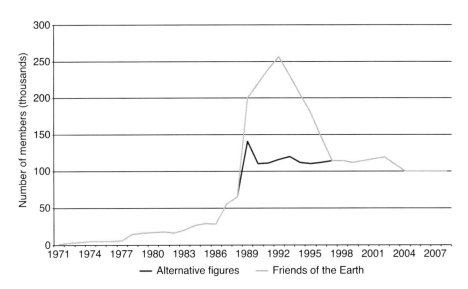

Figure 4.69: Number of members belonging to Friends of the Earth, 1971–2008

Sources: Estimations based on sometimes conflicting sources: Annual reports; *Social Trend* (various years); Neil Carter, *The Politics of the Environment: Ideas, Activism, Policy* (Cambridge, 2007); Francis Sandbach, *Environment, Ideology and Policy* (Oxford: 1980); Paul Byrne, *Social Movements in Britain* (London, 1997); Robert Lamb, *Promising the Earth* (London, 1996); Joe Weston, *The F.O.E. Experience: The Development of an Environmental Pressure Group* (Oxford, 1989); Peter Rawcliffe, *Environmental Pressure Groups in Transition* (Manchester, 1998). For the period around 1989–90, the low estimates are provided by *Social Trends* while the high estimates come from Lamb, Byrne and Rawcliffe.

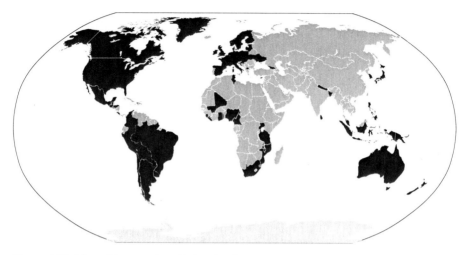

Figure 4.70: Map of international Friends of the Earth affiliates

Source: Friends of the Earth International, www.foei.org/.

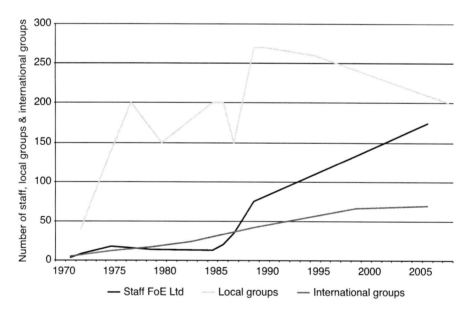

Figure 4.71: Friends of the Earth's staff, local groups and international groups, 1971–2008

Source: Friends of the Earth International, www.foei.org/.

Further reading

Robert Lamb, *Promising the Earth* (London, 1996); Joe Weston, *The F.O.E. Experience: The Development of an Environmental Pressure Group* (Oxford, 1989).

Gingerbread: National Council for One Parent Families

The National Council for the Unmarried Mother and Her Child (NCUMC) was founded by Lettice Fisher in 1918, following an initiative of the Child Welfare Council of the Social Welfare Association. Made up of representatives from the range of organisations concerned with child and maternal welfare, the NCUMC was initially conceived as a campaign and lobbying group. However, it quickly developed a service element, taking on casework and establishing an employment bureau.

The profound social changes of the twentieth century shaped the group. The introduction of the welfare state meant that single mothers needed help to navigate the new, complex and still-inadequate benefits on offer, while the professionalisation of social work in the 1960s and 1970s displaced the need for casework and led the NCUMC to adopt a welfare rights approach. Changing social attitudes to single parenthood were equally significant. During the 1950s, the NCUMC took a moralising tone, in line with the censorious nature of wider society. This did not survive the profound change in attitudes towards sex, women and marriage from the 1960s. In 1973, the NCUMC changed its name to the National Council for One Parent Families (NCOPF), reflecting the relative normalisation of single-parenthood. This normalisation echoed a new self-assertiveness of single parents. 1970 saw the formation of Gingerbread, a self-help group led by single parents, providing both social and practical support, and creating a forum where parents and professionals could come together. In turn, Gingerbread drove the NCOPF to seek a greater representativeness of its client base.

Concurrently, the professionalisation of social work and the growth of social policy as an academic discipline drove a more professional approach within the emergent poverty lobby. In the NCOPF, this was led by Margaret Bramall, general secretary from 1962 to 1979. Campaigning and research capacity across the sector developed enormously in these years, encouraged by the changing statutory context of social policy, and particularly the appointment in 1969 of the Finer Commission, to consider the situation of one-parent families. The Commission, which reported in 1974, encouraged both hope and action in the poverty lobby. The NCOPF joined with peers such as Shelter, the Child Poverty Action Group, Mind and Gingerbread, to form the Finer Joint Action Committee. Despite this effort, the Finer Report was largely ignored by government, resulting in only incremental benefit for one-parent families, and not the fundamental change that was hoped for. The climate chilled further during the 1980s, when the liberal social attitudes of the previous two decades gave way, in government at least, to a renewed moralism, which saw single mothers cast as scapegoats for social dysfunction.

In 2007 Gingerbread and the NCOPF merged, relaunching in 2009 under the Gingerbread name, but retaining the latter body's legal and organisational identity.

Key dates

1918   NCUMC formed
1969   Finer Commission appointed; reports in 1974
2007   Merger of Gingerbread and NCOPF

Key figures

Lettice Fisher: founder and initial chair of NCUMC
Margaret Bramall: general secretary of NCUMC/NCOPF, 1962–78
Jane Streather: director, 1979–83
Sue Slipman: director, 1986–95
Karin Pappenheim: director, 1995–97
Maeve Sherlock: director, 1997–2000
Kate Green: director, 2000–04
Chris Pond: chief executive, NCOPF, subsequently One Parent Families/Gingerbread
Tessa Fothergill: founder of Gingerbread
Fiona Weir: chief executive, Gingerbread, 2008–

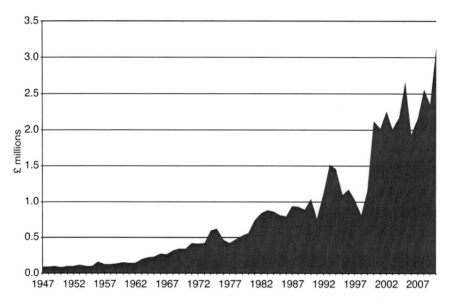

Figure 4.72: Income of One Parent Families, 1947–2009 (adjusted for inflation, 2009), including Gingerbread from 2007 onwards

Sources: Annual Reports and accounts, One Parent Families; Charity Commission.

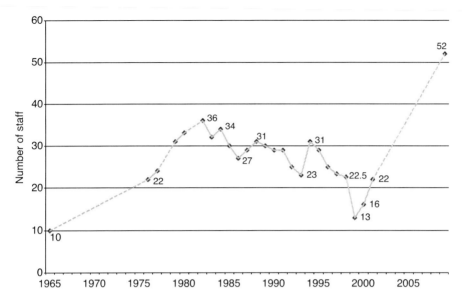

Figure 4.73: Number of staff working for One Parent Families, 1965–2009

Notes: (a) The figures for the 1980s reflect the 'average number of employees'; from the 1990s, they reflect 'full-time equivalent'. (b) The figure for 2009 is for the merged organisation One Parent Families/Gingerbread.

Source: Annual reports and accounts, One Parent Families; Top 3000 Charities.

Further reading

Sue Graham Dixon, *Never Darken My Door: Working for Single Parents and Their Children 1918–1978* (London, 1981); Tanya Evans and Pat Thane, *Unmarried Motherhood in Modern England* (Oxford, 2011); Hilary Macaskill, *From the Workhouse to the Workplace: 75 Years of One Parent Family Life* (London, 1993).

Greenpeace

Greenpeace (UK) is the British member of Greenpeace International, the environmental campaign organisation. Distinctive for its combination of daring direct action protests and a high media profile, Greenpeace campaigns on a wide range of environmental issues, including climate change, biodiversity and opposition to nuclear power.

The origins of Greenpeace lie in the Canadian 'Don't Make a Wave' committee, formed at the beginning of the 1970s to protest against nuclear testing. These early efforts were based around the activism of US ex-pats Jim and Marie Bohlen, and Irving and Dorothy Stowe. The latter couple's Quaker faith, and particularly the notion of bearing witness against injustice, would have lasting significance for Greenpeace's later development. Subsequent direct action protests against nuclear tests by the American and French governments, with Greenpeace sailing its boats into exclusion zones around the blast sites, gained international media attention.

Confrontation with the French government would later have deadly consequences in the darkest episode of the organisation's history. In 1985, the Greenpeace vessel *Rainbow Warrior* was bombed and sunk while anchored in Auckland harbour, killing photographer Fernando Pereira. At the time, the vessel was preparing for another challenge to French nuclear tests, and despite initial denials, it soon emerged that the bombing was the work of the French secret service.

In the mid 1970s, Greenpeace's hitherto exclusive campaign focus on nuclear testing broadened out to include the threats from commercial whaling. The subsequent 'Save the whale' activism was perhaps the organisation's best-known work with the wider public during the 1970s and 1980s. This was also a period of considerable international expansion. The UK branch was established in 1977, and the umbrella grouping Greenpeace International in 1979. It has since grown into one of the largest and most visible international environmental NGOs.

In 1995, the organisation made its highest-profile intervention in Britain when Greenpeace confronted the oil company Shell and the British government over the fate of the Brent Spar oil platform. Company plans for the retired platform to be disposed of at sea were endorsed by the government, and in response Greenpeace launched a daring occupation, accompanied by a European-wide boycott of the company. Despite controversy over the NGO's use of statistics, the campaign was a resounding success as the company was eventually forced to back down and dismantle the platform on land.

Box 4.9: Rainbow Warrior legend

'When the Earth is sick and the animals have disappeared, there will come a tribe of peoples from all creeds, colours and cultures who believe in deeds not words and who will restore the Earth to its former beauty. This tribe will be called the "Warriors of the Rainbow".'

Native American legend, cited in Greenpeace promotional leaflet, c. 1986.

Like its fellow product of 1970s radical environmentalism, Friends of the Earth, Greenpeace enjoyed dramatic expansion during the 1980s on the back of growing public concern and increasingly sophisticated marketing techniques. This growth stalled in the 1990s, but the organisation remains a high profile and distinctive campaigning presence.

Key dates

1970   Don't Make a Wave committee formed
1971   Direct action protests against US nuclear testing in Alaska
1972   Direct action protests against French nuclear testing in South Pacific
1977   Greenpeace UK established
1984   Greenpeace UK launches its anti-fur campaign, with the slogan 'It takes up to forty dumb animals to make a fur coat. But only one to wear it.'
1985   Bombing of *Rainbow Warrior*
1995   Brent Spar protests

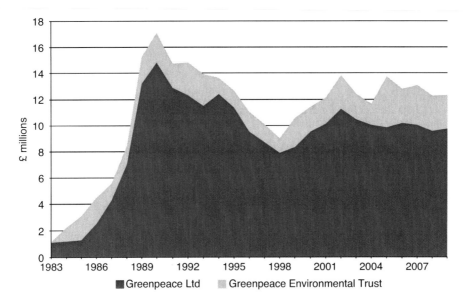

Figure 4.74: Income of Greenpeace Ltd and Greenpeace Environmental Trust, 1983–2009 (adjusted for inflation, 2009)

Sources: Annual reports and accounts, Greenpeace Ltd and Greenpeace Environmental Trust; Charity Commission.

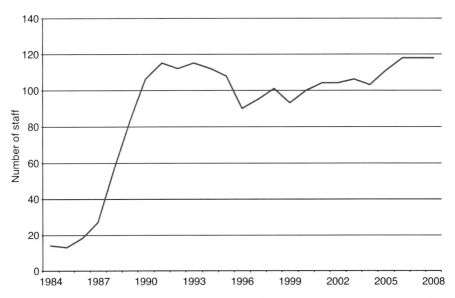

Figure 4.75: Staff working for both Greenpeace Ltd and Greenpeace Environmental Trust (average weekly number of employees), 1984–2008

Sources: Annual reports and accounts, Greenpeace Ltd and Greenpeace Environmental Trust; Charity Commission.

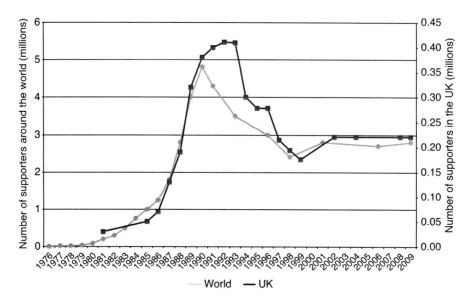

Figure 4.76: Number of Greenpeace supporters (UK and World), 1976–2009

Sources: Annual reports and accounts, Greenpeace Ltd and Greenpeace Environmental Trust; *Social Trends* (various years); Neil Carter, *The Politics of the Environment: Ideas, Activism, Policy* (Cambridge, 2007); Paul Byrne, *Social Movements in Britain* (London, 1997); Peter Rawcliffe, *Environmental Pressure Groups in Transition* (Manchester, 1998); Pierre Kohler, *Greenpeace: Le Vrai Visage Des Guerriers Verts* (Paris, 2008); Greenpeace website.

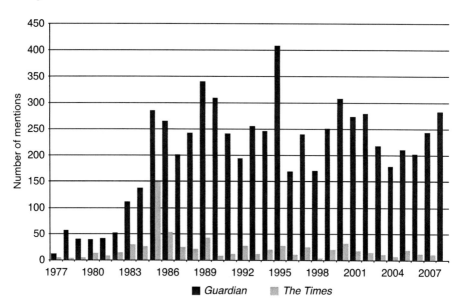

Figure 4.77: Number of mentions of Greenpeace in the *Guardian* and *The Times*, 1977–2008

Source: *Guardian* & *The Times*.

Further reading

Michael Brown and John May, *The Greenpeace Story* (London, 1989); Chris Rose, *The Turning of the 'Spar'* (London, 1998); Frank Zelko, '"Make it a Green Peace": The History of an International Environmental Organization', *German Historical Institute Bulletin,* 34 (2004), pp. 127–35.

Howard League for Penal Reform

The Howard League campaigned not just for the abolition of capital punishment but also for the reform of many criminal law and penal practices. Initially known as the Howard Association, its merger with the Penal Reform League in 1921 led to a renaming as the Howard League for Penal Reform. The Howard Association was established in 1866 and took its name from prison reformer John Howard, an eighteenth-century high sheriff of Bedfordshire who had collated material on the state of prisons in England and Wales. This desire for empirical rigour underpinned the group's ethos. However, it failed to achieve anything of note until the imprisonment of middle-class conscientious objectors during the First World War, and their experiences of the brutality of the system reinvigorated the group. Likened to His Majesty's Official Opposition for all questions of penal policy from the interwar years and until the 1960s, it was the dominant campaigner on penal reform. It has been credited with the creation of various agencies and organisations such as the Magistrates' Association, Victim Support and the Prisoners' Advice Service.

In the mid 1940s the abolition campaign was revived, not least because of the perceived greater sympathy from the Labour Party. A Royal Commission was appointed in 1949 (reporting in 1953), with its chair Ernest Gowers admitting by the end that he had been converted to the abolitionist case. The Bentley, Evans and Christie, and Ellis trials and subsequent executions also aroused public concern. Abolition was eventually won in 1957.

It is a centralised, London-centric organisation – drawing members from the professional middle classes who have direct experience of the penal system. Membership is relatively small, being approximately 1,300 in 1975, and is largely passive, although in recent decades it has been able to draw upon the support of celebrities such as Michael Palin and Sheila Hancock. The Howard League Centre for Penal Reform was opened by former House of Commons speaker Betty Boothroyd in 2001 and the League now bases its 28 staff at the Hackney site.

Well connected within Whitehall, the small leadership was very much the 'insider' organisation – its pre-eminence was challenged from the 1970s by groups that emerged outside and which were less conformist, like Radical Alternative to Prison (RAP) and Women in Prison (WIP). It can sometimes be difficult to establish where the League's influence ends and the government's begins. For example, George Benson MP and League chair mooted the idea of a first offenders bill in the 1950s. The Home Office then appointed a subcommittee to consider the issue, of which Benson and Margery Fry were members, and then drew up a bill which was introduced by Benson in the Commons and Viscount Templewood in the Lords.

During the 1960s, as rehabilitation became the fashion, the League moved in line with the Home Office. But by the 1970s it was so concerned with the institutional side of penal reform that it was unable to see the possibility that prison did not work and the need to reform or rehabilitate offenders – critics felt it did too little to provide practical help to offenders. From the late 1970s the League's influence declined. Its liberal agenda appeared at odds with Thatcher's more strident and populist approach to law and order, and even under New Labour it appeared little better, with Home Secretary Jack Straw likening the 1998 Crime and Disorder Bill to being a victory for local communities rather than the liberal metropolitan elites. It suggests that the League's failure to engage with the public means that it is now just reacting to punitive populist responses from politicians and the media. However, since 2000, the League has sought to refocus its message – its campaigning emphasis is upon the benefits of community sentences over custodial (since 2005 it has a Weekly Prison Watch totalling the numbers in jail), and it places particular weight on the penal system's impact on children, young people and women. In 2002 it launched a legal service for children and young people in custody and has launched an All Party Group on Women in Prison. It has also secured consultative status with the United Nations and Council of Europe.

Key figures

Margery Fry (1874–1958): honorary secretary, 1919–26; chairman and vice-chairman
Viscount Templewood, Samual Hoare (1880–1959): home secretary, 1937–39;
    Howard League president, 1947–59
Hugh Klare (1916–): secretary, 1950–71

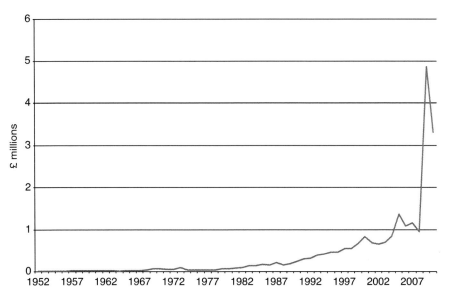

Figure 4.78: Total income of the Howard League for Penal Reform, 1952–2010 (adjusted for inflation, 2009)

Note: The very high figure for 2009 is due to a donation of £4 million from Lord Parmoor's trustees.

Sources: Annual reports and accounts, Howard League for Penal Reform; *Yearbook of International Organisations*; Charity Commission.

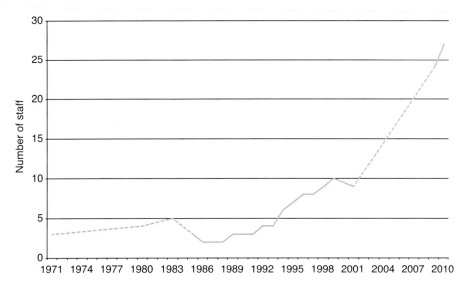

Figure 4.79: Number of staff working for the Howard League for Penal Reform, 1971–2010

Sources: Annual reports and accounts, Howard League for Penal Reform; Charity Commission.

Further reading

Gordon Rose, *The Struggle for Penal Reform* (London, 1961); Mike Ryan, *Penal Policy and Political Culture in England and Wales* (Winchester, 2003); Mike Ryan, *The Acceptable Pressure Group: Inequality in the Penal Lobby: A Case Study of the Howard League and RAP* (Farnborough, 1978); Gordon Rose, *The Struggle for Penal Reform: The Howard League and its Predecessors* (London, 1961); James B. Christoph, *Capital Punishment and British Politics* (London, 1962).

Indian Workers' Association

Indian Workers' Associations (IWAs) first appeared in London in the 1930s and in Coventry in 1938. These were largely concerned with Indian politics and disappeared after independence in 1947. Following the influx of Punjabi immigrants in the 1950s, new branches were formed in Southall, Wolverhampton and Birmingham, uniting together in 1958.

The IWA is a broad-ranging organisation. It has been concerned with politics back in India, while also attaching itself to the concerns of the British labour and trade union movement. It has politically committed itself to anti-racist struggle, while also serving as a social, cultural and welfare organisation for its members. It has therefore participated in certain shopfloor disputes, such as Imperial Typewriters (1974) and Grunwick (1976–78), but its role within the wider labour movement has been restricted due to its position as an organisation of Punjabi males.

These functions, as well as political differences and the two power bases in Southall and Birmingham, have been the basis for division. The Southall branch did not formally affiliate with the IWA (GB) based in Birmingham, choosing instead to link up with the Campaign Against Racial Discrimination. But in 1967 the politics of India's war with China caused the IWA (GB) itself to split. One faction, led by Prem

Singh, supported the Communist Party of India (Marxist), while the other assumed a pro-Chinese Marxist-Leninist character and was associated with Jagmohan Joshi, Teja Sahota and Avtar Jouhl. The Singh faction forged links with the Black People's Alliance in 1968 after Enoch Powell's 'rivers of blood' speech and initiated the Campaign Against Racist Laws. The Joshi-Jouhal group sought political alliances with West Indian groups such as those connected to the black power movement and with other Marxist black groups.

Yet at the everyday level, the IWAs have maintained their social and welfare role which has meant they have been connected to a particular cohort of often first-generation Punjabi immigrants. As such they have been in something of a decline since the 1980s. Significantly, a second generation of British Asians has looked to new forms of socio-political organisation. When 18-year-old Gurdip Singh Chaggar was murdered close to the IWA Southall's offices in 1976, the IWA supported the resulting protests, as they did the emerging Anti-Nazi Leagues. Yet at the same time, the event was an important trigger for the creation of an Asian Youth Movement which highlighted some of the generational differences emerging in black and Asian politics. Some of the IWAs are still active but they no longer play the leadership role they had once assumed for the British Punjabi community.

Key figures

Prem Singh
Jagmohan Joshi
Avtar Jouhl
Teja Singh Sahota

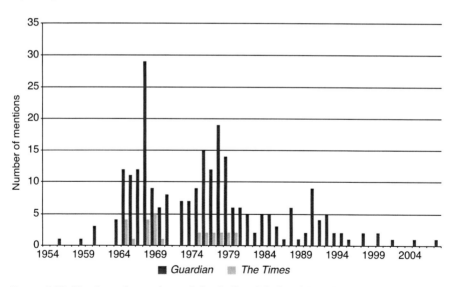

Figure 4.80: Number of mentions of the Indian Workers' Association in the *Guardian* and *The Times*, 1954–2008

Source: *Guardian* & *The Times*.

Further reading

Terri Sewell, *Black Tribunes: Black Political Participation in Britain* (London, 1993); Gurharpal Singh and Darshan Singh Tatla, *Sikhs in Britain: The Making of a Community* (London, 2006); Sasha Josephides, *Towards a History of the IWA* (University of Warwick, 1991).

Institute for Fiscal Studies

An economic and financial think tank that was incorporated in 1969, the Institute for Fiscal Studies (IFS) enjoys a significant media profile in Britain, frequently offering comment on budgetary and economic affairs, and being commissioned to undertake independent academic and policy-related research. It has established a particular reputation for its expertise on taxation. Its genesis was the 1965 Finance Act which introduced capital gains tax and a corporation tax. This so appalled a group of city financiers (Will Hopper, Bob Buist, Nils Taube and John Chown), that they began to consider the best manner in which to challenge the assumptions upon which these tax changes had been proposed. This led to the four publishing the *Charter for Tax Reform* in *The Times* (see Box 4.10) which encouraged Jeremy Skinner and Halmer Hudson to join the fledgling discussions.

The outcome was the proposal made in July 1968 to form a research institute with a view to commissioning financial research that would influence British fiscal policy. It conceived itself as a 'shadow' Inland Revenue and Treasury. Organisational reforms took place in 1971 that led to the creation of council of the Institute (under president Sir Richard Powell and vice-presidents Roy Jenkins and Selwyn Lloyd – both former Chancellors of the Exchequer) and the following year its first full-time staffers were appointed, including a research director. Ex-IFS staffers include, amongst others, Mervyn King (governor of the Bank of England) and Thelma Liesner (research director until 1979). The publication of the 1978 Meade Report established the IFS's reputation; not only did it secure considerable publicity and generate new sources of corporate revenue for the organisation, it also contributed to the awarding of the Nobel Prize to Professor Meade.

Still in 1979, aside from the director, there were only two full-time staff, but by the time the organisation celebrated its thirtieth anniversary it had 34 economists on the permanent staff, 19 research fellows and associates in the UK and 23 overseas.

Box 4.10: *A Charter for Tax Reform*

'More than £10,000m, or 38 per cent of our national income, is collected each year as taxes, rates and national insurance contributions and spent on our behalf by central and local government on various public services. This is an enormous sum, and both politicians and citizens much surely be concerned to ensure that it is collected with a minimum of pain and disbursed with a maximum of benefit. Taxes should be equitable, readily understood by the taxpayer, simple and cheap to collect, and should hinder as little as possible the production of wealth within the economy ... What is needed is for a philosophy of taxation to be developed which will then lead to a sympathetic but gradual programme of reform ... Tax reform should never be put through in such a hurry.'

The Times, 10 April 1967, p. 17.

Its reputation for academically based independent research was confirmed when in 1990 the Economic and Social Research Council (ESRC) agreed to fund the Centre for Fiscal Policy within the IFS, directed by Richard Blundell. The 1990s also saw the creation of a Tax Law Review Committee. The IFS does not consider itself a think tank but rather an independent financial research institute; but no matter which, it has established an international reputation and has over its history persisted in its essential messages on fiscal neutrality and the need to rationalise and simplify the tax system.

Early key publications

1979   *Fiscal Studies* – launched as a peer review journal published quarterly
1978   Meade Report into the structure and reform of direct taxation
1980   Armstrong Report on UK budgetary reform
1982   Report series launched and first Green Budget
1984   *Reform of Social Security* proposed benefits be administered through tax system and concentrated on the poorest

Directors

Dick Taverne, 1970–79
John Kay, 1979–86
Bill Robinson, 1986–91
Andrew Dilnot, 1991–02
Robert Chote, 2002–10
Carl Emmerson, 2010–

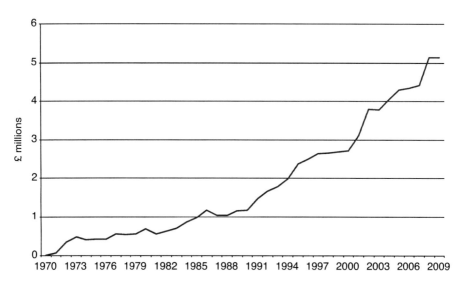

Figure 4.81: Income of the Institute for Fiscal Studies, 1970–2009 (adjusted for inflation, 2009)

Sources: Annual reports and accounts, IFS; Charity Commission; Top 3000 Charities.

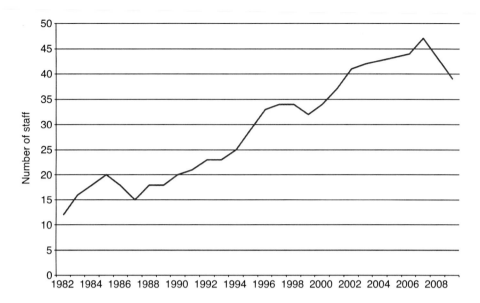

Figure 4.82: Number of staff working for the Institute for Fiscal Studies, 1982–2009

Sources: Annual reports and accounts, IFS; Top 3000 Charities; Charity Commission.

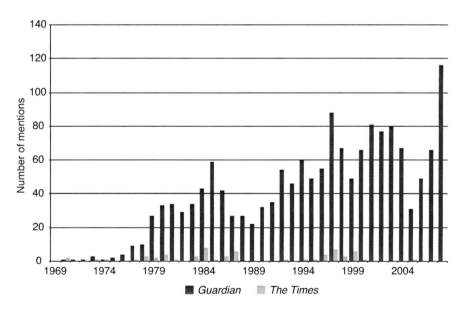

Figure 4.83: Number of mentions of the Institute for Fiscal Studies in the *Guardian* and *The Times*, 1969–2008

Source: *Guardian* & *The Times*.

Further reading

Michael Kandiah and Anthony Seldon (eds), *Ideas and Think Tanks in Contemporary Britain, vols 1–2* (Newbury, 1996–97); Richard Cockett, *Thinking the Unthinkable: Think Tanks and the Economic Counter-Revolution 1931–83* (London, 1995); Martin Daunton, *Just Taxes: The Politics of Taxation in Britain 1914–79* (Cambridge, 2002).

The Institute's website also has reflections from its first four directors: www.ifs.org.uk/aboutIFS.

Joint Council for the Welfare of Immigrants

The Joint Council for the Welfare of Immigrants (JCWI) was set up in 1967 specifically to focus on the relief of hardship and poverty faced by many immigrants arriving in Britain. In the 1960s, many umbrella organisations for blacks and Asians were divided along political lines. The executive of the Campaign Against Racial Discrimination therefore decided to establish a deliberately apolitical organisation dedicated to a single issue that could attract broad consensual support. It was founded at a meeting of 240 people representing a variety of immigrant groups, and Vishnu Sharma of the Southall Indian Workers' Association became its first secretary-general. Within a few years, 115 immigrant organisations had affiliated.

The JCWI helped families and individuals arriving in Britain. It first began working at Heathrow airport, assisting those immigrants regarded as not meeting the skills level and resident family requirements of the 1962 Commonwealth Immigrants Act. The passing of the 1968 Commonwealth Immigration Act meant it changed its focus to helping families on the sub-continent to obtain the newly required entry clearance certificates. Its casework increased substantially with the arrival of immigrants from Kenya and Uganda in the early 1970s.

As the official checks on age and marriage have increased, the JCWI has increasingly come to advise immigrants seeking to gain entry for family members. It has also worked with asylum seekers and refugees. In addition to individual advice, it has also published literature, including the influential *Immigration, Nationality and Refugee Law Handbook*.

Although primarily a resource NGO, it has engaged in political campaigning. It supported the Migrant Action Group which opposed passport raids on migrant workers in 1973. It campaigned against the 1981 Immigration Act for imposing tougher conditions on Asian and Chinese immigrants, establishing the No Pass Laws Here! Group. During the Gulf War of 1991 it helped obtain the release of all national security detainees. It has continued to lobby parliament during all subsequent passing of legislation relating to immigrants and refugees. Most recently, in 2010, it launched the 'I Love Migrants' campaign to help emphasise the positive impacts migration has had on the UK.

Key figures

Ann Dummett: co-founder and author of *A Portrait of English Racism* (1973)
Sir Michael Dummett: philosopher; co-founder and chair, 1970–71
Vishnu Sharma: first general secretary, 1967–77
Claude Moraes: director, 1992–99
Habib Rahman: director, 1999–

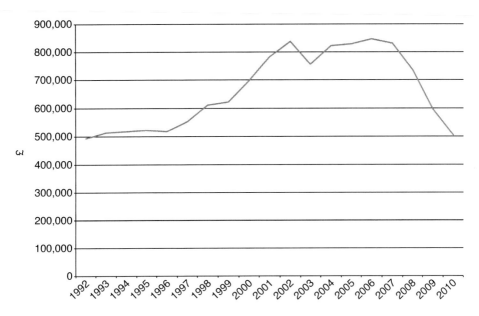

Figure 4.84: Income of the Joint Council for the Welfare of Immigrants, 1992–2010 (adjusted for inflation, 2009)

Source: Annual reports and accounts, Joint Council for the Welfare of Immigrants.

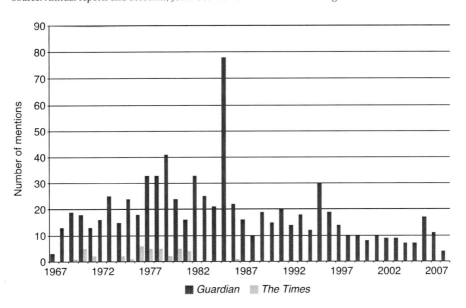

Figure 4.85: Mentions of the Joint Council for the Welfare of Immigrants in the *Guardian* and *The Times*, 1967–2008

Source: *Guardian* & *The Times*.

Further reading

Peter Barberis, John McHugh and Mike Tyldesley, *Encyclopedia of British and Irish Political Organizations* (London, 1999); Terri Sewell, *Black Tribunes: Black Political Participation in Britain* (London, 1993).

Liberty

Liberty originated as the National Council for Civil Liberties (NCCL) in 1934. In 1932, police arrested the leader and stole the petition of a hunger march, as well as using agents provocateurs to incite violence. Ronald Kidd worked to bring together prominent writers, lawyers and journalists to act as observers to ensure such civil liberties were not infringed again at the arrival in London of the next march in 1934. He convinced E.M. Forster to act as president, and assembled an impressive collection of vice-presidents (which included Clement Attlee, Aneurin Bevan, Alduous Huxley, J.B. Priestley and Bertrand Russell); some of whom, such as H.G. Wells, agreed to act as observers.

The organisation adopted a non-party political stance, but as its actions frequently brought it into conflict with the government it increasingly assumed a left-wing character. This led to some – not entirely – unfounded accusations of Communist Party bias, and the organisation consequently struggled in the 1940s and 1950s with the onset of the Cold War.

Its fortunes, however, revived with the birth of new social movements, the respectable, middle-aged NCCL observers serving to protect the civil liberties of younger protesters connected to organisations such as the Campaign for Nuclear Disarmament (CND). NCCL's work in the 1950s protecting the rights of the mentally ill were followed by increasingly prominent campaigns in the 1960s defending minority groups, especially immigrants, children, gypsies and caravan dwellers, and prisoners. In 1963 it also set up the Cobden Trust to undertake research into civil liberties.

From the late 1960s it continued to do important work with the women's movement, gay liberation and civil rights in Northern Ireland. For instance, in 1972, it collected 600 witness statements from the 'Bloody Sunday' demonstration, and it investigated the death of Blair Peach at an Anti-Nazi League demonstration in Southall in 1979. As it engaged with human rights activists, and following international fashion, its language of civil liberties gradually gave way to one of human rights. In 1989 it changed its name to Liberty and adopted the tagline 'Working to protect civil liberties and promote human rights for everyone.' It's prominence in British public life has continued through the high media profile of Shami Chakrabarti, director since 2003.

Key secretaries and directors

Ronald Kidd, 1934–41
Elizabeth Acland Allen, 1941–60
Martin Ennals, 1960–66
Tony Smythe, 1966–71
Patricia Hewitt, 1975–83
Shami Chakrabarti, 2003–

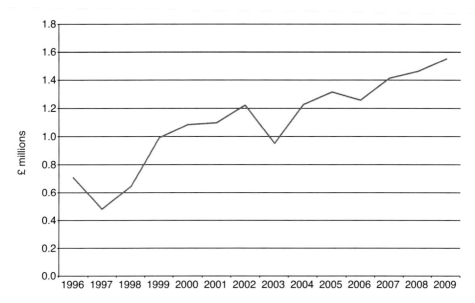

Figure 4.86: Income of Liberty, 1996–2009 (adjusted for inflation, 2009)

Source: Annual reports and accounts, Liberty.

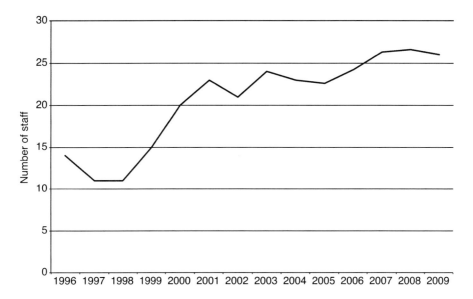

Figure 4.87: Number of staff working for Liberty, 1996–2009

Source: Annual reports and accounts, Liberty.

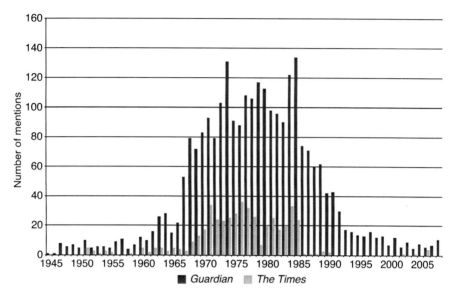

Figure 4.88: Number of mentions of Liberty in the *Guardian* and *The Times*, 1945–2008

Source: *Guardian* & *The Times*.

Further reading

Mark Lilly, *The National Council for Civil Liberties: The First Fifty Years* (Basingstoke, 1984); Brian Dyson, *Liberty in Britain 1934–1994: A Diamond Jubilee History of the National Council for Civil Liberties* (London, 1994); Chris Moores, 'The Progressive Professionals: The National Council for Civil Liberties and the Politics of Activism in the 1960s', *Twentieth Century British History*, 20:4 (2009), pp. 538–60; Janet Clark, 'Sincere and Reasonable Men? The Origins of the National Council for Civil Liberties', *Twentieth Century British History*, 20:4 (2009), pp. 513–37.

Mencap

Mencap is Britain's leading learning disability charity. The organisation was formed in 1946 as the National Association of Parents of Backward Children. Its founder, Judy Fryd, who herself had a child with learning disabilities, sought to improve the services available in such cases, and appealed through *Nursery World* magazine for parents in similar circumstances to get in touch. Within a month hundreds did so, forming the initial core of what would become Mencap. The organisation's name was altered in 1955 to the National Society for Mentally Handicapped Children, with the shortened form, Mencap, coming into use in the late 1960s.

These changes of name, and the gradual eschewal of pejorative terms such as 'backward' and 'handicapped', are reflective of changing attitudes to learning disability in society more generally. The often overcrowded and authoritarian asylums of the Victorian period, initially conceived as an improvement on the harsh social conditions of urban Britain, characterised those with learning disabilities as separate from society, as 'problems' needing 'solutions'. The popularity of eugenicist thought around the turn of the century compounded this lack of sympathy and integration, while institutionalisation remained the norm well into the twentieth century. It was not until the 1950s and 1960s that an understanding of the severe drawbacks and deficiencies of institutional care began to be widely accepted, and it was later still before services actually caught up with this new understanding.

This changing understanding can be traced through legislative developments. The 1959 Mental Health Act began the shift of thinking away from hospital-based care, a trend complemented by the 1990 National Health Service and Community Care Act. The 1971 Education (Handicapped Children) Act, meanwhile, rejected the notion that those with learning disabilities could not benefit from education, and that any provision should be met privately by the family, or though institutionalisation. Subsequently, an appreciation for the rights of those with learning disabilities has developed alongside the service-based approach, something exemplified by the 1995 Disability Discrimination Act.

Much of this change in attitudes and service provision can be credited to the work of Mencap. In 1958 the organisation conducted its groundbreaking Brooklands experiment; a demonstration, through observing cohorts of children with learning disabilities over two years, that small-scale, family-based care had marked developmental superiority over institutionalisation. Judy Fryd was also central to the lobbying that resulted in the 1971 Education Act. Moreover, Mencap has pioneered services, since it first opened a short-stay residential home in 1955. Its Pathway employment service commenced in the 1970s, while in the 1990s, people with learning disabilities were elected to Mencap's national assembly in order to become fully involved with the running of the organisation.

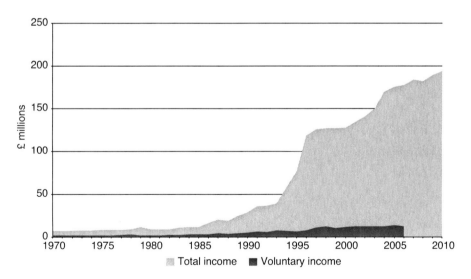

Figure 4.89: Total and voluntary income of Mencap, 1970–2010 (adjusted for inflation, 2009)

Note: There are no data regarding voluntary income after 2006.

Sources: Wells Collection; Charity Statistics; Annual reports and accounts, Mencap; Charity Commission.

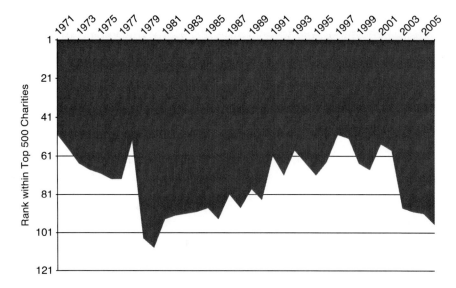

Figure 4.90: Mencap's charitable ranking by voluntary income, 1970–2006

Source: Charity Statistics.

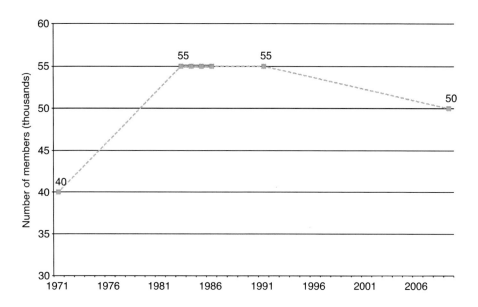

Figure 4.91: Number of members (including affiliated members) belonging to Mencap, 1971–2006

Sources: *Social Trends*; contact with Mencap (April 2009).

Further reading

www.mencap.org.uk/
'Mental Health Charity Plans National Inquiry into Hospitals', *Guardian*, 24 March 1982;
'Obituary: Judy Fryd', *Guardian*, 24 October 2000.

Mind

Mind is Britain's leading mental health charity. It was formed as the National Association for Mental Health (NAMH) in 1946, through the merger of three existing mental health bodies: the Central Association for Mental Welfare (established 1913); the National Council for Mental Hygiene (established 1922) and the Child Guidance Council (established 1927). The amalgamation had been recommended in 1939 by the Feversham Committee on the voluntary mental health associations, and served as a clear example of the ongoing contribution of voluntary social services in the era of the post-war welfare state.

The NAMH was an early champion of the move towards community-based care, and away from institutionalisation. The desirability of this goal was accepted by Minister of Health Enoch Powell in the early 1960s, following years of campaigning by the sector. The early 1960s also saw the development of the NAMH's local network: there are currently around 200 local affiliated associations, providing a range of services complementing statutory provision.

The second major development of the 1960s was the adoption of a more explicitly user-oriented, rights-based approach by the NAMH. 1971 saw the launch of the Mind campaign, focused on forcing mental health up the political agenda, improving services, and challenging the apathy and ignorance surrounding the issue. (The campaign's success led the NAMH to adopt Mind as its official name the following year.) This focus on rights was strengthened under the directorship of Tony Smythe during the 1970s, previously an activist in the human rights field. The themes of challenging mindsets and standing up for service users have fed into the campaigns Mind has run since, on topics as diverse as anti-discrimination, user-centricity, the side-effects of drugs, and housing and service provision.

Mind also runs an annual awards series, designed to recognise significant contributions to the public understanding of mental health issue in the fields of journalism, books (see Box 4.11) and public life. Awards have also been used to challenge discrimination: from 1995 to 2003, Mind ran a 'Bigot of the Year' award, twice won by journalist and former Conservative politician David Mellor. This then became its 'Mind Champion' award, recognising contributions to challenging

---

Box 4.11: Recent winners of the Mind Book of the Year award

2010   John O'Donoghue, *Sectioned: A Life Interrupted*
2009   Sathnam Sanghera, *The Boy with the Topknot: A Memoir of Love, Secrets and Lies in Wolverhampton*
2008   Martin Townsend, *The Father I Had*
2007   Michele Hanson, *Living with Mother*
2006   Valerie Mason-John, *Borrowed Body*

discrimination against those with mental health issues. Winners have included prominent personalities who have talked openly about their mental health, including Frank Bruno, Stephen Fry and Alastair Campbell.

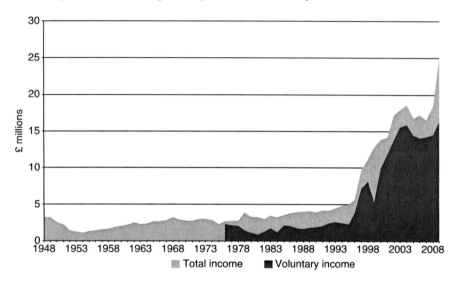

Figure 4.92: Voluntary and total income of Mind, 1948–2008 (adjusted for inflation, 2009)

Note: Voluntary income figures are only available from 1976 onwards.

Sources: Annual reports and accounts, Mind; Charity Commission; Charity Statistics.

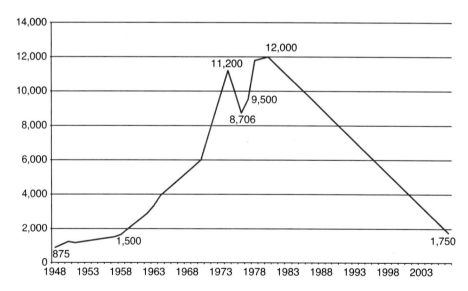

Figure 4.93: Number of members (individuals) belonging to Mind, 1948–2007

Sources: Annual reports and accounts, Mind; Share Community, *Guide to Self-Help Groups* (London, 1980); contact with Mind (2007).

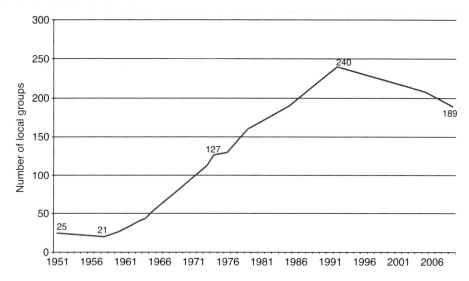

Figure 4.94: Number of local groups (Local Mind Associations), 1951–2009

Source: Annual reports and accounts, Mind.

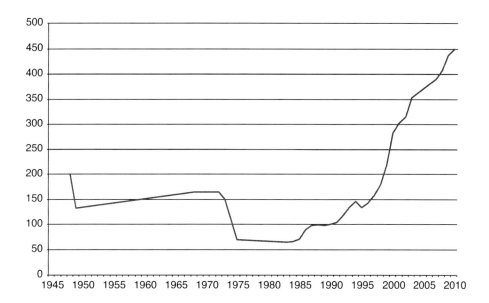

Figure 4.95: Number of staff working for Mind, 1948–2008

Sources: Annual reports and accounts, Mind; Charity Statistics.

Further reading

History of Mind, the National Association for Mental Health, available from: www.mind.org.uk/help/research_and_policy/history_of_mind-the_national_association_for_mental_health.

Mothers' Union

The Mothers' Union was started in 1876 by Mary Sumner, wife of an Anglican vicar in Winchester, when her first grandchild was born, though it was not formally established until 1885. She wanted to create an organisation that would support new mothers in a manner of which she herself had earlier felt deprived. In 1896 the Central Council of Mothers Unions was formed in close collaboration with the Anglican Communion: branches are usually based on parishes, and higher level interactions often follow Church structures.

By 1900 the Mothers' Union already had 169,000 members, but it is its growth as an imperial and global organisation that has been most impressive. By 1950, worldwide, there were 500,000 members. While its popularity in Britain peaked in the 1930s, today there are around 4 million members: 1.9 million are based in India, 1.3 million in Africa (principally Tanzania) and around 93,000 in the UK.

The organisation aimed to be a socially conservative force. It promoted Christianity and motherhood and regarded home and family as the main priorities for women. It viewed abortion as a mortal sin and barred divorced women from membership. However, as with the Women's Institutes, the Mothers' Union also engaged on single issues that showed a more tolerant and understanding side. By the 1940s it recognised that many women regretted losing their financial independence after marriage and they campaigned to ensure that women were treated fairly under divorce law.

It also recognised the need to change with the times. In the 1960s it established Away From It All Holidays to enable poor families to have a break that they would otherwise not be able to afford. In 1969 it set up a commission to review its work and principles, and the resulting 1972 report, *New Dimensions*, allowed the entry of divorced women into the organisation and it spoke of the need to respond more quickly to social and political issues.

Precisely because of its global membership, the Mothers' Union has become something of a development organisation, linking up with its members in Africa and India to support micro finance schemes, promote literacy and good parenting, and campaign against violence against women and trafficking. In the UK, it became an active participant in Jubilee 2000 and Make Poverty History. It remains linked to the Anglican Church but in a manner, like Christian Aid, that makes many of its approaches to global issues indistinguishable from overtly secular organisations.

Box 4.12: The Mothers' Union Prayer

Loving Lord
We thank you for your love so freely given to us all.
We pray for families around the world.
Bless the work of the Mothers' Union
as we seek to share your love
through the encouragement, strengthening and support of marriage and family life.
Empowered by your Spirit, may we be united in prayer and worship,
and in love and service reach out as your hands across the world.
In Jesus' name. Amen.

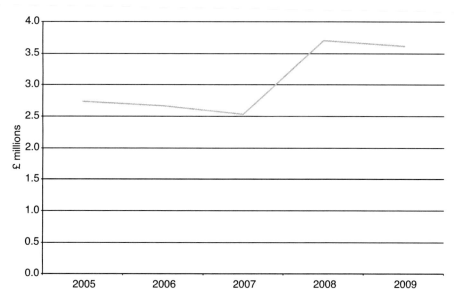

Figure 4.96: Income of the Mothers' Union, 2005–2009 (adjusted for inflation, 2009)

Source: Charity Commission.

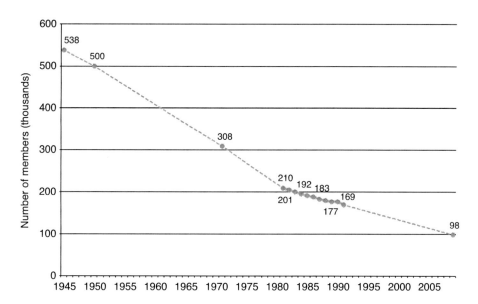

Figure 4.97: Mothers' Union membership in the UK, 1945–2009

Sources: *Social Trends*; Caitriona Beaumont, 'The Women's Movement, Politics and Citizenship, 1918–1950s', in Ina Zweiniger-Bargielowska (ed.), *Women in Twentieth Century Britain* (Harlow, 2001), pp. 262–77; contact with Mothers' Union (2009).

Further reading

Cordelia Moyse, *A History of the Mothers Union: Women, Anglicanism and Globalisation, 1876–2008* (London, 2009); Caitriona Beaumont, 'Citizens not Feminists: The Boundary Negotiated between Citizenship and Feminism by Mainstream Women's Organisations in England, 1928–1939', *Women's History Review*, 9:2 (2000), pp. 411–29; Caitriona Beaumont, 'Housewives, Workers and Citizens: Voluntary Women's Organisations and the Campaign for Women's Rights in England and Wales during the Postwar Period', in Nick Crowson, Matthew Hilton and James McKay (eds), *NGOs in Contemporary Britain: Non-State Actors in Society and Politics since 1945* (Basingstoke, 2009).

National Anti-Vivisection Society

The National Anti-Vivisection Society (NAVS) is the world's oldest group campaigning against animal experimentation.

The Society was formed in 1875 as the Victoria Street Society, by activists and leading figures including Lord Shaftesbury, Frances Power Cobbe and Cardinal Manning, and adopted its current name in 1897. The following year, the fissiparous nature of the anti-vivisection movement asserted itself, as the group split over tactical questions. The NAVS narrowly adopted a policy that favoured campaigning for measures short of the total abolition of vivisection, as a way of both advancing towards that ultimate cause and alleviating the suffering of laboratory animals in the meantime. For some in the movement, however, this was unacceptable. Frances Power Cobbe immediately left the Society she had helped to found, and set up a rival, the British Union for the Abolition of Vivisection (BUAV), committed solely to immediate and total abolition. The NAVS continued with its staged policy (as it does to this day), under the leadership of Stephen Coleridge, while remaining committed to total abolition as an ultimate goal.

The Society came to particular prominence through its part in the Brown Dog affair at the beginning of the twentieth century. In 1903, two Swedish anti-vivisectionists enrolled as students at London University in order to investigate laboratory work. Their account of the vivisection of a brown terrier dog, publicised by Coleridge, then became the focus of a libel action. Although Coleridge and the NAVS lost the action, the publicity from the case generated significant public support, and more than enough money to cover the damages awarded against him. A statue in Battersea Park commemorating the brown dog at the centre of the dispute,subsequently became the focus of disturbances involving medical students and researchers, and was removed by the local council in 1910. A replacement statue carrying the same inscription (see Box 4.13) was erected in 1985.

The anti-vivisection cause met with very limited legislative impact through the twentieth century, at least until the banning of cosmetics testing on animals in 1998. In spite of this, the Society has successfully maintained a campaigning presence. Along with other anti-vivisection groups, it benefited from the reassertion of animal rights thinking from the 1960s onwards, brought to prominence by philosophers such as Tom Regan and Peter Singer. The rise of local activism around this time can be seen in the boost in numbers of local NAVS groups during the late 1960s and early 1970s. Numbers rose to between 50 and 60, although they had dwindled again to around 30 by the end of the 1970s. Non-animal research is funded through the Lord Dowding Fund for Humane Research, established in 1973 in honour of the Second World War hero and former NAVS president. In 1979, the Society established a World Day for Laboratory Animals on 24 April (Lord Dowding's birthday), an event now recognised by the United Nations. The Society has also established another group, Animal Defenders International, to work on a broader set of campaigns.

Box 4.13: Inscription on the Brown Dog Statue

'In memory of the Brown Terrier Dog done to Death in the Laboratories of University College in February 1903, after having endured Vivisection extending over more than two months and having been handed from one Vivisector to another till Death came to his Release. Also in Memory of the 232 dogs vivisected at the same place during the year 1902. Men and Women of England, how long shall these things be?'

Key legislation and inquiries

1875   Royal Commission on Vivisection appointed, reports following year
1876   Cruelty to Animals Act establishes system for regulation of vivisection
1906   Second Royal Commission on Vivisection appointed, reports 1912
1963   Departmental Committee on Experiments on Living Animals (Littlewood Committee) established, reports 1965
1986   Animals (Scientific Procedures) Act updates 1876 governance regime
1998   Animal testing for cosmetic purposes banned in UK

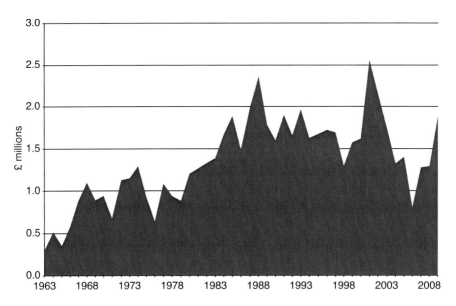

Figure 4.98: Income of National Anti-Vivisection Society, 1963–2009 (adjusted for inflation, 2009)

Source: Annual reports and accounts, NAVS.

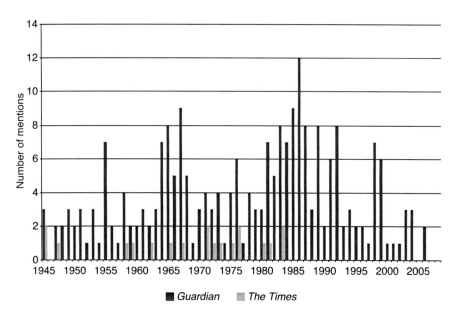

Figure 4.99: Number of mentions of the National Anti-Vivisection Society in the *Guardian* and *The Times*, 1945–2007

Source: *Guardian* & *The Times*.

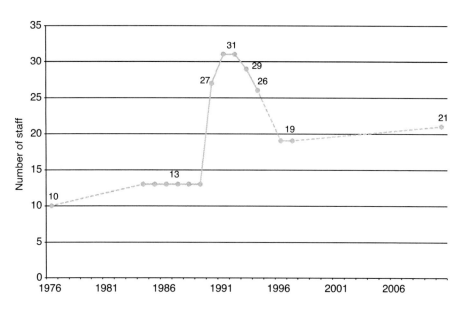

Figure 4.100: Number of staff working for the National Anti-Vivisection Society, 1976–2010

Sources: Annual reports and accounts, NAVS; Guardian Directory of Pressure Groups; contact with NAVS (2011).

Further reading

Robert Garner, *Political Animals: Animal Protection Politics in Britain and the United States* (London, 1998); Hilda Kean, *Animal Rights: Political and Social Change in Britain since 1800* (London, 1998).

National Federation of Women's Institutes

The Women's Institutes (WIs) originated with the support of the state. Modelled on a Canadian initiative begun in 1897, local WIs were set up by the Agricultural Organisation Society and the Board of Agriculture in 1915 in order to revitalise rural communities and to encourage women to become involved in food production. Within two years, 137 WIs had been formed, and the National Federation of Women's Institutes (NFWI) was created in 1917, launching its magazine, *Home and Country*, in 1919. It was funded by a government grant so that it could take over responsibility for the creation of new branches. By 1928 it oversaw 4,244 WIs with a total of 240,000 members.

Usually associated with social, if not political, conservatism, WIs have frequently betrayed their 'jam and Jerusalem' image ('Jerusalem' was first sung at the annual meeting in 1924). In the interwar period it campaigned on issues such as equal pay, public housing, improved maternity services and the general rights of citizenship, as well as supporting the work of the League of Nations in promoting peace. These may well have been undertaken with a strong sense of the domestic role of women, but it nevertheless demanded respect for women's work and, at the level of the specific campaign, made the organisation indistinguishable from more radical, even feminist organisations.

During the Second World War, along with the Mothers' Union and Townswomen's Guild, the WIs became a major feature of national public life. They served on bodies such as the 1941 Inter-Departmental Committee on Social Insurance and Allied Services and the 1942 Ministry of Health's Design of Dwellings Sub-Committee, as well as successfully opposing, alongside Eleanor Rathbone, plans to pay the new Family Allowance to fathers.

After the war, the WIs expanded their social and cultural role and saw their primary role in supporting wives and mothers. Yet they recognised also the need and desire of many women to go out to work and they supported further equal pay campaigns and lobbied on key measures relating to women's status following

---

Box 4.14: Women's Institute recipe for strawberry jam

'*Ingredients*: 1kg/2lb 2oz jam sugar; 2kg/4¼lb strawberries; Juice of ½ lemon
Method: 1. Put the sugar into a preserving pan; 2. Hull and pick through the strawberries, discarding any blemished fruit; 3. Put the fruit and lemon juice into the pan and stir gently. Leave for 1 hr; 4. Put the pan on a medium heat, bring to the boil and boil rapidly for 15–18 mins, skimming off any scum as it appears; 5. Test for a set; 6. When ready, turn off the heat and leave to stand for 15–20 mins to prevent the fruit rising in the jars; 7. Spoon into jars.'

marital breakdown. Participation in WI meetings also became a training ground for many local authority councillors and even MPs.

The number of WIs peaked in the 1970s at around 9,300. There has been a subsequent decline, though they have maintained their high profile through their support for fair trade and international development issues, as well as the publicity surrounding the slow handclap given to Tony Blair when he tried to make party political points when addressing the Triennial General Meeting in 2000.

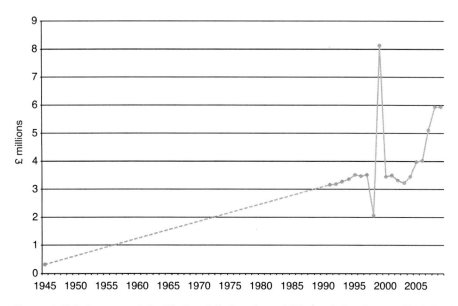

Figure 4.101: Income of the National Federation of Women's Institutes, 1945–2009 (adjusted for inflation, 2009)

Note: The exceptionally high income in 1998/99 is due to the one-off transfer of Denman College's funds to the NFWI as a result of Denman College being redefined as a subsidiary charity of the NFWI by the Charity Commission during the course of the year.

Sources: Annual reports and accounts, NFWI; Top 3000 Charities; Charity Commission; H.A. Mess, G.R. Williams and C. Braithwaite, *Voluntary Social Services since 1918* (London, 1947).

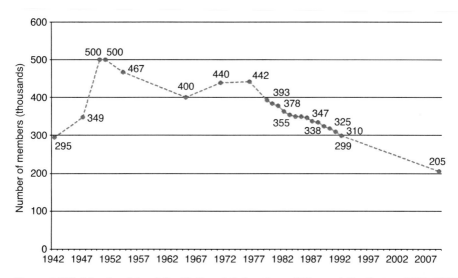

Figure 4.102: Membership of the National Federation of Women's Institutes, 1942–2009

Sources: *Social Trends*; Guardian Directory of Pressure Groups; Anne F.C. Bourdillon, *Voluntary Social Services: Their Place in the Modern State* (London, 1945); Beveridge 1949; Caitriona Beaumont, 'The Women's Movement, Politics and Citizenship, 1918–1950s' in Ina Zweiniger-Bargielowska (ed.), *Women in Twentieth Century Britain* (Harlow, 2001), pp. 262–77; Caitriona Beaumont, 'Housewives, Workers and Citizens: Voluntary Women's Organisations and the Campaign for Women's Rights in England and Wales during the Postwar Period', in Nick Crowson, Matthew Hilton and James McKay (eds), *NGOs in Contemporary Britain: Non-State Actors in Society and Politics since 1945* (Basingstoke, 2009); NFWI's website (2009).

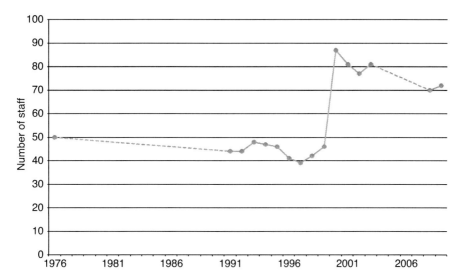

Figure 4.103: Number of staff working for the National Federation of Women's Institutes, 1976–2009

Sources: Annual reports and accounts, NFWI; Top 3000 Charities; Charity Commission; Guardian Directory of Pressure Groups.

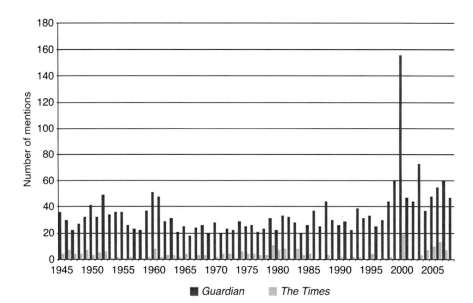

Figure 4.104: Number of mentions of the National Federation of Women's Institutes in the *Guardian* and *The Times*, 1945–2007

Source: *Guardian* & *The Times*.

Further reading

Maggie Andrews, *The Acceptable Face of Feminism, the Women's Institute as a social movement* (London, 1997); Caitriona Beaumont, 'Citizens not Feminists: The Boundary Negotiated between Citizenship and Feminism by Mainstream Women's Organisations in England, 1928–1939', *Women's History Review*, 9:2 (2000), pp. 411–29; Caitriona Beaumont, 'Housewives, Workers and Citizens: Voluntary Women's Organisations and the Campaign for Women's Rights in England and Wales during the Postwar Period', in Nick Crowson, Matthew Hilton and James McKay (eds), *NGOs in Contemporary Britain: Non-State Actors in Society and Politics since 1945* (Basingstoke, 2009).

National Society for the Prevention of Cruelty to Children

From 1884 the National Society for the Prevention of Cruelty to Children (NSPCC) pioneered child protection in the UK. Thomas Agnew founded the Liverpool Society in 1883. He was invited to London and as a result the London Society was formed on 8 July 1884 with Lord Shaftesbury as president, and Rev. Edward Rudolph and Rev. Benjamin Waugh as joint secretaries. Branches rapidly spread through England and Wales, and Queen Victoria served as patron. Over its lifetime the society has secured a semi-public status as a private charitable campaigning group that has enshrined legal status and works alongside the police and social services.

Throughout its history the NSPCC has pioneered the construction of the criminality of child abuse, particularly through initial visual representation (pioneering use of photography) before it became enshrined in legal judgement.

It started to employ child inspectors (often ex-policemen), the 'Cruelty Men', and by 1889 had dealt with 3,947 cases of child brutality and neglect. Its first political success was the 1889 Children's Charter Act. Further legislative successes followed, all of which gave the NSPCC increased legal rights to intervene in the private sphere in defence of the child.

After 1945, the NSPCC continued to expand nationally, merging or absorbing other regional child protection groups. But the overlapping of its services with some state provision resulted in professional tensions. During the 1960s the Society redirected itself towards more specialised services in therapies, child protection training and policy research. It also established pre-school playgroups and modernised its child protection network. During the 1960s the notion of child abuse was discovered and it became a moral panic of the 1970s. Social work practise came under increased public and media scrutiny during the 1970s following a number of high-profile child deaths. In 1973 it launched the Battered Child Advisory Centre offering a range of specialised services for children, families and professionals nationwide.

The NSPCC has provided statistics showing that since the 1980s there have been increases in the numbers of children at risk. The majority of referrals to the NSPCC derive from public as opposed to social service referrals. Heightened public awareness increases the probability of referrals, which consequentially increases consciousness of the problem. By 1991 it had over 120 Child Protection Teams and Projects offering a range of services, some specialised child protection issues or to provide assessments for the courts and other professional agencies. Child Protection Helpline was launched in 1991, the first of its kind in Europe, offering free 24-hour access with an experienced telephone counsellor at the end of the line. By 1999 it had taken 74,000 calls.

The 1990s also saw campaigning and parliamentary work, with an emphasis on redirecting resources towards prevention of abuse and cruelty. It led the NSPCC to the conclusion that child cruelty could be ended in the UK and that it should reorient its structure and campaigning message towards this goal with the FULL STOP campaign. Critics have pointed out that it is bound to fail as child cruelty will persist, and point to recent tragic cases such as those of Victoria Climbie and 'Baby Peter'. Since 1989 it is the only charity authorised by law to take legal action to protect children, and is credited with inspiring the 1989 Children's Act and the 1996 Family Law Act. Analysis of its annual financial audits showed that in 2000, 60 per cent of the organisation's total costs were due to 'administration', which aroused considerable criticism at the time.

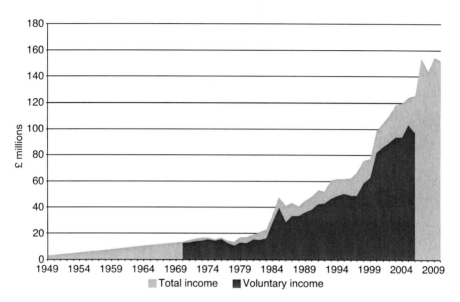

Figure 4.105: Total and voluntary income of NSPCC, 1949–2009 (adjusted for inflation, 2009)

Note: The total income between 1949 and 1970 is inferred, and there are no data for voluntary income before 1970 or after 2006.

Sources: Beveridge 1949; Wolfenden 1978; Wells Collection; Charity Statistics; Charity Commission.

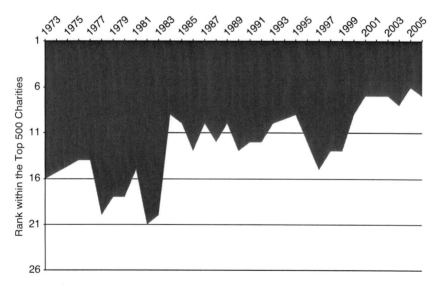

Figure 4.106: NSPCC's charitable ranking by voluntary income, 1973–2005

Source: Charity Statistics.

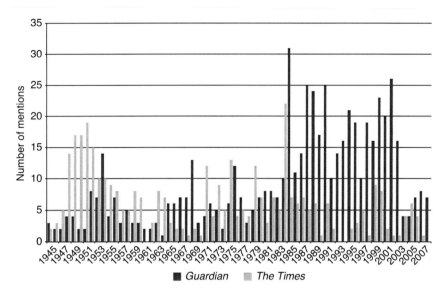

Figure 4.107: Number of mentions of the NSPCC in the *Guardian* and *The Times*, 1945–2007

Source: *Guardian* & *The Times*.

Further reading

George K. Behlmer, *Child Abuse and moral reform in England 1870–1908* (Stanford, CA, 1982); NSPCC, *NSPCC: The First Hundred Years, 1884–1984* (London, 1984).

National Trust

The National Trust for Places of Historic Interest or Natural Beauty is one of Britain's leading conservation bodies. A major landowner in its own right, the Trust holds more than 200 historically significant buildings and gardens, 700 miles of coastline, and 250,000 hectares of countryside, across England, Wales and Northern Ireland. It is also one of the country's largest membership organisations, with more than 3.5 million supporters.

The Trust was established in 1895 by Octavia Hill (see Box 4.15), Sir Robert Hunter and Canon Hardwicke Rawnsley, and formed part of a wider movement to protect Britain's heritage and countryside from what were seen as the ravages of industrialisation and urbanisation. Hill and Hunter had previously been involved in the Open Spaces Society (1865). Together with other groups, such as the Royal Society for the Protection of Birds (RSPB) (1889) and the Royal Society of Wildlife Trusts (1912), the Trust therefore formed part of an initial wave of conservation and environmental groups in Britain, characterised both by a concern for preservation, and the socially elite nature of their leadership and support.

The motivation behind the Trust's foundation was the urge to preserve a London garden, Sayes Court, created by the diarist John Evelyn. It was more than a decade before this initial impetus resulted in the purchase of buildings, the first being Alfriston Clergy House in Suffolk in 1896. The Trust's first nature reserve, Wicken Fen, was purchased three years later.

Since these beginnings, the Trust has made acquisitions of great significance to national and natural heritage. In 1923 it was presented with Great Gable in the Lake District, as a memorial to those who had died in the First World War. Stonehenge Down, purchased following a national appeal in order to protect the prehistoric monument, came in 1927, while two years later, the Trust acquired 4,000 acres of the Lake District's Monk Coniston estate, thanks to the longstanding support of children's author Beatrix Potter. Changing tax regimes in the mid twentieth century led to the disposal of a series of great country houses from private hands, many of which were acquired by the Trust. The period also saw the establishment of the National Land Fund (1946), which again assisted the transfer of great country houses to the Trust. In the 1960s, coastal preservation became a particular priority, with the launch of the Enterprise Neptune project.

During the late twentieth century, the Trust experienced extraordinary membership growth. Membership of 225,000 in 1970 had quadrupled to 1 million by the early 1980s. It reached 2 million by the 1990s, and 3.5 million in 2007. Initially a voluntary organisation, the Trust received statutory recognition with the 1907 National Trust Act, something enhanced by subsequent governments throughout the twentieth century.

Box 4.15: Octavia Hill

Although the National Trust is perhaps the best known cause associated with Octavia Hill (1838–1912), she was principally a housing and social reformer, involved in many of the key developments of social work in the Victorian period.

Brought up by her educationalist mother, Caroline Southwood Hill, and her maternal grandfather, the health reformer Thomas Southwood Smith, Hill was exposed to the harsh social realities of nineteenth-century England from a young age. In the 1860s, with financial support from John Ruskin, Hill began her housing improvement schemes in Paradise Place, London. Over the years, her work became world-famous, as the 'Octavia Hill method'.

Hill was also concerned with social reform more broadly, involved in the Charity Organisation Society and the development of the social work profession, and a member of the 1905 Royal Commission on the Poor Law.

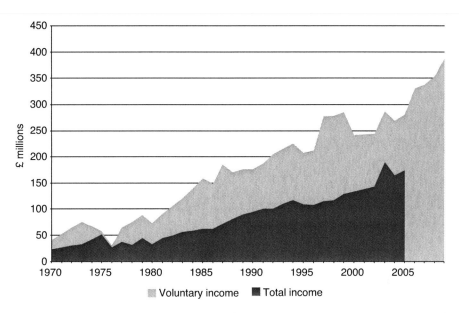

Figure 4.108: Voluntary and total income of the National Trust, 1970–2009 (adjusted for inflation, 2009)

Source: Annual reports and accounts, National Trust; Charity Commission; Charity Statistics.

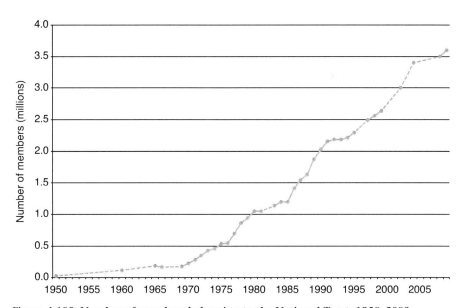

Figure 4.109: Number of members belonging to the National Trust, 1950–2009

Note: The figures for 1950, 1960 and 1965 include members of the National Trust Scotland.

Sources: *Social Trends*; Annual reports and accounts, National Trust; Francis Sandbach, *Environment, Ideology and Policy* (Oxford, 1980), pp. 12–13.

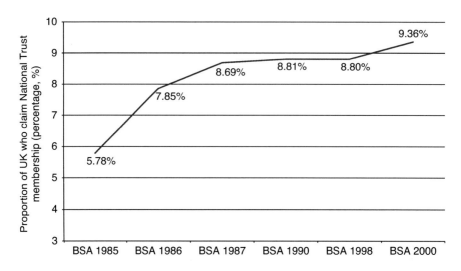

Figure 4.110: Proportion of UK citizens claiming to be a member of the National Trust

Source: British Social Attitudes Survey, percentages answering yes to the question: 'Do you personally belong to any of the groups listed on this card? Yes: National Trust' (data accessed through www.britsocat.com).

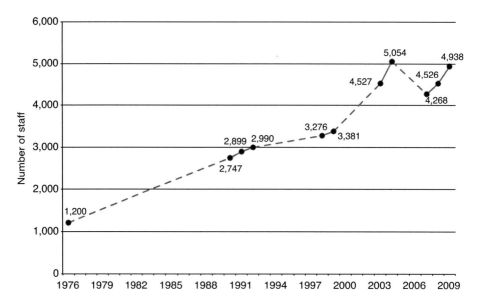

Figure 4.111: Number of staff working for the National Trust, 1976–2009

Sources: Guardian Directory of Pressure Groups; Top 3000 Charities; Charity Commission; Annual reports and accounts, National Trust.

Further reading

www.nationaltrust.org.uk/main/w-trust/w-thecharity/w-history_trust.htm

Gillian Darley, 'Hill, Octavia (1838–1912)', *Oxford Dictionary of National Biography*, Oxford University Press, 2004; online edn, Jan 2011, www.oxforddnb.com/view/article/33873; David Evans, *A History of Nature Conservation in Britain*, 2nd edn (London, 1997); Jennifer Jenkins, 'The Roots of the National Trust', *History Today*, 45:1 (1995); George M. Trevelyan, *Must England's Beauty Perish? A Plea on Behalf of the National Trust for Places of Historic Interest or Natural Beauty* (London, 1929); Merlin Waterson, *The National Trust: The First Hundred Years* (London, 1997).

Oxfam

Oxfam began as the Oxford Committee for Famine Relief, first meeting in October 1942 in the Old Library of the Church of St Mary-the-Virgin in Oxford. As one of many such Committees, Oxfam (the name it would later take from the abbreviation it used for telegraphic purposes) was committed to the humanitarian assistance of Greek civilians for whom official agencies were reluctant to provide relief for fear resources would fall into enemy hands. Once the United Nations Relief and Rehabilitation Administration was established at the end of 1943, many of these committees folded, though Oxfam chose to continue and pursue more generally 'the relief of suffering in consequence of war'.

Oxfam led the way in much development fundraising. In the 1960s it speculatively invested in advertising which meant the other charities regarded Oxfam as 'an anti-establishment upstart brat', though one which showed how high expenditure on publicity images and branding could lead to high returns in voluntary income. It responded quickly to international crises, from Bihar in 1951 to Biafra in 1969, and it grew rapidly, employing around 280 staff by 1970.

Oxfam has pioneered much development thinking, positioning its small-scale, grassroots projects as an alternative to the supposed 'top-down' approach of much official development. It drew on the works of E.F. Schumacher, but also explored the principles of liberation theology and 'conscientisation' which placed the emphasis on the poor themselves having a role in their own path to development. Accordingly, it supported the Gramdam land reform movement initiated by the Gandhian, J.P. Narayan, in India, and the Ujamaa villagisation project of Julius Nyerere in Tanzania, even when the latter became increasingly authoritarian.

At the policy level in the UK, Oxfam has participated in most of the key development campaigns, from the relatively benign Freedom from Hunger Campaign of 1960, initiated by the UN, to the more programmatic Haslemere Declaration of 1968 and the *Manifesto on Aid and Development* in 1969. It has worked with other NGOs to lobby governments, especially to follow the recommendations of key development initiatives such as the Brandt Commission (North–South) in 1980 and, most recently, the Millennium Development Goals. Its prominence and interventions have been such that it has frequently come under the scrutiny of the Charity Commissioners, with right-wing think tanks launching sustained attacks on Oxfam's work in the 1980s in Palestine and apartheid South Africa.

In recent decades, Oxfam has strove to scale up its activities, tying development work to more comprehensive analyses of global trade and the system of international governance. However, it has done so while also employing a language that no longer makes it seem as much an alternative to official development as it once was. Primarily, this has been through the language of human rights, its rights-based approach to development tying the NGO to many of the principles of 'good governance' articulated by official international organisations.

Key texts that have influenced Oxfam's work

Gunnar Myrdal, *Economic Theory and Under-Developed Regions* (1957)
E.F. Schumacher, *Small is Beautiful: A Study of Economics as if People Mattered* (1973)
Paulo Freire, *Pedagogy of the Oppressed* (1968; English translation 1970)
Amartya Sen, *Development as Freedom* (1999)

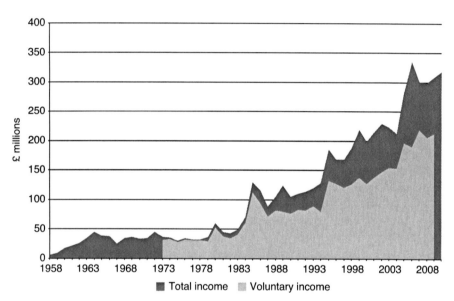

Figure 4.112: Voluntary and total income of Oxfam, 1958–2010 (adjusted for inflation, 2009)

Sources: Annual reports and accounts, Oxfam; Charity Commission; Charity Statistics.

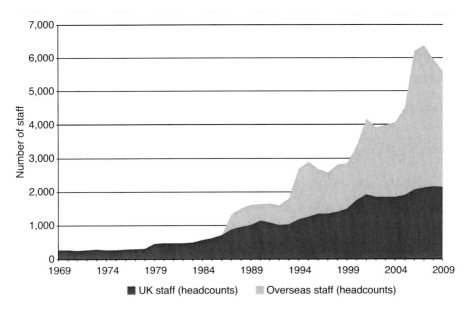

Figure 4.113: Number of staff working for Oxfam, 1969–2009

Sources: Annual reports and accounts, Oxfam; Charity Commission; Charity Statistics; Top 3000 Charities.

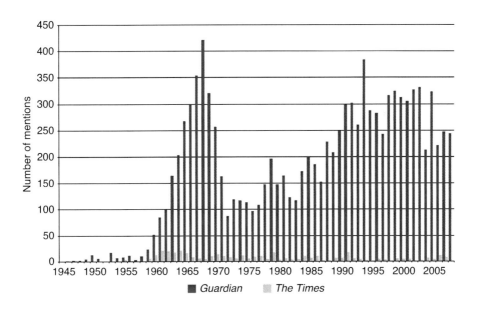

Figure 4.114: Number of mentions of Oxfam in the *Guardian* and *The Times*, 1945–2007

Source: *Guardian* & *The Times*.

Further reading

Maggie Black, *A Cause for Our Times: Oxfam, the First Fifty Years* (Oxford, 1992); Ben Whitaker, *A Bridge of People: A Personal View of Oxfam's First Forty Years* (London, 1983); Michael Jennings, *Surrogates of the State: NGOs, Development and Ujamaa in Tanzania* (Bloomfield, CT, 2008).

Policy Studies Institute

The Policy Studies Institute (PSI) is a think tank that has evolved into one that contracts its research services to outside clients. PSI was formed in 1978 after a merger between PEP (Political and Economic Planning) (created 1931) and the Centre for Studies in Social Policy (established 1972). This was a decision taken because of the similarity of their research interests.

PEP was an intellectual response to the depression and was inspired by Max Nicholson's call in the *Weekend Review*, 1931, for a plan to improve the nation's economic, social and political condition, which gained support from Israel Sieff and Leonard Elmhirst. Whatever the specificity of its impact in the 1930s, what it at least achieved was conditioning political opinion for the upheavals of the 1940s, and many of its early ideas can be seen influencing post-war policy on national statistics, new towns, national parks, integrated transport and the welfare state. It claims that it has no ideological basis, but some scepticism must be attached to this view. Michael Young, PEP's secretary who helped draft Labour's 1945 election manifesto, admits having packed it with as many PEP ideas as he could get past Herbert Morrison.

After the war it became a permanent research organisation, producing research reports inspired by the principles and values of sociology, and pioneered social research technique. The range of topics covered in its history has been vast: from economics, to employment rights, to management issues, to the European Union, to social policy and women's rights. Insiders have, perhaps unsurprisingly, credited the organisation with having considerable impact on policy makers. Its 1937 report on health services directly fed into the reforms that created the National Health Service in 1948. Its 1967 report on racial discrimination convinced the Wilson government of the need for a Second Race Relations Act. Its work on welfare benefits contributed to the introduction of the tax credit system in the 1990s.

It has proved particularly influential in the field of race relations where the multitude of reports on the issue have made it one of the biggest sources of information, ideas and opinions on race relations and the experiences of racial discrimination, such as *Racial Disadvantage* (1977). In fact, one of its trademarks has been longitudinal surveys enabling the PSI to report on changes in subjects such as ethnic diversity and union–employer relations over at least a quarter of a century. A hallmark of its recognised research qualities is that even during the 1980s it continued to receive government commissions despite the often partisan hostility being expressed from Number 10.

In January 1998 it became a wholly-owned subsidiary company of the University of Westminster before fully merging with it in April 2009.

Key publications

PEP, *Report on the British Health Services* (London, 1937)

PEP, *Britain and World Trade* (London, 1947)

PEP, *Growth in the British Economy* (London, 1960)

Bill Daniels, *Racial Discrimination* (London, 1967)

Mayer Hillman, Irwin Henderson and Anne Whalley, *Personal Mobility and Transport Policy* (London, 1973)

Richard Berthoud, *The Disadvantages of Inequality* (London, 1976)

David John Smith, *Racial Disadvantage* (London, 1977)

David Smith, Jeremy Gray and Stephen Small, *Police and People in London* (London, 1983)

Colin Brown, *Black and White Britain: The 3rd PSI Survey* (London, 1985)

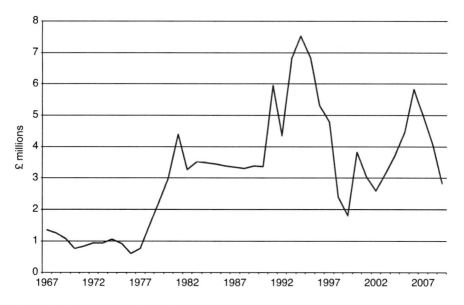

Figure 4.115: Income of the Policy Studies Institute, 1967–2009 (adjusted for inflation, 2009)

Source: Annual reports and accounts, PSI; Top 3000 Charities; Charity Commission.

Figure 4.116: Number of staff working for the Policy Studies Institute, 1966–2009

Source: Annual reports and accounts, PSI; Top 3000 Charities; Charity Commission.

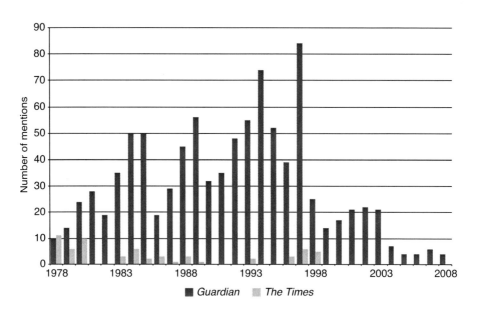

Figure 4.117: Number of mentions of the Policy Studies Institute in the *Guardian* and *The Times*, 1978–2008

Source: *Guardian* & *The Times*.

Further reading

Arthur Marwick, 'Middle Opinion in the Thirties: Planning, Progress and Political "Agreement"', *English Historical Review*, 79:311 (1964), pp. 285–98; John Pinder, '1964–1980: From PEP to PSI', in John Pinder (ed.), *Fifty Years of Political and Economic Planning: Looking Forwards 1931–81* (London, 1981); Abigail Beach, 'Forging a "Nation of Participants": Political and Economic Planning in Labour's Britain', in Richard Weight and Abigail Beech (eds), *The Right to Belong: Citizenship and National Identity in Britain, 1930–1960* (London, 1998), pp. 89–115.

Ramblers

The Ramblers is a national charity devoted to the promotion and protection of recreational walking.

The formation of the National Council of Ramblers' Federations in 1931, and the Ramblers Association four years later, places rambling within a distinct phase of the development of the environment and conservation movement. During the interwar period, groups representing working-class, professional, recreational and amenity interests began to be established. Alongside the Council for the Preservation of Rural England (1926), the Ramblers was therefore clearly distinct from the socially-elite initiatives of the late nineteenth and early twentieth centuries, such as the National Trust (1895) and what would become the Royal Society of Wildlife Trusts (1912).

Despite this social differentiation, the roots of the Ramblers also lay in the nineteenth century, as concern over access to the countryside grew in the face of industrialisation and urbanisation. Early localised initiatives included the Association for the Protection of Ancient Footpaths in the Vicinity of York (1824), while the Commons Preservation Society (1865) would later take on a national campaigning role. This movement gathered pace towards the end of the nineteenth century, and by the 1930s the proliferation of local and regional bodies generated momentum for the formation of a national coordinating body.

The most resonant moment in the rambling movement's history came in 1932, with the mass trespass on Kinder Scout (see Box 4.16). Ironically, the National Council itself did not endorse the trespass, yet Kinder Scout quickly became an iconic symbol of direct-action protest, as hundreds of walkers flouted access laws and invaded the Derbyshire grouse moor, leading to arrests and prison sentences.

Plans for National Parks and long-distance walks gathered pace following the election of the post-war Labour government (leading Labour politician Hugh Dalton was himself president of the Association for a time). The 1949 National Parks and Access to the Countryside Act laid the legislative foundations for these reforms, leading to the creation of the first national park, in the Peak District, in 1951. The Lake District, Snowdonia and Dartmoor parks were created the same year, with a total of ten being established by the end of the 1950s. Access was also enhanced by the creation of official long-distance walks, with the Pennine Way being the first in Britain, opening in 1965.

In 1968, the Countryside Act resulted in the creation of the Countryside Commission, charged with promoting access to, and enjoyment of, the countryside. Finally, decades of campaigning resulted in winning the right to roam at the start of the new century, through the 2000 Countryside and Rights of Way Act (for England and Wales), and the 2003 Land Reform Act (Scotland).

Today, the Ramblers has a membership of around 140,000, and enjoys the affiliation of more than 800 local groups. Separate structures for Scotland and Wales were established in 1967 and 1974 respectively.

Box 4.16: Mass trespass on Kinder Scout

'Four or five hundred ramblers, mostly from Manchester, trespassed in mass on Kinder Scout today. They fought a brief but vigorous hand-to-hand struggle with a number of keepers specially enrolled for the occasion. This they won with ease, and then marched on to Ashop Head, where they held a meeting before returning in triumph to Hayfield.'

Manchester Guardian, 25 April 1932.

Legislative landmarks

1949   National Parks and Access to the Countryside Act
1968   Countryside Act
2000   Countryside and Rights of Way Act
2003   Land Reform Act

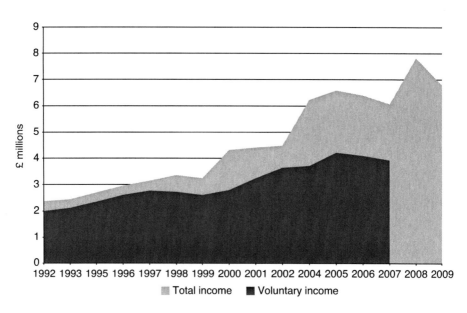

Figure 4.118: Voluntary and total income of the Ramblers, 1992–2009 (adjusted for inflation, 2009)

Note: The voluntary income for the period after 2007 is not known.

Sources: Charity Statistics; Charity Commission.

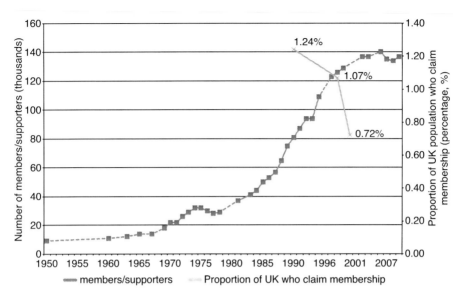

Figure 4.119: Number of members and supporters of Ramblers and proportion of UK who claim membership, 1950–2009

Sources: (a) For the number of members/supporters: Annual reports and accounts; Ramblers' Association Manuscripts, London Metropolitan Archives; Ramblers' Association website. (b) For the percentage of people answering positively to the question: 'Are you currently a member of any of these? Yes: Ramblers Association', British Social Attitudes Survey (data accessed from www.britsocat.com).

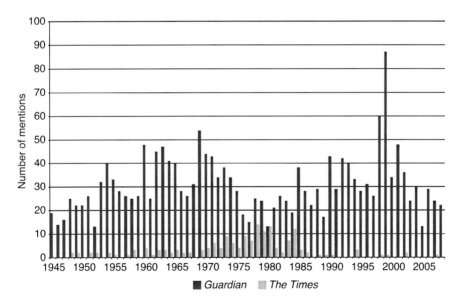

Figure 4.120: Number of mentions of the Ramblers in the *Guardian* and *The Times*, 1945–2007

Source: *Guardian* & *The Times*.

Further reading
www.ramblers.org.uk
David Evans, *A History of Nature Conservation in Britain*, 2nd edn (London, 1997).

Red Cross

The origins of the Red Cross are well known. In 1859, Henry Dunant took pity on the wounded casualties of all combatants at the Battle of Solferino. This led to the creation in 1863 of what would become the International Committee of the Red Cross (ICRC) and the League of Red Cross and Red Crescent Societies. Although not a true NGO itself since the ICRC has always been closely tied to the Swiss Confederation and has come to enjoy a special status with public international law, its affiliated national societies have been more like NGOs. The British Red Cross Society began soon after the outbreak of the Franco-Prussian War in 1870 when Colonel Loyd-Lyndsey wrote to *The Times* calling for the kind of relief organisation that had appeared elsewhere in Europe. Following a public meeting, the British National Society for Aid to the Sick and Wounded in War was formed. It adopted the Red Cross emblem and became formally known as the British Red Cross in 1905. It received its first Royal Charter in 1908.

The Red Cross has relied on a system of organised volunteers since the outset. Voluntary Aid Detachments were formed in every county in England to ensure it could properly mobilise during wartime. In the First World War it combined with the Order of St John to provide relief services and notably was able to supply the first motorised ambulances to the battlefields. During the interwar years, it continued to grow, expanding overseas and extending its peacetime work, such as setting up the first blood transfusion service in the UK. In the Second World War, it again combined with the Order of St John, this time also sending around 20 million food parcels to prisoners of war which it was allowed to do under the terms of the third Geneva Convention.

The operating rationale of the Red Cross has always been one of strict neutrality in times of conflict. This has created the sorts of tensions that would plague many subsequent humanitarian NGOs, especially during the Biafran conflict at the end of the 1960s. Indeed, criticisms have emerged in recent decades over Red Cross complicity during the Second World War, especially relating to its knowledge of Nazi atrocities and the inadvertent ways in which it might have assisted war criminals to flee Germany after the war.

Unlike other NGOs, the Red Cross has also maintained its focus on emergency relief rather than long-term development work. In the post-war period it has been able to mount a sizeable operation in most of the largest disasters, from the crisis in Hungary in 1956 through to the Asian tsunami at the end of 2004. In doing so, it has become one of the largest NGOs with an income of approximately £250 million in 2007–08. In the field, it has cooperated with other NGOs and, in 1963, along with Christian Aid, Oxfam, Save the Children Fund and War on Want, it was one of the founder members of the Disasters Emergency Committee (DEC) that has coordinated fundraising in times of emergency.

Red Cross and neutrality

Neutrality in time of conflict has been the key principal behind Red Cross operations, enabling it to provide services to victims of both sides. Notwithstanding the practical difficulty of ensuring how this occurs in any conflict, the Red Cross has further elaborated on its core mission. In 1965 in Vienna, the Red Cross committed its national organisation to the following 'fundamental principles': Humanity; Impartiality; Neutrality; Independence; Voluntary Service; Unity; and Universality.

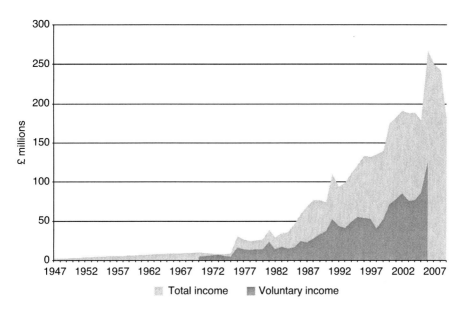

Figure 4.121: Total and voluntary income of the Red Cross, 1947–2009 (adjusted for inflation, 2009)

Note: The income between 1947 and 1970 is inferred.

Sources: Beveridge 1949; Wolfenden 1978; Wells Collection; Charity Statistics; Charity Commission.

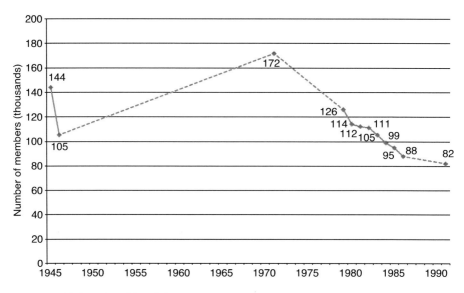

Figure 4.122: Membership of the Red Cross, 1945–1991

Note: The Red Cross is no longer a membership organisation, so it has not been possible to update the figure above. In 2009, the Red Cross claimed it had 30,000 volunteers, 350,000 regular givers and 350,000 active cash donors, but none of these were 'members' as such (source: contact with Red Cross). *Social Trends* also note that due to changes in the method of recording, the 1979 figure is not comparable with 1971.

Sources: Beveridge 1949; *Social Trends*.

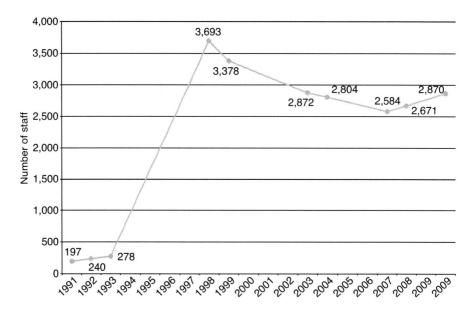

Figure 4.123: Number of staff working for the Red Cross, 1990–2009

Source: Top 3000 Charities.

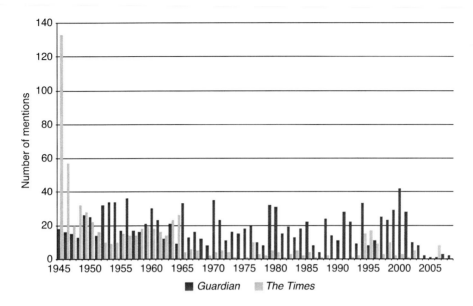

Figure 4.124: Number of mentions of the Red Cross in the *Guardian* and *The Times*, 1945–2007

Source: *Guardian* & *The Times*.

Further reading

David P. Forsythe, *Humanitarian Politics: The International Committee of the Red Cross* (Baltimore, MD, 1977).

Relate

Relate is the UK's largest provider of relationship counselling and support.

At the outbreak of the First World War in 1914, there were 856 divorces that year in England and Wales. By the start of the Second World War, this figure had risen to 8,254. Although these figures would subsequently be dwarfed by statistics from the post-war era, at the time they were a cause of great concern for the institution of marriage.

This concern led clergymen, medics and social workers to come together and form the Marriage Guidance Council (MGC) in 1938. Principal amongst them was Rev. Dr Herbert Gray. The founders sought the provision of marriage preparation and reconciliation services, to combat the rising divorce rate. Despite its concern for the preservation of marriage, the MGC was also notably a progressive force, urging sex education from early childhood onwards as a crucial component in healthy, sustainable relationships. (Gray himself was reported to believe that sex education should commence at the age of one.) The MGC initially began in London; although hampered by the war, counselling services began there in 1943, and opened in Manchester in 1945, the first of a growing number of nationwide centres. As of

2011, the charity ran more than 80 centres across England, Wales and Northern Ireland, with further services in Scotland.

In 1969, the Divorce Reform Act established no-fault divorces, and amidst the wider currents of feminism and societal change, the level of divorce increased dramatically. These changes were felt within the MGC, which in 1988 relaunched as Relate, in recognition that its counselling remit went far beyond married heterosexuals. Alongside relationships counselling, family counselling, sex therapy, young people's services and training workshops are now offered.

In its early years, the MGC was constrained financially, unable to meet the broad demand for its services. Modest government support for its work began to come onstream in the 1950s and 1960s, and has remained a significant proportion of income ever since. The classic model of face-to-face counselling sessions has since been complemented by phone, online and mobile phone services. Alongside this work, Relate also publishes self-help and advice books on topics across its field.

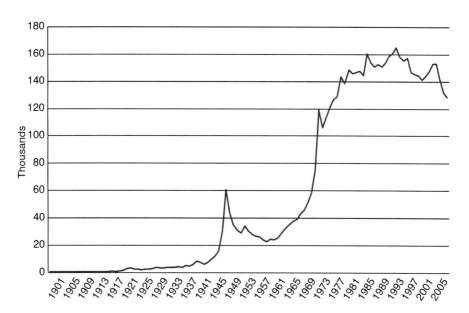

Figure 4.125: Number of divorces in England and Wales, 1900–2007

Source: Historic Divorce Tables, www.statistics.gov.uk/StatBase/Product.asp?vlnk=581.

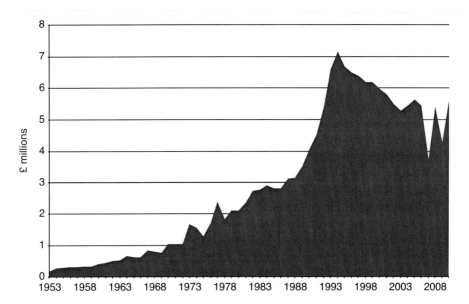

Figure 4.126: Total income of Relate, 1953–2010 (adjusted for inflation, 2009)

Source: Annual reports and accounts, Relate.

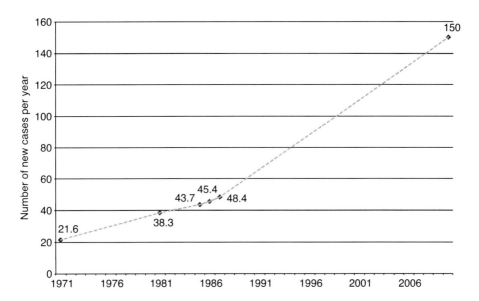

Figure 4.127: Number of 'new cases' dealt with during each year, 1971–2010

Note: The figure for 2011 does not refer only to 'new cases' but to the total number of people seen by Relate during the year.

Sources: *Social Trends*, 16 (1986), p. 180; 17 (1987), p. 173; 19 (1989), p. 183; www.relate.org.uk/relate-the-difference-we-make/index.html.

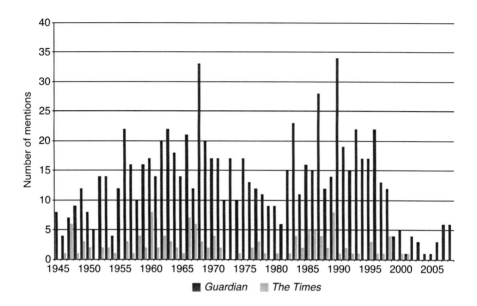

Figure 4.128: Number of mentions of Relate in the *Guardian* and *The Times*, 1945–2007

Source: *Guardian* & *The Times*.

Further reading

www.relate.org.uk/about-us/index.html

Royal British Legion

The Royal British Legion was formed in 1921 from the merger of the Comrades of the Great War, the National Association of Discharged Sailors and Soldiers, the National Federation of Discharged and Demobilised Sailors and Soldiers, and the Officers' Federation. The first president and co-founder was General Douglas Haig. It was granted the 'Royal' title in May 1971, but has had royal patronage since the 1920s.

Remembrance for the fallen has been the principal role of the Legion. From 1919 to 1946, Armistice Day was observed at the 11th minute of the 11th hour of the 11th month with a nationwide two-minute silence. Thereafter it was moved to Remembrance Sunday. By the 1990s, Remembrance Sunday had begun to witness a decline in observation. Sundays had irrevocably changed and become much more active with the relaxation of Sunday trading laws. There were also a series of one-off commemorations (for example, VE and VJ Days in May and August 1995) at which two-minute silences were observed. Although its poppy income was increasing, the Legion was concerned that remembrance was fading, so in September 1995 it began to campaign to return to Armistice Day. Remembrance Sunday still continues but is seen by the Legion as an occasion for local and national services and parades.

The vast majority of Legion members have historically been drawn from the non-commissioned ranks and were predominantly working class, but membership is declining. During the 1990s the Legion began a diversification of fundraising activities; however, the annual Poppy Day appeal remains its principal and most visible revenue generator. This act of remembrance is not without controversy and the wearing of a white poppy by anti-war protesters has been a limited opportunity to defy the overtones of militarism. In August 2010 it emerged that Tony Blair was donating the proceeds from his memoirs to the Legion. Criticised as 'blood money' by some (after Iraq and Afghanistan), it represented the single largest donation to a charity, and is to be used by the British Legion to fund a rehabilitation centre for injured soldiers.

From its inception it has placed emphasis on the duty of care for returning service men and women. During the interwar years it campaigned to improve the rights of the disabled to employment (1944 Disabled Persons Act); it opposed Means Testing in the 1930s and it campaigned for pension rights for ex-servicemen and widows. However, the British Legion did not carry the same level of political influence that similar ex-servicemen's groups possessed in continental Europe.

Since the military campaigns in Iraq and Afghanistan, the Legion has placed considerable efforts on persuading government to 'Honour the Covenant' to its armed forces personnel. Despite the 2005 Armed Forces Compensation Act, the Legion has found itself obligated to continue to highlight the iniquities of the scheme. This has gone a considerable way to fuelling public concern about the welfare of its ex-servicemen that has found expression in campaigns such as 'Help for Heroes'.

Box 4.17: Charles Bushby, RBL chairman, speaking about the need to double the membership and raise extra funds

'We have to bring about a revolution of pride and patriotism in the country. What better organisation to it than the British Legion? We must spread our ideas and ideals, not by exerting political pressure or by being militant or by demonstrating, but by example and by showing in word and deed unselfishness, thought for others, and moderation.'

The Times, 21 May 1977, p. 2.

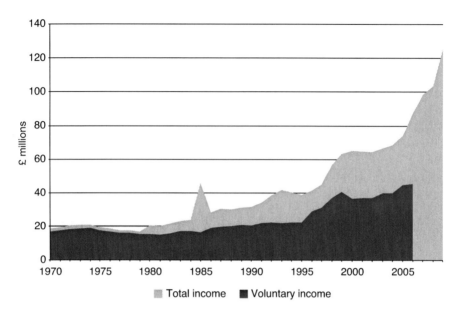

Figure 4.129: Voluntary and total income of the Royal British Legion, 1970–2009 (adjusted for inflation, 2009)

Sources: Wolfenden 1978; Wells Collection; Charity Statistics; Charity Commission.

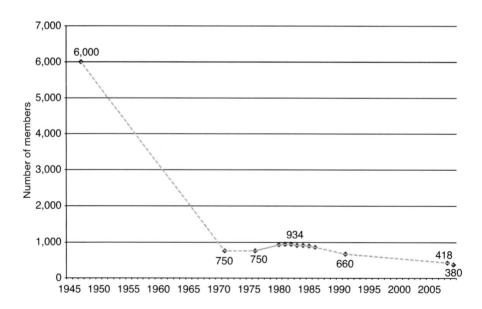

Figure 4.130: Number of members belonging to the Royal British Legion, 1947–2009

Sources: Beveridge 1949; *Social Trends* (various years); *NCVO Almanac*, 2010; Royal British Legion website, www.britishlegion.org.uk/about-us/what-we-do.

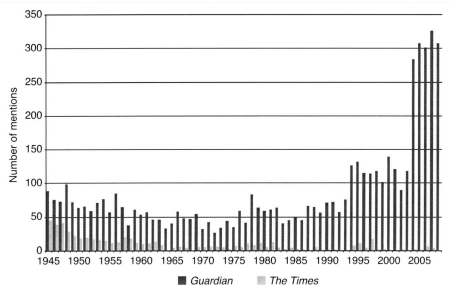

Figure 4.131: **Number of mentions of the Royal British Legion in the *Guardian* and *The Times*, 1945–2007**

Source: *Guardian* & *The Times*.

Further reading

Niall Barr, *The Lion and the Poppy: British Veterans, Politics and Society, 1921–39* (Westport, CT, 2005); Richard Humble, *The Legion: The Official History of the Royal British Legion, 1921–96* (London, 1996); Brian Harding, *Keeping Faith: The History of the Royal British Legion* (London, 2001); Graham Wooton, *The Official History of the British Legion* (London, 1956); Graham Wooton, *The Politics of Influence: British Ex-Servicemen, Cabinet Decisions and Cultural Change, 1917–57* (London, 1963, reprinted 1998).

Royal Institute of International Affairs (previously the British Institute for International Affairs, 1920–26), commonly known as Chatham House

The founders of the British Institute for International Affairs (BIIA) were disillusioned at the re-emergence of old-style diplomacy at the Versailles settlements. Its Charter was 'to advance the sciences of international politics, economics and jurisprudence, and the study, classification and development of the literature of these subjects'. The idealism was to prove unfounded. But the ability to bring together in partnership the politicians, diplomats, academics and journalists for frequent confidential discussion (the so-called Chatham House rule of confidentiality, created in 1927) and collaborative study was an innovation. Membership grew from 714 in 1922 to 1,707 in 1929. Chatham House was acquired in 1923. Its collaborations promoted a sense of understanding between the professionals and the academic communities, and it was seen in some quarters as a 'rival civil service'. The library, press library and study groups were well established by the 1930s, and senior political figures were not afraid to propose topics for study.

When granted a Royal Charter in 1926, 'British' was dropped from the organisational title and replaced with 'Royal'. The RIIA asserted its independence, but links with the Foreign Office were strong. There were only a few documented occasions that Whitehall sought to interfere in the RIIA's activities: in 1938 trying to delay publication of Wiskeman's book on the Czechs and Germans, and in 1978 when officials objected to Smart's *Beyond Polaris*. The Foreign Office's corporate membership means Diplomatic Service members can attend meetings, and it also funds research programmes.

Its research is disseminated through the books and the journals *International Affairs* (1922–) and *The World Today* (1945–). Some critics felt that its historic emphasis towards the Commonwealth, meant it failed to adequately address issues such as American foreign policy, international law and Latin America until the 1990s. 'Eclectic' is how some have described its range of publication topics.

Under the leadership of Lord Tugendhat, a series of large conferences addressed by leading figures as diverse as the Prince of Wales, John Major and Henry Kissinger went some way to restoring its reputation. Critics, including RIIA insiders, felt their integrity was sometimes compromised, as with their inability to influence the list of speakers for John Major's EC Presidency Conference which was hosted in their name in 1992.

After 1945, not only did it face a rival from the Foreign Office's research department but it also faced opposition from new pace-maker institutions that were often more specialised, such as the International Institute for Strategic Studies (IISS). But also more established organisations made themselves relevant, such as the Royal United Services Institute for Defence Studies (RUSI). During the 1990s, financial cuts, not least to its library and press cuttings department, and its links with America seriously undermined its reputation for original authoritative works. It was suggested that it spread itself too thinly when rival think tanks were developing strong research teams on the key urgent complex challenges. Some in Whitehall thought it had become detached from policy and too interested in academia. Consequently, it has sometimes been marginalised at critical periods in international affairs and unable to compete effectively with other organisations with strong connections in Washington.

Box 4.18: *The Times'* **reaction to the British Institute of International Affairs' inaugural meeting**

'We therefore welcome the Institute as likely to be a useful educational agency, and as coming at a time when there never was more needed a corrective to the intolerance and exacting claims of nationalities. It is a paradox of our times that, with the ever increasing facilities of intercourse between nations and their closer interdependence, social and economical, rivalries, jealousies, and disintegrating influences were rarely rifer and stronger than today.'

The Times, 5 July 1920 p. 15.

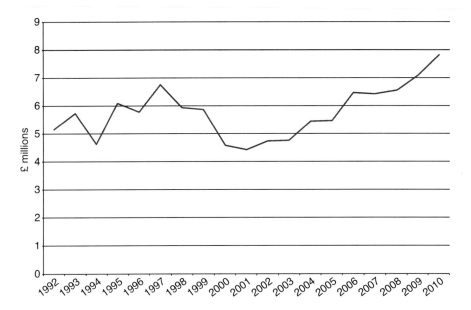

Figure 4.132: Income of Chatham House, 1992–2010 (adjusted for inflation, 2009)

Sources: Top 3000 Charities; Charity Commission.

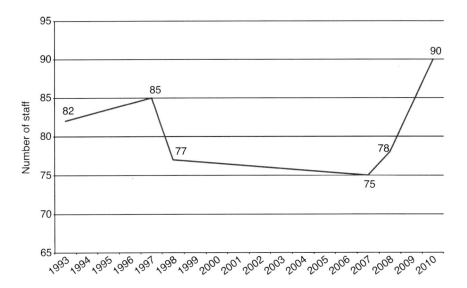

Figure 4.133: Number of staff working for Chatham House, 1993–2010

Sources: Top 3000 Charities; Charity Commission.

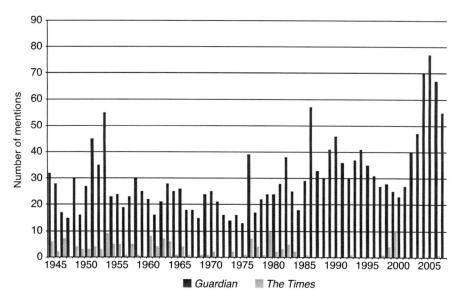

Figure 4.134: Number of mentions of Chatham House in the *Guardian* and *The Times*, 1945–2007

Source: *Guardian* & *The Times*.

Further reading

John Dickie, *The New Mandarins: How British Foreign Policy Works* (London, 2007); Richard Higgott and Diane Stone, 'The Limits of Influence: Foreign Policy Think Tanks in Britain and the USA', *Review of International Studies*, 20:1 (1994), pp. 15–34; Stephen King Hall, *Chatham House: A Brief Account of the Origin, Purpose and Methods of the RIIA* (Oxford, 1937); Laurence Martin, 'Chatham House at 75: The Past and the Future', *International Affairs*, 71:4 (1995), pp. 697–703; Inderjeet Parmar, 'Anglo-American Elites in the Interwar Years: Idealism and Power in the Intellectual Roots of Chatham House and the Council on Foreign Relations', *International Relations* , (2002) 16:1, pp. 53–75.

Royal National Institute of Blind People

The Royal National Institute of Blind People (RNIB) is the UK's leading sight-loss charity. The organisation was formed by Thomas Rhodes Armitage in 1868. Armitage was an affluent Christian and medical practitioner when his sight began to fail in his mid-thirties. Abandoning his vocation in order to protect what sight remained, Armitage dedicated himself to improving the poor social provision for blind people. In particular, he sought ways to enhance education as a route to employability and self-sufficiency.

From the outset, the RNIB was characterised by this concern with blind and partially-sighted people taking control of their own lives. Armitage recruited a small committee composed of blind men, and spent two years investigating the various systems of embossed type that existed at that time, painstakingly consulting with blind people who used these systems. The guiding principle of the committee's work was that the suitability of services for blind people should be determined by blind people themselves. Louis Braille's system was finally decided upon, owing to it enabling blind people to write as well as read, and the society devoted itself to the promotion of Braille.

As Braille grew in popularity, the RNIB expanded its work into education and training more generally. In 1915 it absorbed the National Institution for Massage by the Blind, work which continues to this day. Subsequently, training in telephony, secretarial work and, later, computer programming was developed.

Alongside its work in education and training, the RNIB has developed a broad range of support and services for blind people. These include social support, a helpline and research facilities, and perhaps most famously the Talking Books service. Launched in 1935, the service merged in 2007 with the National Library for the Blind to form the RNIB National Library Service.

Box 4.19: What's in a name?

The organisation has been known by a variety of names. Formed as the British and Foreign Society for Improving Embossed Literature for the Blind, it subsequently became the British and Foreign Blind Association, the National Institute for the Blind (1914), and later, the Royal National Institute for the Blind (1953). Subsequent changes, to the Royal National Institute of the Blind (2002) and the Royal National Institute of Blind People (2007) may appear subtle, but indicate an ongoing commitment to inclusion and self-determination, and particularly moves in the 2000s to enhance the organisation's representative legitimacy by reforming it from a group *for* blind people, into a group *of* blind people.

Key dates

1868   RNIB first formed
1918   First schools open
1935   Talking Books service begins
1940   First rehabilitation centre opened by Captain Sir Beachcroft Towse
1962   National Eye Donor scheme begins
1997   RNIB helpline launched

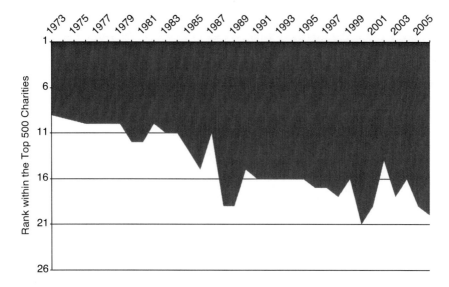

Figure 4.135: The RNIB's charitable ranking by voluntary income, 1973–2006

Source: Charity Statistics.

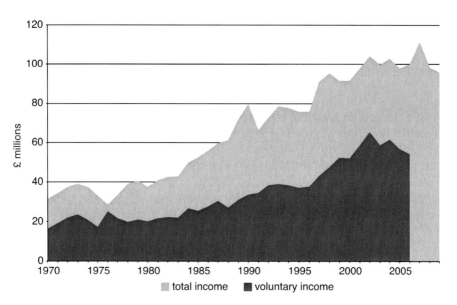

Figure 4.136: Total and voluntary income of the RNIB, 1970–2009 (adjusted for inflation, 2009)

Note: Voluntary income data after 2006 are missing.

Sources: Wolfenden 1978; Wells Collection; Charity Statistics; Charity Commission.

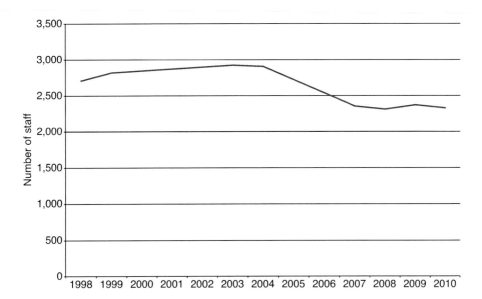

Figure 4.137: Number of staff working for the RNIB, 1998–2010

Sources: Top 3000 Charities; Charity Commission.

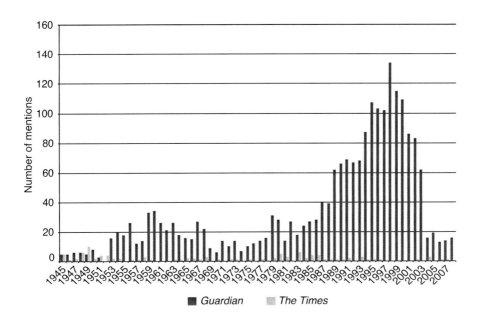

Figure 4.138: Number of mentions of the RNIB in the *Guardian* and *The Times*, 1945–2007

Source: *Guardian* & *The Times*.

Further reading

www.rnib.org.uk/aboutus/Pages/about_us.aspx
Darren Halpin, *Groups, Representation and Democracy: Between Promise and Practice* (Manchester, 2010).

Royal National Lifeboat Institution

The Royal National Lifeboat Institution (RNLI) is one of Britain's largest and most high-profile charities, responsible for the rescue of seafarers and welfare of sea-users. It maintains 235 lifeboat stations around Britain, Ireland and the Channel Islands as well as providing, since 2001, beach lifeguards at 140 locations. It rescues around 6,000 people annually.

Formed by Sir William Hillary as the National Institute for the Preservation of Life from Shipwreck on 4 March 1824, it quickly secured royal patronage, a relationship which continues – Queen Elizabeth II opened their new Poole headquarters in 2004. Since inception it has saved over 140,000 lives. It is an archetypal voluntary organisation relying both on voluntary labour and on voluntary donations. As of 2009 it had 7,500 operational volunteers and 35,000 helpers. In addition, there is a paid staff of 1,400. Its lifeboat crews have close local community ties often with generational links – which means that tragedies when they occur are profoundly felt (for example, Penlee in 1981 when eight crew members were lost, and Fraserburgh in 1918, 1953 and 1970). Around 20 per cent of volunteer crews have a nautical background, and since the 1960s women have been recruited. The only full-time member of the crew is usually the boat mechanic. The physical demands of crewing mean that the retirement age for members of inshore boats is 45, and all-weather offshore, 55.

The RNLI plays strongly on its voluntary ethos and the 'nobility of the cause'. From the outset bravery awards have played an important part of the organisation's history. Gallantry medals of bronze, silver and gold are awarded. All of this contributes to the high visibility of the organisation amongst the public. One 'trust' survey from 2010 ranked it as the most reputable charity in Britain, ahead of the RSPCA and British Red Cross (ICSA survey). This is important because as an organisation it consistently derives two-thirds of its income from legacies. In 2009 it secured 590 legacies under £500. It pioneered street collections, the first of which was held in Manchester in October 1891 to raise funds for the RNLI families of the *Mexico* disaster off the Lancashire coast. It also has 118 charity shops, manned by 1180 volunteers, whilst another revenue stream has been its dedicated credit card, launched in 1988.

Some critics complain that the RNLI's high profile means the public ignore the other independent rescue organisations that are located around the country, but which are as much a part of the network likely to be called upon by the coastguard. The RNLI does incur substantial operational costs and is at the forefront of research and development into lifeboat and sea-safety technology, and is aware of its reliance on legacy funding – this means that it invests on the stock market, but this is not without danger – as in 2000 when its £11 million investment saw a 20 per cent fall.

Key dates

1854 Royal National Lifeboat Institution name is adopted
1854 Cork lifejacket is invented by RNLI inspector Captain Ward
1886 27 RNLI crew lost in rescue of the *Mexico* off Lancashire coast
1907 456 rescued from liner *Suevic* off Cornish coast
1970 Beaufort lifejacket adopted
2001 First inland waterway lifeboat station opened, Enniskillen
2002 Four lifeboat stations opened on River Thames
2003 Rod MacDonald becomes first lifeguard to receive a gallantry medal (Bronze)
2005 Aileen Jones becomes first female crew member to win a medal (Bronze) for *Gower Bride* rescue

Key figures

Grace Darling (1815–1842): lighthouse keeper's daughter who, as a 22-year-old, took part in the 1838 rescue of *Forfarshire* and became the first female medallist, despite not being an RNLI crew member

Henry Blogg (1876–1954): lifeboatman, Cromer; gold medal winner three times, and silver medal winner four times

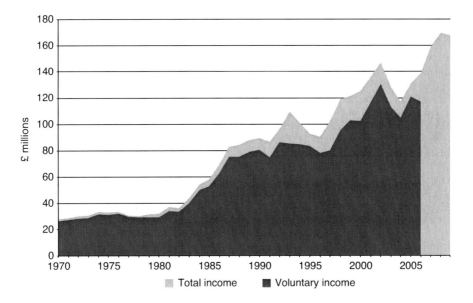

Figure 4.139: Total and voluntary income of the RNLI, 1970–2009 (adjusted for inflation, 2009)

Note: Figures for voluntary income after 2006 were not available.

Sources: Wolfenden 1978; Wells Collection; Charity Statistics; Charity Commission.

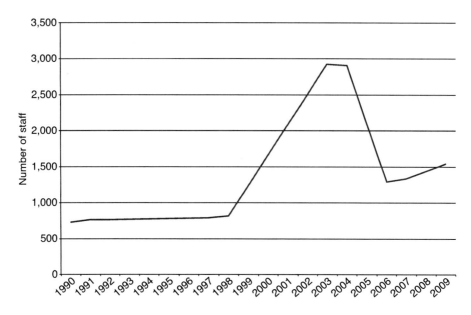

Figure 4.140: Number of staff working for the RNLI, 1990–2009

Sources: Top 3000 Charities; Charity Commission.

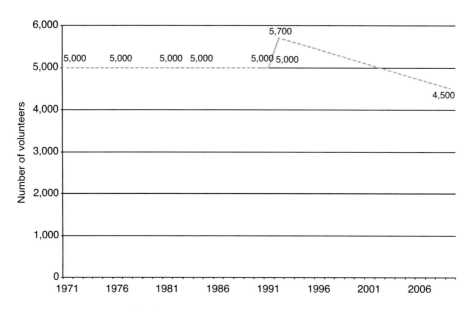

Figure 4.141: Number of volunteers working for the RNLI, 1971–2009

Source: *Social Trends* (various years).

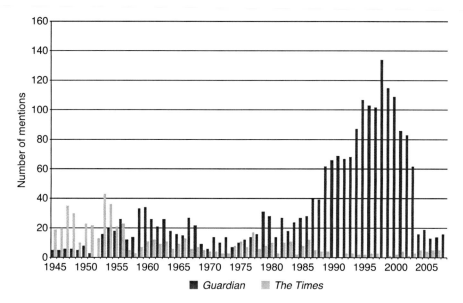

Figure 4.142: Number of mentions of the RNLI in the *Guardian* and *The Times*, 1945–2007

Source: *Guardian* & *The Times*.

Further reading

Ray Kipling and Suzannah Kipling, *Never Turn Back: The RNLI since the Second World War* (Stroud, 2006).

Royal Society for the Prevention of Cruelty to Animals

The Royal Society for the Prevention of Cruelty to Animals (RSPCA) is the UK's leading animal protection charity, with an annual income in excess of £120 million.

The organisation was formed in 1824 as the Society for the Prevention of Cruelty to Animals, gaining its 'Royal' prefix in 1840 following patronage from Queen Victoria. Pioneering in its time, the Society was founded at the beginning of a long period of concern for animal welfare: two years previously had come the groundbreaking Martin's Act, outlawing cruel treatment of cattle, and the Society was quickly followed by the formation of the Animal Friends' Society and the Rational Humanity Group.

The Society's studied moderation has been a constant source of controversy and tension within the wider animal protection movement, and it has faced repeated attempts at conversion towards a rights-based approach, away from the Society's longstanding welfarism. It frustrated the anti-vivisection groups which emerged in the nineteenth century, so much so that during the early twentieth century the leader of the National Anti-Vivisection Society, Stephen Coleridge, attempted unsuccessfully to infiltrate the Society. Entryist tactics were revived with the growing popularity of the animal rights paradigm from the 1960s, led by Richard Ryder, who became chair of the Society's council in 1977. Although the attempt to turn the Society into a rights-based group ultimately failed, stances on issues such as hunting and factory farming were notably strengthened, as was the group's campaigning work.

Despite this, the Society is not primarily a campaigning organisation. Through a broad network of local branches, the organisation provides a wide range of services including subsidised veterinary treatment, advice, and animal rehoming. Its inspectors and animal welfare officers also seek to enforce the law around animal protection, both through preventing and prosecuting abuse – a function that harks back to the founding motive of the organisation, seeking to ensure that protective legislation was properly enforced. Within this continuity however, the focus of the Society's work has evolved with broader changes in the relationship between humans and domesticated animals. Pit ponies, and work to protect animals used in fashion and entertainment, have become less relevant with the passage of time, while modern farming and growing pet ownership have created new sources of work.

Unlike many of its peers in the animal protection and environmental sector, the RSPCA is not heavily reliant upon membership subscription; rather, legacies and donations form the great majority of its income.

Key animal protection legislation

1822   Martin's Act, forbidding cruel treatment of cattle
1835   Pease's Act, extending protection to domestic animals, and outlawing some blood sports
1911   Protection of Animals Act extends protection afforded to domestic and captive animals
1986   Animals (Scientific Procedures) Act requires Home Office licensing of scientists working with laboratory animals
2004   Hunting Act outlaws hare coursing and strictly regulates hunting with hounds
2006   Animal Welfare Act updates the 1911 legislation and imposes a duty of care on pet owners

---

Box 4.20: RSPCA centenary poem

Extract from Thomas Hardy's 'Compassion: An Ode in Celebration of the Centenary of the Royal Society for the Prevention of Cruelty to Animals', January 1924:

> Cries still are heard in secret nooks,
> Till hushed with gag or slit or thud;
> And hideous dens whereon none looks
> Are blotched with needless blood.
> But here, in battlings, patient, slow,
> Much has been won – more, maybe than we know –
> And on we labour stressful. 'Ailinon!'
> A mighty voice calls: 'But may the good prevail!'
> And 'Blessed are the merciful!'
> Calls yet a mightier one.

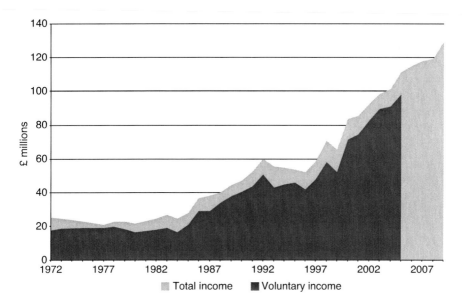

Figure 4.143: Total and voluntary income of the RSPCA, 1972–2009 (adjusted for inflation, 2009)

Note: Data on voluntary income were unavailable after 2005. The data do not include RSPCA Scotland and Northern Ireland.

Sources: Wells Collection; Charity Statistics; Charity Commission.

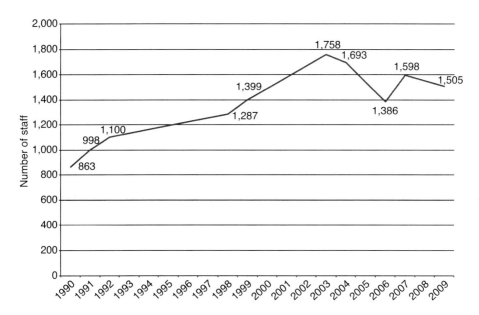

Figure 4.144: Number of staff working for the RSPCA, 1990–2009

Source: Top 3000 Charities.

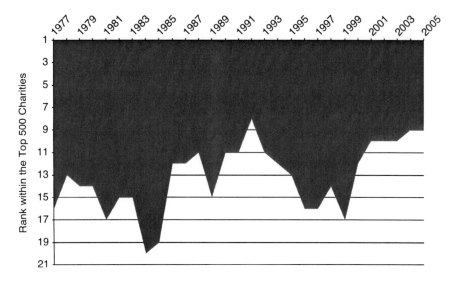

Figure 4.145: The RSPCA's charitable ranking by voluntary income, 1977–2005

Source: Charity Statistics.

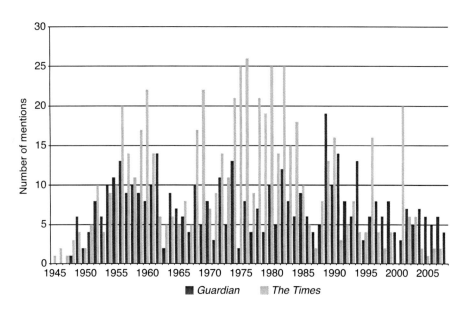

Figure 4.146: Number of mentions of the RSPCA in the *Guardian* and *The Times*, 1945–2007

Source: *Guardian* & *The Times*.

Further reading

Anthony Brown, *Who Cares for Animals? 150 Years of the RSPCA* (London, 1974); Robert Garner, *Political Animals: Animal Protection Politics in Britain and the United States* (London, 1998); Hilda Kean, *Animal Rights: Political and Social Change in Britain since 1800* (London, 1998); Arthur W. Moss and Royal Society for the Prevention of Cruelty to Animals, *Valiant Crusade: The History of the RSPCA* (London, 1961).

Royal Society for the Protection of Birds

The Royal Society for the Protection of Birds (RSPB) is Europe's largest wildlife conservation charity.

The organisation was founded in Didsbury, Manchester, in response to the near extinction of the Great Crested Grebe and other birds, notably egrets, due to trade in their feathers for use in millinery. Other groups with a similar focus quickly joined, giving the organisation national scope.

Established in 1889, the RSPB is often seen as one of the 'Big Three' conservation groups, the others being its near contemporaries the National Trust (1895) and the Society for the Promotion of Nature Reserves (now the Royal Society of Wildlife Trusts) (1912). Like these groups, the RSPB was distinguished by the affluence and prominence of its initial supporters: the Duchess of Portland became president in 1891 (remaining in post until her death in 1954), while the Society gained royal patronage in 1904, just 15 years after being established.

The original campaign focus on the plumage trade was remarkably successful, with legislation introduced during the interwar period, notably the 1921 Importation of Plumage (Prohibition) Act. The Society thereafter diversified its interests, with the dangers posed by oil pollution receiving particular attention. In 1931, for example, the Society successfully prosecuted an oil company for a spill near Stockholm. Pollution threats also became a more general priority, such as those posed by agricultural pesticides. The banning of lead shot in England in 1999 is demonstrative of the ongoing relevance of these concerns.

The Society has been consistently innovative in its approach to campaigning, fund raising and conservation work. In 1898 it launched its line of Christmas cards, selling 4,500, while nesting boxes were sold from 1906. The Society made its first film in 1950, and established a film unit in 1952, five years prior to the BBC setting up its own natural history unit. Membership groups were introduced in 1969, the first being in Epping Forest. The Society is also a major landholder, with an extensive network of nature reserves. The first, in Romney Marsh, was acquired in 1930. The 100th reserve, at Wood of Cree, came in 1984, while the 200th reserve came in 2007 with the acquisition of Sutton Fen.

Perhaps its most distinctive contribution to public awareness, however, has been the Big Garden Bird Watch, originally launched in 1979. The event harnesses the labour and expertise of volunteers across the country to provide an annual snapshot of the British wild bird population. In 2011, 600,000 people took part, recording the details of more than 10 million birds.

The Society is today one of Britain's leading membership organisations. Although it would be 70 years before it gained 10,000 members, from then on growth was vertiginous. With membership standing at 925,000 in 1996, the Million Member Campaign was launched, achieving its goal the following year.

Since 1993, the RSPB has been a partner of BirdLife International, the global conservation network. Together, the two organisations successfully lobbied for an EU-wide ban on the import of wild birds, introduced in 2007.

Key legislation

1921   Importation of Plumage (Prohibition) Act
1933   Protection of Birds Act
1954   Protection of Birds Act
1981   Wildlife and Countryside Act
2007   EU ban on import of wild birds

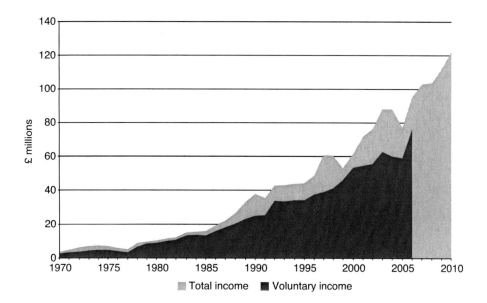

Figure 4.147: Voluntary and total income of the RSPB, 1970–2010 (adjusted for inflation, 2009)

Sources: Annual reports and accounts, RSPB; Wolfenden 1978; Wells Collection; Charity Statistics; Charity Commission.

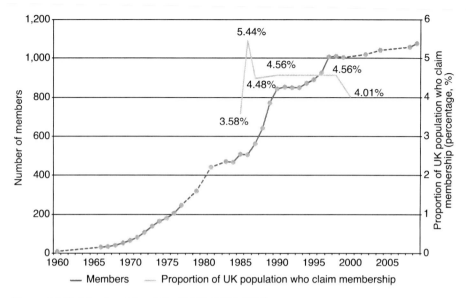

Figure 4.148: Membership of the RSPB, 1960–2009

Sources: (a) For the number of members/supporters: RSPB website; Annual reports and accounts, RSPB; *Social Trends*; Francis Sandbach, *Environment, Ideology and Policy* (Oxford, 1980); Paul Byrne, *Social Movements in Britain* (London ; New York, 1997); Peter Rawcliffe, *Environmental Pressure Groups in Transition* (Manchester, 1998). (b) For the percentage of people answering positively to the question: 'Are you currently a member of any of these? Yes: RSPB', British Social Attitudes Survey (data accessed through www.britsocat.com).

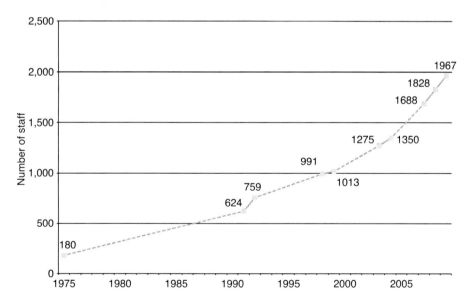

Figure 4.149: Number of staff working for the RSPB, 1975–2009

Sources: Guardian Directory of Pressure Groups; Top 3000 Charities; Charity Commission.

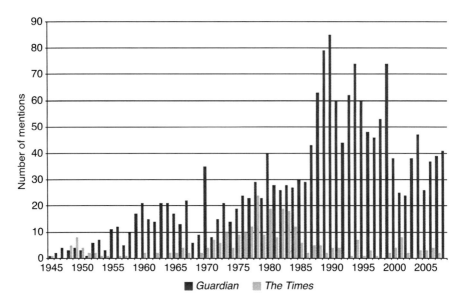

Figure 4.150: Numbers of mentions of the RSPB in the *Guardian* and *The Times*, 1945–2007

Source: *Guardian* & *The Times*.

Further reading

www.rspb.org.uk
David Evans, *A History of Nature Conservation in Britain*, 2nd edn (London, 1997).

Runnymede Trust

Amidst a context of rising racial tension, sparked especially by Enoch Powell's 'rivers of blood' speech, the Runnymede Trust was set up in 1968 by the journalist and former intelligence officer, Jim Rose, and the then Labour MP, Anthony Lester. Other initial supporters included academics associated with race relations, Nicholas Deakin and Dipak Nandy, as well the Liberal politician and chair of the Race Relations Board, Mark Bonham Carter. The suggestion for the name came from Phillip Mason of the Institute for Race Relations and referred to the field in which the Magna Carta was signed, implying that all citizens are equal.

Distinguishing itself from other organisations focused on race, the Trust deliberately set out to be a think tank, receiving funding from the Joseph Rowntree Charitable Trust and the New World Foundation in New York. Modelling itself on the American Anti-Defamation League, which tackles anti-semitism, the Trust has worked to combat racism and discrimination targeted at all minority groups in the UK.

As with other think tanks, the Runnymede Trust works by providing briefs and background papers for politicians, journalists and civil servants. It has published its *Bulletin* since 1969 and has sought to respond quickly to public issues. One of its first publications was entitled *Colour and Citizenship* and was a rebuttal to the popular anti-immigration policies associated with Powell.

In later decades, it has worked more closely with governments to interpret policy to a wider audience and to advise on a more regular basis. In the early 1990s it organised an influential commission on anti-semitism, followed by one on anti-Muslim sentiments, which was launched by the then Home Secretary, Jack Straw, in 1997.

It has operated with a small staff but has attempted to marshal some of the key intellectual figures associated with race. Its patrons include the cultural theorist Stuart Hall and the political philosopher, Lord Bhikhu Parekh. The latter chaired one of the Trust's most famous commissions, that on *The Future of Multi-Ethnic Britain*, which was set up in 1997 and published its findings in 2000. It was to be a major influence on the racial policies of the Labour government.

Key publications

Colour and Citizenship (1969)
A Very Light Sleeper: The Persistence and Dangers of Anti-Semitism (1994)
Islamaphobia: A Challenge for Us All (1997)
The Future of Multi-Ethnic Britain: The Parekh Report (2000)

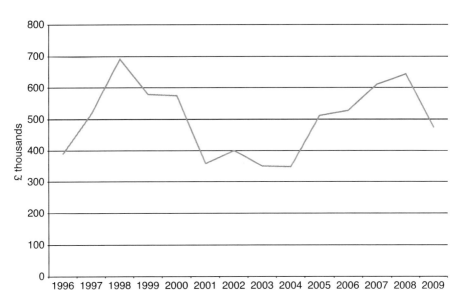

Figure 4.151: Income of the Runnymede Trust, 1996–2009 (adjusted for inflation, 2009)

Sources: Annual reports and accounts, Runnymede Trust; Charity Commission.

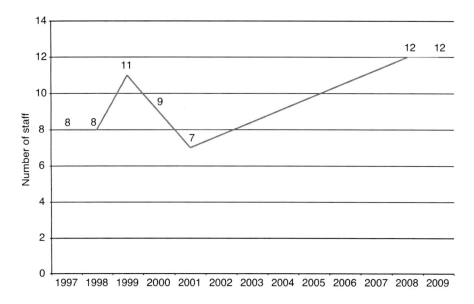

Figure 4.152: Number of staff working for the Runnymede Trust, 1997–2009

Sources: Annual reports and accounts, Runnymede Trust; Charity Commission.

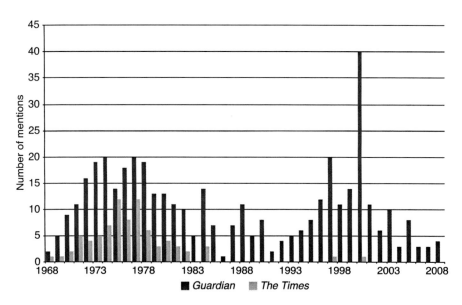

Figure 4.153: Number of mentions of the Runnymede Trust in the *Guardian* and *The Times*, 1968–2008

Source: *Guardian* & *The Times*.

Further reading

Anthony Lester, 'Nailing the Lie and Promoting Equality', Jim Rose lecture, 15 October 2003, available from: www.runnymedetrust.org/uploads/events/aLesterSpeech.pdf; Peter Barberis, John McHugh and Mike Tyldesley, *Encyclopedia of British and Irish Political Organizations* (London, 1999).

Save the Children

Save the Children emerged out of the Fight the Famine Council which had been set up in the First World War to protest against the Allied blockade of Germany. In 1919, two sisters, Eglantyne Jebb and Dorothy Buxton, created the organisation to send aid and assistance to children starving partly because of the blockade. From the start, this was an international response, an equivalent organisation (Rädda Barnen) being set up in Sweden at the same time. In 1920, an International Save the Children Union was established in Geneva, to be followed in 1977 with the International Save the Children Alliance, an organisation now based in London but representing 28 national Save the Children organisations.

Straight after its formation, it undertook to provide emergency relief during the Greco-Turkish War (1919–22) and the Russian famine of 1921. In the 1930s it suffered a fall in its income, though it began to work beyond Europe, opening a nursery school in Addis Ababa in 1936. Its fortunes revived in the 1940s and it worked with many other humanitarian agencies to deal with the wartime refugee crisis. Post-1945 it has developed into one of the largest aid and development NGOs in the UK and has followed many of the same trends. It has been involved in all the key emergency incidents, has collaborated with other NGOs through the Disasters Emergency Committee (DEC) and has transformed itself into an organisation that caters to long-term development projects as much as emergency relief. Today it draws on an annual income of over £200 million and a paid staff of over 5,000.

What distinguishes Save the Children as a development NGO is its focus on rights. Jebb committed the organisation to the protection of children's rights, and she played a key role in drafting the Declaration of the Rights of the Child

---

Box 4.21: Declaration of the Rights of the Child, 1924

1. The child must be given the means requisite for its normal development, both materially and spiritually;
2. The child that is hungry must be fed; the child that is sick must be nursed; the child that is backward must be helped; the delinquent child must be reclaimed; and the orphan and the waif must be sheltered and succoured;
3. The child must be the first to receive relief in times of distress;
4. The child must be put in a position to earn a livelihood, and must be protected against every form of exploitation;
5. The child must be brought up in the consciousness that its talents must be devoted to the service of fellow men.

that was passed by the League of Nations in 1924. The worsening international situation in the 1930s made the organisation aware that there was still a need for a convention on the treatment of children in wartime, but the outbreak of hostilities prevented this. Persistent campaigning in the post-war period, together with a growing ascendancy of rights talk for specific groups such as women and minorities, eventually led to the passing of the UN Convention on the Rights of the Child in 1989. As other NGOs have come to adopt a rights-based approach, Save the Children is now firmly located in the mainstream of development work, acting as a critical NGO but also engaging in contract work with official agencies.

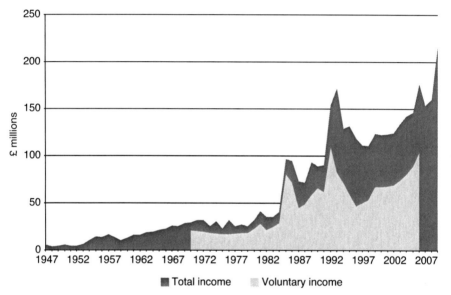

Figure 4.154: Voluntary and total income of Save the Children, 1947–2008 (adjusted for inflation, 2009)

Sources: Annual reports and accounts, Save the Children; Charity Statistics; Charity Commission.

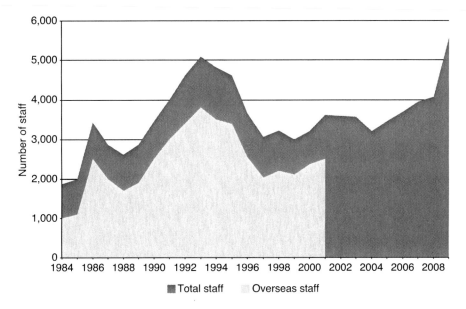

Figure 4.155: Number of staff working for Save the Children, 1984–2009

Sources: Annual reports and accounts, Save the Children; Charity Statistics; Charity Commission; Top 3000 Charities.

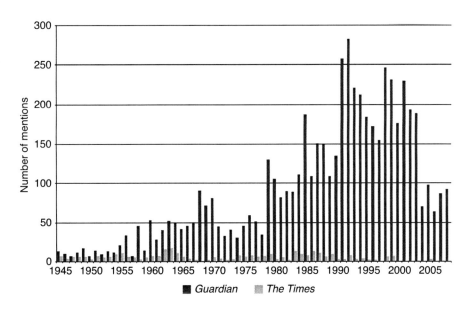

Figure 4.156: Number of mentions of Save the Children in the *Guardian* and *The Times*, 1945–2007

Source: *Guardian* & *The Times*.

Further reading

Clare Saunders, 'British Humanitarian, Aid and Development NGOs, 1949–Present', in Nick Crowson, Matthew Hilton and James McKay (eds), *NGOs in Contemporary Britain: Non-State Actors in Society and Politics since 1945* (Basingstoke, 2009), pp. 38–58; Matthew Hilton, 'International Aid and Development NGOs in Britain and Human Rights since 1945', *Humanity*, forthcoming 2013.

Shelter

Shelter was formed by a coalition of voluntary homeless groups (the National Federation of Housing Societies, British Churches Housing Trust, Christian Aid, the Catholic Housing Aid Society and the Notting Hill Housing Trust) that realised coordinated fundraising would serve them better. Launched from the crypt of St Martin-in-the-Fields in December 1966 and benefiting from the controversy around the play *Cathy Come Home,* Shelter succeeded in making homelessness a major socio-political issue.

Shelter's objective was to relieve hardship and distress amongst the homeless and those in need who were living in adverse housing conditions. Initially it raised funds to support housing associations and other bodies involved in charitable relief of the homeless. In 1968 Des Wilson lost patience with the housing association movement and Shelter began supporting its own aid projects. After 1972 it began a conscious effort to influence housing policy. The redirection was due to a realisation that many of the claims it was making about actual success and impact were being undermined by independent research which showed that homelessness was increasing. This signalled the end of its Christian charitable intents and instead it had become a housing pressure group commenting on all aspects of housing policy.

Shelter joined the Joint Charities Group in 1974 that succeeded in introducing the 1977 Housing (Homeless Persons) Act. This provided a statutory definition of homelessness. Although significant elements of this legislation were unsatisfactory in Shelter's mind, it provided the basis for all homelessness legislation until the 2002 Homelessness Act.

Through the 1980s and 1990s Shelter campaigned via research publications, a parliamentary lobby, and offered advice and housing aid, although it was unpopular with government. Homelessness re-emerged as an issue in the 1990s with the concern about sleeping rough. Shelter saw its influence grow in legislative and policy terms, as with the Rough Sleepers Programme (1990–) and the Foyers (1992–) programme.

Since 1997, Shelter's annual reports have trumpeted the successes that it has had in lobbying government, reducing the numbers sleeping rough and the impact that it has had on legislation. Longer-term things might not be so good: in 1966, the year Shelter formed, the government built 180,000 social rented properties. In 2006 it managed to build only 28,000, and sold off a further 38,000 under the 'right to buy' scheme. And regardless of how homelessness is defined, the numbers have continued to increase. Nevertheless, by 2009, at the end of Adam Sampson's directorship, Shelter felt it had 'propel[led] housing from the periphery to the centre of UK politics'.

> **Box 4.22: The Shelter story**
>
> 'Three years have passed since a small number of men already involved in the voluntary housing movement met to establish Shelter – a National Campaign for the Homeless. They were united in certain convictions. First, they were convinced that the tragedy of Britain's homeless deserved far more urgent action than it seemed likely to get. Second, they believed that large sums of money had to be raised in order that volunteers could make an immediate and direct impact on the needs of homeless families. Third, they believe that fundraising could be an effective way of convincing a lot more people, and especially young people, not only that the problem of the homeless was urgent but that there were effective ways of alleviating the misery it brought.'
>
> Lewis E. Waddilove, Chairman of Trustees, *The Shelter Story* (London, 1970).

Key figures

Rev. Bruce Kenrick: founder
Des Wilson: director, 1967–70
John Willis: director, 1971–72
Geoffrey Martin: director, 1973
Douglas Tilbe: director, 1974–77
Neil McIntosh: director, 1976–84
Shelia McKechnie: director, 1985–94
Chris Holmes: director, 1995–2002
Adam Sampson: director, 2003–09
Campbell Robb: chief executive, 2010–

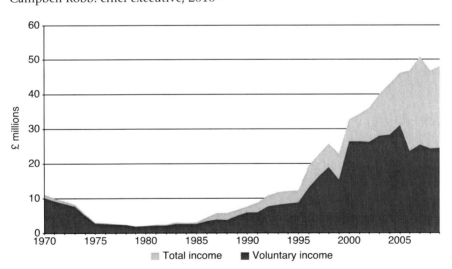

Figure 4.157: Total and voluntary income of Shelter, 1970–2009 (adjusted for inflation, 2009)

Sources: Wolfenden 1979; Wells Collection; Annual reports and accounts, Shelter; Charity Statistics; Charity Commission.

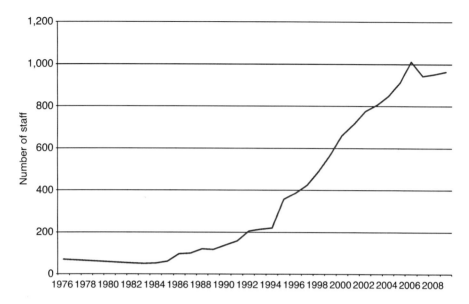

Figure 4.158: Number of staff working for Shelter, 1976–2009

Sources: Guardian Directory of Pressure Groups; Annual reports and accounts, Shelter.

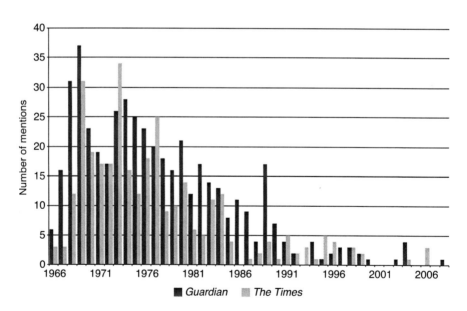

Figure 4.159: Number of mentions of Shelter in the *Guardian* and *The Times*, 1966–2007

Note: A search in the *Guardian* with the keyword 'Shelter' was impossible as it brought too many irrelevant results, so the search was conducted instead using the phrase 'National Campaign for the Homeless'.

Sources: *Guardian* & *The Times*.

Further reading

Patrick Seyd, 'Shelter: The National Campaign for the Homeless', *Political Quarterly*, 46:4 (1975), pp. 418–31; Shelter, *The Shelter Story* (London, 1970).

Soil Association

The Soil Association exists to promote and accredit organic agriculture, through a blend of campaigning, community programmes, educational work and inspection.

The Association was formed in 1946 by Lady Eve Balfour and others, following on from the success of Balfour's book *The Living Soil* (see Boxes 4.23 and 4.24). Positioning itself against the rapid development of intensive agriculture (a trend confirmed by the 1947 Agriculture Act), the Association had four main concerns: soil erosion and depletion; declining nutritional content; the treatment of animals in intensive systems; and the impact of intensive farming on the wider countryside.

Based at Balfour's Suffolk farm, the Association's original focus was research, following on from its founder's own extensive experimentation. Standards and frameworks for organic produce were initially developed in the 1960s, and accreditation began in the 1970s. Today, the Association accredits around 80 per cent of British organic produce. Its standards prohibit the use of artificial chemical fertilisers and genetically modified crops, as well as closely restricting pesticide and drug use, and laying down strict conditions for the treatment of animals.

In the late 1990s, the Association began a period of extraordinary growth, fuelled by fast-growing public interest in organic agriculture (see Figures 4.160–163). Contributory factors behind this dramatic growth include the introduction of government grants to encourage and support farmers to make the switch to organic agriculture, high-profile and adverse media coverage of the issue of genetically modified food, and a developing interest in so-called 'ethical consumerism', amid a period of more general affluence. The growth has also undoubtedly been facilitated by the increasing presence of organic produce on supermarket shelves.

Box 4.23: Lady Eve Balfour

Born in 1898 into an aristocratic family (her father was the second Earl of Balfour; her uncle, prime minister), Eve Balfour studied agriculture during the First World War. With her sister, she subsequently purchased a farm in Haughley, Suffolk, which in time became the site of her famous experiments with organic agriculture. These had developed out of her growing discontent with mainstream farming methods, and were published in 1944 as *The Living Soil*. The volume became a founding text of the organic movement, reprinted nine times. After establishing the Soil Association in 1946, Balfour remained closely involved in the organisation into her mid-eighties. She died in 1990.

Box 4.24: *The Living Soil*

'My subject is food, which concerns everyone; it is health, which concerns everyone; it is the soil, which concerns everyone – even if he does not realise it – and it is the history of certain recent scientific research linking these three vital subjects.'

From *The Living Soil* (1944).

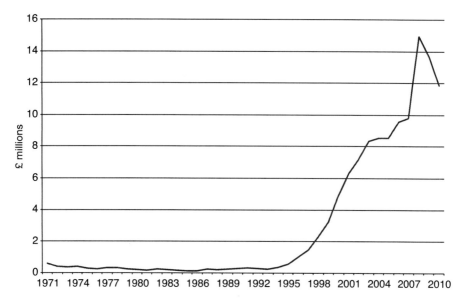

Figure 4.160: Income of the Soil Association Ltd, 1971–2009 (adjusted for inflation, 2009)

Sources: Annual reports and accounts, Soil Association; Charity Commission.

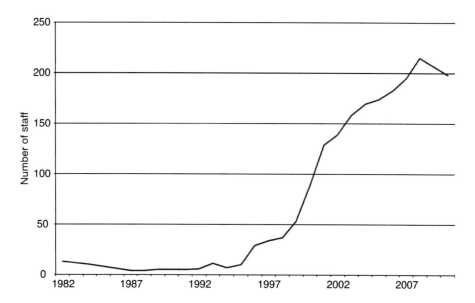

Figure 4.161: Staff working for the Soil Association Ltd, 1982–2010

Sources: Annual reports and accounts, Soil Association; Charity Commission.

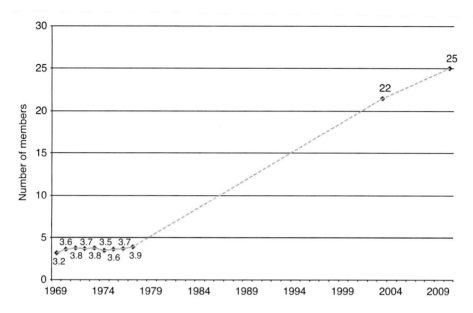

Figure 4.162: Members belonging to the Soil Association, 1969–2010

Sources: Annual reports and accounts, Soil Association; Francis Sandbach, *Environment, Ideology and Policy* (Oxford, 1980); Soil Association website.

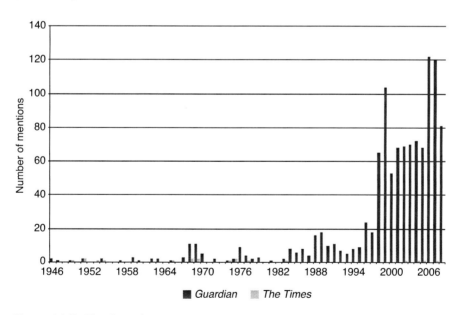

Figure 4.163: Number of mentions of the Soil Association in the *Guardian* and *The Times*, 1946–2007

Source: *Guardian* & *The Times*.

Further reading

www.soilassociation.org

Eve Balfour, *The Living Soil: Evidence of the Importance to Human Health of Soil Vitality, with Special Reference to National Planning* (London, 1944); Michael Brander, *Eve Balfour: The Founder of the Soil Association and the Voice of the Organic Movement* (Haddington, 2003); James Cornford, 'Saturated with Biological Metaphors: Professor John Macmurray (1891–1976) and the Politics of the Organic Movement', *Contemporary British History*, 22:3 (2008), pp. 317–34; John Martin, 'Balfour, Lady Evelyn Barbara (1898–1990)', in H. Matthew and B. Harrison (eds), *Oxford Dictionary of National Biography* (Oxford, 2004).

Stonewall

Stonewall is a lesbian, gay and bisexual (LGB) lobbying and campaign group, named in honour of the 1969 act of resistance in New York that launched the modern gay rights movement.

The group was formed in response to the introduction of Section 28, the notorious clause within the 1988 Local Government Act forbidding the promotion of homosexuality by local authorities in schools, or teaching in state schools that presented homosexuality 'as a pretended family relationship'. The legislation appeared in the context of heightened homophobia surrounding the HIV/AIDS epidemic. In the face of such overt discrimination, the gay community reacted strongly. Established initially by a group of figures from politics and the arts – including *Guardian* theatre critic Nicholas de Jongh, Matthew Parris, Ian McKellan, Michael Cashman and Peter Mandelson, Stonewall has become Britain's leading gay rights group. It has grown from having just one paid member of staff in 1990, to ten in 2000, to 49 in 2009.

Stonewall embodies in many ways the elite, discreet lobbying groups of the 1950s and 1960s, and has carefully pursued a policy of political non-alignment. As chief executive Ben Summerskill commented in 2010, 'Stonewall has never pretended to be a democratic member organisation. We have never said we speak for all lesbian, gay and bisexual people.' It thereby stands in contrast to more radical and participative elements within the LGB movement, such as the Gay Liberation Front (GLF) and OutRage! Yet the difference is mainly one of style, rather than being indicative of any major disagreement over the goal of equality: former GLF activists such as Lisa Power and Angela Mason have played a key role in the group's success.

Section 28 was finally repealed in the UK in 2003 (2000 in Scotland). In the intervening period, Stonewall had been closely involved in campaigning on a range of gay rights issues. During the early 1990s it successfully lobbied Prime Minister John Major to allow a free vote on the equalisation of the age of consent, resulting in the lowering of the gay age of consent from 21 to 18 in 1994, before being finally equalised with the heterosexual age of consent by the 2000 Sexual Offences (Amendment) Act. With the successful attainment of much of the legal equality agenda, consolidated by the 2010 Equality Act, the group has also diversified its work into fields such as homophobic bullying, hate crime and workplace accreditation.

Key dates

1988   Section 28 introduced (repealed 2003)
1989   Stonewall formed
1994   Gay age of consent lowered from 21 to 18
2000   Gay age of consent lowered to 16

Key figures

Angela Mason: executive director, 1992–2002
Ben Summerskill: chief executive, 2003–

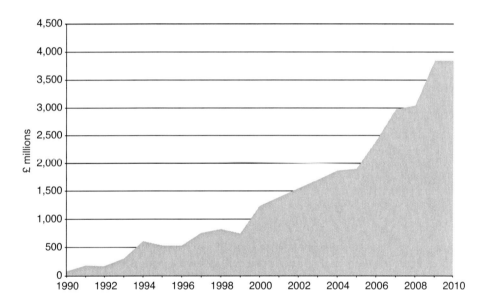

Figure 4.164: Income of Stonewall, 1990–2010 (adjusted for inflation, 2009)

Source: Annual reports and accounts, Stonewall.

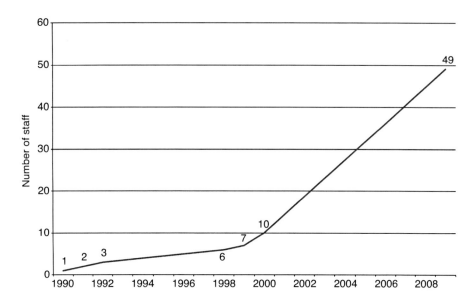

Figure 4.165: Number of staff working for Stonewall, 1990–2009

Sources: Annual reports and accounts, Stonewall; Charity Commission.

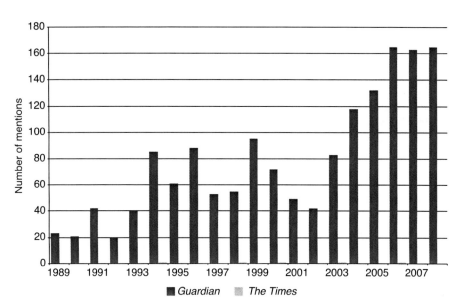

Figure 4.166: Number of mentions of Stonewall in the *Guardian* and *The Times*, 1989–2008

Source: *Guardian* & *The Times*.

Further reading

Pat Thane, *Unequal Britain: Equalities in Britain since 1945* (London, 2010); Matthew Waites, 'Lesbian, Gay and Bisexual NGOs in Britain: Past, Present and Future', in Nick Crowson, Matthew Hilton and James McKay (eds), *NGOs in Contemporary Britain: Non-State Actors in Society and Politics since 1945* (Basingstoke, 2009).

Sue Ryder

Sue Ryder Care is a leading social care charity, providing palliative and long-term care for the sick and disabled.

Born into an affluent, service-minded family in the 1920s, Sue Ryder volunteered for the First Aid Nursing Yeomanry at the outbreak of the Second World War and was rapidly moved to work with the Special Operations Executive (SOE). The extraordinary bravery and sacrifice she witnessed during the war years was what initially made her contemplate establishing some kind of 'living memorial' to commemorate their efforts. After the war, she remained in mainland Europe, working with relief agencies supporting prisoners and displaced persons unable, through age or infirmity, to resettle themselves; she continued this work alone once the relief agencies withdrew in the early 1950s, as the vision of her living memorial took shape. The Sue Ryder Foundation was registered on a return to England in 1951/52; in 1953 Ryder purchased a house in Cavendish, Suffolk, as an initial care home and headquarters. Her work became famous, and in 1955 she was invited by decorated war veteran Leonard Cheshire to visit the similar convalescent and care homes he had established. The two married in 1959, and while they continued with their separate organisations, they also formed the Ryder Cheshire Foundation for joint ventures.

Ryder's work exemplified notions of Christian voluntarism and service. Neglected properties were renovated into care homes with the help of impromptu, voluntary support; Green Shield Stamps were collected to ship a van to India; and a vast network of volunteer-run charity shops sprang up across the country in the 1960s and 1970s to support the Foundation's work. Her Christian faith gave Ryder a trust in Providence, and she always viewed herself as a fieldworker rather than an administrator: in her 1975 memoirs, she noted that 'I really dislike the word "money"'. Regardless, the organisation she founded took on a life of its own. As Ryder later recalled, 'The national press took a great interest, and later, much to my embarrassment and surprise, I was confronted by the television programme *This Is Your Life*, of which I had never heard.'

Perhaps inevitably, Ryder's dogged voluntarism eventually collided with the demands of running a large and diverse organisation. She retired as a trustee in 1998, but subsequently claimed to have been forced out, and was fiercely critical of modernisation and professionalisation measures taken by her successors. In response, Ryder established a rival organisation not long before her death: the Bouverie Foundation (now the Lady Ryder of Warsaw Memorial Trust). Today, Sue Ryder Care employs 2,000 staff, along with 6,500 volunteers in the UK, and has recently reoriented its work from the residency model to providing care in people's homes.

Key figures

Sue Ryder, 1923–2000
Leonard Cheshire, 1917–1992

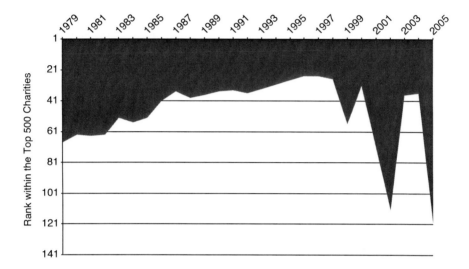

Figure 4.167: Sue Ryder Care's charitable ranking by voluntary income, 1979–2006

Source: Charity Statistics.

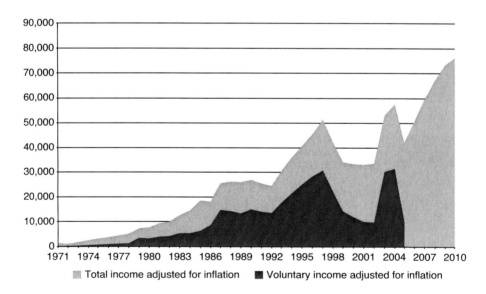

Figure 4.168: Total and voluntary income of Sue Ryder, 1971–2010 (adjusted for inflation, 2009)

Source: Annual reports and accounts, Sue Ryder; Charity Statistics; Charity Commission.

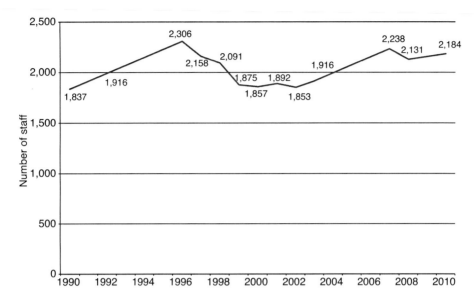

Figure 4.169: Number of staff working for Sue Ryder, 1990–2010

Sources: Top 3000 Charities; Annual reports and accounts, Sue Ryder.

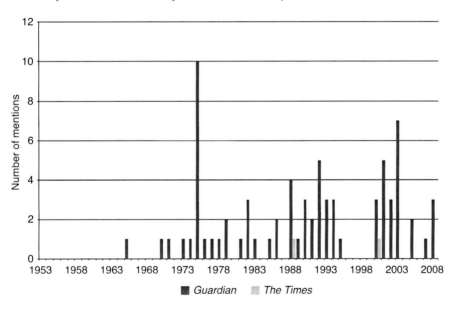

Figure 4.170: Number of mentions of Sue Ryder in the *Guardian* and *The Times*, 1965–2008

Source: *Guardian* & *The Times*.

Further reading

Sue Ryder, *And the Morrow is Theirs: The Autobiography of Sue Ryder* (Bristol, 1975); Sue Ryder, *Child of My Love* (London, 1986).

Tearfund

Tearfund is an evangelical Christian international aid and development (IAD) organisation, emerging out of Britain's Evangelical Alliance (EA) in the 1960s. Drawing upon EA relief activity, which dated back to the stimulus of the 1960 World Refugee Year initiative, it was established in 1968 as an initiative of the EA's general secretary, Morgan Derham, and was led into the late 1980s by George Hoffman. Initially called the Evangelical Alliance Relief Fund, it quickly adopted the acronym TEAR Fund, which had settled into its present form, Tearfund, by the late 1990s.

The evangelical Christian nature of the NGO is key to understanding both the context of its formation, and its subsequent development. It emerged at a time when the external face of evangelicalism was characterised by political conservatism, and a strong suspicion of the liberal-minded 'social gospel' path, followed by other activist organisations in the Christian community. As such, it self-consciously formed part of a broader move within evangelicalism to engage more with social issues, characterised by the thinking and writings of, amongst others, John Stott in the UK, Ron Sider in the US, and the stance of the 1974 International Congress on World Evangelisation in Lausanne, Switzerland.

Unlike comparable Christian IAD NGOs, however (for example, Christian Aid), Tearfund has sought to engage with its social mission in explicitly evangelical terms. On the one hand, its work has reflected the intellectual trends within contemporaneous IAD activism, such as a preference for long-term development over short-term relief, engagement with ideas such as Fritz Schumacher's of appropriate technology, and emphasis during the 1980s on the role of women in development. It also played a key role in the creation of the fair trade movement, through its Tearcraft subsidiary. At the same time, it has maintained a strongly evangelising character, seen through its fundraising techniques, its choice of Southern partners, and its stance on issues of sexuality and morality, such as the challenge of HIV/AIDS.

The broadly separatist thinking that characterised the NGOs early decades (a product of the political conservatism and commitment to evangelical values cited above) has, more recently, given way to a greater engagement with joint campaigning, over issues such as international taxation, debt relief and climate change policy. Significant here was the role Tearfund played in the Jubilee 2000 mobilisation of the 1990s, which has paved the way for a wider endorsement of public and political advocacy.

Key dates

1960   World Refugee Year triggers Britain's Evangelical Alliance to engage with international relief efforts
1968   Formation of Evangelical Alliance Relief Fund (later Tearfund)
1974   Tearcraft established
1974   Lausanne Congress on World Evangelisation
1990s Participation in the Jubilee 2000 coalition

Key figures

Morgan Derham: general secretary, Evangelical Alliance, 1960s
George Hoffman: director of Tearfund until 1988
John Stott: writer and theologian; Tearfund president from 1983

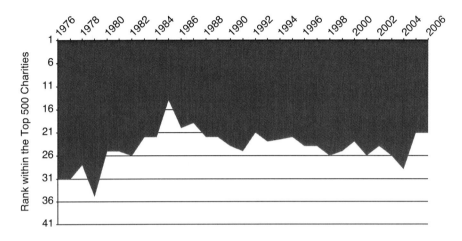

Figure 4.171: Tearfund's charitable ranking by voluntary income, 1976–2006

Source: Charity Trends.

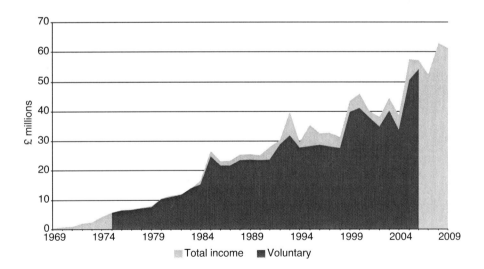

Figure 4.172: Total and voluntary income of Tearfund, 1969–2009 (adjusted for inflation, 2009)

Sources: Annual reports and accounts, Tearfund; Charity Commission; Mike Hollow, *A Future and a Hope: The Story of Tearfund and Why God Wants the Church to Change the World* (Oxford, 2008); Tearfund website, www.tearfund.org/About+us/The+Tearfund+story/ (accessed in 2008 – the page has changed since then).

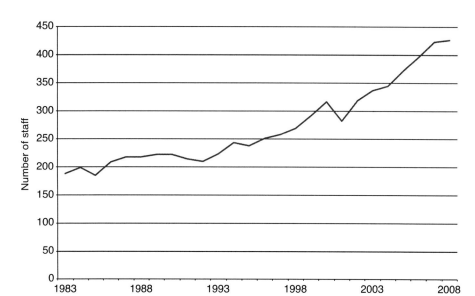

Figure 4.173: Number of staff working for Tearfund, 1983–2008

Sources: Top 3000 Charities; Annual reports and accounts, Tearfund.

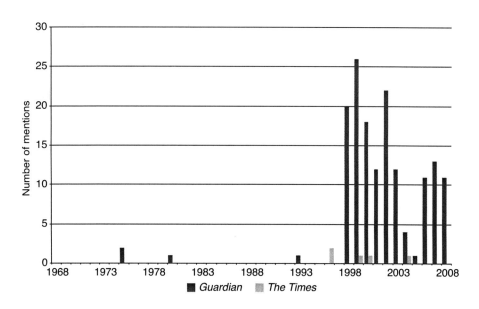

Figure 4.174: Number of mentions of Tearfund in the *Guardian* and *The Times*, 1975–2008

Source: *Guardian* & *The Times*.

Further reading

Mary Endersbee, *They Can't Eat Prayer: The Story of Tearfund* (London, 1973); Melanie Symonds, *Love in Action: Celebrating Twenty Five Years of Tearfund* (Guildford, 1993); Mike Hollow, *A Future and a Hope: The Story of Tearfund and Why God Wants the Church to Change the World* (Oxford, 2008).

Terrence Higgins Trust

The Terrence Higgins Trust (THT) is Britain's leading charity working in the fields of human immunodeficiency virus (HIV) and sexual health.

The Trust was formed by Rupert Whitaker and Martyn Butler, respectively the partner and friend of Terry Higgins, who was one of the first people in Britain to die with acquired immunodeficiency syndrome (AIDS). Higgins' death in St Thomas' Hospital in July 1982 was at the time understood to be a result of gay-related immune deficiency (GRID). The Trust emerged as part of efforts to raise awareness and research funding for GRID, and was formally established during 1983/84.

The issue of HIV/AIDS achieved rapid and high public salience during the 1980s and early 1990s, due to a combination of factors. The close relationship between AIDS and sexuality, particularly homosexuality, as well as its links to intravenous illegal drug use, meant that the subject was immediately complicated by fraught debates over sexual morality and permissiveness. For a time, AIDS was seen by some social conservatives as a useful weapon in these ideological arguments, and assertions that the 'gay plague' was divine retribution for homosexuality were not uncommon.

Amid growing public concern, particularly widespread fear and misunderstanding over how AIDS was transmitted, the UK government launched a major public health campaign, 'Don't die of ignorance'. During 1987, leaflets were delivered to every household in the country, and hard-hitting cinema and television adverts were produced. While the campaign undoubtedly enhanced public awareness, the doom-laden tone of the campaign also contributed to the atmosphere of fear surrounding the disease (see Box 4.25).

Deaths of high-profile individuals with AIDS also kept it in the public eye, including actor Rock Hudson (1985), pop singer Freddie Mercury (1991), tennis player Arthur Ashe (1993) and film-maker Derek Jarman (1994). Over this period, the initial government engagement with the issue faded; the cabinet committee on AIDS was disbanded in 1989, while in 1993 central funding for THT's work was cut by two-thirds. However, as combination drug therapy and improved public health began to improve prospects in the Western world during the mid 1990s, the scale of devastation facing the developing world, particularly sub-Saharan Africa, was increasingly clear, and AIDS became a major international development issue.

Despite the relative withdrawal of government support, THT has expanded significantly, particularly since the mid 1990s. In part this has been driven by a series of mergers with local and regional groups around the turn of the century. In 1999, THT merged with Oxford's OxAIDS, Coventry's HIV Network, Leeds' Bridgeside,

Brighton's Sussex AIDS Trust and London's Red Admiral project. The following year saw mergers with the Aled Richards Trust and the London Lighthouse project.

Box 4.25: From 'Tombstone' public information film, 1987

'There is now a danger that has become a threat to us all.
It is a deadly disease and there is no known cure.
The virus can be passed during sexual intercourse with an infected person.
Anyone can get it, man or woman.
So far it has been confined to small groups. But it is spreading …
If you ignore AIDS it could be the death of you. So don't die of ignorance.'

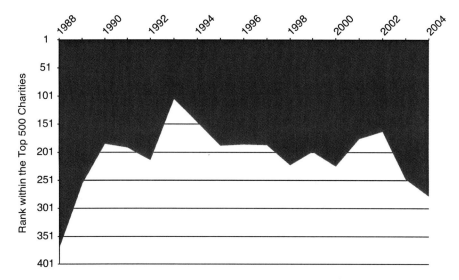

Figure 4.175: The Terrence Higgins Trust's charitable ranking by voluntary income, 1988–2004

Source: Charity Commission.

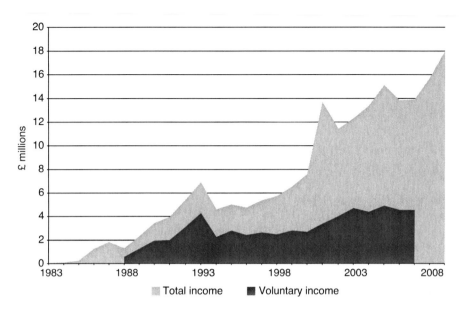

Figure 4.176: Total and voluntary income of the Terrence Higgins Trust, 1983–2009 (adjusted for inflation, 2009)

Note: Data for voluntary income before 1988 and after 2007 are missing.

Source: Annual reports and accounts, Terrence Higgins Trust; Top 3000 Charities; Charity Statistics; Charity Commission.

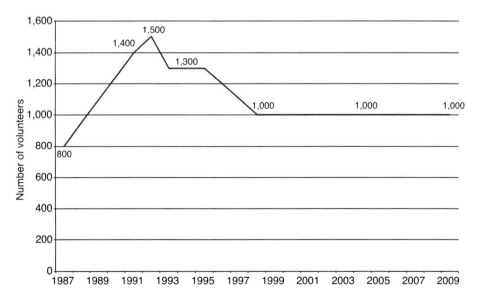

Figure 4.177: Number of volunteers working for the Terrence Higgins Trust, 1987–2009

Source: Annual reports and accounts, Terrence Higgins Trust.

Further reading

www.tht.org.uk/aboutus
Virginia Berridge, 'AIDS and the Rise of the Patient? Activist Organisation and HIV/AIDS in the UK in the 1980s and 1990s', *Medizin, Gesellschaft, und Geschichte*, 21 (2002), pp. 109–23; Virginia Berridge, *AIDS in the UK: The Making of Policy, 1981–1994* (Oxford, 2006).

Vegetarian Society

The Vegetarian Society was the UK's first expressly vegetarian organisation established in September 1847 in Ramsgate, and which held its first Annual General Meeting in Salford in 1848. A London branch of the organisation broke away in 1888, but a merger of their publications, *The Vegetarian Messenger* and *Vegetarian News*, in 1958, paved the way for an organisational reunion in 1969, with its headquarters based in Altrincham. During the 1950s Dr Frank Wokes established the Vegetarian Nutritional Research Centre, and in collaboration with the Society sought to provide 'expert' scientific and medical evidence for the benefits of vegetarian food on health. The Society also established in 1982 the Cordon Vert Cookery School.

The move into the mainstream of vegetarianism (with restaurants, vegetarian sections in supermarket freezers and the labelling of food) would appear to signal success for the Vegetarian Society, as would the growth in numbers of vegetarians (now estimated at 5 per cent of the UK population). However, the Society's membership has not grown, and direct involvement in the Society's activities has declined. This in part may be because there can be a difference between a vegetarian diet and a vegetarian ideology, and what a vegetarian means differs from person to person and over time. The term 'vegetarian' ideologically is one that views eating meat as being wrong, and has a moral underpinning that considers the use of animals for food and the justifications for the health benefits of meat in a diet to be wrong. But the justifications for vegetarian habits are varied, from animal welfare, to environmental degradation, to taste and cost (the latter two of which are not ideological). The Society has been one of a number of organisations that have promoted the diet for a range of food, health and moral reasons. It has also been linked to ideas of self-sufficiency and the animal rights movement. In 1944 schism led to the breakaway formation of the Vegan Society, which rejects the use of all animal-derived produce.

As both a limited company and a registered charity, the Society promotes the diet and ideology of vegetarianism to the wider public. Since 1986 it has licensed the 'V' symbol which food producers use on their product packaging, and this provides a key source of income and also an awareness indicator for vegetarianism. Under the articles of association, the organisation considers dairy produce and eggs as suitable for vegetarian consumption, but the organisation has also helped define vegetarian food further. In the 1980s it decided that only 'free range' eggs were suitable, and withdrew the 'V' symbol licence from products using genetically modified foodstuffs. During the course of the twentieth century there were 187 products that the Society redefined as being unsuitable for vegetarian consumption. Despite the overlap of vegetarianism and other ethical consumption issues, collaborations with other NGOs have sometimes proved difficult, as with the RSPCA over animal welfare, because of divergent ideological views. Difficulties also arise over matters relating to fair trade, vivisection, environmentalism and natural or health foods. The Society has transformed from being a club-like membership organisation into a professionalised consumer campaigning group that has developed relations with the food industry in order to serve the needs of the vegetarian consumer.

Box 4.26: Poster slogan for National Vegetarian Week, 1995

'Vegetarians have 30 per cent less risk of heart disease according to the Oxford Vegetarian Study, one of the most detailed surveys ever conducted into health and diet.'

From Andrew Smart, 'Adrift from the Mainstream: Challenges facing the UK Vegetarian Movement', *British Food Journal* (2004), p. 87.

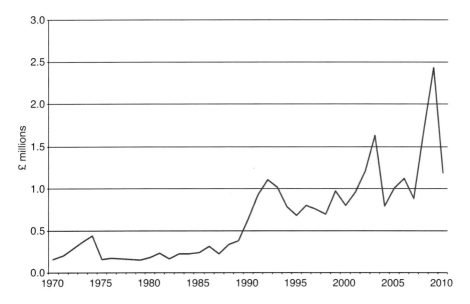

Figure 4.178: Income of the Vegetarian Society, 1970–2010 (adjusted for inflation, 2009)

Sources: Annual reports and accounts, Vegetarian Society; Charity Commission; Top 3000 Charities.

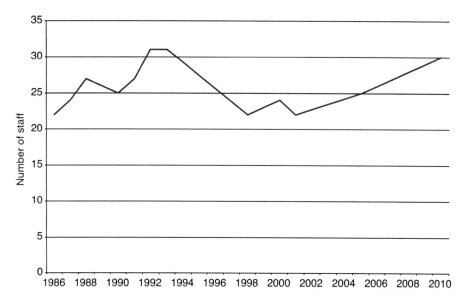

Figure 4.179: Number of staff working for the Vegetarian Society, 1986–2010

Sources: Annual reports and accounts, Vegetarian Society; Charity Commission; Top 3000 Charities.

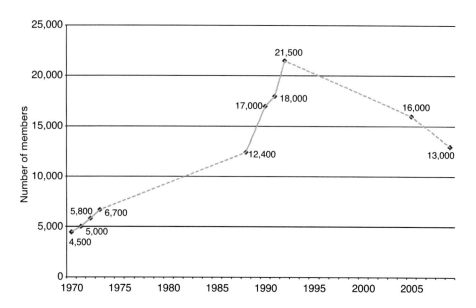

Figure 4.180: Membership of the Vegetarian Society, 1970–2009

Sources: Annual reports and accounts, Vegetarian Society; Guidestar UK; email contact with Vegetarian Society (June 2009).

Further reading

Andrew Smart, 'Adrift from the Mainstream: Challenges Facing the UK Vegetarian Movement', *British Food Journal*, (2004), pp. 79–92; Leah Leneman, 'No Animal Food: The Road to Veganism 1909–44', *Society and Animals*, 7:3 (1999), pp. 219–28.

Victim Support (formerly the National Association of Victim Support Schemes)

Victim Support is a charity that aims to help the victims of crime by raising awareness of their needs and delivering services to them. The first Victim Support scheme was launched in Bristol in 1974 (founded by Christopher Holtom of NACRO (a criminal justice charity), and Bristol University's Social Administration department, Martin Guy, a psychiatrist, and Susan Thomas, a doctor), and within four years 30 similar schemes were in operation across England and Wales. This led to the creation of the umbrella body, the National Association of Victim Support Schemes (NAVSS), in 1979 with private trust funding and support from the Home Office's Voluntary Services Unit. This development was representative of part of a wider emerging concern for the rights of the victim of crime during the 1970s which had seen the emergence of groups like Erin Pizzey's National Federation of Women's Aid for the victims of domestic violence, and the emergence of Rape Crisis Centres from 1976 onwards. The experience and neglect of the victim, and the need for coordinated policy from the police and judiciary, has underpinned many of its research reports, such as *Rights for Victims of Crime* (London, 1995) and *Criminal Neglect* (London, 2002).

Since the 1990s, Victim Support's service delivery has come in three ways. It supports the victims of crime in the community by talking about their experience and offering practical advice, such as how to apply for compensation. Its Witness Service scheme offers emotional and practical support to those appearing as witnesses in court. It also offers a telephone support service through which those who have experienced crime may speak with a trained volunteer.

Although the NAVSS was viewed as 'commendable' by the Home Office, politicians were reluctant until the mid 1980s to provided additional funding incentives, suggesting the limited influence of the organisation. There was also a Whitehall tendency to lump together compensation, recognition and support as a single issue. This explains the three-pronged development of Victim Support's services. Critics have also felt that although the rapid expansion of local Victim Support schemes suggested it was one of the most successful of voluntary organisations, the organisation has failed to capitalise on this and give itself a sufficiently visible presence in the minds of both the public and the politicians.

Key dates

1974　First Victim Support scheme set up in Bristol
1979　National Association of Victim Support Schemes established
1980　First national paid member of staff and part-time secretary appointed and headquarters located in Brixton

1981   National code of conduct introduced, and NAVSS holds first national conference
1986   Every county in England and Wales now covered by at least one Victim Support scheme
1987   Registered as a charitable company limited by guarantee and given core funding by Home Office
1989   Her Royal Highness, The Princess Royal, becomes patron
1991   Home Office agrees to fund Crown Court Witness Service after campaigning and research from NAVSS, although not launched until 1994
1998   Telephone helpline service Victim Supportline launched
2006   Victim Support's 'sun and clouds' logo is revised and updated
2007   Extraordinary General Meeting agrees to replace existing NVASS federation with a single national charity, Victim Support, from 1 January 2008
2008   National volunteer awards ceremony held at Buckingham Palace

Chief executives, 1979–2011

Helen Reeves, 1979–2005
Gillan Guy, 2006–2010
Owen Sharp (acting chief executive), 2010
Javed Khan, 2010–

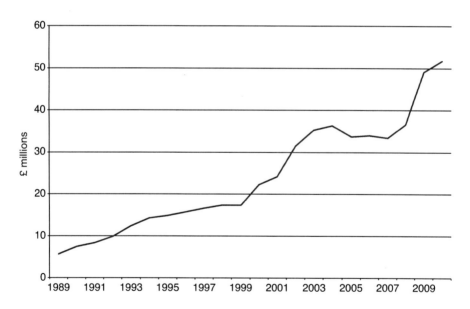

Figure 4.181: Income of Victim Support, 1989–2010 (adjusted for inflation, 2009)

Sources: Annual Reports and accounts, Victim Support; Top 3000 Charities; Charity Commission.

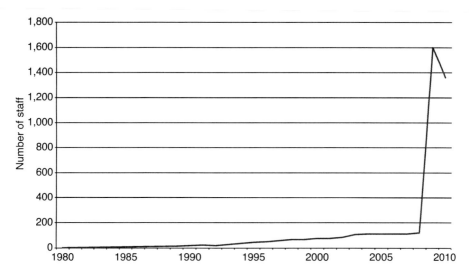

Figure 4.182: Number of staff working for Victim Support, 1980–2010

Note: In 2008, Victim Support completed the process of merging its 77 local charities into one national organisation. This explains the very high rise in the number of employees between 2007 and 2008.

Sources: Annual reports and accounts, Victim Support; Top 3000 Charities; Guidestar UK; Victim Support's website.

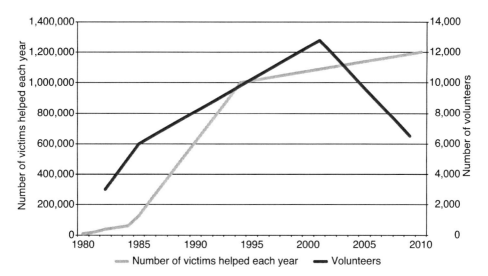

Figure 4.183: Number of volunteers and number of victims helped by Victim Support each year, 1980–2010

Sources: (a) For volunteers: *Social Trends*, 14 (1984); 16 (1986); Annual report, Victim Support, 2001 and 2008. (b) For number of victims: Victim Support website; *Social Trends*, 14 (1984); 16 (1986); Annual report, Victim Support, 2010.

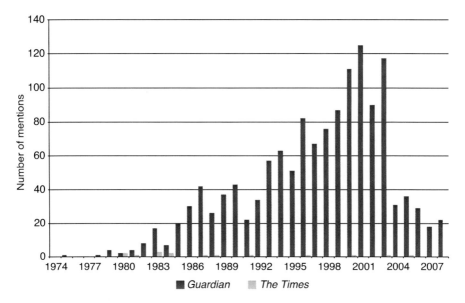

Figure 4.184: Number of mentions of Victim Support in the *Guardian* and *The Times*, 1974–2008

Source: *Guardian* & *The Times*.

Further reading

Paul Rock, *Helping Victims of Crime: The Home Office and the Rise of Victim Support in England and Wales* (Oxford, 1990); Mike Ryan, *Penal Policy and Political Culture in England and Wales* (Winchester, 2003).

War on Want

The history of War on Want falls into distinct phases. Its origins lie in a letter by Victor Gollancz to the *Manchester Guardian* in 1951, written against the backdrop of the Korean War and appealing for a renewed effort at international peace and development. The positive response to this letter led to the establishment of the Association for World Peace, with the support of leading left-wing activists such as Sir Richard Acland, Fenner Brockway, Canon Collins and Leslie Hale. The following year a booklet was produced under the lead authorship of future prime minister, Harold Wilson, entitled *War on Want*. An organisation of the same name was loosely established, without a formal footing, and drifted without clear direction into the 1950s.

The history of War on Want as an independent NGO properly got underway when Frank Harcourt-Munning, a Christian Socialist of private means, took it over in the late 1950s. Modestly styled as an administrator, and noticeably influenced by his religious faith, Harcourt-Munning ran the body on largely voluntarist lines, subsidising it out of his own fortune, yet failing to construct durable and sustainable organisation. This voluntarist approach was in marked contrast to the technocratic, expert-led solutions the NGO was at that time promoting to the developing world through its publications.

Harcourt-Munning's forced departure at the end of the 1960s triggered both a professionalisation and a shift to the left: a general secretary replaced the administrator post, numbers of paid staff were increased, and campaigning and advertising was noticeably sharpened. More striking, however, was the intellectual and ideological shift that took place: macro-level solutions regarding aggregate aid flows were replaced with a focus on issues such as grassroots development, the malign effects of multinational companies, liberation movements and the rights of women. This trend built pace into the 1980s when, along with the Labour Party, War on Want went into domestic opposition, campaigning against poverty in the UK, and increasingly attracting the hostile attention of the Charity Commission. Led for some of these years by future MP George Galloway, the NGO became swashbuckling and radical, but arguably attracted as much trouble for itself as it did attention for its causes. A financial crisis at the start of the 1980s forced a harsh restructuring; another at the end of the decade came within an inch of destroying the NGO completely.

A smaller, chastened War on Want emerged from the wreckage of the 1980s. Aspirations to being a grassroots mass movement, always somewhat over-exaggerated by the NGOs literature, are today much less in evidence. Nevertheless, War on Want continues to provide a distinctive, if quieter, voice in the sector, with an ongoing concern for workers' rights that is testament to its labour movement roots.

Key dates

1951   Gollancz writes to the *Manchester Guardian*
1952   Publication of *War on Want: A Plan for World Development*
1974   Publication of Mike Muller's *The Baby Killer: A War on Want Investigation into the Promotion and Sale of Powdered Baby Milks in the Third World*
1987   George Galloway resigns as general secretary following his election as an MP, amid internal strife and critical media coverage of his conduct
1991   Charity Commission publish a highly critical report into War on Want mismanagement, against a backdrop of the NGO's near-collapse

Key figures

Victor Gollancz: author of the 1951 *Manchester Guardian* letter that eventually led to the establishment of the NGO
Harold Wilson: lead author of the 1952 report *War on Want*
Frank Harcourt-Munning: Christian Socialist who led the NGO through its first phase, until the end of the 1960s
George Galloway: flamboyant and controversial general secretary, 1983–87

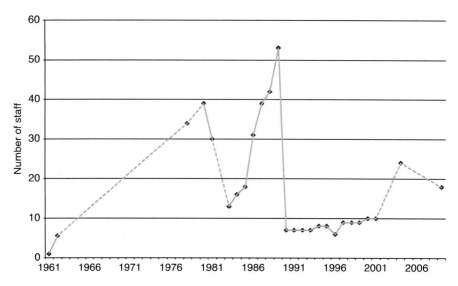

Figure 4.185: Number of staff working for War on Want, 1961–2009

Sources: Annual reports and accounts, War on Want; *Yearbook of International Organizations*; Charity Commissioners for England and Wales, *War on Want: Report of an Inquiry Submitted to the Commissioners, 15th February 1991* (London, 1991); Mark Luetchford and Peter Burns, *Waging the War on Want: Fifty Years of Campaigning against World Poverty: An Authorised History* (London, 2003); Charity Commission.

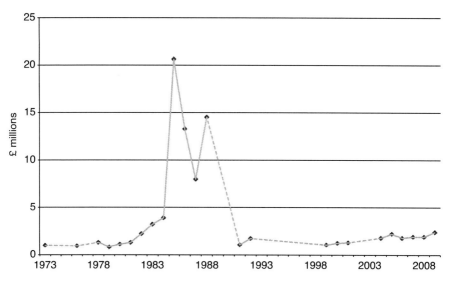

Figure 4.186: Voluntary income of War on Want, 1973–2009 (adjusted for inflation, 2009)

Sources: Annual reports and accounts, War on Want; *Yearbook of International Organizations*; Charity Commissioners for England and Wales, *War on Want: Report of an Inquiry Submitted to the Commissioners, 15th February 1991* (London, 1991); Mark Luetchford and Peter Burns, *Waging the War on Want: Fifty Years of Campaigning against World Poverty: An Authorised History* (London, 2003); Charity Commission; Charity Statistics.

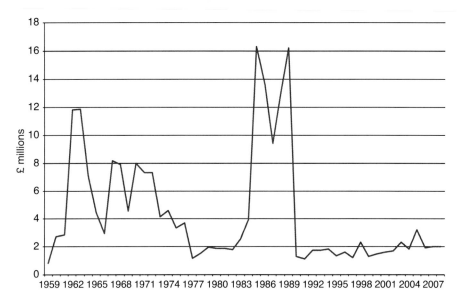

Figure 4.187: Total income of War on Want, 1959–2009 (adjusted for inflation, 2009)

Sources: Annual reports and accounts, War on Want; *Yearbook of International Organizations*; Charity Commissioners for England and Wales, *War on Want: Report of an Inquiry Submitted to the Commissioners, 15th February 1991* (London, 1991); Mark Luetchford and Peter Burns, *Waging the War on Want: Fifty Years of Campaigning against World Poverty: An Authorised History* (London, 2003); Charity Commission; Charity Statistics.

Further reading

The Association for World Peace, *War on Want: A Plan for World Development* (London, 1952); Charity Commissioners for England and Wales, *War on Want: Report of an Inquiry Submitted to the Commissioners, 15th February 1991* (London, 1991); Mark Luetchford and Peter Burns, *Waging the War on Want: Fifty Years of Campaigning against World Poverty: An Authorised History* (London, 2003).

Which?

Which? began life as the Consumers' Association. In the early 1950s, the recently married Dorothy and Ray Goodman, the director of PEP (Political and Economic Planning), became frustrated that there existed no guide to buying as existed in *Consumer Reports* in their native US. They called an initial meeting of prominent individuals including the sociologist Michael Young, and produced a dummy test magazine. The Consumers' Association was established in 1956 and the first issue of *Which?* came out in 1957.

The success of the magazine was almost instantaneous. It had 47,000 subscriber/ members by the end of its first year, a figure which rose steadily until it peaked in 1987 at the 1 million mark. Moreover, its other publishing ventures proved highly popular: in 1979 there were 575,000 separate subscriptions to *Money Which?*, 531,000 to *Handyman Which?*, and 460,000 to *Motoring Which?* The appeal of the objective comparative testing of branded goods lay in its 'best buys': the professional ethos of *Which?* offered a comforting guide through the high street at a time when the traditional skills of the consumer-housewife were of no relevance in the selection of a whole range of technical goods associated with the age of affluence.

Yet *Which?* has been much more than just a shopper's guide. It quickly realised that value for money could not be determined by choice alone. Often major changes were needed in the regulation of the market and it has lobbied hard for many state interventions. By 1980, *The Times* was able to claim that the Consumers' Association had 'filled more pages of the statute book than any other pressure group this century.'

Which? has also spearheaded something of a social movement. By the end of the 1960s there were over 100 local consumer groups around the country. Internationally too, organised consumerism has become a significant force in the NGO world, largely funded by Which? and the other largest consumer group, the Consumers' Union, in the US. The International Organisation of Consumers' Unions was created in 1960. Today it represents consumer groups from over 100 different countries and has been an important critic of the global trade system.

The consumer movement has pursued a rights-based (to choice, to information, to redress, to safety) and non-political agenda. It has done much to protect the individual shopper, but it has avoided more difficult issues concerning public or private provision. In recent decades it has also faced increased competition from commercial publishers who have taken advantage of the obvious and high demand for comparative testing.

Key UK consumer protection legislation

1968   Trade Descriptions Act
1973   Fair Trading Act
1974   Consumer Credit Act
1977   Restrictive Trade Practices Act
1978   Consumer Safety Act
1987   Consumer Protection Act
1998   Competition Act
2002   Enterprise Act
2008   Consumer Protection from Unfair Trading Regulations

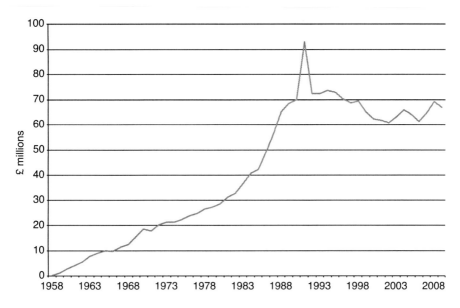

Figure 4.188: Total and voluntary income of Which?, 1958–2009 (adjusted for inflation, 2009)

Sources: Annual reports and accounts, Which?; Charity Commission; Top 3000 Charities.

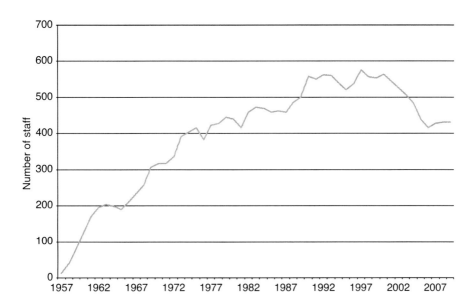

Figure 4.189: Number of staff working for Which?, 1957–2009

Sources: Annual reports and accounts, Which?; Charity Commission; Top 3000 Charities.

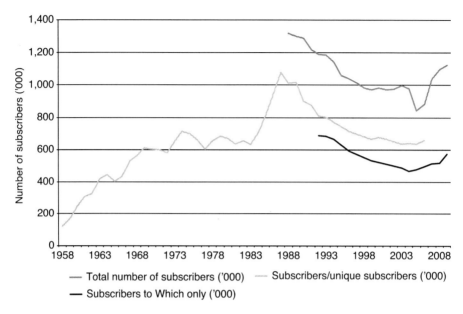

Figure 4.190: Membership of Which?, 1958–2009

Note: From 1999, the line showing the number of subscribers only shows the number of 'unique subscribers' (that is, people who receive *Which?* and one of the other Which? specialised magazines are counted only once).

Sources: Annual report and accounts, Which?.

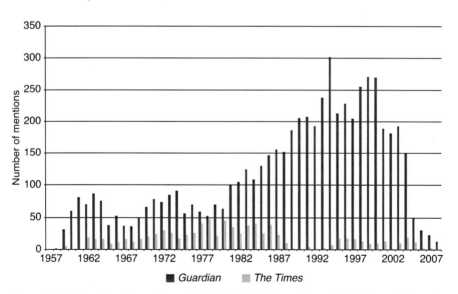

Figure 4.191: Number of mentions of Which? in the *Guardian* and *The Times*, 1957–2007

Source: *Guardian* & *The Times*.

Further reading

Matthew Hilton, *Consumerism in Twentieth-Century Britain: The Search for a Historical Movement* (Cambridge, 2003); Lawrence Black, '*Which?*craft in Post-War Britain: The Consumers' Association and the Politics of Affluence', *Albion*, 36:1 (2004), pp. 52–82.

Women's Aid Federation

In 1971 Erin Pizzey established the world's first refuge for battered women in Chiswick, West London. She attracted considerable attention for it, even appearing on the Jimmy Young television show, and within a couple of years around 40 refuge services had been formed around the country. In 1974, the Women's Aid Federation was established to coordinate these services, subsequently splitting into four separate organisations for each of the constituent parts of the UK.

The impetus to establish refuge services for victims of domestic violence clearly owed much to the inspiration provided by second-wave feminism. Yet precisely because women were victims, the Federation also attracted much mainstream support, obtaining funding from charitable trusts, government and private donors. Nevertheless, refuges were almost exclusively staffed by feminists and Women's Aid became a central pillar of the Women's Liberation Movement, sharing the same objectives and many of the key principles, such as a non-hierarchical structure and an assumption that no woman was to be turned away.

As a service, the refuges have grown rapidly. There were 179 refuges in England alone operating in 1986. Today, the Federation consists of 370 local domestic violence organisations which together provide over 500 refuges, outreach, advocacy and children's support services. It has also run, since 1987, a National Domestic Violence Helpline with Refuge.

Political campaigning has been a key function. Soon after its formation, the Labour MP Jo Richardson introduced a private member's bill and the Domestic Violence Act was passed in 1976. Women's Aid also lobbied to ensure that the 1977 Housing (Homeless Persons) Act defined women and children at risk of violence as homeless to ensure they had the right to state help with temporary accommodation.

On single issues, such as the defence of Child Benefit in the 1980s, Women's Aid has worked with non-feminist organisations such as the Women's Institute, the Mothers' Union and the Church of England Children Society. It has continued to raise public awareness of domestic violence, and its closer links with government (particularly through Sarah Brown, the wife of Gordon Brown) following the election of Labour in 1997 eventually resulted in the Domestic Violence Crime and Victims Act 2004.

Key figure: Erin Pizzey

The Women's Aid Federation has had a troubled relationship with its original leading figure. Erin Pizzey was regarded as too much of a self-publicist by her colleagues and it was felt she wanted too much personal control over the organisation. At the second Annual General Meeting in 1975, Pizzey stormed out, and her Chiswick centre has largely gone its own way ever since. More controversially, she has subsequently gone on to claim that many women are 'prone to violence' and actually seek out abusive relationships. Furthermore, she has claimed that much domestic violence is reciprocated. She has bemoaned much of the feminist direction that Women's Aid has taken and, although still regarded as an authority on domestic violence, she stands entirely separately from an organisation that she had played a prominent role in establishing.

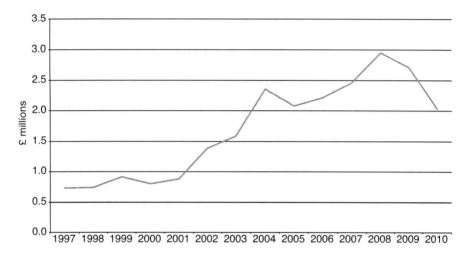

Figure 4.192: Income of the Women's Aid Federation, 1997–2010 (adjusted for inflation, 2009)

Sources: Annual report and accounts, Women's Aid Federation; Charity Commission.

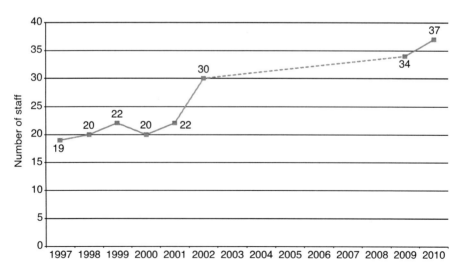

Figure 4.193: Number of staff working for the Women's Aid Federation, 1997–2010

Sources: Annual report and accounts, Women's Aid Federation; Charity Commission.

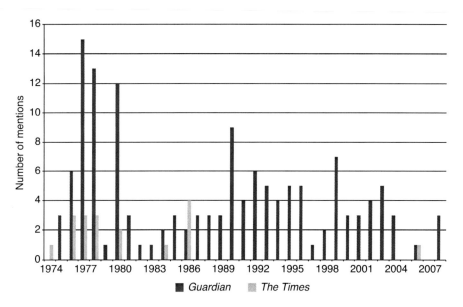

Figure 4.194: Number of mentions of the Women's Aid Federation in the *Guardian* and *The Times*, 1974–2008

Source: *Guardian* & *The Times*.

Further reading

Anna Coote and Beatrix Campbell, *Sweet Freedom* (Oxford, 1987); J. Sutton, 'Growth of the British Movement for Battered Women', *Victimology*, 2:3–4 (1977–78), pp. 576–84.

Workers' Educational Association

In 1903 Albert Mansbridge, an Anglican lay preacher, established an Association to Promote the Higher Education of Working Men. It drew on support from the churches, the cooperative movement, the trade unions and the University Extension Movement. In 1905 it was renamed the Workers' Educational Association (WEA) and had eight branches by the end of the year. By 1919 the number had risen to 219, and by 1945 there were 800, further rising to around 1,000 by the end of the century.

The purpose of the WEA was to create a 'partnership between labour and learning' where workers would be taught to think for themselves about the society in which they lived and worked. Its actual impact on the working class as a whole has been limited. One study conducted in the mid 1960s in Chester and Eccles found that only 5 per cent of adults had ever taken a WEA or extramural course. But its real influence came through its impact on the labour movement: indeed, it has been described as the 'university of the Labour Party'. One investigation into the careers of WEA students found that 2,300 were holding public office, including 15 MPs and nearly 1,500 local councillors. In 1945, 14 members of the new Labour government were former WEA tutors or executives (including Clement Attlee) and over 100 Labour MPs had benefited from adult education.

Its influence might have been greater had it cooperated with, rather than competed with, other forms of adult education, such as the National Council of Labour Colleges and other trade-affiliated bodies. However, it has worked with Oxford University and Ruskin College, and in the 1940s it joined with the Co-operative Union, the Trades Union Congress and the National Union of Teachers to form a Council for Educational Advance which pushed for a fair and just education system that was ushered in through the 1944 Education Act.

After 1945, the WEAs thrived through the continued willingness of key individuals to become tutors: the literary scholar, Raymond Williams, for instance, used WEA tutorials to disseminate the new field of cultural studies. But they have also been eclipsed, to an extent, through new institutions such as the Open University as well as the general social and economic changes that have helped create a mass higher education system.

Some WEA tutors

R.H. Tawney
G.D.H. Cole
Harold Laski
Hugh Gaitskell
Frank Pakenham
Richard Crossman
E.P. Thompson
Richard Hoggart
Raymond Williams

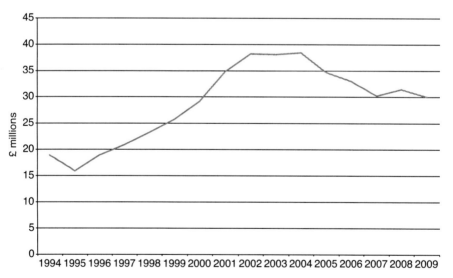

Figure 4.195: Income of the Workers' Educational Association, 1994–2009 (adjusted for inflation, 2009)

Sources: Top 3000 Charities; Charity Commission.

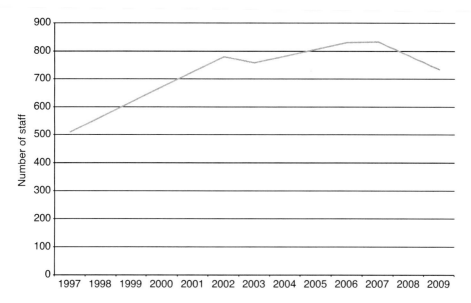

Figure 4.196: Number of staff working for the Workers' Educational Association, 1997–2009

Sources: Top 3000 Charities; Charity Commission.

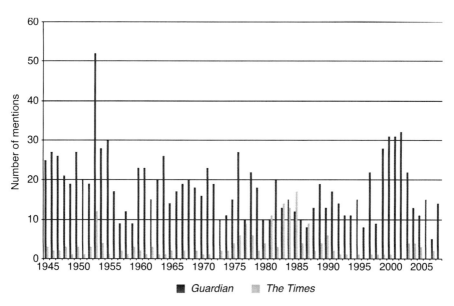

■ *Guardian*   ▨ *The Times*

Figure 4.197: Number of mentions of the Workers' Educational Association in the *Guardian* and *The Times*, 1945–2007

Source: *Guardian* & *The Times*.

Further reading

Stephen Roberts (ed.), *A Ministry of Enthusiasm: Centenary Essays on the Workers' Educational Association* (London, 2003); Roger Fieldhouse, *The Workers' Educational Association: Aims and Achievements, 1903–1977* (Syracuse, 1977); Lawrence Goldman, *Dons and Workers: Oxford and Adult Education since 1850* (Oxford, 1995); Tom Steele, *The Emergence of Cultural Studies, 1945–1965: Cultural Politics, Adult Education and the English Question* (London, 1997).

World Development Movement

In 1969, several charities, led by Christian Aid and Oxfam, decided to build on the momentum begun by numerous local World Development and Poverty Action Groups to create Action for World Development. It launched in that year its *Manifesto on Aid and Development* which reflected the NGO sector's growing disappointment with government cuts in aid and its realisation that it would have to be more political. To avoid a confrontation with the Charity Commissioners, though, the following year the non-charitable body, the World Development Movement (WDM), was formed.

WDM has enabled the development charities to have a political voice. It has grown as an independent entity, such that by the end of the 1980s its cross-party membership consisted of 5,000 individuals at the national level plus 180 local action groups. WDM has been particularly effective at mobilising the public around key events. Following the publication of the findings of the Brandt Commission in 1981, it organised a mass lobbying of parliament attended by 10,000. Michael Foot addressed them, pledging the Labour Party to meet the 0.7 per cent target of the proportion of GDP to be spent on aid. Two years later, ahead of the North–South summit in Cancun, WDM sold 100,000 copies of its letter-writing guide, resulting in such pressure that 400 MPs wrote to either the prime minister or the foreign secretary for clarification on the government's position.

The WDM has helped politicise aid in a way that charities were not able to. It campaigned with some success to get its members to support the Independent Group on British Aid's proposals in the 1980s to target official aid at the poorest members of society, regardless of the strategic needs of British diplomacy. This culminated in another mass lobbying of parliament in 1985, the sale of 100,000 copies of its pamphlet, *Africa in Crisis*, and the collection of 750,000 signatories to its 'Famine in Africa' petition.

Yet there have been limits to this politicisation, highlighting an issue faced by NGOs as a whole. One survey of WMD members in 1988 found that while there was general support for development, one-third wished to avoid tackling the more problematic – and obviously political – situations in Nicaragua and South Africa.

Nevertheless, WDM has been successful in a variety of initiatives, from securing market access into the EU for developing world sugar producers in 1970, to helping to defeat the proposed Multilateral Agreement on Investment in 1996. It was a co-founder of the Fairtrade Foundation and a leading participant in the coalitions

(Jubilee 2000, Trade Justice, Make Poverty History) that were to have a direct influence on the Labour government's approach to debt and aid.

World Development Movement Trust

WDM is not a charity. However, it has set up its own charitable body, the WDM Trust, to enable it to undertake small-scale, grassroots projects in the developing world in a manner similar to the larger development charities. WDM itself is then free to engage in political campaigning, unencumbered by charity legislation. In 2005 WDM claimed that 'the fundamental causes of world poverty cannot be overcome without changes to the policies and practices of governments and business interests in wealthy industrialised countries like Britain. So, free from charity law, WDM undertakes campaigns that change the policies of governments and companies which keep the poor marginalised.'

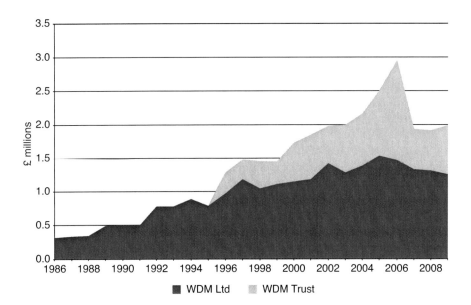

Figure 4.198: Income of WDM Ltd and WDM Trust (charity), 1986–2009 (adjusted for inflation, 2009)

Note: A large proportion of the income of the WDM Trust is donated back to WDM Ltd.

Sources: Annual reports and accounts, WDM; Charity Commission.

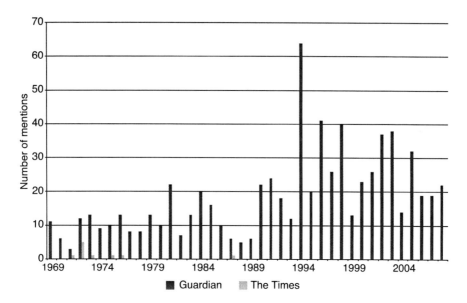

Figure 4.199: Number of mentions of the World Development Movement in the *Guardian* and *The Times*, 1969–2008

Source: *Guardian* & *The Times*.

Further reading

World Development Movement, *A Brief History of WDM* (London, 1997); Peter J. Burnell, *Charity, Politics and the Third World* (London, 1991); Chris Rootes and Clare Saunders, 'The Global Justice Movement in Britain', in Donatella della Porta (ed.), *The Global Justice Movement: Cross-national and Transnational Perspectives* (Boulder, CO, 2007), pp. 128–56.

World Wide Fund for Nature

The World Wide Fund for Nature, UK (WWF-UK) is the British branch of the major international conservation charity with offices in 35 countries.

The organisation emerged out of developing international conservation through the twentieth century. While earlier attempts at coordination came to little (such as the international Consultative Commission for the International Protection of Nature (1913) and the International Office for the Protection of Nature (1934)), efforts gained more traction with the establishment of the United Nations, and particularly its scientific and educational programme, UNESCO. UNESCO's interest in nature protection, under the leadership of British biologist Julian Huxley, led in1948 to the formation of the International Union for the Protection (later Conservation) of Nature (IUCN).

The World Wildlife Fund itself was founded in Morges, Switzerland, by Huxley, along with Guy Mountfort, ornithologist and painter Peter Scott (designer of the now world-famous panda logo) and Max Nicholson. The resulting 'Morges Manifesto' originally conceived of the organisation as a fundraising mechanism for the IUCN. National appeals were initiated to raise money, with the UK appeal becoming WWF-UK. Launched in 1961, this became the first of the national chapters making up the international group.

Although the Fund soon developed a life of its own, its international focus was significant at a time when conservation groups often had a more parochial focus. As such, WWF has been seen as something of an institutional bridge between older, anthropocentric approaches, and the more globally aware environmental movement that emerged in the 1960s and 1970s. Over the course of the 1970s, and in line with these intellectual changes, the WWF expanded its remit from its original focus on habitat and wildlife conservation, to encompass broader questions of humanity's impact on the global environment.

In 1980, the organisation launched its World Conservation Strategy, warning that conservation must be prioritised if humans were to enjoy a viable future. In doing so, it anticipated the notion of sustainable development (see Box 4.27), popularised by the 1987 report of the Brundltand Commission, *Our Common Future*.

In 1986 the organisation changed its name to the World Wide Fund for Nature, emphasising its concern with the entirety of biodiversity, rather than just animals. Generally, however, the body uses the WWF initials, and its focus remains the fate of endangered species in the wild.

Box 4.27: Sustainable development

'Sustainable development is development that meets the needs of the present without compromising the ability of future generations to meet their own needs. It contains two key concepts:

- the concept of "needs", in particular the essential needs of the world's poor, to which overriding priority should be given; and
- the idea of limitations imposed by the state of technology and social organization on the environment's ability to meet present and future needs.'

Our Common Future (1987), p. 43.

Key programmes and initiatives

1972   Operation Tiger, seeking to establish nine Indian national parks as tiger reserves

1976   TRAFFIC programme (Trade Records Analysis of Flora and Fauna in Commerce) launched with the World Conservation Union

1980   World Conservation Strategy

1991   Caring for the Earth launched with the World Conservation Union and the United Nations Environment Programme, continuing the sustainable development agenda

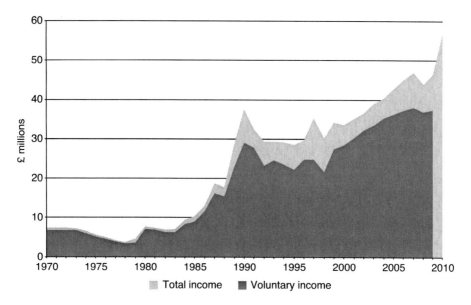

Figure 4.200: Voluntary and total income of the WWF, 1970–2010 (adjusted for inflation, 2009)

Sources: Wolfenden 1978; Wells Collection; Charity Statistics; Annual reports and accounts, WWF; Charity Commission.

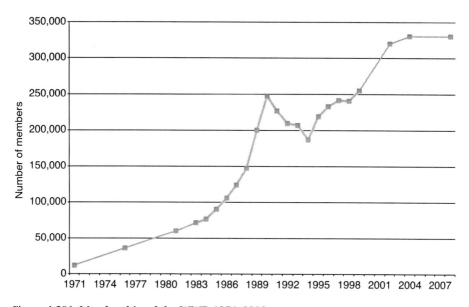

Figure 4.201: Membership of the WWF, 1971–2008

Sources: *Social Trends*; Peter Rawcliffe, *Environmental Pressure Groups in Transition* (Manchester, 1998); WWF website.

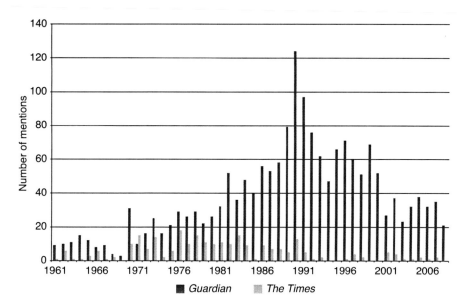

Figure 4.202: Number of mentions of the WWF in the *Guardian* and *The Times*, 1961–2008

Source: *Guardian* & *The Times*.

Further reading

www.wwf.org.uk

John McCormick, *The Global Environmental Movement*, 2nd edn (Chichester, 1995); Christopher Rootes, 'Environmental NGOs and the Environmental Movement in England', in Nick Crowson, Matthew Hilton and James McKay (eds), *NGOs in Contemporary Britain: Non-State Actors in Society and Politics since 1945* (Basingstoke, 2009); World Commission on the Environment and Development, *Our Common Future* (Oxford, 1987).

5
Key Players

Ann Pettifor

Ann Pettifor represents a recent type of British-based global activist that has campaigned on a variety of fronts and through several different organisations. If a programmatic ideology has not driven their political interventions there has nevertheless been an attempt to bring a certain unity of perspective to a range of topics: tackling global poverty, debt, climate change, and reform of the world trade system. In Pettifor's case it means she has worked with progressive think tanks, faith-based communities, and organisations established to explore alternative approaches to economics and finance.

Born in South Africa, Pettifor first worked in Britain in the 1980s as an advisor to Ken Livingstone's Greater London Council and to the Labour MP, Margaret Beckett. However, she turned away from the more formal political arena in the 1990s and became most closely associated with Jubilee 2000 from 1994. This biblically-inspired campaign aimed with some success to cancel $100 billion of debts from 42 of the world's poorest countries. Leading the campaign, Pettifor arranged a series of high-profile events including the formation of a 70,000-strong human chain that surrounded the G8 summit in Birmingham in 1998. With much celebrity support, the campaign also mobilised many international aid and development charities in alliance with a considerable cross-section of faith-based organisations. By 2000, the network consisted of 27 coalitions in Europe and North America, 17 in Central and Latin America, 15 in Africa and 10 in Asia. There were 110 NGOs connected to the UK coalition alone and, collectively, Jubilee 2000 was able to produce a petition of 24 million signatures from over 60 different countries.

The tactics of Jubilee 2000 would be imitated by other global campaigns, especially Make Poverty History. Pettifor herself would go on to attempt a similar strategy for environmentalism. Operation Noah, for which she currently serves as advisor and part-time director, is trying to mobilise the faith communities around climate change in the same way that Jubilee 2000 did with debt.

In 2001 she joined the New Economics Foundation (NEF), a think tank set up in 1986 which has sought a 'new model of wealth creation, based on equality, diversity and economic stability'. From there she edited *The Real World Economic Outlook* in 2003 which suggested a financial crisis loomed over the West – a point further elaborated upon in her 2006 work, *The Coming First World Debt Crisis*. With the NEF she also set out the Green New Deal in 2008 which marries many of the concerns of what has been inadequately termed the 'anti-globalisation movement': for instance, climate change, trade and financial regulation. It has also served as the model for her work at Operation Noah.

In addition, Pettifor set up Advocacy International with Janet Bush in 2004, based in London and New York. This advises governments from the developing world on debt management issues, offering them expert advice on how to negotiate with the major global financial institutions.

To some extent, Pettifor has joined a band of global celebrity NGO leaders who campaign and write on a number of issues and whose books have a guaranteed readership across the NGO sector. Yet Pettifor also recognises the importance of the traditional political sphere. In 2010, in a move which perhaps points the way for other NGO leaders in the future, she sought (unsuccessfully) the Labour candidacy for the North West Durham parliamentary seat.

Further reading

On Jubilee 2000, see Paolo Grenier, 'Jubilee 2000: Laying the Foundations for a Social Movement', in John Clark (ed.), *Globalising Civic Engagement: Civil Society and Transnational Activism* (London, 2003), pp. 86–108. Of Pettifor's own writings, see *The Real World Economic Outlook* (London, 2003) and *The Coming First World Debt Crisis* (London, 2006).

William Henry Beveridge

William Beveridge, the principal architect of the post-Second World War welfare state, is, at first glance, an odd choice as a key player in the history of NGOs, voluntary societies and charities. Yet his 1948 work, *Voluntary Action: A Report on the Methods of Social Advance*, has been a key reference point for those wishing to think about the role of NGOs and other bodies in modern society.

Beveridge himself had long worked with the sector. As a volunteer at Toynbee Hall, an Oxford outreach settlement in a deprived area of London, he came into contact with reformers of many different persuasions who were all pressing for increased governmental intervention on social questions. Beveridge was particularly interested in the application of social science remedies to social problems. As a civil servant in charge of rationing during the First World War, and then as director of the London School of Economics (LSE), he was able to pursue these interests, though in an increasingly academic manner. The Second World War provided him with his greatest opportunity, and his 1942 report, *Social Insurance and Allied Services*, provided the blueprint for state welfarism.

However, this work was complemented by Beveridge's later report, *Voluntary Action* (1948). Concerned that an all-powerful Leviathan might overreach itself, Beveridge sought to remind policy makers of the 'vigour and abundance' of voluntary action; that is, those forms of civic engagement that he held to be 'the distinguishing marks of a free society' and one of 'the outstanding features of British life'. Here Beveridge sought to rein in the reforms that followed in the wake of his first report. He worried about 'the coming of the social service state' that threatened the traditional role played by many voluntary organisations, but social changes had adversely affected the sector too.

In this sense, Beveridge harked back to a prior golden era of voluntarism that continues to inform policy debates about the sector to this day. He celebrated philanthropists of the Victorian decades: 'a time of private enterprise not only in pursuit of gain, but also in social reform' and to which British citizens were indebted. Accordingly, in his public life (following a brief stint as a Liberal MP, he entered the Lords in 1946), Beveridge continued to be vocal against what he felt to be the marginalisation of voluntary organisations in service provision.

As the rest of this volume demonstrates, he ought not to have been so concerned. His welfare state did not bring about the end of volunteering, and the rise of the modern NGO is testament to the continued adaptability and flexibility of a sector willing to reflect the needs, interests and desires of citizens. Indeed, in *Voluntary Action*, amidst Beveridge's overall pessimism, he did actually note:

> In face of these changes philanthropy has shown its strength of being able perpetually to take new forms. The Charity Organisation Society has passed over to Family Welfare. Within this century entirely new organizations have arisen, such as the Boy Scouts and Girl Guides, Women's Institutes, the Workers' Educational Association, the National Council of Social Service, Training Colleges for the Disabled, Women's Voluntary Services, and Citizens' Advice Bureaux. The capacity of Voluntary Action inspired by philanthropy to do new things is beyond question.

Further reading

Jose Harris, *William Beveridge: Biography*, 2nd edn (Oxford, 1997). All quotations above are taken from William Beveridge, *Voluntary Action: A Report on the Methods of Social Advance* (London, 1948).

Des Wilson

Des Wilson has had one of the more idiosyncratic careers in the NGO sector, though he very much began as typical of a new wave of activist associated with the 1960s and the so-called 'rediscovery' of poverty.

Born in New Zealand, Wilson began his career in Britain in 1960 as a journalist. This would prove crucial to his later work as an NGO leader. Taking advantage of the portrayal of homelessness in the November 1966 BBC play, *Cathy Come Home*, Wilson would help found Shelter on 1 December 1966. The launch drew on all of Wilson's experience in the media. He utilised as many contacts in the press as he could, as well as coordinating publicity, fundraising calls and the connections between existing homelessness charities, such that Shelter's explosion into the public consciousness was a far cry from the quiet discussions that had originally taken place among sympathisers who met at St Martin-in-the-Fields. The NGO soon gained a reputation for hard-hitting pamphlets that drove home the message in stark detail, while the research that went into Shelter's work also meant that Wilson was respected by the civil servants that the organisation sought to persuade.

It is this professionalism that has characterised Wilson's contribution to the NGO sector. Although he was known as a radical product of the 1960s (indeed, it has been suggested that Edward Heath closed down the government's Consumer Council in 1970 partially because Wilson was being touted as a director), he brought to activism a level of professional competence that made Shelter much admired by NGOs working in very different fields. The careers of Wilson and others attest to the extent to which the skills needed to run a modern NGO have become increasingly similar no matter what the object of concern, even to the point at which movement between the private and charitable sectors has become commonplace.

Wilson's career trajectory has incorporated all of these trends. His skills have been in demand by very different types of organisation, such that he has worked for the Royal Shakespeare Company, BAA plc, Carphone Warehouse and the England and Wales Cricket Board. He continued to pursue his journalistic work, combining his interests in his editorship of *Social Work Today* in the late 1970s. And after leaving Shelter in 1971 he went on to support a whole range of new NGOs. Most prominently, he applied what he had learnt in the homelessness sector to environmentalism as he headed Friends of the Earth from 1982 to 1986. But in the 1980s he also led the CLEAR campaign for lead-free petrol, he chaired the Campaign for Freedom of Information from 1984 to 1991, as well as assisting in various capacities a range of single-issue groups including Citizen Action, the National Council for Civil Liberties, the Child Poverty Action Group and Parents Against Tobacco.

At the same time, he has also been aware of the importance of party politics. He stood unsuccessfully as the Liberal Party candidate at the Hove by-election in 1973. Although never entering parliament, he remained keenly interested in the work of the Liberal Party, serving at various times on its Council, National Executive and as president (1987), and was an enthusiastic supporter of its merger with the Social Democratic Party, even serving as campaigns manager for the Liberal Democrats at the 1992 election.

His activities since retirement might serve to consolidate the image of an unorthodox maverick. He has participated in several poker competitions and become a noted writer and authority on the game. But such a personal liking for gambling betrays the influence of an activist who very much brought a level of sure-footed professional competence to many an organisation, if not the sector as a whole.

Further reading

For a study of the work of Shelter, see Paul Whiteley and Stephen Winyard, *Pressure for the Poor* (London, 1987); P. Seyd, 'Shelter: The National Campaign for the Homeless', *Political Quarterly*, 46:4 (1975), pp. 418–31. On Wilson himself, see his autobiography, *Memoirs of a Minor Public Figure* (London, 2011).

Fenner Brockway

Fenner Brockway, who died in 1988 just six months short of his 100th birthday, was engaged with a variety of peace and anti-colonial movements throughout the twentieth century. Although strongly associated with party politics (he was a staunch supporter of the Independent Labour Party (ILP), and a Labour Party MP from 1929 to 1931 and again from 1950 to1964), his activism attests to the close links between the formal and informal political arenas. The variety of organisations he became involved in also points to the continuities and changes in socio-political action.

Brockway was a committed labour movement activist, though his interest in world peace saw him branch out into other – often associated – organisations. He played a leading role in the ILP's opposition to the First World War, and in 1914 he founded the No Conscription Fellowship to oppose the introduction of compulsory service in the army. Once conscription was introduced, Brockway launched a full-scale campaign against it and he himself was convicted four times, serving a total of 28 months in prison before being finally released in April 1919.

During the interwar years, his efforts were mainly channelled through the leadership of the labour movement. He supported the ILP's shift further to the left and its disaffiliation from the Labour Party in 1932. But as the ILP's fortunes declined, he rejoined the Labour Party after the war, and the outlet for his varied interests came to be expressed through other organisations.

His interest in anti-colonialism was longstanding. In 1919 he had been joint secretary of the British Committee of the Indian National Congress, and editor of *India*. In 1942 he was chair of the British Centre for Colonial Freedom, an organisation which would be absorbed by the Congress of Peoples Against Imperialism in 1948, another body he had established in 1945. He became a frequent visitor to Africa and used his position as an MP to raise various issues related to decolonisation. In 1954, he transformed the Congress into the Movement for Colonial Freedom (now known as Liberation) and served as its first chair from 1954 to 1957.

His anti-colonialism was bound up with anti-racism and a continued support for world peace. He introduced several bills into parliament outlawing discrimination, and he continued to lend his support to specific causes. In 1965, for instance, he started the British Committee for Peace in Vietnam, and in 1967 he established a similar body devoted to the same goal in Nigeria. Along with many other leading figures, he was a founder member of the Campaign for Nuclear Disarmament in 1958 and, later, with Philip Noel-Baker in 1979, the World Disarmament Campaign which worked for the implementation of the policies agreed at the 1978 Special Session on Disarmament of the UN General Assembly. In addition, as a lifelong humanist he was also a member of the Advisory Council of the British Humanist Association.

Brockway accepted a peerage in 1964 seemingly against his socialist principles. Crucially, though, it gave him a voice in parliament and ensured that the sorts of issues he pushed though his peace and civil rights groups could also be expressed at the political centre. He continued to do so into his nineties just as, in the final decades of his life, he continued to attend world peace conferences, as a figure who represented the concerns of both the party political system and the more disorganised world of NGO campaign groups.

Further reading

Brockway published countless books, articles and pamphlets as well as four volumes of autobiography: *Inside the Left* (London, 1942); *Outside the Right* (London, 1963); *Towards Tomorrow* (London, 1977); *98 Not Out* (London, 1986). See also the entry for Brockway in the *Dictionary of National Biography* by David Howell, as well as the article by Josiah Brownell, 'The Taint of Communism: The Movement for Colonial Freedom, the Labour Party, and the Communist Party of Great Britain (1954–1970)', *Canadian Journal of History*, 42:2 (2007).

Jonathon Porritt

A writer, broadcaster and environmentalist, Jonathon Porritt has forged a career right at the heart of the modern environmentalism that emerged in the 1960s and 1970s.

Initially working as a teacher in London, Porritt was also a regular election candidate for the Ecology Party (which later became the Green Party) during the late 1970s and early 1980s, including in the 1979 and 1983 general elections. He also chaired the party for several years over this period. The dramatic spike of support for the Green Party at the 1989 European elections heightened a party debate over whether it should be internally remodelled to focus on electoral goals and a more professional approach to campaigning. Porritt, along with Sara Parkin and Jean Lambert, was a key advocate of such changes, under the Green 2000 banner, seeking Westminster representation for the party by the millennium. Although a disastrous performance at the 1992 election effectively killed off Green 2000 in formal terms, the impact of its overall philosophy can be seen in recent party history, including the election of its first leader in 2008, and winning its first Westminster seat in 2010.

In 1984 Porritt took over the helm at Friends of the Earth. Despite initial concerns regarding his political background, and how appropriate this was in an NGO that needed to reach out to all parties, it soon became clear he had arrived at the beginning of a time of extraordinary growth for the environmental movement. Public concern swelled in response to high-profile news stories, including disasters at Bhopal (1984) and Chernobyl (1986), alongside domestic crises such as the Bovine spongiform encephalopathy (BSE) epidemic. Coupled with increasingly sophisticated marketing techniques, this broader context created a boom time for environmental groups, including Friends of the Earth. His period in charge has also been noted for the relative internationalisation of the environmental agenda, as issues such as rainforest depletion, the ozone layer and global warming, began to seriously impact upon the public and political consciousness.

Since leaving Friends of the Earth, Porritt's career has increasingly focused on the notion of sustainable development, brought to public attention by the 1987 Brundtland Report, *Our Common Future*, and the 1992 Rio Earth Summit. In 1996, along with his former Green Party colleague Sara Parkin, Porritt established Forum for the Future, an NGO working with businesses and the statutory sector to transform their methods of working. From 2000 to 2009, he was also chair of the British government's Sustainable Development Commission, a publicly funded watchdog charged with promoting, reporting on and monitoring adherence to sustainable development principles. This body was in itself a direct result of the 1992 Earth Summit, developing as it did from the previous roundtable on sustainable development in England and Wales.

Awarded a CBE in 2000 for services to environmental protection, Porritt has also been closely involved with a range of other environmental organisations, including The Prince of Wales's Business and Environment Programme, the South West Round Table for Sustainable Development, and WWF-UK.

Some books by Jonathon Porritt

Seeing Green: The Politics of Ecology Explained (Oxford, 1984)
(ed.) *The Friends of the Earth Handbook* (London, 1987)
(co-authored with David Winner) *The Coming of the Greens* (London, 1988)
Where on Earth are We Going? (London, 1991)
Capitalism: As if the World Matters (London, 2005)

Further reading

www.forumforthefuture.org
Neil Carter, 'The Green Party: Emerging from the Political Wilderness?', *British Politics*, 3 (2008), pp. 223–40; Robert Lamb, *Promising the Earth* (London, 1996); Peter Rawcliffe, *Environmental Pressure Groups in Transition* (Manchester, 1998).

Martin Ennals

Although largely associated with his tenure as general secretary of Amnesty International between 1968 and 1980, Martin Ennals' career was marked with a consistent faith in political activism that embraced minority rights, civil liberties and human rights. As a campaigner and organiser, Ennals' achievements were substantial. His work centred on his belief that governments, politicians and bureaucrats could be influenced by well-researched, informed and truthful criticism. His work also demonstrated a dedication to fighting against persecution and discrimination.

Throughout his life Ennals demonstrated a profound commitment to a sense of international justice. In some respects this appeared a family trait. His father had been a regional officer in the United Nations' Association and both his brothers presided over that organisation at different points in their lives. Indeed, all three Ennals brothers would be involved in the Anti-Apartheid Movement. Unsurprisingly then, Ennals graduated from the LSE with a degree in international relations. From there he worked for the National Union of Students as assistant secretary before moving to Paris as president of UNESCO's staff association. In that position he led a successful defence of American UNESCO workers who were targeted during the McCarthy witch-hunts.

Ennals returned to London in 1959 to become organising secretary of the National Council for Civil Liberties (NCCL), and within nine months he had become the organisation's general secretary. Demonstrative of his capacity for inspiring organisations, Ennals played a vital role in re-establishing the NCCL as an independent, professional and credible organisation during the 1960s. His work in the NCCL saw the group embrace numerous minority rights issues. He was particularly eager that the organisation tackle gender and racial discrimination.

During this period Ennals was also associated with the Anti-Apartheid Movement, having organised the Boycott Movement against South African goods in 1959. After leaving the NCCL in 1966, Ennals took up a position as information officer in the National Committee for Commonwealth Immigrants to pursue his interests in race relations and the welfare of immigrants. He resigned from this quasi-governmental organisation in protest against the Labour government's handling of Kenyan Asians and the Commonwealth Immigration Act of 1968.

Ennals' commitment to human rights, his international outlook and his skill as an activist meant that he was a perfect appointment as general secretary of Amnesty International in 1968. For all that Amnesty owed much to its founder Peter Benenson's campaigning zeal, it was Ennals who built the organisation into a truly global player. Amnesty's staff expanded from 9 to 150, and its annual budget increased from £20,000 to £1.6 million under his leadership. It was during his tenure, in 1977, that Amnesty won the Nobel Peace Prize.

Such interests were products of Ennals' concerns for the rights of those that appeared most threatened. Outside of Amnesty he was outspoken in favour of gay rights, both in the NCCL and later whilst serving as a vice-president of the Campaign for Homosexual Equality. In 1987 he helped found Article 19, an NGO aiming to promote freedom of expression all over the world, and in 1986 he was a founder and then general secretary of International Alert, a global NGO. Typical of his interests, this group aimed to end violent conflict across the world through dialogue, advocacy, research and training. He also returned to more traditional civil liberties concerns by acting as an advisor to the Greater London Council's Police Committee during the 1980s.

Ennals worked in and between conventional and non-conventional bodies, and his activism demonstrated a coherent and longstanding commitment to human rights, civil liberties and international justice both at international and national levels.

Further reading

Martin Ennals, 'Amnesty International and Human Rights', in Peter Willetts (ed.), *Pressure Groups in the Global System* (London, 1982), pp. 62–83. See also the entry for David Ennals, which briefly covers Martin, in the *Dictionary of National Biography* by Howard Glennester. For Ennals at the NCCL, see Chris Moores, 'The Progressive Professionals: The National Council for Civil Liberties and the Politics of Activism in the 1960s', *Twentieth Century British History*, 20:4 (2009), pp. 538–60. For Amnesty during the 1970s, see Stephen Hopgood, *Keepers of the Flame* (London, 2006).

Mary Whitehouse

The career of Mary Whitehouse as an activist helps to unpick a few myths about social movements, NGOs and the nature of campaigning. Firstly, it makes clear that social movements can be reactionary as much as they are radical. Secondly, it reminds us that the 1960s inspired new strands of conservatism as well as the ideologies associated with the young and the political left. Thirdly, it shows that political action can stem from the comfortable surroundings of the middle-class suburb just as it does from the streets of the city. And, fourthly, it demonstrates that a morality inspired by religious belief has persisted as a key motivator for socio-political organising.

As with many an NGO, Whitehouse likes to present the origins of the National Viewers and Listeners' Association (NVLA) as the outcome of the concern of amateur, ordinary citizens. Upset at the emerging cultural revolution of the 1960s, and, more specifically, at the airing of a discussion about premarital sex on the TV programme *Meeting Point* on 8 March 1963, Whitehouse wrote a series of letters to the BBC that were frequently ignored. The following year, when the BBC licence was up for renewal, she therefore organised a meeting at Birmingham Town Hall and the 'Clean-up TV' campaign was launched.

Whitehouse, however, was no mere ordinary viewer. She was an experienced secondary school teacher who even had some background in broadcasting, having fronted a famine relief appeal in 1945 and presented her thoughts as a housewife on the coronation in 1953. Moreover, she had a long-term interest in public morality, having met her husband through the Oxford Group which later became Moral Re-Armament in 1938. And she soon transformed her campaign into a more professional outfit. 'Clean-up TV' soon became the National Viewers and Listeners' Association in 1965, with Whitehouse serving as general secretary until 1980 and president until 1993.

Whitehouse was often derided in the media as an interfering busybody, and certainly the frustrated BBC did much to encourage further public ridicule. Yet others have rightly come to see her as one of the 'populist heroines of the right'. Moreover, her activism was not out of step with other trends in the voluntary sector. While the NVLA owed its origins to a reactionary impulse, its demands to have licence-fee payers' views taken into account and for greater public participation in the running of public bodies locates it firmly among those consumer groups that sought greater consumer protection and representation. Indeed, it is in this sense that Whitehouse was most influential. Her presence and views were felt every time the BBC licence fee came to be renewed, and a number of concrete outcomes might be attributed to her organisation. These include the 1982 Indecent Displays Act, and the mechanisms through which the public could influence the content of TV and radio: the establishment of the Broadcasting Complaints Commission in 1981 and the Broadcasting Standards Council in 1988.

In addition, her own charisma helped galvanise various faith-based organisations around her cause, making the NVLA into something of a social movement, though one of the retired and the middle-aged rather than the young (indeed, she was 53 when she began her campaign). In one sense the NVLA might be imagined as the vanguard for the New Right as the Campaign for Nuclear Disarmament had once been imagined as the vanguard of the New Left. Certainly, it helped promote other forms of social activism. Whitehouse was a major figure behind the launch of the Festival of Light in 1971, the Christian revivalist movement that targeted moral pollution not only on television but across society as a whole, and which was able to bring 10,000 supporters into Trafalgar Square in September of that year at one of its many early rallies.

Because, from her perspective, standards on TV have continued to deteriorate, it might easily be assumed that she was ultimately unsuccessful. But she ought not to be ignored, and historians and sociologists are beginning to recognise her contribution to socio-political action.

Further reading

Whitehouse published three volumes of autobiography: *Who Does She Think She Is?* (London, 1971), *A Most Dangerous Woman?* (Tring, 1982) and *Quite Contrary: An Autobiography* (London, 1993). More scholarly assessments of her role can be found in Mary Warnock's entry on Whitehouse in the *Dictionary of National Biography* and in Lawrence Black, 'There was Something about Mary: The National Viewers and Listeners' Association and Social Movement History', in Nick Crowson, Matthew Hilton and James McKay (eds), *NGOs in Contemporary Britain: Non-state Actors in Society and Politics since 1945* (Basingstoke, 2009), pp. 182–200.

Michael Young

The list of voluntary organisations, pressure groups, think tanks and NGOs associated with Michael Young is quite extraordinary. As the original 'social entrepreneur', he created around 40 consumer, self-help and educational bodies that have profoundly shaped modern Britain. As more of an instigator rather than a manager, he is not generally acknowledged as an important figure in the voluntary sector, yet his ideas, energy and commitment to small-scale action has been critical in shaping modern British civil society.

Born in 1915, Young was the product of the progressive educational establishment at Dartington School. His first entry into the world of NGOs was through the policy think tank, Political and Economic Planning (PEP), of which he was the director during the Second World War. From there he was recruited into the Labour Party research department and contributed significantly to the 1945 election manifesto. Disillusioned with the statist policies of the Attlee administration, he turned to academic sociology, publishing pioneering works on family and kinship, as well as coining the term 'meritocracy' in his 1957 satire, before taking up the first lectureship in sociology at Cambridge University.

More significant, though, was the Institute of Community Studies (ICS) that he established in Bethnal Green in 1953 which he used as the base for both his academic research and his social organisations. It was from here that he launched the Consumers' Association in 1956, the publishers of *Which?* magazine from 1957. This would be a crucial cause throughout Young's career, its empowerment of the individual against the 'bigness' of capitalist and public sector organisations forming a central plank of his left-leaning humanist liberalism.

Other ventures soon followed. Many of these would follow the consumer model, such as the Advisory Centre for Education in 1960 which aimed to empower parents through access to greater information about schools. Education, though, was not a commodity: it was a lifelong learning experience. In 1962 he established the National Extension College, an open learning institution that would expand into the International Extension College in 1971. It was also a forerunner to the Open University, the establishment of which also owes much to Young's thinking. Education was to continue into retirement: Young's University of the Third Age continues to educate through self-managed lifelong learning co-operatives.

Some of his ventures were small scale and downright quirky. In the late 1970s, he set up Bulk Buying Clubs, and Language Line provided a telephone-interpretation service. He established a Mutual Aid Centre to assist citizens in taking control over their lives, be it motor vehicle repairs, playschool groups, and even education through the Brain Train, a study club for rail commuters. The College of Health (1983) followed the Patients' Association in empowering the ill, again along the consumer activist model, as well as setting up the first national AIDS helpline.

All this activity fitted into a coherent strategy for somebody who wished to empower individuals in society overseen by a democratic and fair state. To this end he was a founder member of the Social Democratic Party (SDP) and in 1982 he launched the Tawney Society as the SDP counterpart to the Fabian Society.

Towards the end of his life, he sought to create a new generation of activists such as himself. In 1997 he secured substantial funding for a School for Entrepreneurs, again to be run from the ICS in Bethnal Green, which aims to teach people how to direct their creative abilities to new institutional forms that improve society. Such a goal came from a rich tradition of liberal socialism within the Labour Party. Since the 2010 election, it now finds itself fashionable with the Conservative Party, and a model for what has been promoted as the 'Big Society'.

Further reading

The main biography is Asa Briggs, *Michael Young: Social Entrepreneur* (Basingstoke, 2001). See also Geoff Dench, Tony Flower and Kate Gavron (eds), *Young at Eighty: The Prolific Public Life of Michael Young* (Manchester, 1995), and the essays by Martin Daunton, Peter Hennessy, Matthew Hilton, Hilary Perraton and Pat Thane in the special issue of *Contemporary British History*, 19:3 (2005).

Peter Tatchell

Peter Tatchell (1952–) is an Australian-born human rights activist, whose high-profile career has embraced both party and non-party politics. Best known for his work on gay rights, Tatchell has long been a leading and at times controversial exponent of direct-action protests.

Tatchell came to Britain in 1971 at the age of 19. Within five days he had joined the newly formed Gay Liberation Front (GLF), established by LSE students Aubrey Walter and Bob Mellors, and modelled on its US counterpart. He quickly became involved with the GLF's trademark 'zaps', protest and awareness-raising stunts that combined humour and assertiveness with a sure grasp of what would play well in the media. Although the GLF itself was relatively short-lived, activists from it went on to play leading roles in subsequent gay rights and support groups, such as Stonewall, the London Lesbian and Gay Switchboard, and Tatchell's own campaign group, OutRage!

Following the GLF, Tatchell studied sociology at North London Polytechnic, becoming involved with student protests there. It was his party-political activism, however, that would first bring him to national prominence. In 1983, Tatchell was the Labour Party candidate in the Bermondsey by-election, triggered by the resignation of the sitting Labour MP Bob Mellish. The by-election became infamous for the unpleasantness with which it was conducted. Tatchell represented a bitterly divided party, received hate mail and death threats, and was denounced in the Commons by Labour leader Michael Foot. In the event, the Alliance candidate Simon Hughes won the seat with a landslide victory. Tatchell eventually left Labour, subsequently joining the Green Party.

Following the murder of Michael Booth in 1990, Tatchell was one of the founders of OutRage!, a loose network of direct-action activists, comparable in many ways to the GLF of the 1970s. The group quickly became controversial for its advocacy of outing those public figures it saw as promoting discrimination against gays, while secretly leading homosexual or bisexual lifestyles. MPs and Anglican bishops were particular targets for the group, which faced hostility for its stance from both within and outside the gay movement. Tatchell caused further controversy when he was one of several activists to invade the pulpit during the Archbishop of Canterbury's Easter sermon, in protest at the archbishop's attitudes towards gay rights. For his troubles, he was prosecuted under the 1860 Ecclesiastical Courts Jurisdiction Act.

Tatchell has been highly critical of what he sees as a commercialised, shallow and ultimately oppressive gay culture, failing to assert itself in the struggle for civil rights. Ultimately, he sees gay identity, however positive, as a defensive position in the face of homophobia, and argues that the real goal for gay activists is a situation where everyone's human rights are respected, allowing differentiation on the grounds of sexuality to fade into irrelevance.

Although best known for his work on gay rights, Tatchell's human rights campaigning has embraced a wide range of causes. Twice in his career he has attempted to arrest the Zimbabwean dictator Robert Mugabe for human rights abuses. On the second occasion, in Paris in 2001, he was badly beaten by Mugabe's entourage, leaving him with permanent brain damage. As a result of the ongoing incapacitating effects of these and other injuries sustained during campaigning, Tatchell announced in 2009 that he was standing down as the Green Party parliamentary candidate in Oxford East constituency.

Further reading

Peter Tatchell, *The Battle for Bermondsey* (London, 1983); Ian Lucas, *OutRage! An Oral History* (London, 1998).

Frank Field

Frank Field (1942–) is a poverty and welfare campaigner and Labour politician. Field has never been a 'natural insider', and despite his close association with the Labour Party he appears as being a 'rebel with a cause'. He rose to prominence when he became director of the Child Poverty Action Group (CPAG) in 1969, a post he would retain until his election to parliament as Labour MP for Birkenhead in 1979. Field broke the partisan relationship his predecessors Tony Lynes and Richard Titmuss had established with Labour and questioned the effectiveness of their Fabian-informed approach. Instead, he favoured a non-partisan strategy that meant establishing relations with both the Conservatives and the trade unions, in order to bring greater pressure to bear on Labour. He was motivated by Crossman's understanding of politics and believed that to achieve results in party politics there needed to be a distinction between myth and reality. For Field, the idea that Labour was the party of the poor was the myth, and he decided that CPAG would challenge this with a campaign 'The Poor Get Poorer under Labour'. Although his executive approved the campaign, it caused disquiet within the ranks, not least for Peter Townsend. During the 1970s Field developed the view that pressure could be applied more effectively to ministers by the media, and so he evolved a strategy that involved utilising different papers to target different audiences: the *Guardian* to attract the support of trade unionists; *The Times* to get to ministers and civil servants. He focused CPAG's efforts more narrowly on winning influence in the corridors of Whitehall and Westminster, and was prepared to allow others, such as Shelter, to bask in the glare of public opinion. CPAG began to re-determine its campaign message away from one of anti-poverty towards the more specific targets related to welfare rights. CPAG's campaign for Child Benefit reform in the mid 1970s was mired in controversy because Field became the recipient of leaks of cabinet minutes detailing its volte-face on the matter, which he then publicised in an article for *New Society* in June 1976. Whilst leading CPAG he also developed its casework role through its Citizens' Rights Office. He founded the Low Pay Unit in 1974, which was concerned with protecting the rights of workers on wage councils, and began a campaign along with Rodney Bickerstaffe, the trade unionist, for a national minimum wage (something finally achieved in 1998).

Field secured election to Westminster in 1979, and in 1980 was appointed shadow education and social security spokesman. He lost his frontbench post for voting against the ban on trade unions at GCHQ, the Cheltenham monitoring headquarters, rather than abstaining as the leadership requested. But Field found himself locked in a desperate battle with militant activists in Birkenhead who were trying to deselect him. He forced the leadership's hand by announcing he would stand as an Independent in the event of de-selection, and he was 'imposed' upon the local party. In 1997 Field was appointed as minister for welfare reform. But despite direct access to Tony Blair and a remit to think the unthinkable, he clashed with his boss Harriet Harman and Chancellor Gordon Brown and within a year he was returned to the backbenches. There he continued to campaign for welfare reform, objected to the abolition of the 10p tax band, urged a referendum on the European Union Constitution, and became a trenchant critic of the leadership of Gordon Brown.

Outside parliament he became chair of the Church Conservation Trust, 2001–07, helped found the Pension Reform Group, a think tank for reform of the pension system, and established the environmental NGO Cool Earth which buys up rainforest in trust for local indigenous populations. He has also served on the advisory board of free-market think tank Reform. But welfare reform has remained his secular religion, and in 2010 he accepted an invitation from David Cameron to chair the 'Review on Poverty and Life Chances'. Field, now labelled the 'Poverty Tsar' by the media, presented a report which argued that the life opportunities for each generation were determined by their formative childhood years. In doing so he was challenging the former Labour administration's emphasis on anti-poverty measures based on material income. He was also sceptical of the likelihood that child poverty could be eradicated by 2020.

Further reading

Frank Field, *Poverty and Politics: The Inside Story of the Child Poverty Action Group's Campaigns in the 1970s* (London, 1982); Michael McCarthy, *Campaigning for the Poor: CPAG and the Politics of Welfare* (London, 1986).

Pat Arrowsmith

Pat Arrowsmith (1930–) is a peace activist and campaigner. After completing her Cambridge history degree (where she became involved in the Crusade for World Government), Arrowsmith turned to the social sciences, completing postgraduate qualifications in Ohio and Liverpool. She began working for Liverpool's Family Service Unit as a social caseworker, then as a childcare officer before a period as a nursing assistant, before being sacked for getting patients and staff to sign an anti-nuclear petition. Her natural compassion and life experiences inevitably fed into her move towards political activism.

After reading a *Guardian* article about an anti-nuclear protester planning to sail to a nuclear test zone, she decided that banning the nuclear bomb was the central issue facing her generation. In 1958 she became organiser for several anti-nuclear campaigns, including the Committee of 100, the Direct Action Committee Against Nuclear War (DAC) and the Campaign for Nuclear Disarmament (CND). She helped organise the Aldermaston marches in 1958, and was intimately involved in the struggles within the anti-nuclear movement about the best tactics to adopt. She favoured direct action and was viewed as one of the radical militants of DAC. She was critical of those pacifists who allowed themselves to be distracted from campaigning about the nuclear bomb by matters such as opposing British membership of NATO. She frequently clashed with Canon Collins of CND. During the 1960s she combined her social care work with other forms of political activism, including editing the newspaper *Peace News*. Despite her commitment to direct activism, she also saw potential in the parliamentary route to publicise her causes: she stood frequently as a parliamentary candidate: Fulham in 1966 for Radical Alliance, Hammersmith in 1970 as an anti-Vietnam War candidate, and Cardiff in 1979 as Independent Socialist against Jim Callaghan, barracking him throughout his acceptance speech. When she was given an entry in *Who's Who* in 1976 because of her CND work, she used it to highlight her sexuality.

As her range of parliamentary candidatures suggests, Arrowsmith did not confine herself solely to the anti-nuclear cause. From 1969 to 1971 she became interested in race relations, becoming a researcher for the Society of Friends Race Relations Committee, and she took a range of menial hourly-paid jobs through the 1970s to fund her activism. In 1971 she joined Amnesty International as an assistant editor, a role she kept until 1994, and whilst there, formed its first trade union. Between 1958 and 1985 she was jailed eleven times, including an 18-month sentence for sedition after leafleting soldiers urging them not to serve in Northern Ireland (she escaped from prison several times), and was twice adopted as a prisoner of conscience by Amnesty. She has been named several times in the House of Commons, including in October 1961 after she went on hunger strike in Gateside Prison and was being forcibly fed. From the outset she complained that the police were using arcane and obscure laws to jail her and other peace activists; however, when she took the British Government to the Council of Europe's Court of Human Rights in 1975, arguing that this was contrary to her human rights, she lost her case.

Further reading

Aside from her political activism, Arrowsmith has written a number of fictional books and poetry. She also wrote a short memoir of her anti-Vietnam War activities, *To Asia in Peace* (London, 1972). Her role in the anti-nuclear movement features heavily in Richard Taylor, *Against the Bomb: The British Peace Movement 1958–65* (Oxford, 1988).

Tariq Ali

Tariq Ali (1943–) is a Renaissance man of the British left, first coming to national prominence as a radical student leader in the 1960s, and later establishing himself as a leading writer and cultural critic.

Ali was born into a wealthy and influential Pakistani family, his grandfather having served as prime minister of the Punjab. He came to Britain in the 1960s to study at Oxford University.

As a student, Ali began to develop a reputation as an activist. He was disciplined by the university following a protest against the South African ambassador Dr Carel de Wet. While president of Oxford Union in 1965, he was acquitted on a threatening behaviour charge following involvement in a protest against the Vietnam War which took place near the US embassy.

Later in the decade, Ali became a significant figure in the British counter-culture. During 1967/68, he was one of the founders of the radical socialist journal *Black Dwarf*. The journal experienced a tumultuous life, including high-profile raids by the police, and internal tensions over an alleged attempted takeover by the Trotskyist International Marxist Group (IMG), which Ali had joined. He departed *Black Dwarf*, and set up and edited the socialist journal *Red Mole*, renamed *Red Star* in 1973. Later in the 1970s he edited the Trotskyist paper *Socialist Challenge*.

It was Ali's leading involvement with the Vietnam Solidarity Campaign (VSC) that brought him to national prominence. The activities of the VSC, most notably the violent anti-war protests outside the US embassy in March 1968, triggered calls for Ali to be deported, and led the Home Secretary, James Callaghan, to describe him as a 'spoiled, rich playboy'. Although British student activism in 1968 never reached the levels of elsewhere, Ali was seen in the media as a comparable figure to continental student leaders Rudi Dutschke and Daniel Cohn-Bendit. His activities with the VSC were immortalised in the Rolling Stones song, 'Street Fighting Man'.

During the 1970s, Ali participated in electoral politics under the IMG banner. He unsuccessfully contested Sheffield Attercliffe during the February 1974 general election, and continued to contest national and European elections for the party later in the decade. By the early 1980s, however, he had left the IMG and attempted to join the Labour Party. His application was opposed by Michael Foot, Neil Kinnock and the party's National Executive Committee, amidst much broader concern in the party at the role of far-left entryism. Despite having the support of his local party, backed by future Labour MP Jeremy Corbyn, his application was definitely rejected by the annual conference in 1983.

Notwithstanding his forays into party politics, by the 1970s Ali's name was more likely to be spotted in newspaper by-lines than headlines. He has maintained a prolific output as a writer and commentator, and his wide-ranging work embraces fiction, history and politics, particularly international affairs. Since 1983, he has sat on the editorial board of the *New Left Review*.

Further reading
Tariq Ali, *Street Fighting Years: An Autobiography of the Sixties* (London, 1987).

Victor Gollancz

Publisher and activist Victor Gollancz (1893-1967) was a central figure in twentieth-century Britain's progressive politics.

After being dismissed as a classics master at Repton School for being too radical (thereby having the distinction of being sacked by the future Archbishop of Canterbury, Geoffrey Fisher), Gollancz joined the publishing firm Benn Brothers in 1921. He developed his expertise within the firm, and subsequently founded his own publishing house in 1927.

Gollancz quickly established a reputation for the groundbreaking design and marketing of his books, as well as making some of the time's most prominent writers available in affordable formats. Throughout his publishing, his passion for progressive politics, and socialism particularly, shone through.

In 1936 Gollancz launched the venture for which he is most famous: the Left Book Club. Conceived as part of Popular Front efforts to combat Nazism, the Club provided a mass-market platform for writers such as Arthur Koestler, George Orwell and Sidney and Beatrice Webb. The Club became a key institution of interwar progressive politics, with 57,000 members at its height, and 1,500 discussion groups nationwide. Despite its popularity, and the wider political and educational activities it generated, the Club faded following the defeat of Nazism and the election of a socialist government in 1945, publishing its final book in 1948.

After the War, Gollancz turned to more direct campaigning. In 1945 he had established Save Europe Now (SEN), a humanitarian relief effort on behalf of those displaced and left destitute in central Europe. SEN was credited with ensuring the survival of local wartime relief coordinating efforts (such as what would become Oxfam), and closed in 1948, following the establishment of the Marshall Plan. He was further involved in a wide range of progressive causes in the post-war decades, from the Campaign for Nuclear Disarmament to efforts to abolish the death penalty (even unsuccessfully seeking to persuade the Israeli government not to hang Adolf Eichmann in 1961).

Arguably his most lasting campaigning legacy was the international development charity War on Want (WOW). On 12 February 1951, Gollancz wrote a letter to the *Manchester Guardian*. The letter itself was not principally concerned with development, beginning with a sketch of the international situation dominated by the Korean War, massive rearmament, and the catastrophic decline in international relations. However, he went on to call for

> a great international fund ... for improving the conditions of those fellow human beings who, to the number of hundreds of millions, are starving, destitute, and in despair. I should like to see our own country, by the size of its proposed contribution, challenging the world to a new kind of rivalry, a rivalry in the works of peace ... So at last might swords be turned into ploughshares.

Gollancz received 10,000 postcards in support of his call, leading to the establishment of the Association of World Peace (AWP), which issued its first leaflet on 12 March 1951. Although its initiator quickly faded from the organisation, the AWP went on to commission Labour politician Harold Wilson to write a report on development, published as *War on Want* (1952), and leading directly to the establishment of the body of the same name.

Further reading

Gollancz published two autobiographical volumes, *My Dear Timothy* (1952) and *More for Timothy* (1953). For the foundation of War on Want, see Mark Luetchford and Peter Burns, *Waging the War on Want: Fifty Years of Campaigning against World Poverty* (London, 2003).

6
Membership and Volunteering

Introduction: the Big Society

In May 2010, Britain's new coalition government took office, committed to introducing the 'Big Society'. It was an idea that David Cameron had chosen to make his defining offer to the British people, since being elected leader of the Conservative Party in December 2005. The phrase was a self-conscious neologism, an attempt to distinguish Cameron's Conservative Party both from what was characterised as New Labour's statism, and from the Conservative Party's own hitherto unsympathetic public image. As a concept, the Big Society was embraced and derided, adopted and rejected in equal measure across party lines: it raised the suspicions of many more traditional Conservatives, while the left were divided between those who saw it as a cover for cuts to public spending, and those who wished to embrace community activism as a long-term way of revitalising their political fortunes. And yet, the novelty of the phrasing and the mixed reaction to the idea notwithstanding, the Big Society is in many ways a contemporary expression of longstanding ideas, embedded within much older debates over the respective roles of voluntarism and the state in British society.

In constructing his notion of the Big Society, Cameron melded liberal, conservative and progressive critiques of contemporary Britain, in order to demonstrate to the widest possible audience that current ways of doing things were irretrievably broken. From traditional Conservatism, he took the idea that the state had become too large, an overbearing presence that was stripping people of their sense of personal and social responsibility. He invoked a golden age of community and kindness, which had been smothered by the expansion of big government. From liberalism, Cameron introduced the idea that in its bloated form, the state was no longer accountable to its citizens, and thus co-opted civil libertarian concerns over surveillance and unchecked state power into his overall theme. From the left, meanwhile, he used the failure of the progressive dream against the centralising, Fabian bureaucracy the public were invited to see before them, while distinguishing himself from Thatcherism by asserting that the Big Society could be no simple exercise in rolling back the state. Society would not automatically flower in the ground vacated by government.

Instead, government was needed to coax society back into life. The state, it was conceded, had made enormous progressive strides, at least up until the late 1960s. But in recent years, social mobility and progress had stalled, despite ever larger amounts of taxpayers' money being spent. The logic was that a different approach was now needed, in the face of state failure. Decentralisation, transparency and accountability were to be the methods. The means would be found in social entrepreneurs, community activists, and by giving people once again the means and encouragement to participate in the running of their country. The relationship between the state and society should be reversed, the overbearing master being transformed into the faithful servant.

The idea of the Big Society takes its place as the latest in a long line of critiques of the relationship between society and the state. It is relatively unusual amongst these narratives in that it deliberately seeks to borrow from a variety of political traditions. At the same time, it is entirely typical. Its central premise is that things were once different, society was once ordered in a better way, and that somehow government and citizens have since lost the path of righteousness. In other words, the Big Society is normative in that it takes a particular time and place, real or imagined, and argues that diversions from this norm are necessarily wrong. The first part of this chapter briefly reviews how common such thinking has been amongst those who have thought and written about voluntarism, campaigning and participation. As will be clear, the evidence base for assessing the wide range of voluntary activity is not ideal. However, such evidence that does exist suggests that change, not decline (or even revival) is the key to understanding the reality of social activism in Britain. The main part of the chapter is given over to reviewing the evidence that does exist and concluding that ultimately, activism reflects the society from which it comes. As society changes and develops, so does activism. Change is the key.

Tunnel visions

Commentary on associational life, volunteering and citizen engagement is dominated by four broad concepts. Firstly, there is a conservative critique that sees the advance of the state in the twentieth century as having stifled voluntary and informal activity. Secondly, and in some ways complementing the conservative critique, there is a body of literature that champions the importance of associational life to liberal democracies, and which has recently focused on the question of whether associational life has declined since the mid twentieth century. (The impact of both of these schools of thought can be seen in the concept of the Big Society.) A third school of thought, much of it coming from a more radical perspective, looks to the social changes of the mid century, particularly increased levels of affluence and education, and detects a more confident, critical citizenry. And finally, there is a diverse body of work on apathy and disengagement, which argues that people have become detached from the traditional processes of engagement and accountability in society, or, alternatively, were never particularly engaged in these processes in the first place.

These four are the dominant interpretations of engagement and associational life, and they each look in different directions. That is not to say, however, that they are mutually exclusive. They all offer important truths about the current nature of society; their collective weakness is that they each, to a greater or lesser degree, privilege particular aspects of that society, and therefore individually present an incomplete view. Each perspective carries with it its own form of tunnel vision. By bringing them together, though, it is possible to come to a more balanced view of how society has changed and continues to do so, shaping and creating new forms of engagement and association as it goes.

The conservative critique of the state's impact on voluntarism and association has its eyes firmly fixed on the Victorian era. Here, it is held, a small state, laissez-faire economics and Christian faith blended together to give people the freedoms, incentives and inclinations necessary to improve society for themselves, rather than sit back and expect state provision to do it for them. However, these perfect conditions began to break down in the twentieth century, with the rise of the state in both the economic and the social sphere, and the long, seemingly inexorable emptying of the pews. Although these processes played out over a long period, it is the post-war decades that have a particular reputation for infamy, when a comprehensive welfare state was established, and new cults of youth and permissiveness undermined deference and religious observance. The New Right, born in think tanks like the Institute for Economic Affairs, and later taken into Downing Street by Margaret Thatcher, sought to challenge this shift, and assert what was seen as the deeply moral case for rolling back state frontiers. The state had infantilised the country by smothering the proper roles of charity, citizenship and association – only by pushing back against the state could these things be revived. The conservative critique overextends itself by claiming that voluntarism was necessarily harmed by the rise of the state. Nevertheless, it provides a key insight – the shape and nature of the state is of fundamental importance to voluntarism. As the state grew and developed over the twentieth century, the social contribution of voluntarism was reshaped accordingly.

Liberal associational thought on this topic is particularly associated with the United States and, to a lesser extent, Britain. The basic premise, which goes back to the nineteenth-century reportage of Alexis de Tocqueville, is that the coming together of citizens in associations and shared endeavour is a crucial part of a healthy liberal democracy, because it provides them with the skills, confidence and inclination to participate in the running of their societies. The theme was revived in the mid century, when it was found that Britain and the US were peculiarly good examples of such a society, and correspondingly well-functioning democracies. By the end of the twentieth century, however, work was emerging that carried a more worrying message. By now, the links and bonds of associational life had been conceptualised as 'social capital'. It was reported that while mid-century America had indeed been rich in such capital, stocks had dwindled dangerously since then, as social networks closed inwards and shrank. The drawback of this school of thought is that it privileges as its norm a particular type of community and associational life, that which was common from the 1920s to the 1960s. It neglects the fact that the clubs, teams and neighbourhoods of that era were shaped by a particular set of societal circumstances. Its key insight, however, is incredibly valuable: the way in which we link with people and causes has changed fundamentally over the twentieth century and beyond. The predictable, committed and face-to-face association of clubs, leagues and institutes has long been in decline. In its place have come more individualised, irregular and distant methods of interaction.

While Conservatives critique the role of the state, and liberals look to the role of association, the radical perspective on this topic focuses upon the changing nature of the individual. Unlike the previous two perspectives, it tells a story of hope, not despair. In common with them, it has a key time, in this case the late 1960s. Under the overlapping headings of post-materialism, middle-class radicalism, the new politics, and new social movements, this school looks to how rising levels of affluence, education and social security have changed the way citizens engage with the world around them. Relieved of the material concerns over food on the table and a roof overhead, people have been liberated to consider issues of identity and quality of life, in areas such as gender and sexuality, peace, racial equality, and the state of the environment. As well as new topics coming to the fore, new ways of tackling these topics have emerged. Out are bureaucracy and formality; in are more fluid networks based around the primacy of the individual conscience and experience. Counter-intuitively, this vision of a new cadre of confident, critical citizens is complemented by a literature which points to people's inexorable disengagement with the traditional forms and structures of politics: voting in elections; joining political parties and trade unions; attending political meetings. They are two sides of the same coin, as a new politics has displaced the old.

The different approaches to questions of association and participation therefore leave us with three key insights. Firstly, the context: the changing nature of the state has been a crucial determinant of the shape and role of voluntary activity. Secondly, the manner in which voluntary and associational activity is undertaken has changed dramatically, away from the face-to-face and the collective, towards a far more individualised model. And finally, to complement the changes to the context and the manner of association, the participants have changed too: richer, smarter and more self-assured, these new citizens each have their own distinctive agendas and are increasingly disinclined to subsume their social and political identity within a larger whole. Individually, these insights are limited. Collectively, they provide the key to understanding how membership, volunteering and association have changed over recent decades.

The ever-changing nature of associational life

Those wishing to understand changing trends in membership and volunteering face a twofold challenge. Firstly, the data available seem to point to different conclusions – optimism and pessimism, continuity and change. Secondly, much of the data that exists – and there is a great deal of it – does not lend itself to easy comparison over time. Surveys start and stop, questions are asked in significantly different ways, and researchers work to constantly changing definitions. Drawing firm conclusions from such material is an incredibly difficult task. And yet the diversity of material can tell its own story. For every clear narrative – be it decline, revival, or enduring apathy – there is a mass of contradictory evidence. Simplistic stories do not stand up to serious scrutiny. Instead, we should understand that some indicators point in one direction, while others point in entirely another. By integrating these varying perspectives, we can get an overall sense of change over time.

It is undoubtedly true that many of the habits and institutions classically associated with active citizenship have declined dramatically over recent decades. The various figures in Chapter 2 summarised the main trends. Voting at general and local elections has dropped from a peak in the 1950s. Membership of the main political parties has fallen considerably: the combined memberships of the Labour and Conservative Parties were over 3 million in 1964, but fewer than 500,000 in 2006. And trade union figures have likewise fallen, though here membership did expand through to the 1970s before collapsing sharply in the 1980s.

Clearly, then, major behaviours and forms of association classically associated with an individual being politically active are in serious decline, and have been so for decades. However, this is not in itself conclusive evidence of apathy and disassociation. For one thing, none of these sets of data are unproblematic. Voting in elections, of course, is not in itself an infallible measure of interest in politics. Historic (and current) party membership data are less than transparent: estimates are heavily reliant upon disclosures by parties themselves, and historic requirements for local parties to have a given level of membership in order to qualify for affiliation may also have created an incentive to artificially inflate figures. Further, the decline in trade union membership can be supposed to be closely linked to events in 1980s Britain, and the perceived efficacy and social norm of belonging to such a group. Nevertheless, collectively these datasets suggest that there has been a turning away – not from politics and engagement as such – but rather from particular, historically specific ways of organising that involvement.

Beyond the political arena, other classic sites of membership and association have also experienced striking decline. Chapter 2 also showed how membership of traditional women's organisations, that thrived in the early and mid twentieth century, has fallen dramatically. Since the 1950s, cumulative membership of these groups has fallen by approximately 60 per cent. Precipitous decline appears to have set in with the advent of second-wave feminism in the late 1960s, and the general trend of women's (particularly middle-class women's) entry into the paid workforce. In amongst this general decline are women's groups such as the Mothers' Union and the Church of Scotland Women's Guild. Their decline is a fate shared by Christian observance more generally (see Figure 6.1, and Chapter 2, Figure 2.4).

While the decline in recent decades has not been as precipitous as for women's organisations, there has clearly been a steady thinning of the pews. The overall picture, of course, is more complicated than that presented here. In the Christian community, charismatic denominations have seen significant growth in recent years, while other faiths again show different results: in a multicultural society,

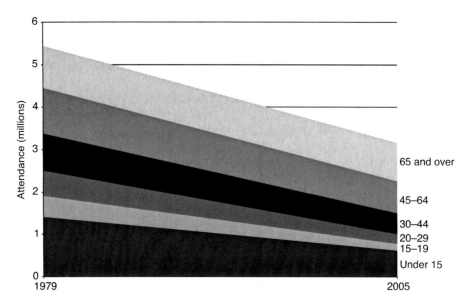

Figure 6.1: Attendance at churches by age, 1979–2005

Sources: *Social Trends*, 37 (2007), p. 181; data from English Church Census, Christian Research.

religious observance is informed by ethnicity alongside other social factors such as age and class. Yet even with these qualifications, these figures in themselves do not demonstrate that there has been a generalised socio-political disengagement in Britain. Rather, they are indicative of a particular historical change, the significance of which should be neither downplayed nor exaggerated: the available data suggest that as a whole, we are doing rather less often those specific things that our parents and grandparents used to do as a matter of course. Undoubtedly, we are significantly less likely than our forebears to go to church, vote, join a party, get involved with the Mothers' Union, or do any number of things that once defined socio-political engagement. But this does not in itself demonstrate that nowadays we are less socio-politically engaged. In order to assess that, we need to ask: what, if anything, are we doing instead?

The evidence that there has been a growth in membership, association and engagement is just as good – and just as in need of careful qualification – as the evidence for decline. Previous chapters attest to the rising number of organisations Britain hosts, and the growing number of people who join or support those organisations. The overall framework of association and membership, therefore, is healthy. However, there is considerable debate over what this actually means for the individuals who do join, volunteer or otherwise support their chosen groups – the nature of association has changed dramatically over recent decades, in no area more so than how we choose to affiliate and support our favourite causes. A key question is whether membership and association has been devalued and damaged by these changes, or if it is more benignly reflective of new social realities.

Organisations do not, of course, necessarily require association and membership, and therefore we need to look down a level, at the supporter base, to get a fuller picture. Decline in certain areas is being offset by dramatic membership and supporter growth in other areas, such as environmental groups (see Figure 6.2).

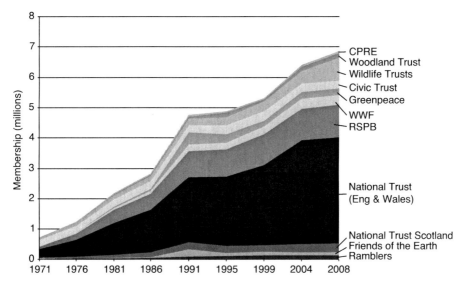

Figure 6.2: Membership of environmental organisations, 1971–2008

Sources: *Social Trends*; Annual reports and accounts, organisations concerned.

Figure 6.2 encompasses a wide range of organisations with different causes and approaches. Some, such as the National Trust and the Royal Society for the Protection of Birds (RSPB), were born in the first wave of interest in environmental preservation, from the mid nineteenth century onwards, when urbanisation and industrialisation were seen as key threats to Britain's natural and built heritage. In the interwar period, the socially elite nature of the earlier groups was complemented by groups of professionals, like the planners and architects of the Campaign to Protect Rural Britain (CPRE), and those, like the Ramblers, capturing the affordable leisure opportunities offered by the countryside. Later groups, including Greenpeace and Friends of the Earth, brought with them the ecological and global environmental concerns of the 1970s, and a distinct campaigning bias. And yet, as the figure demonstrates, the 1970s was a key point of development for all groups, traditional and modern, recreational and campaigning alike.

At this time, the environment was just one of a number of causes associated with activism, particularly amongst young people and those benefiting from the expansion of tertiary education. The 'new social movements', encompassing themes such as civil rights, peace activism, sexuality and sexual politics, have been credited with harnessing a generalised upswing of activism from the 1960s onwards, with particular emphasis on the radical, the progressive and the confrontational. Clearly, the causes and styles that came to prominence in these years are significant in the history of activism and engagement. But they formed only one aspect of one period in our recent history. The new social movements, then, did not form a rupture with the past, but rather add to the ongoing nature of change.

Rather than dramatic decline, or rebirth, there is good reason to believe that membership and volunteering has remained a relatively constant presence in Britain's socio-political life, as an overall phenomenon. Certainly, when asked by the British Household Panel Survey, respondents have showed a degree of consistency (though with a slight decline) in the number of types of organisations they have claimed to be a member of (see Figure 6.3).

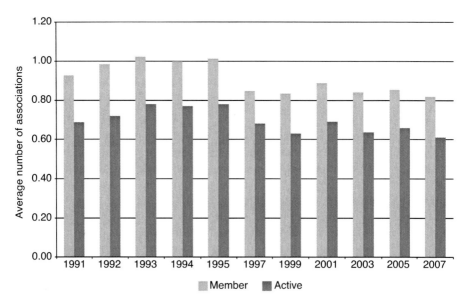

Figure 6.3: Average number of types of associations people belong to or are active in, 1991–2007

Source: University of Essex, Institute for Social and Economic Research, *British Household Panel Survey: Waves 1–18, 1991–2009* (computer file), 7th edn, Colchester, Essex, UK Data Archive (distributor) July 2010, SN: 5151.

The more significant trend to capture is that of the changes in the topics people are engaged with, and the ways they engage with them (see Figure 6.4). As can be seen, some causes and forms of association have declined since the Second World War – women's organisations and service groups most notably. Youth groups seem to have had a post-war renaissance, followed by a decline that has left them roughly at their post-war level. At the same time, outdoor organisations and environmental groups have flourished. The overall picture that emerges is of a society experiencing change, rather than decline or revival.

This impression is borne out when one looks at overall levels of volunteering over recent decades, depicted in Figure 6.5 which shows a general upwards trend

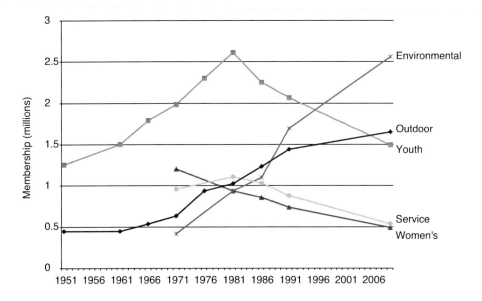

Figure 6.4: Membership of various sectors, 1951–2009

Sources: Compilation of figures from many different sources, principally *Social Trends* (various years), Peter A. Hall, 'Social Capital in Britain', *British Journal of Political Science*, 29 (1999), pp. 417–61; Annual reports and accounts, organisations concerned.

in volunteering (though the figures are not unproblematic). Looking in more detail, in Figure 6.6 the top line shows rates of informal voluntary activity over the past year (that is, ad hoc help and assistance outside of one's family, but not formally organised by groups or associations). The middle line shows the number of respondents reporting formal volunteering (that is, through a club or association) over the past year, while the bottom line shows reported rates of formal volunteering over the last month.

Over the last 30 years, these indicators have remained remarkably steady. As would be expected, more people volunteer informally than formally, and more volunteer formally over the space of a year than do so over a single month. Nevertheless, it seems that succeeding generations are not strikingly less likely to get involved with wider society than their forebears. The stories of decline come from a mis-understanding: they focus on the fact that we stop doing some things (going to church, joining the Women's Institute), but neglect the fact that we are doing other things instead. Indeed, over the past 30 years, members of the British public have continued to raise money, campaign, provide advice, join committees and offer their services in countless other ways to sustain the life of voluntary associations, charities and NGOs (see Figure 6.7). And they have continued to join for all the reasons that motivated a volunteer in the 1950s (see Figure 6.8).

There is also a relatively predictable pattern to when in our lives we carry out this volunteering (see Figure 6.9). Generally speaking, young adults show a strong

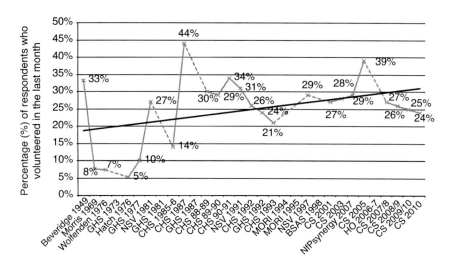

Figure 6.5: Number of people volunteering in the past month, according to various surveys, 1949–2010

Key: GHS = General Household Survey; NSV = National Survey of Volunteering; CHS = Charity Household Survey; BSAS = British Social Attitudes Survey; HO = *Helping Out*; CS = Citizenship Survey.

Sources: 'Beveridge 1949': Beveridge 1949, p. 33; 'Morris 1969': Mary Morris, *Voluntary Work in the Welfare State* (London, 1969), p. 252; 'GHS 1973': *Social Trends*, 6 (1975), p. 98; 'Wolfenden 1976': Wolfenden 1978, p. 35; 'Hatch 1976': Stephen Hatch, *Voluntary Work: A Report of a Survey* (Berkhamsted, 1978); 'GHS 1977': Stephen Humble, *Voluntary Action in the 1980s: A Summary of the Findings of a National Survey* (London, 1982), p. 5; 'NSV 1981': Humble, *Voluntary Action in the 1980s*; 'GHS 1981': *Social Trends*, 14 (1984), p. 153; 'CHS 1985-6' and 'CHS 1987': *Charity Statistics*, 12 (1989); 'GHS 1987': *The 1991 National Survey of Voluntary Activity in the UK* (Berkhamsted, 1993), p. 19; 'CHS 88-89', 'CHS 89-90', 'CHS 90-91': *Charity Statistics* (1995), p. 53; NSV 1991: *The 1991 National Survey of Voluntary Activity in the UK*; 'CHS 1992': *Charity Statistics* (1995), p. 53; 'GHS 1992': *Charity Statistics* (1997), p. 232; 'CHS 1993': *Charity Statistics* (1995), p. 53; 'MORI 1994', 'MORI 1995': *Charity Statistics* (1996), p. 36; 'NSV 1997': *National Survey of Volunteering 1997*; 'BSAS 1998': *Social Trends*, 30 (2000), p. 218; 'CS 2001', 'CS 2003', 'CS 2005': Citizenship Survey, data from www. communities.gov.uk/communities/research/citizenshipsurvey; 'HO 2006-7': *Helping Out: A National Survey of Volunteering and Charitable Giving* (London, 2007); 'NfpSynergy 2007': 'Who Volunteers? Volunteering Trends: 2000–2007: A Briefing from nfpSynergy', January 2008, available at: www.nfpsynergy.net/includes/documents/cm_docs/2008/v/volunteeringtrendsjan08.pdf; 'CS 2007/8', 'CS 2008/9', 'CS 2009/10', 'CS 2010': Citizenship Survey.

interest in membership and volunteering, and this interest strengthens as they reach middle age. This propensity declines somewhat as we approach retirement, and continues to do so with the onset of old age.

Contrary to the expectations of those who lament the relative secularisation of Britain over the twentieth century, it would further seem that faith (or at least, the presence or absence of Christian faith) does not have a strong connection with the propensity to volunteer (see Figure 6.10). This is in spite of the strong contribution of faith groups to associational and campaigning life for centuries, from the abolition of the slave trade, through social service and temperance movements, to advocacy of international development. There is clearly some variation between faiths – the differences between Muslims and Buddhists is particularly striking, although these

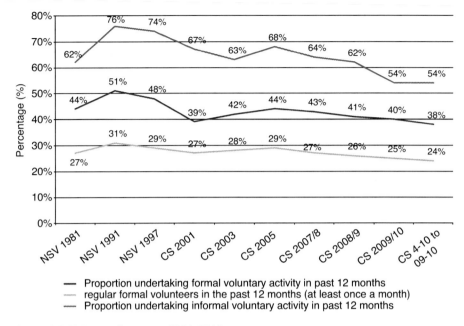

Figure 6.6: Volunteering rates, 1981–2010

Sources: National Survey of Volunteering (1981, 1991, 1997); Citizenship Surveys (2001–10), data from www.communities.gov.uk/communities/research/citizenshipsurvey.

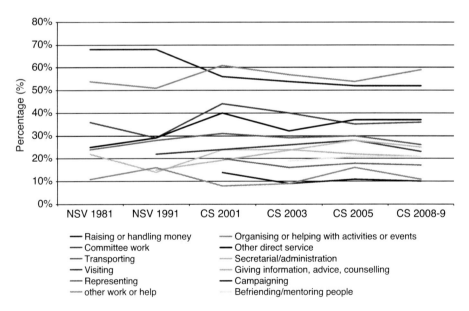

Figure 6.7: Volunteering by type of tasks done within charities/organisations, 1981–2009

Sources: National Survey of Volunteering (1981); Citizenship Surveys (2001–08), data from www.communities.gov.uk/communities/rcscarch/citizenshipsurvey.

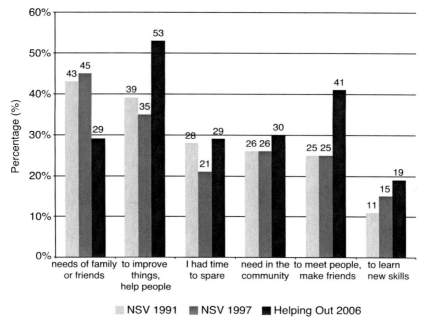

Figure 6.8: Reasons for volunteering, 1991–2006

Sources: National Survey of Volunteering (1991, 1997); *Helping Out: A National Survey of Volunteering and Charitable Giving* (London, 2007).

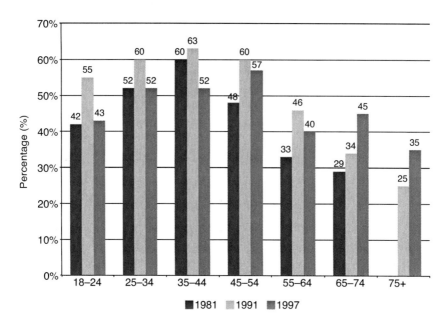

Figure 6.9: Volunteering by age, 1981–97

Source: National Survey of Volunteering (1981, 1991, 1997).

may be explicable through different cultural norms of social engagement. However, the most interesting finding is that there is little real difference between Christians and those with no religion.

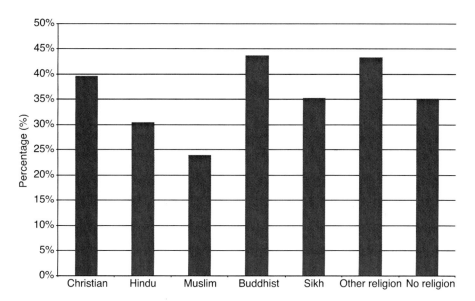

Figure 6.10: Rates of volunteering by faith, 2007–08 to April–September 2010 (formal volunteering at least once in the last year (%))

Source: Citizenship Survey: Headline Findings – April–September 2010, England, www.communities.gov. uk/publications/corporate/statistics/citizenshipsurveyq2201011.

Given all the change that has taken place in British associational life, one can therefore be relatively confident that the quantity of interaction has neither dramatically declined nor spectacularly revived. But what of the quality of that interaction? If one considers the startling rise of environmental groups since the 1970s, the criticism has been made that this, somehow, is not *real* participation. At one time, the argument goes, we used to get together face to face, and do things collectively for the greater good. Now, we just sign direct debit forms, and are only 'members' of an organisation in a tenuous, financial sense. We rarely (knowingly) meet other financial supporters, nor seem to have much wish to do so. We simply want to pay a small sum, calm our troubled consciences, and then get back to the business of getting on with our lives. In this way, the social has been degraded in a way concealed by membership statistics and the growth of large organisations – it is just not the same any more.

Although this is a caricature, there is a truth to be confronted here. The internet, direct mail, direct debits, ethical consumption – all of these phenomena have facilitated the rise of an atomised activism, less centred on face-to-face engagement. But there are three main reasons why these concerns are less valid than they might at first seem. Firstly, a statement is still being made. If we choose to sign a direct debit to Friends of the Earth, or boycott Nestlé products when stood in front of a vending machine, we are still making a choice. We are acting in a political, discriminatory way, to express support or displeasure through the medium of our everyday lives. These are hardly the actions of an apathetic generation. Secondly, by doing so, we contribute to broader social norms. Personal decisions become collective, if not strictly associational, when repeated en masse. Public scrutiny and engagement is increased, and politicians, businesses and campaign groups respond accordingly. Finally, this is clearly not all we are doing, nor is it all we will do in the future. Social and technological change will continue to shape activism and associational life, just as it has done over the last century. But new developments – direct debits, Facebook, and so on – do not sweep away the old overnight. Rather, they add to the rich mix of association and activism, so churchgoers might check their Twitter feed during a tedious sermon, before sharing a Fairtrade coffee with other parishioners after the service, before dropping some wine bottles in the bottle bank on the way back home, and then picking the kids up from Sunday League football. All of these activities are social and/or political. Some are old, some new, but they sit alongside each other (at the moment, at least) in the kaleidoscope of membership, volunteering and activism.

Conclusion

For decades, people have been bemoaning the decline of associational life. Some have done so from a conservative perspective, others have been progressive. The state, or television, or women's liberation, or political correctness, or educational dumbing-down – the list of supposed reasons for this supposed decline goes on and on. And in response to this chorus of despair, politicians regularly step forward with plans to revive society – the Big Society is but the latest example of this trend. Others, meanwhile, have argued that we are actually witnessing a great revival in our society, that we are more engaged, and more active, than ever before, and it is simply the political system that has been left behind. Even this revivalism is a narrative of decline, of course, but one that looks to the decline of formal politics rather than other areas of society.

All of these stories contain some truth. But equally, they are all myopic. They focus on one particular aspect without considering the whole picture. And that picture is, and always will be, one of change. Today's fashionable cause will be neglected tomorrow, yesterday's way of engaging bears little relation to how we do things now, and less still to how we will do them in the future (see Figure 6.11 for data on the types of activity supported by volunteers). Volunteering, membership and associational life is subject to constant and extraordinary flux. And yet, overall, it continues. It manages this seemingly remarkable feat because there is so much diversity, so much going on, in different places, with different people, in different ways, that single trends and social innovations, however powerful, can only change the makeup of the overall picture, not seriously undermine it as a whole. As a nation, we quite like to get involved. That fact remains remarkably constant. It is the how, and the why, that changes.

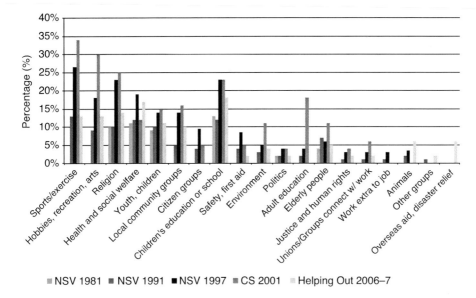

■ NSV 1981 ■ NSV 1991 ■ NSV 1997 ■ CS 2001 ▪ Helping Out 2006–7

Figure 6.11: Volunteering by types of sector, 1981–2007

Sources: National Survey of Volunteering (1981, 1991, 1997); Citizenship Survey (2001); *Helping Out* (2006): *Helping Out: A National Survey of Volunteering and Charitable Giving* (London, 2007).

Further reading

An overview of the changing nature of voluntarism in the twentieth century can be found in Matthew Hilton and James McKay (eds), *The Ages of Voluntarism: How We Got to the Big Society* (London, 2011). Other key texts include Jose Harris (ed.), *Civil Society in British History: Ideas, Identities, Institutions* (Oxford, 2003), and Brian Harrison, *Peaceable Kingdom: Stability and Change in Modern Britain* (London, 1982).

David Cameron's 2009 Hugo Young Memorial Lecture provides an excellent overview of the Big Society concept, available at: www.conservatives.com/News/Speeches/2009/11/David_Cameron_The_Big_Society.aspx. The conservative critique of the state's impact on voluntarism and association has been most elegantly put by Frank Prochaska: see *The Voluntary Impulse: Philanthropy in Modern Britain* (London, 1988), and *Christianity and Social Service in Modern Britain: The Disinherited Spirit* (Oxford, 2000). An excellent introduction to Conservative thought on civil society can be found in Ewen H.H. Green, *Ideologies of Conservatism: Conservative Political Ideas in the Twentieth Century* (Oxford, 2002).

On associational life in liberal democracies, the starting point remains Alexis de Tocqueville, *Democracy in America*, trans. Henry Reeve (London, 1946 [1835, 1840]). See also Gabriel A. Almond, and Sidney Verba, *The Civic Culture: Political Attitudes and Democracy in Five Nations* (Princeton, NJ, 1963). The key contribution to the contemporary social capital debate is Robert Putnam, *Bowling Alone: The Collapse and Revival of American Community* (New York, 2000). For a British perspective, see

Peter Hall, 'Social Capital in Britain', *British Journal of Political Science*, 29 (1999), pp. 417–62.

Accounts of the new politics can be found in Frank Parkin, *Middle Class Radicalism: The Social Bases of the British Campaign for Nuclear Disarmament* (Manchester, 1968); Ronald Inglehart, *The Silent Revolution: Changing Values and Political Styles among Western Publics* (Princeton, NJ, 1977), and Pippa Norris, *Democratic Phoenix: Reinventing Political Activism* (New York, 2002).

The literature on apathy and disengagement is diverse, but useful starting points include Colin Hay, *Why We Hate Politics* (Cambridge, 2007); Kevin Jefferys, *Politics and the People: A History of British Democracy since 1918* (London, 2007), and Grant Jordan and William Maloney, *The Protest Business: Mobilizing Campaign Groups* (Manchester, 1997).

On secularisation, see Callum Brown, *The Death of Christian Britain: Understanding Secularisation, 1800–2000* (London, 2001), and Hugh McLeod, *Religion and the People of Western Europe, 1789–1989*, 2nd edn (Oxford, 1997).

Of the many datasets that exist covering volunteering and associational life, particularly useful are *Social Trends* (London, published annually since 1970); *NCVO Almanacs* (published since 1996, initially every two years and then annually since 2006); see in particular NCVO's *Participation: Trends, Facts and Figures, An NCVO Almanac*, March 2011, available at: www.ncvo-vol.org.uk/sites/default/files/ participation_trends_facts_figures.pdf; *Helping Out: A National Survey of Volunteering and Charitable Giving* (London, 2007); the 1981, 1991 and 1997 National Survey of Volunteering – the results of these have been reported in Julia Field and Barry Hedges, *A National Survey of Volunteering* (London, 1984), and Stephen Humble, *Voluntary Action in the 1980s: A Summary of the Findings of a National Survey* (London, 1982); Peter Lynn and Justin Davis Smith, *The 1991 National Survey of Voluntary Activity in the UK* (Berkhamsted, 1991), and Justin Davis Smith, *The 1997 National Survey of Volunteering* (Berkhamsted, 1998). There are also specific data relating to volunteering in the Citizenship Surveys, conducted since 2001 and available at: www.communities.gov.uk/communities/research/citizenshipsurvey/.

7
NGO Income Streams and Giving

Overall income

We saw in Chapter 2 that the overall income of all charities has increased from around £12 billion in 1970 to over £50 billion today (see Figure 7.1). Another way of seeing the sheer scale of the sector is in the total assets all charities have acquired. In 1980, 'general charities' held around £30 billion in total assets, a figure which tripled over the next 30 years. If we take a looser definition to incorporate all NGOs and 'civil society organisations', the levels of overall income are extremely impressive: around £50 billion in 1990 and around three times that amount 20 years later. As is well known, the charitable sector is dominated by many of its leading organisations: a few hundred are enormous compared to the many other tens of thousands. The income of the top 500 charities has continued to dominate, rising to well over £10 billion since the turn of the millennium (see Figure 7.2). For all that the sector remains incredibly diverse, populated by tens of thousands of organisations, it is clearly led by some enormous NGOs that are able to draw on vast resources to pay for many hundreds of staff, projects and campaign initiatives.

This trend is all the more noticeable if we examine the income figures for any one sector. If we take international aid and development sector, for instance, we can see that the sheer scale of some organisations eclipses the income-earning capacities of the numerous smaller organisations. The growth in incomes of Oxfam, Save the Children and the British Red Cross makes even established bodies such as Tearfund and Christian Aid appear small, never mind the numerous tiny organisations devoted to international relief work (see Figure 7.3). Likewise, similar trends can be discerned in other sectors, with the British Heart Foundation and Cancer Research dominating their peers in the field of health and medicine (see Figure 7.4).

It might be expected that the types of organisation that have seen their incomes expand are the new players on the scene, often associated with the new social movements of the 1960s and 1970s. Undoubtedly, many of these organisations have prospered, but what is also remarkable is the persistence of the older established organisations. The fledging environmental groups, Friends of the Earth and Greenpeace, had a negligible impact on the overall income levels for

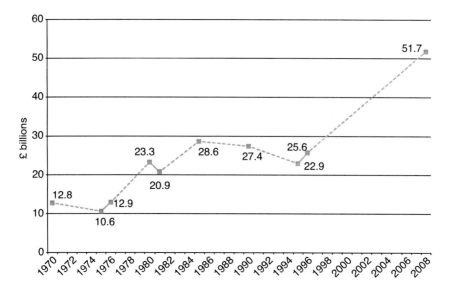

Figure 7.1: Total income of all registered charities, 1970–2008 (adjusted for inflation, 2009)

Sources: Wolfenden 1978; Charity Statistics (various years); Charity Commission.

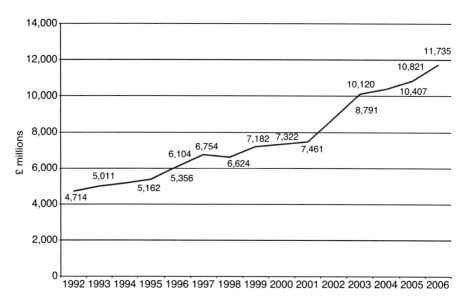

Figure 7.2: Income of top 500 charities, 1992–2006 (adjusted for inflation, 2009)

Source: Charity Statistics (various years).

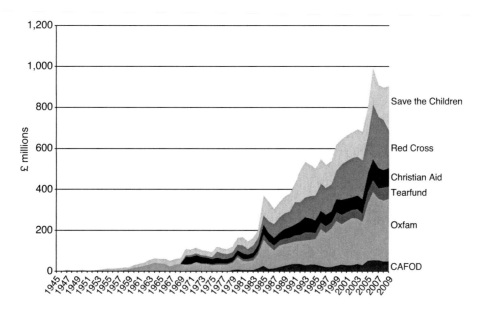

Figure 7.3: Cumulated income of international aid and development NGOs, 1945–2009 (adjusted for inflation, 2009)

Source: Annual reports and accounts, organisations concerned.

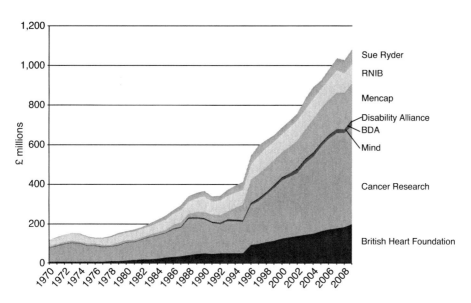

Figure 7.4: Cumulated income of nine health and medicine charities, 1970–2009 (adjusted for inflation, 2009)

Source: Annual reports and accounts, organisations concerned.

the environmental and conservation sector in 1982. While this had increased to an extent 25 years later, it still only amounted to less than 2 per cent each (see Figure 7.5). If any encroachment was made upon the territory occupied by the traditional giant in conservation, the National Trust, this came more from the revival of other established charities, such as the Royal Society for the Protection of Birds (RSPB), rather than from radical climate change protesters.

(a) **In 1982**

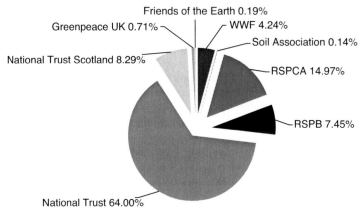

(b) **In 2006**

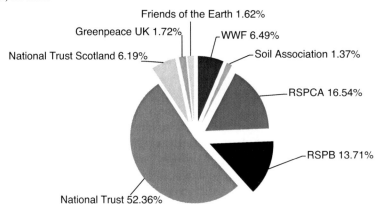

Figure 7.5: Income of environmental NGOs, 1982 and 2006 (proportion within total of environmental NGOs in sample) (adjusted for inflation, 2009)

Sources: Annual reports and accounts, organisations concerned; Charity Statistics; Charity Commission.

The more important point to make about the income levels of NGOs, charities and voluntary sector organisations is the way in which their incomes have been generated. While they still all rely on voluntary donations from members of the public, there have been important changes in the ways in which the public has provided an income. In addition, over the last quarter century, most sectors have been transformed by the often massive injection of funding from official government sources.

State funding

Voluntary organisations and charities have always worked in partnership with central and local government. As the welfare state emerged in the early twentieth century, commentators spoke of the need for a 'new philanthropy' in which charities were better equipped to undertake public services. It is a thinking that has not gone away. The architect of the modern welfare state, Beveridge, also wrote of the need to encourage the voluntary social services, and even committed proponents of nationalisation such as the post-war Labour governments saw a continuing role for civic action.

In the 1970s, though, this relationship came to be increasingly formalised by successive governments, resulting in the transfer of funds from the public to the voluntary sector. When the Wolfenden Committee reported on the state of the voluntary sector in 1978, it provided some data that showed the increasing importance of government funding from across various departments. From an admittedly small level (£19.2 million in 1974–75), official financing of voluntary groups had almost doubled to £35.4 million just two years later (see Table 7.1).

Table 7.1: Government funding of the voluntary sector, 1974–77

Central government departments	£m 1974/75	£m 1975/76	£m 1976/77
DES	5.2	6.5	7.2
DHSS	1.8	2.2	2.8
VSU (including WRVS)	2.4	3.4	4.5
Home office (excluding VSU)	0.9	1.5	1.8
Dept. Of Employment	3.4	5.8	8.6
DOE	1.6	1.7	2.5
Scottish Office	1.2	1.7	1.7
Northern Ireland Office	2	4	4.6
Welsh Office	0.1	0.2	0.2
Dept. of Prices & Consumer Protection	0.4	0.8	1.2
Other departments	0.2	0.2	0.3
Total	19.2	28	35.4

Note: DES = Department of Education and Science; DHSS = Department of Health and Social Security; VSU = Voluntary Services Unit; WRVS = Women's Royal Voluntary Service; DOE = Department of the Environment.

Source: Wolfenden 1978, p. 255.

Crucial to this change was the establishment of the Voluntary Services Unit (VSU) in the Home Office by Edward Heath's Conservative government which coordinated government–charity relations. The subsequent Labour administration expanded its work (see Table 7.2) and may have done so still further had the Conservatives again not come into power in 1979. The latter though, also maintained a commitment to the voluntary sector. Its iconic Manpower Services Commission was clearly intended to massage down unemployment figures, but its Community Programme nevertheless drew an increasing number of organisations into the state's orbit. Although this would come to an abrupt halt at the end of the 1980s, shocking many organisations who had come to rely on its funding, it nevertheless precipitated a more general expansion of government outsourcing from which the voluntary sector has substantially increased its income. Contracting, compacting, partnership and co-funding arrangements have been the subsequent hallmarks of both the Labour and Conservative administration's dealing with the sector, as well as the myriad funding arrangements organised at the local level by local governments. While the acceptance of funding from government to provide specific services has not been unproblematic, it has nevertheless clearly transformed the sector.

Table 7.2: Grants distributed through the Voluntary Services Unit, 1974–86

	Grants (£)	*'Grant-in-Aid' (£)*	*Grand total (£)*
1974–75	565,145	268,300	833,445
1975–76	3,469,059	319,800	3,788,859
1976–77	1,880,569	2,433,000	4,313,569
1978–79	2,637,430	3,429,000	6,066,430
1979–80	2,435,486		
1981–82	2,689,901	4,520,000	7,209,901
1983–84			16,693,120
1984–85			17,110,140
1985–86			9,694,829

Sources: Parliamentary questions relating to VSU funding, in HC Deb 10 November 1975 vol 899 cc522-4W; HC Deb 21 January 1977 vol 924 cc348-50W; HC Deb 25 May 1977 vol 932 cc498-500W; HC Deb 02 July 1979 vol 969 cc387-9W; HC Deb 13 July 1979 vol 970 cc315-6W; HC Deb 31 March 1980 vol 982 cc30-2W; HC Deb 21 April 1982 vol 22 cc96-7W; HC Deb 04 December 1984 vol 69 cc129-31W; HC Deb 06 February 1986 vol 91 cc223-5W; HC Deb 28 January 1986 vol 90 cc476-80W (data accessed through http://hansard.millbanksystems.com).

Official funding has been particularly influential on the sorts of charities, voluntary organisations and NGOs dealing with general welfare matters. It has meant the proportion of their income derived from voluntary sources has fallen quite dramatically. Figure 7.6, for instance, shows the level of voluntary income as a proportion of total income for several leading general welfare organisations: The Royal National Lifeboat Institution (RNLI), Shelter, the Royal British Legion, Action for Children, the National Society for the Prevention of Cruelty to Children (NSPCC), the Children's Society, Help the Aged and Age Concern. Whereas voluntary income accounted for most of their incomes in the 1970s, by the mid-1990s it was less than half. These charities still rely on voluntary funds, and these have continued to expand, but the modern NGO has drawn on other sources of income, with the lion's share ultimately coming from government. Even NGOs with established campaigning reputations have not been able to escape the allure of guaranteed funding streams. In line with the rest of the sector, Shelter, for instance, has seen its voluntary income occupy a less prominent place in its overall funding profile (see Figure 7.7).

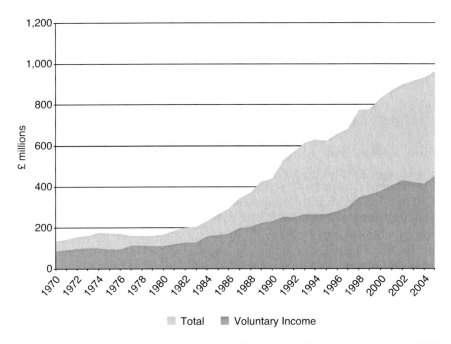

Total   Voluntary Income

Figure 7.6: Voluntary versus total income, 1970–2005 (adjusted for inflation, 2009), of selected welfare charities (RNLI, Shelter, the Royal British Legion, Action for Children, the NSPCC, the Children's Society, Help the Aged, Age Concern)

Sources: Annual reports and accounts, organisations concerned; Charity Statistics (1977–2006); Wells Collection; Wolfenden 1978.

Internationally, much of the discussion about the potential pitfalls of accepting official funding has been directed at the aid and development NGOs. In Britain, government funding of this sector occurred around the same time as it did for domestic affairs. In the same year as the VSU was created in the Home Office, the newly-elected Labour government of 1974 went on to establish a Disaster Unit in the Overseas Development Ministry to work with the leading relief and development NGOs, particularly those combined through the Disasters Emergency Committee (DEC). The next year, a Joint Funding Scheme (JFS) was launched which funded up to 50 per cent of new projects submitted by the NGOs. In 1977, guaranteed block grants were also introduced to the larger NGOs, beginning with Oxfam and Christian Aid that year and extended to the Catholic Agency for Overseas Development (CAFOD) in 1979 and Save the Children Fund in 1985. The importance of the JFS,

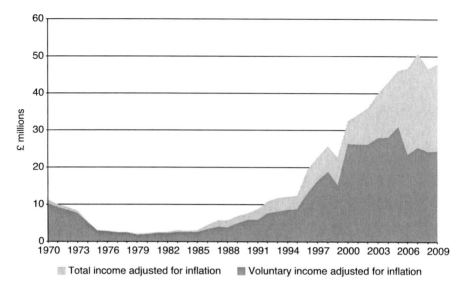

Figure 7.7: Income of Shelter, 1970–2009 (adjusted for inflation, 2009)

Sources: Annual reports and accounts, Shelter; Charity Statistics; Wells Collection; Wolfenden 1978.

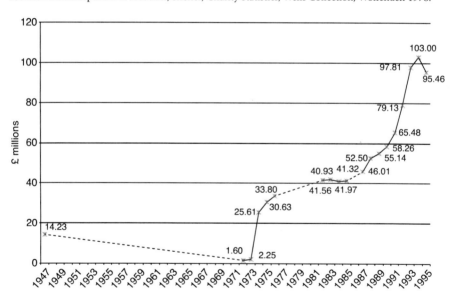

Figure 7.8: Grants distributed by the Home Office (including through the VSU) to voluntary organisations, 1947–1995 (adjusted for inflation, 2009)

Sources (chronological order): Beveridge 1949, pp. 91–8; HL Deb 07 March 1973 vol 339 cc1139-41; Wolfenden 1978, p. 255; HC Deb 01 December 1983 vol 49 c603W; HC Deb 04 December 1984 vol 69 cc129-31W; HC Deb 30 January 1986 vol 90 c576W; HC Deb 02 March 1987 vol 111 cc462-3W; HL Deb 16 May 1989 vol 507 cc1169-70WA; HC Deb 11 May 1990 vol 172 cc254-6W; HC Deb 22 March 1991 vol 188 cc235-6W; HC Deb 16 July 1992 vol 211 cc868-9W; HC Deb 17 June 1993 vol 226 cc682-3W; HC Deb 13 April 1994 vol 241 cc178-9W; HC Deb 19 July 1995 vol 263 cc1445-7W; HC Deb 28 February 1997 vol 291 cc393-6W (data accessed through http://hansard.millbanksystems.com).

and the block grant within it, has increased gradually. By the end of the 1980s, the scheme was supporting over 900 projects in around fifty countries with more than 100 charities benefiting from public sector assistance.

Presenting data on overall government funding is difficult. Funds come from many sources, are channelled through various bureaucracies and are reported with varying degrees of accuracy. Attempts at collation have often proved contradictory. It is, however, relatively easier to collect data from any one ministry. Figure 7.8 shows how the Home Office, a particularly important financer of NGOs, has expanded its funding arrangement to what, historically, are extraordinarily high levels. Figure 7.9 does attempt to trace overall levels of funding, but there are so many caveats that the data should be read with extreme caution. For more recent years, more consistent efforts have been made to track voluntary sector income from various sources. Figure 7.10, for instance shows data from 2001 to 2008 collected by the National Council of Voluntary Organisations (NCVO) which again demonstrates the increasing importance of official funds to the sector.

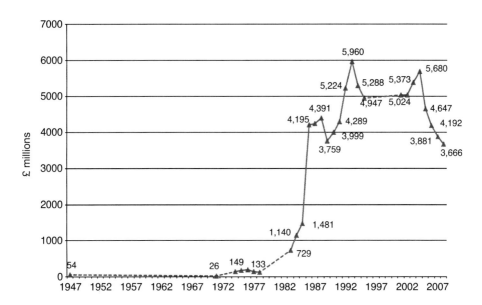

Figure 7.9: Grants distributed by the central government, 1947–2008 (cumulated, adjusted for inflation, 2009)

Sources (chronological order): Beveridge 1949 (figure calculated from table pp. 91–8); HC Deb 08 July 1975 vol 895 cc345-405; Wolfenden 1978, p. 255; HL Deb 17 July 1978 vol 395 c139WA; HL Deb 17 July 1978 vol 395 c139WA; HC Deb 01 December 1983 vol 49 c603W 603W; *Charity Statistics*, 14 (1991), p. 111; HC Deb 16 July 1992 vol 211 cc868-9W; HC Deb 17 June 1993 vol 226 cc682-3W; HC Deb 13 April 1994 vol 241 cc178-9W; HC Deb 19 July 1995 vol 263 cc1445-7W; HC Deb 28 February 1997 vol 291 cc393-6W; *NCVO Almanac* (2010) (tables accessed through www.ncvo-vol.org.uk/access-tables-behind-almanac).

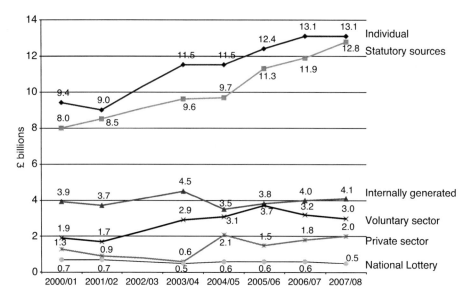

Figure 7.10: Sources of income of voluntary organisations, 2000/01–2007/08 (adjusted for inflation, 2009)

Source: *The UK Civil Society Almanac 2010* (London, 2010), table Q20 (accessed through www.ncvo-vol. org.uk/access-tables-behind-almanac).

Giving

Figure 7.10 showed that while state funding has helped drive the rapid expansion of NGOs from the 1980s, Britain has also continued to be a nation of givers. The NCVO has estimated that in 2009 around one-quarter of the total income of the entire charitable sector came from individual donations. The Charity Household Survey found that the average annual donation per household has been reasonably steady over the last quarter-century, at around £200 per year. Another study, again conducted by the NCVO, found that there has been a slight rise in the mean amount each person has claimed to have donated in the past four weeks (see Figure 7.11). According to the Family Expenditure Survey, the average weekly donation (adjusted for inflation) increased from just under £1 in 1978 to £2.34 in 2008, with much of the growth coming during the economic boom of the later 1980s.

The most obvious manifestation of this trend is in the rise in levels of voluntary income that can be seen across the sector. Overall, the voluntary income of the top 500 charities has risen substantially. Just as government funding enabled a rapid expansion from the 1970s, so too did new forms of donating, especially direct debits, standing orders as well as – later and more controversially – affinity credit cards and the use of 'chuggers' (that is, 'charity muggers') in the high street. It has meant that the big NGOs have done particularly well, with overall voluntary income rising from less than £1 billion in the late 1970s to approaching £6 billion by 2004 (see Figure 7.12).

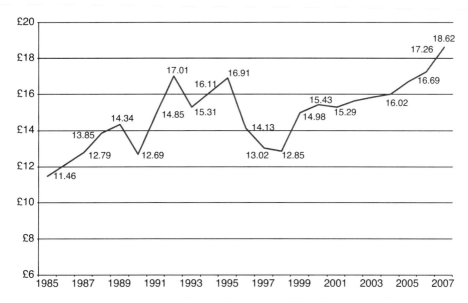

Figure 7.11: Mean amount donated in past four weeks, 1985–2007 (adjusted for inflation, 2009)

Sources (chronological order): *Charity Statistics*, 9 (1985), p. 130; 12 (1989), p. 34; 1999, p. 115; 15 (1992), p. 8; 1995, p. 12; *The UK Civil Sector Almanac 2004* (London, 2004), p. 92; *UK Giving*, 2004, p. 12; *The UK Civil Society Almanac 2007, 2008* and *2009*.

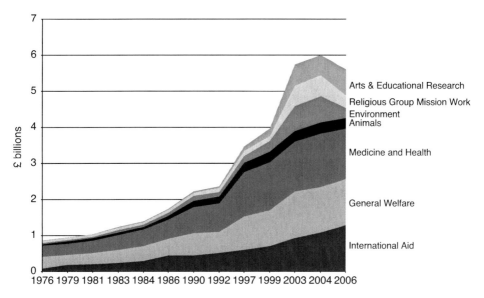

Figure 7.12: Cumulated voluntary income of top 500 charities (by sector), 1976–2006 (adjusted for inflation, 2009)

Source: Charity Statistics (1976–2006).

Again, the trend can be seen across sectors, with the big players in the welfare, international development and medicine and health sectors doing particularly well. Indeed, the latter has remained particularly dependent on voluntary donations. Taking a sample of eight NGOs dealing with health and medicine, the total share of their income from voluntary sources has generally been over two-thirds. By 2005, for instance, while total income reached over £900 million, the amount from the public was over £600 million (see Figure 7.13). The health and medicine charities have not been able to rely on government contracts in quite the same way. Despite these impressive rises in voluntary income, therefore, this has to be contrasted with the falling share of total charitable income (voluntary and official) that the sector has enjoyed. For much of the 1970s through to the 1990s, the proportion of total income of the top 500 charities that was taken up by health and medicine NGOs was around one-third. Subsequently, it has fallen dramatically, to around one-quarter in the new millennium (Figure 7.14).

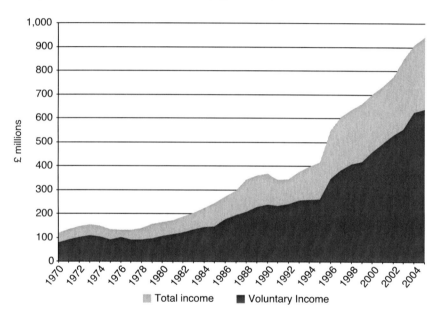

Figure 7.13: Total and voluntary income of selected sample of health and medicine charities, 1970–2005 (Sue Ryder, Royal National Institute of Blind People (RNIB), Mind, Mencap, British Deaf Association, Cancer Research, British Heart Foundation) (adjusted for inflation, 2009)

Sources: Annual reports and accounts, organisations concerned; Charity Statistics (1977–2006); Wells Collection; Wolfenden 1978.

Nevertheless, there have been some consistent patterns over the last few decades. The top fundraisers in 1977–78 were remarkably similar to those a quarter of a century later, with the persistent presence of the household names such as Oxfam, the National Trust and Cancer Research (in its various guises) (see Table 7.3). Generally, it seems, the big NGOs have been able to hold their own, drawing on their professional and established fundraising resources and methods, often bucking the trends in giving that are apparent for sectors as a whole. Accordingly, while the British Heart Foundation and Cancer Research might well be able to maintain high levels of income, the rest of their sector's hold on the purse strings of the public has declined, amidst the increasing competition of a whole range of NGOs (see Figure 7.15). Likewise, while international aid and development NGOs have done increasingly well in their ability to attract funds voluntarily, this has perhaps been at the expense of general welfare charities.

Figure 7.14: Income of medicine and health charities as a proportion of the total income of Top 500 charities, 1976–2006 (adjusted for inflation, 2009)

Source: Charity Statistics (1976–2006).

Table 7.3: Top 10 fundraising charities in 1977–78 and 2003–04 by voluntary income

Rank	Charity	Voluntary income 1977–78 (£m)	Charity	Voluntary income 2003–04 (£m)
1	Imperial Cancer Research	6.6	Cancer Research UK	184.4
2	Oxfam	6	National Trust	160.6
3	RNLI	6	Oxfam	131.1
4	Dr Barnardo's	6	British Heart Foundation	112
5	Cancer Research Campaign	5.4	RNLI	95.6
6	Save the Children Fund	5.2	Salvation Army	91.5
7	Help the Aged	5.2	NSPCC	79.5
8	National Trust	5.1	Comic Relief	73.7
9	Spastics Society	5	Macmillan Cancer Relief	71.1
10	RNIB	4.7	RSPCA	68.2
		55.2		1,067.7

Source: Charity Statistics (1978, 2004).

(a) **In 1976**

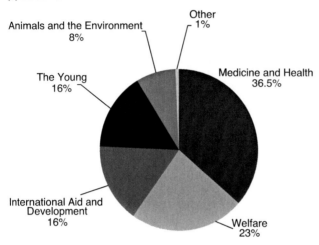

(b) **In 2006**

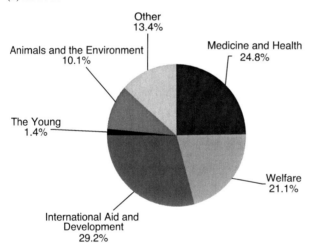

Figure 7.15: Breakdown of voluntary income of top 200 charities, 1976 and 2006 (adjusted for inflation, 2009)

Source: Charity Statistics (1977, 2006).

Overall, then, it might easily be argued that the sector continues to do well from a public keen to part with its money. However, a number of caveats are required as there are some competing trends if we look in more detail at the nature of giving. One report, based on an analysis of the Family Expenditure Survey (now known as the Living Costs and Food Survey) from 1978 has found that while overall contributions have increased in real terms, this has tended to come from a declining pool of charitable givers. The proportion of people interviewed in the survey who claimed to have given money to charity within the past two weeks fell from over 30 per cent in the 1970s to as low as 25 per cent in 1999 (see Figure 7.16). It is a trend that has been captured by other survey data. A study commissioned by the Charities Aid Foundation and the NCVO found that the proportion of all adults claiming to have given to charity in the past month fell even more dramatically, from 89 per cent in 1985 to 54 per cent in 2008–09 (see Figure 7.17).

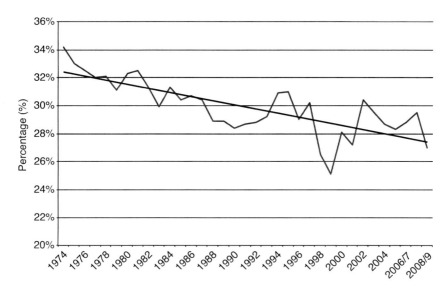

Figure 7.16: Proportion of people giving to charities in the past two weeks, 1974–2009

Sources: Edd Cowley, Tom McKenzie, Cathy Pharoah and Sarah Smith, *The New State of Donation: Three Decades of Household Giving to Charity 1978 – 2008* (Bristol, 2011), p. 50 (www.bristol.ac.uk/cmpo/publications/other/stateofdonation.pdf); *Charity Statistics* (1997), p. 60; ultimate source: Living Costs and Food Survey/Family Expenditure Survey.

Some care needs to be taken with such data. Surveys do not necessarily capture all forms of charitable giving, and falling levels of stated donations might coincide with the more unreflecting trend to increased use of direct debit. Also, even the more reliable Family Expenditure Survey data show fluctuations based on a low standard deviation. Although a declining trend can be seen, this is offset by the substantial levelling off since the turn of the millennium.

That said, other patterns of giving are discernible. Firstly, those people who do give to charity have been giving more over recent decades. According to the Family Expenditure Survey, the average size of a donation, even adjusted for inflation, has tripled from £3.05 in 1978 to £8.66 in 2008. This is the reason why certain NGOs have seen their voluntary incomes expand, and giving as a whole has been in line with gross domestic product (GDP) growth, while the actual number of donors among the public has declined. Figure 7.18 shows how donations as a proportion of overall expenditure have remained relatively stable (though with a gradual rise), while among those who give, the rise has been much more substantial.

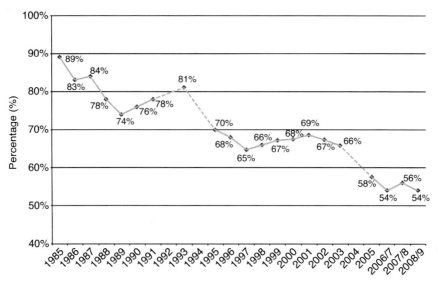

Figure 7.17: Proportion of people giving to charities in the past month, 1985–2009 (all adults)

Sources: Charity Statistics (1985–95); Andrew Passey and Les Hems, *Charitable Giving in Great Britain 1996* (London, 1997); *NCVO Almanac* (1996, 2004, 2007, 2009, 2010).

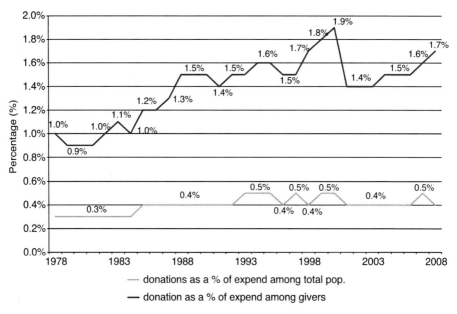

Figure 7.18: Donations as a percentage of household expenditure, 1978–2008

Sources: Edd Cowley, Tom McKenzie, Cathy Pharoah and Sarah Smith, *The New State of Donation: Three Decades of Household Giving to Charity 1978 – 2008* (Bristol, 2011), p. 55 (www.bristol.ac.uk/cmpo/publications/other/stateofdonation.pdf); ultimate source: Family Expenditure Survey.

Secondly, there has been an increasing reliance on older people for charitable giving. The proportion of retired people regularly donating to charity has increased since the 1970s which, coupled with increases in the size of their donations, has meant the share of total donations given by the over-65s has risen from 24 per cent in 1978–82 to 35 per cent in 2003–08. At the same time, the level of giving among younger cohorts of the population has fallen, though the trend has been reversed over the last decade. It may well be that new habits of giving were inspired by the new technologies of giving in the 1980s. While the middle-aged were most likely to adopt direct debit, and continue such behaviour until older age, young people only slowly came round to these new forms of giving.

Thirdly, the rich have increasingly accounted for a larger share of all donations to charities. Intriguingly, such a trend may well reflect rising levels of inequality between the rich and the poor. The richest 10 per cent of the population accounted for 16 per cent of all donations reported in the Family Expenditure Survey in 1978–82, but as much as 22 per cent in 2003–08. While the number of rich givers has remained relatively stable, the proportion of those in the poorest 10 per cent of society who give has fallen from 17 per cent in 1978–82 to 10 per cent in 2003–08. Again, the technologies of giving may be relevant, with charities targeting those who can give most easily through direct debit and other such means. But for those poor who have continued to give, they have remained more generous. The poorest 10 per cent that were seen to be donors gave 3.6 per cent of their expenditure in 2008, while the richest 10 per cent gave only 1.1 per cent.

The advantages and disadvantages of different forms of giving were made apparent to a number of environmental NGOs in the late 1980s. On the back of heightened discussion of environmental issues in politics and the media (not least because of a number of catastrophes that had captured the public imagination), a number of environmental and conservation organisations stepped up their marketing to encourage donations and subscriptions through direct debit. The results were quite spectacular: Figure 7.19 shows the sudden surge in membership of four of the leading NGOs. But just as significant were the falls in membership straight afterwards when unsustained promotion, matched with the shift to an economic recession, saw significant losses for, in particular, Greenpeace and Friends of the Earth.

The so called 'greenrush' proved to be only a blip, and the sector as a whole has recovered since. But the shift to new techniques of obtaining money from the public has had to be carefully monitored. Charitable giving has proven itself to be remarkably recession-proof. Dips in giving generally tend to be short term, and overall levels of voluntary incomes have followed increases in standards of living. Nevertheless, what the greenrush shows is the potential fragility of these donations if not organised correctly. Given that charities seem to have been collecting from a potentially smaller pool of givers (at least up until these trends levelled off around ten years ago), it is perhaps unsurprising that those who have done well have been those better able to marshal the techniques of the modern marketing professional in courting that public's support.

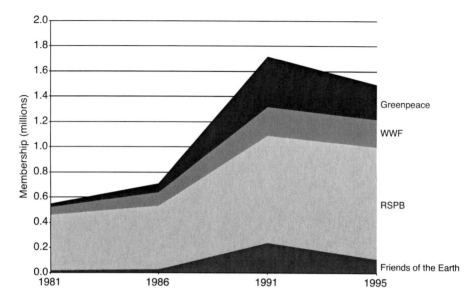

Figure 7.19: Membership of environmental organisations, 1981–1995

Sources: Estimations based on sometimes conflicting sources: Annual reports, organisations concerned; *Social Trends,*(various years); Neil Carter, *The Politics of the Environment: Ideas, Activism, Policy* (Cambridge, 2007); Francis Sandbach, *Environment, Ideology and Policy* (Oxford: 1980); Paul Byrne, *Social Movements in Britain* (London, 1997); Robert Lamb, *Promising the Earth* (London, 1996); Joe Weston, *The F.O.E. Experience: The Development of an Environmental Pressure Group* (Oxford, 1989); Peter Rawcliffe, *Environmental Pressure Groups in Transition* (Manchester, 1998).

Further reading

The income levels of NGOs have been tracked annually by the Charities Aid Foundation (CAF) in *Charity Statistics*, published more or less yearly since the mid 1970s. This publication has now been superseded by *Top 3000 Charities*, which has been published annually by Caritas Data since 1993. Data for the present can be obtained from the websites of the NCVO (www.ncvo-vol.org.uk) and the Charities Aid Foundation (www.cafonline.org). There is also scattered information on the income of charities in William H. Beveridge, *The Evidence for Voluntary Action* (London, 1949) (figure calculated from table on pp. 91–8); Wells International Donors Advisory Service, *1973 Supplemental Edition of the 1971 Wells Collection of U.K. Charitable Giving Reports* (London, 1975); John Wolfenden, *The Future of Voluntary Organisations: Report of the Wolfenden Committee* (London, 1978).

For useful surveys of the statistics of giving, see especially Edd Cowley, Tom McKenzie, Cathy Pharoah and Sarah Smith, *The New State of Donation: Three Decades of Household Giving to Charity, 1978–2008* (Bristol, 2011), available at: www.bristol.ac.uk/cmpo/publications/other/stateofdonation.pdf. CAF and the NCVO have published yearly reports on giving, entitled *UK Giving*, since 2004. These reports can be downloaded from the NCVO or CAF websites at: www.cafonline.org/Default.aspx?page=17922.

For up-to-date surveys of giving, see Charities Aid Foundation/National Council of Voluntary Organisations, *UK Giving 2010* (London, 2010), available at: www.ncvo-vol.org.uk/sites/default/files/101201_UKGivingReport_FINAL.pdf. Other surveys of historical data include Andrew Jones and John Posnett, 'Charitable Donations by UK Households: Evidence from the Family Expenditure Survey', *Applied Economics*, 23 (1991), pp. 343–51; Natalie Low, Sarah Butt, Angela Ellis Paine and Justin Davis Smith, 'Helping Out: A National Survey of Volunteering and Charitable Giving' (London, 2007); Cathy Pharoah and Sarah Tanner, 'Trends in Charitable Giving', *Fiscal Studies*, 18:4 (1997), pp. 427–43. For historical data on voluntary income during times of recession, see John Mohan and Karl Wilding, 'Economic Downturns and the Voluntary Sector: What can we Learn from Historical Evidence', *History & Policy* (2009), available at: www.historyandpolicy.org/papers/policy-paper-85.html.

8
The Impact of NGOs

The ultimate goal of NGOs, charities and voluntary associations is to have some impact upon the subjects they were organised to tackle. Impact, however, can be measured in various ways. Ideally, many organisations would like to think they could impact upon long-term change. The actions of the Coal Smoke Abatement Society and Smoke Abatement League, for instance, led to the 1956 Clean Air Act which in turn influenced Des Wilson's CLEAR campaign for lead-free petrol and the Council for the Protection of Rural England's (CPRE's) campaign against stubble burning in the 1980s. These actions paved the way for the 'Big Ask' coalition of environmental and development groups that helped condition the debate that led to the 2008 Climate Change Act. Other groups campaign in favour of or against particular issues and problems. Campaigning by the morality lobby in the 1980s is acknowledged to have encouraged the tightening of restrictions on video recordings and sex education, as well as the controversial Section 28 legislation that restricted local authorities' promotion of homosexuality. Or it may be that a more general impact on public opinion and political attitudes is proposed. Reviewing a decade of achievements in 2004, the National Society for the Protection of Cruelty to Children (NSPCC) believed that it had persuaded government to allocate significant resources to internet safety and awareness for young people whilst also influencing eight pieces of parliamentary legislation. Data tracking of the impact of NGO campaigns on MPs appeared to reinforce this verdict with the NSPCC's 'Full Stop' campaign consistently being the most recalled campaign between 2000 and 2004, topping seven out of the eight six-monthly surveys, and at its peak being noticed by 35 per cent of MPs.

Success, therefore, comes in various forms. And the impact of NGOs on, say, specific pieces of legislation or government policies is by no means easy to measure. The Campaign for One Parent Families (COPF, now Gingerbread) had contributed a lengthy report to the Finer Committee on social welfare in 1971. When this committee reported, COPF was delighted that the vast majority of its recommendations had been accepted. However, its main campaigning point, non-means-tested benefits, had been rejected. Furthermore, government then shelved the report, and despite many of the campaigning groups with an interest in family coming together to form the Finer Joint Action Committee, they still only managed to secure the implementation of a few of the less important recommendations of the original Finer Report.

It would be incredibly difficult to make firm conclusions about the impact of so many organisations on public opinion, legislation, policy and actual change. Moreover, to provide hard data and to separate out apparent 'impact' from the general context of reform, to which an organisation might have contributed, can prove even more difficult. However, the impact aims of NGOs as a whole are generally clear. They seek, first of all, to influence public opinion through media and public relations strategies. They seek also to influence parliament and Whitehall through lobbying and campaigning and by fostering close links with officials in the various government departments. This chapter will deal with each of these two broad forms of impact in turn, offering quantitative evidence where possible that points to how impact might be measured.

Public opinion and the media

Gaining publicity for a cause is one of the key challenges for any NGO not least because the proliferation of organisations has made it a congested space. In 1989 the Royal Society for the Prevention of Cruelty to Animals (RSPCA) warned its supporters that it was 'now one of dozens of charities seeking support by progressively more sophisticated and persuasive means. The RSPCA must compete to survive.' In the 1960s a new breed of media-savvy NGOs had emerged better able to exploit the media and public relations more generally. Pioneers such as Oxfam recognised that image and brand were increasingly important, especially the need to exploit that image to raise resources and launch campaigns. This in part required the co-option of the media. Shelter was given the rights to the Jeremy Sandford BBC broadcast docu-drama film *Cathy Come Home*, about the plight of one single homeless mother, and screened it widely around Britain to successfully raise funds. Its 1966 advertisement in *The Times* described one family's 'Home Sweet Hell' and provoked public donations of £50,000 (equivalent to £700,000 in 2011) in one month alone. Not every NGO had such budgetary prowess. The Child Poverty Action Group (CPAG), like many others in the 1960s and 1970s, operated on a limited budget. Nevertheless it also turned to the media to help fundraise, often relying on sympathetic journalists. It once tipped off the *Guardian* about its parlous finances, and when an article duly ran predicting their extinction, a donor stepped forward.

The oxygen of publicity that the media offers NGOs can be vital, and increasingly from the 1970s, and especially since the 1980s, these groups have sought to professionalise their media operations. Some organisations have perhaps been slower than others to adapt to the demands of the modern media. In 1975 the Council for the Protection of Rural England decided that it no longer required the services of a full-time media/press officer and instead transferred the duties to the organisation's president. However, the rise of a press officer within many such organisations has seen an apparent increase in column inches devoted to NGOs. Figures 8.1–8.3 show, despite fluctuations, that the amount of attention cumulatively devoted to

NGOs in the *Guardian* and *The Times* has gradually increased. By the turn of the millennium, the 63 NGOs profiled in Chapter 4 were being referred to over 4,500 times per year in these two newspapers alone.

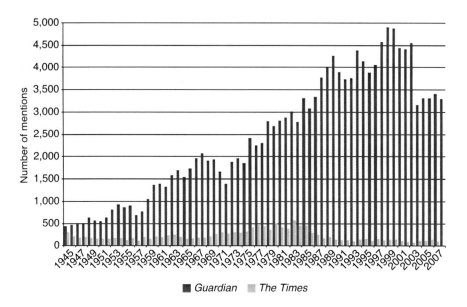

Figure 8.1: Number of mentions in the *Guardian* and *The Times*, 1945–2007, of the key NGOs profiled by the NGOs in Britain project

Note: The use of the paper index for *The Times* explains the much lower figures for that newspaper. The drop in the number of occurrences in the *Guardian* after 2003 is due to a change in the databases used, from ProQuest to Nexis. It does not necessarily reflect a drop in the number of mentions of NGOs.

Source: *Guardian* & *The Times*.

These NGOs have a range of publics they wish to communicate with and will accordingly adopt differing strategies. In the 1970s, for instance, if CPAG wished to get its message across to trade unionists it would plant stories in the *Guardian*. If it wanted the attention of civil servants or politicians it would use *The Times*. And if it sought to reach a non-working or female audience it would try to obtain airtime on Jimmy Young's BBC Radio 2 show or pioneering afternoon television programmes. Likewise, Gingerbread would seek to exploit the willingness of agony aunt columns, like Marjorie Proops' advice page in the *Daily Mirror* in the 1970s and 1980s, to make contact with their clients' groups, who otherwise might be deemed unworthy of broader mainstream press coverage.

The sophistication of some campaigning organisations has reached new levels of professionalism, as they target not just the traditional print media and TV and radio but also seek to exploit the new media of the internet. When 35 Greenpeace activists occupied the Range Rover production line in Solihull in May 2005 protesting about the emissions from 4x4 vehicles, journalists arriving at the plant were greeted by a Greenpeace media production van that could provide footage of the activists chained to the chassis, whilst Greenpeace's executive director provided mobile phone updates direct from the occupation, including one from inside a police van after his arrest. Conducting campaigns in the full media glare can be counter-productive, as the controversy over Greenpeace's use of science after the 1995 Brent Spar oil platform occupation demonstrated.

Specific sector analysis shows that the *Guardian* and *The Times'* coverage of international aid and development (IAD) groups likewise grew from the 1960s. This was the point when a number of key organisations were founded (Catholic Agency for Overseas Development (CAFOD), 1960; Tearfund, 1968) and also when international disaster and famine relief became an increasingly coordinated activity through groups like the World Development Movement (WDM) and the Disasters Emergency Committee (DEC). The August 1966 Turkish earthquake was DEC's first appeal, and the troughs and peaks of media attention (see Figure 8.2) for these IAD NGOs do mirror the range of international disasters. For example, the dip in 1972 may be explained by the absence of any significant appeal until the December of that year, and similarly in 1978 and 1979. If the hypothesis is that increased publicity for IAD NGOs leads to increased resources, then the scales of success from DEC appeals broadly match the upward ebb and flow of the graphic.

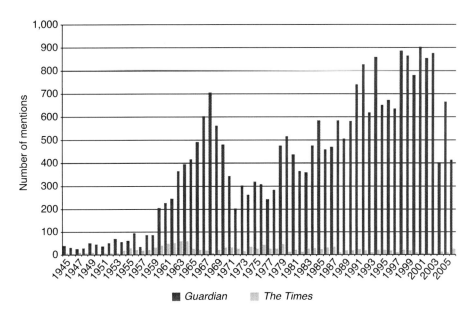

Figure 8.2: Number of mentions of IAD organisations in the *Guardian* and *The Times*, 1945–2008

Note: Organisations sampled: CAFOD; Christian Aid; Save the Children; Tearfund; War on Want; WDM; British Red Cross.

Source: *Guardian* & *The Times*.

The upward trend of citations for general welfare charities is also evident (see Figure 8.3). However, the starting point is not so low, and is probably reflective of the general concern for the welfare state and because so many of the profiled NGOs sought to alleviate the condition of the most vulnerable in society, concerns that have always been prominent in the *Guardian*. But it also points to better media publicity by many of the organisations concerned. Organisations such as this also sought to co-opt sympathetic journalists onto their management committees, and the poverty lobby particularly during the 1970s and 1980s, more so than today, created links that made the broadsheet media more susceptible to their lobbying.

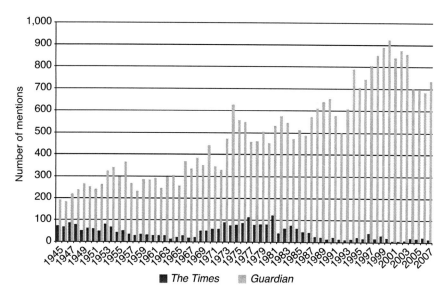

Figure 8.3: Number of mentions of general welfare charities in the *Guardian* and *The Times*, 1945–2008

Note: Organisations sampled: Age Concern; Baby Milk Action; CPAG; Children's Society; Help the Aged; RNLI; NSPCC; National Children's Homes; Royal British Legion; Shelter; Workers' Educational Association.
Source: *Guardian* & *The Times*.

NGOs try to associate their names with a particular cause. A search of *The Times* from 1966 to 1985 for the phrase 'child benefit' found 722 articles; 10 per cent of these referred to CPAG and 3 per cent to Gingerbread (and its earlier name incarnations). A similar search for the phrase 'family allowances' yielded 292 articles, of which 23 (8 per cent) mentioned CPAG and 16 (5 per cent) cited Gingerbread. A similar search of the *Guardian* and the *Observer* from 1966 to 2003 found 2,974 articles on 'child benefit', of which 275 (9 per cent) mentioned CPAG and 71 (2 per cent) referred to Gingerbread. The same search for 'family allowance' yielded 1,194 articles, of which 158 (13 per cent) mentioned CPAG and 12 (1 per cent) Gingerbread.

Other such searches are easily possible thanks to new online resources. To give another example, the phrase 'Climate Change Bill' in all electronically indexed

British newspapers over the period 5 December 2007 to 5 December 2008 yielded 677 articles; 198 (29 per cent) of these mentioned Friends of the Earth, though intriguingly only 30 (4 per cent) referred to Greenpeace, suggesting the former was more successful in attaching its name to a campaign which was the concern of a whole variety of NGOs.

In recent years, the internet has assumed an extraordinary prominence for the public relations and campaigning work of NGOs. How to maximise the potential of the internet, and also the related growth in technological developments, as with social networking and smart phones, have become key development areas for many NGOs. The most basic level is the organisational webpage. The costs associated with such web developments means that the relative wealth of an organisation can determine how slick a website appears; however, it also depends upon the purpose of the website. Some organisations, like the Disability Alliance, clearly see their webpage as a resource database and have eschewed fancy graphics, perhaps in response to the needs of its users, and have instead concentrated on text-based pages that direct readers to resource, advice and publications pages and to details of the Alliance's latest campaign responses. The need to move beyond having a webpage presence has led some organisations to enlist the support of PR consultants, as they seek to think of different ways of campaigning and fundraising. Many groups now have presences on Twitter and Facebook, whilst Shelter, amongst others, has exploited the use of the viral marketing techniques. The growth in popularity of YouTube has also been exploited. Again, to use Shelter as just one example, it uploaded its internet film, *House of Cards*, in 2008, featuring a soundtrack by Radiohead and a voiceover by actress Samantha Morton, quickly securing over 55,000 viewings in the year of its launch. Its website was by 2009 getting over 100,000 hits per month and it benefited by £100,000 from the Facebook campaign that propelled Rage Against the Machine to the UK music chart's Christmas number-one spot in 2009.

It is difficult to assess whether all this media work has translated into a greater public awareness of an NGO's cause. In other words can NGOs be seen to be transforming the agenda, at least at the level of public debate? The rediscovery of poverty in the 1960s appears to have in part been mediated by the emergence of groups like CPAG, Shelter and Gingerbread, and also the older established welfare groups such as the Salvation Army and the NSPCC. But the growing public awareness of these issues was also dependent upon wider socio-cultural changes, a growing sense of affluence for the middle classes, immigration and an expanding but also ageing population, and debates within the political parties, which reflected that cultural situation. The saliency of an issue can be a difficult matter to track despite opinion polls regularly asking questions about what were the most pressing issues facing the country. Figures 8.4–8.8 illustrate the growing awareness of environmental issues, in part prompted by disasters such as oil spills or extreme acts of nature, but indicate that the environment rates much more lowly in the electorate's mind than immediate material concerns. Given the increased press coverage of environmental matters, it suggests that the environmental NGOs still have a considerable way to go to convince the wider public that significant lifestyle changes are required if the environment is to be afforded greater protection.

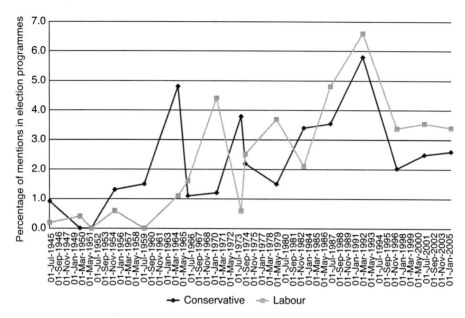

Figure 8.4: The political saliency of environmental protection, 1945–2005

Sources: Ian Budge et al., *Mapping Policy Preferences: Estimates for Parties, Electors and Governments, 1945–1998* (Oxford, 2001); Hans-Dieter Klingermann et al., *Mapping Policy Preferences II: Estimates for Parties, Electors, and Governments in Central and Eastern Europe, European Union and OECD, 1990–2003* (Oxford, 2006).

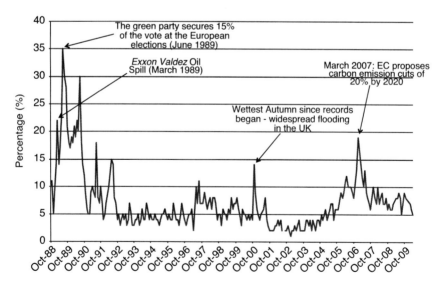

Figure 8.5: What do you see as the most important issue facing Britain today? Pollution/environment, 1988–2010

Source: Ipsos-MORI, Issues Index, 'The Most Important Issues Facing Britain Today', www.ipsos-mori.com/researchpublications/researcharchive/poll.aspx?oItemId=56&view=wide#2009.

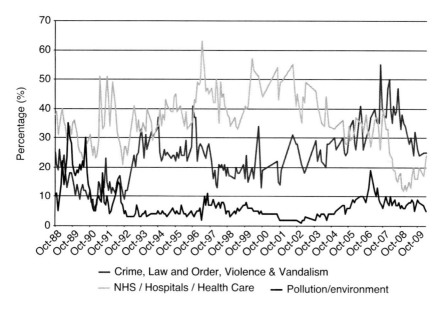

Figure 8.6: Most important issues facing Britain today: environment mapped against crime and the NHS, 1988–2010

Source: Ipsos-MORI, Issues Index, 'The Most Important Issues Facing Britain Today', www.ipsos-mori.com/researchpublications/researcharchive/poll.aspx?oItemId=56&view=wide#2009.

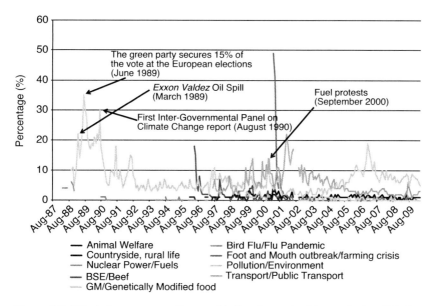

Figure 8.7: What do you see as the most/other important issues facing Britain today? Environmental-related issues, 1988–2010

Source: Ipsos-MORI, Issues Index, 'The Most Important Issues Facing Britain Today', www.ipsos-mori.com/researchpublications/researcharchive/poll.aspx?oItemId=56&view=wide#2009.

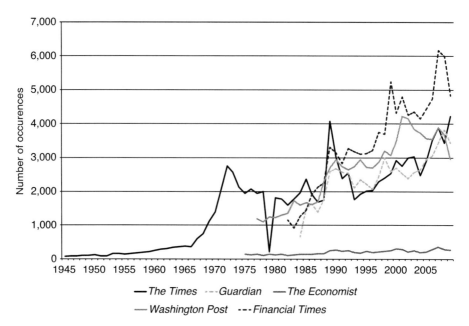

Figure 8.8: Number of mentions of the word 'environment' in newspapers, 1945–2010

Sources: For *The Times*: Gale's *The Times Digital Archives 1785–1985* (for the period 1945–85); from 1985: Nexis online database. For the *Guardian*, *The Economist*, the *Financial Times*, the *Washington Post*: Nexis.

If NGOs, charities and voluntary organisations have not always been able to make their issue the most important subject of the day, there is evidence to suggest that they have been successful in getting the public to trust them; a crucial relationship that can bolster the authority of an organisation when it enters the political affray. Opinion polls have been asking about the 'trust' the public have in British institutions since the 1960s. These polls have shown an apparent decline in the trust with which politicians, the media and national government are held. Although the data are highly problematic due to differing methodology, definitions and questions, there is some suggestion that the public has come to trust NGOs more, implying that the media strategies they had adopted may well have paid off, in this regard at least.

In 1996 the Henley Centre, which had been monitoring trust in public institutions since 1983, asked people the extent to which they had confidence in charities, with one-third of respondents agreeing that they had a 'great deal' or 'quite a lot' of confidence in charities. This was significantly less than their confidence in the armed forces (74 per cent) and the police (58 per cent), but significantly better than government (11 per cent). In 1997 the Henley Centre altered the wording of its question to one of 'trust' and found that 56 per cent expressed such a view. From 2000, a range of other polling organisations have begun to ask the question of the public's perception of 'trust' in charities, NGOs and pressure groups (see Figure 8.9). It is clear that the public in the UK, as with the wider EU, hold charities in relatively high esteem compared to political institutions (political parties, government, civil service, EU) and the media.

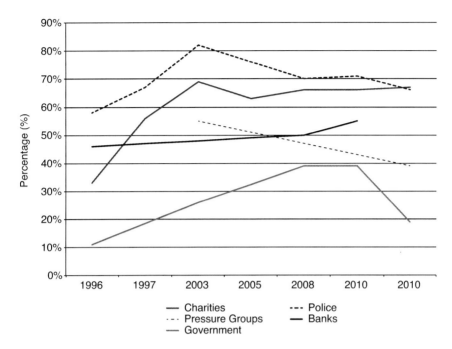

Figure 8.9: Public trust in charities versus pressure groups, the police, government and banks, 1996–2010

Sources: NCVO, 'Blurred Vision – Public Trust in Charities', *Research Quarterly* (London, 1998); Centre for Civil Society, NCVO and William Plowden, *Next Steps in Voluntary Action: An Analysis of Five Years of Developments in the Voluntary Sector in England, Northern Ireland, Scotland and Wales* (London, 2001), p. 11; 'Whom do the Public Trust?', YouGov Trust tracker, http://today.yougov.co.uk/sites/today.yougov.co.uk/files/PKPublicTrustAug2010.pdf; *Standard Eurobarometer*, 55 (2001), p. 10, http://ec.europa.eu/public_opinion/archives/eb/eb55/eb55_en.pdf.

On the other hand, the public also holds a much less positive view of campaigning pressure groups or NGOs. Yet there is a problem here. The public may not hold environmental pressure groups in great 'trust', but when asked a question about from where the public expects to get information about pollution problems, pressure groups top the poll. They are followed by independent scientists, whilst the government was held in considerable low esteem (Figure 8.10).

There is also a problem about definitions. 'Trust' is not the same thing as 'confidence', whilst it is evident that the public are not always clear what they consider charities and pressure groups to be. Reports commissioned by the National Council of Voluntary Organisations (NCVO) and the Charity Commission have indicated that the public has equated charity with 'caring' and helping the needy in society, independent of government and crucially having non-profit-making motives (see Figure 8.11). Yet they appear unaware that the boundaries between business, government and charity are closely entwined (see Chapter 9 for a further explanation of the legal and statutory status that can be adopted by NGOs). The situation has been complicated further because some PR consultancies talk less about 'trust' and instead have adopted the language of business and seek to describe NGOs as 'brands'. Again this is problematic and at times controversial (or at least in the eyes of rival consultancies), but what it all ultimately reveals (as with Tables 8.1 and 8.2) is that the British public are most confident in recognising organisations that are concerned with animal welfare, health and children. Furthermore, they are supportive of NGOs that have a welfare or relief orientation, but are more anxious about those that may be perceived as having a more political campaigning role.

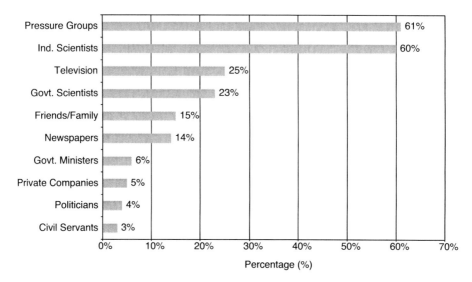

Figure 8.10: Trust on pollution: Q: 'Thinking now about pollution, which two or three, if any, of these sources would you trust most to advise you on the risks posed by pollution?'

Source: Audit Commission and MORI Social Research Institute, *Exploring Trust in Public Institutions, Report for the Audit Commission* (London, 2003), p. 38, www.ipsos-mori.com/DownloadPublication/1180_sri_trust_in_public_institutions_2003.PDF.

Table 8.1: Top five 2010 UK charities by reputation, 2010

1. RNLI
2. RSPCA
3. British Red Cross
4. Cancer Researches
5. British Heart Foundation

Source: Reputation Institute, *2010 Global Reputation Pulse Study – UK Results* (ICSA, London, May 2010), report available from the Reputation Institute, http://reputationinstitute.com.

Table 8.2: 'Are there any specific charities or types of charities that you would trust more than others?', 2005, 2008, 2010

	2005 (%)	2008 (%)	2010 (%)
Cancer Research UK	12	15	12
NSPCC	4	9	6
British Heart Foundation	3	4	5
Oxfam	6	9	4
Macmillan Cancer Relief	1	6	3
RSPCA	2	6	3
British Red Cross	4	4	3
RNLI	1	4	2
The Salvation Army	2	2	2
Save the Children	2	3	1
Age Concern	1	2	1
Barnardo's		2	1
Christian Aid	1	2	1
RNIB		2	1
Marie Curie		2	1
British Legion		2	1
Children in Need		2	1
Breakthrough Breast Cancer		1	1
Guide Dogs for the Blind		1	1
Imperial Cancer Research Fund		1	1
UNICEF	1	1	1
WWF		1	1
Amnesty International	1	1	1
Air Ambulance	1	1	1
Great Ormond Street		1	1
Greenpeace		1	1
RSPB		1	1
ChildLine	1	2	1
MS Society			1
Scope			1
Dogs Trust			1
Help for Heroes			1
St John Ambulance			1
Help the Aged		2	1
Charities by type			
Animal charities	3	4	4
Well-known charities	1	4	4
Health-related charities	2	2	4
Local charities	3	5	3
Religious charities	2	3	2
Children's charities	3	3	2
Big Charities	3	2	2
Small charities		2	2
Cancer charities	3	2	2
International charities	2	1	1
Blind charities		1	1
Hospital/hospice charities			1
UK/British-based charities			1
Don't know/None	50	34	39

Plus 'other' responses – not shown (11% in 2010, inc. responses of less than 1%)

Source: *Public Trust and Confidence in Charities*, MORI/Charity Commission 2010 report, Q4A p. 59, www.ipsos-mori.com/DownloadPublication/1373_sri-third-sector-public-trust-in-charities-july-2010.pdf.

Figure 8.11: Public Trust in Charities to … (mean scores of respondents to the question 'On a 0–10 scale [where 0 shows no trust and 10 absolute trust], how much would you trust charities to …'), 2005, 2008, 2010

Note: The question relating to 'Make independent decisions …' was not asked before 2010.

Source: *Public Trust and Confidence in Charities*, MORI/Charity Commission 2010 report, p. 10, www.ipsos-mori.com/DownloadPublication/1373_sri-third-sector-public-trust-in-charities-july-2010.pdf.

Politics and the state

In one sense, it is rather arbitrary to separate measures of the impact NGOs have on the public with the impact they could be said to have had on government. Much of the public relations work is directed at both. In particular, the strategy and target audience of the many publications published by NGOs is important to understand. Some are intended specifically for supporters to enable them to understand more fully the issues about which the NGO is interested in; others are intended for wider public consumption as part of a wider education programme. Some are targeted specifically at the decision makers or the media, perhaps highlighting detailed research that may have been undertaken by the NGO, as part of a wider agenda-changing campaign. Sometimes, the publications are the result of government-funded research and may form part of an official report.

Undoubtedly, though, many NGO publications are targeted at the policy making process. The NGOs hope they are read by politicians and people of influence and will ultimately impact upon government legislation, regulation and policy. Such a logic must certainly lie behind the tremendous outpouring of NGO publications over the last few decades. The output of printed books and pamphlets of the leading NGOs is staggering. Figure 8.12 only counts those publications that have been stored at the British Library. Many other pamphlets and printed ephemera can be found in NGOs' own archives.

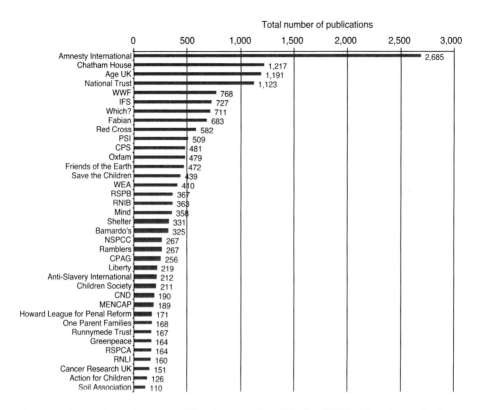

Figure 8.12: Total numbers of publications produced by key NGOs (showing only those NGOs that have published more than 100 titles)

Note: For Which? only the 'Consumers' Association' could be used as a search term due to the high number of erroneous results produced by using the search term 'Which?'. Similarly, only the search term 'National Council for Civil Liberties' could be used for Liberty.

Source: British Library Catalogue.

If one considers research reports or findings mentioned in early day motions in the House of Commons it would appear that some NGOs have a much better ratio of publications to mentions (for example, Age UK) than others (such as Amnesty). Figure 8.13, for instance, shows how different homelessness NGOs have been cited in Early Day Motions (EDMs) from 1989 to 2010.

The reception for such publications is not always positive. During the 1970s the floors of the House of Commons and Lords often heard speakers bemoaning the exaggerations and accuracy of Shelter reports. Shelter had from the outset sought to break the mould with its publications, making innovative use of photographs to highlight the plight of the homeless. The internet has revolutionised the means of publishing NGO research, any cursory examination of organisational homepages will quickly reveal pdfs of reports and publications freely downloadable, but at the same time it also means that there is even more material out there and questions are raised about who actually reads them.

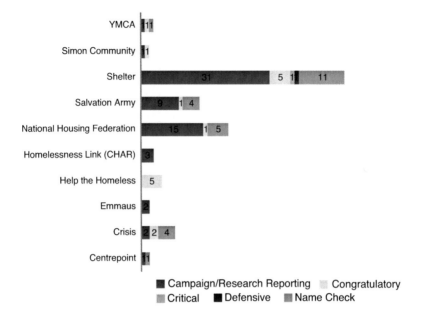

Figure 8.13: Categories of EDMs associated with homeless NGOs, 1989–2010

Note: Categorisation of EDMs: 'Campaign/Research Reporting': citing evidence from NGOs or mentioning individual campaigns and reports; 'Congratulatory': paying tribute to sustained work in a particular area or an NGO's anniversary; 'Critical': critical of an NGO's policy or its internal workings; 'Defensive': defending NGOs in light of action against NGOs; 'Name Check': using an NGO as an example to aid a motion. No individual campaign or report is mentioned.

Sources: House of Commons Early Day Motion database, http://edmi.parliament.uk/edmi/; Early Day Motions website, www.edms.org.uk/.

Those NGOs that adopt a parliamentary strategy have a number of options before them in order to influence the agenda. Aside from the parliamentary function of the initiation and scrutiny of legislation (private members' bills, amendments tabled in the committee stages), NGOs can use representative assemblies to promote their research (through mention in debates, evidence to parliamentary committees, EDMs, All Party Parliamentary Groups), to assist in their own research through eliciting information from government (parliamentary questions), and generally heighten awareness of their cause through mass lobbies of parliament and lobbying of individual elected representatives by NGO supporters (letter writing, emails, constituency surgery visits). Much of this is directed towards creating a group of sympathetic elected representatives who will be prepared to act, and lobby fellow MPs and government, upon their behalf. Although there is no formula for success, in that access can be ensured, certainly there is evidence to show that certain NGOs, or NGO sectors, have proved adept at ensuring they have a presence in parliament. Figure 8.14, for instance, tracks the number of mentions of environmental NGOs in the House of Commons from 1945.

Some NGOs' publications have obtained a reputation for accuracy and rigour. The reports of the big IAD NGOs, such as Oxfam, have a reputation that ensures their

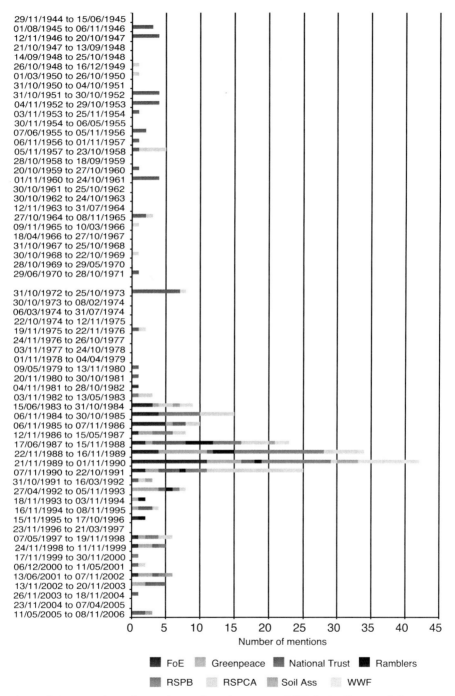

Figure 8.14: Number of mentions of environmental NGOs in House of Commons, 1945–2006

Source: Hansard: House of Commons Debates: Index.

work is often read by staff at key intergovernmental institutions. Within a domestic context the Consumers' Association's reputation has rested on the authority of its publications which in turn has made it easier to secure policy initiatives. While in the 1960s it could present evidence that entered a more general mix behind such pieces of legislation as the 1968 Trade Descriptions Act, by the 1970s its published investigations were taken up by MPs and show a direct link from NGO to Act of Parliament. Key impacts of the organisation in this decade included the Unsolicited Goods and Services Act (1971), the Litigants in Person (Costs and Expenses) Act (1975) and the Unfair Contract Terms Act (1977).

The complexity of political influence can be seen in specific examples. In the Westminster parliamentary session of 2002–03, Joan Ruddock tabled a Friends of the Earth-inspired EDM (No. 333) calling for curbside household recycling; 320 MPs signed in support after Friends of the Earth urged its supporters to contact their MPs on the matter. Ruddock then agreed to introduce, on behalf of Friends of the Earth, a private member's bill which sought to obligate English and Welsh local authorities to introduce doorstep recycling for a minimum of two recyclables to every home by 2010. It secured royal assent in October 2003 after 450 MPs supported the Act.

Box 8.1: Diabetes UK and elected assemblies

This NGO has been particularly active in recent years, with a quarterly parliamentary bulletin, awarding an annual Diabetes Parliamentary Champion prize, and sponsoring All Party Groups on Diabetes at Westminster, the Scottish parliament and the Welsh Assembly. In 2010 they, and their research campaigns, were mentioned in three Westminster EDMs (Nos 445, 8 July; 901, 26 October; 1002, 12 November). During the 2009–10 Westminster session, ten parliamentary questions were asked relating to diabetes (six by Keith Vaz) and Diabetes UK's collaboration with the Department of Health was specifically acknowledged in one ministerial reply (26 November 2009).

Box 8.2: World Development Movement and the 1981 Brandt Report mass lobby of Westminster

The World Development Movement organised a mass lobbying of parliament on 5 May 1981 in support of the Brandt Report. It was estimated that between 8,000 and 10,000 people attended, and Michael Foot, leader of the opposition, addressed the lobby, pledged Labour's commitment to meeting the 0.7 per cent figure of the proportion of GDP to be spent on aid. The *Guardian* reported:

'... ministers, who were clearly surprised by the depth of popular support expressed at Westminster yesterday, were quick to stress that the Government's new found liking for the Brandt Commission did not mean that it saw any reason to change its policies on overseas aid and development. As queues for the mass lobby began to grow around Parliament yesterday, the Government took the unusual step of calling a briefing for journalists to explain its position. Earlier, the Foreign Office had circulated a six page paper to MPs specifically to counter the criticisms of British policy which were made at the lobby by speakers ...'

James Erlkichman, 'Tories' Change of Heart on Brandt Report', *Guardian*, 6 May 1981, 2.

Although some NGOs have become sceptical about the value of parliamentary lobbying, it is evident that others still consider this a worthwhile option. The continued growth in EDMs, many of which cite specific NGOs and their research campaigns and which are widely acknowledged as having been ghosted by the organisations themselves, points to this. The House of Commons Information Office has observed the extent to which NGOs go to persuade MPs to sign 'their' motion. Figure 8.15 illustrates how EDMs between 1989 and 2010, related to key

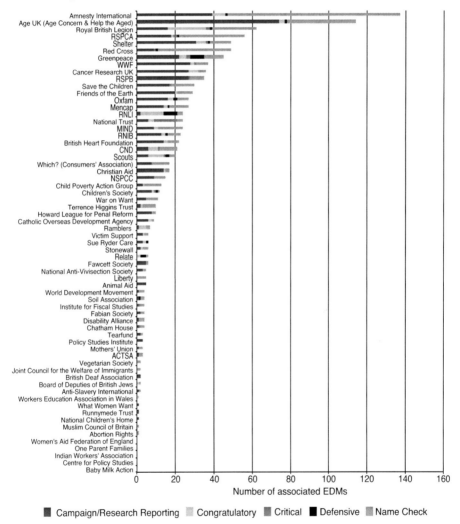

Figure 8.15: Number of mentions in Westminster EDMs, 1989–2010, of the key NGOs profiled by the NGOs in Britain project

Note: On categorisation of EDMs, see note to Figure 8.13.

Sources: House of Commons Early Day Motion database, http://edmi.parliament.uk/edmi/; Early Day Motions website, www.edms.org.uk/.

NGOs, shows the popularity of this method of publicity, and that it is clearly seen as an opportunity to highlight research or campaigns. Those that have been cited over 20 times are the big 'brand' NGOs, both charitable and campaigning, that have a resource base to devote time to maintaining a parliamentary profile. Others are sceptical of the value of EDMs, as with John Belcrow, speaker of the House of Commons, in January 2011 when he labelled them as 'toilet paper'. Looking at those EDMs that have secured significant backbench support (with over 300 signatures) the influence of NGOs is discernible: disability, drugs, rights (children and sexual), health campaigning and road safety all feature frequently.

The wider prevalence of NGOs in British society and the growth in post-materialist concerns can be seen when comparing Labour MPs elected in 1945 with those who were elected in 1997. From entries in *Who's Who*, 20 per cent of the 1945 cohort had a connection during their lifetime, whilst this had grown to 35 per cent by 2007. But the range of NGOs has dramatically expanded. The Fabians still remain the most popular, with the Workers' Educational Association still in second place, if substantially reduced, but below these the range of issues covered stretches from human rights, to old-age matters, to race, to poverty, to the environment. Figure 8.16 shows the general trend of these connections, but an individual example shows the crossover between the two spheres of action. Christopher Pond, for instance, entered parliament in 1997 after a career spanning over 20 years at the Low Pay Unit. He subsequently returned to the NGO sector, bringing his political experience to such organisations as Gingerbread and End Child Poverty.

Select committees have provided an opportunity for 'expert' NGO engagement with the legislator. The numerical growth in NGOs has also been replicated in the numbers giving evidence to parliamentary committees. In 1952 the sixth report of the Select Committee on Estimates on Child Care had drawn evidence from four children's groups (Barnardo's, Crusade of Rescue, National Children's Home and Orphanage, and the Children's Society) in addition to ten government or local authority bodies. By 2001 when a select committee considered the Adoption and Children's Bill, 15 NGOs presented evidence, alongside a further total of 15 government and professional bodies.

Reviewing the evidence presented to the Select Committee on Overseas Aid[1] between 1968 and 2010 demonstrates both the growth of the influence of NGOs and the shift in priorities over 40 years. Before 1983 the committee was much more likely to take evidence from British diplomats and officials than it was NGOs, and its reports were concerned more with the mutually beneficial aspects of international aid and trade (see Figures 8.17 and 8.18). From 1997, NGOs become the dominant source of evidence, and the committee reports are more concerned with humanitarian issues, subjects to which the NGOs are better able to speak (see

---

1 The name of this committee changes frequently: 1968 Select Committee on Overseas Aid, 1973–79 Select Committee on Overseas Development, then in 1979 it became a sub-committee of the Foreign Affairs Select Committee. Between 1983 and 1997 there was no specific meeting of the select committee on the matter of international aid. In 1997 it was reborn as the International Development Select Committee.

Figures 8.17 and 8.19). Furthermore, the independence of these NGOs at scrutinising the work of the Department of International Development appears to be highly valued by the committee.

(a) MPs elected in 1945

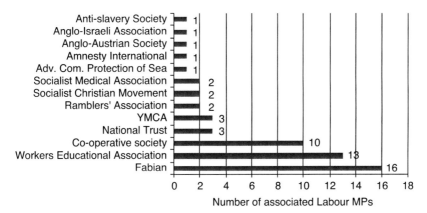

(b) MPs elected in 1997

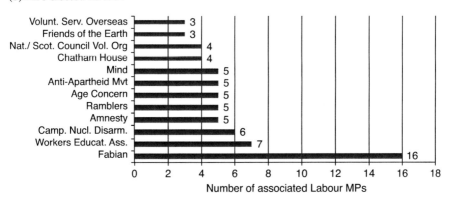

Figure 8.16: Top twelve NGOs with which Labour MPs were associated in 1945 and 1997

Source: *Who's Who* and *Who Was Who*, online edition, www.ukwhoswho.com.

The expertise of NGOs has also been called upon by Royal Commissions. Since 1945 there have been 34 on a range of topics from equal pay (1946), to the press (1949 and 1962), to the NHS (1979). Overall, 5,550 organisations have contributed evidence to one or more commission. Table 8.3 and Figure 8.21 show some of the most prominent NGO contributors, as well as the most prominent sectors called upon to give evidence.

Table 8.3: Contributions to Royal Commissions by different sectors

Royal Commission	Business, professional and trade unions	Government, statutory & public sector	Voluntary organisation	Grand total
1944 Equal Pay	68	45	19	132
1944 Population	5	1	30	36
1946 Justices of the Peace	23	44	6	73
1947 Capital Punishment	9	26	5	40
1947 The Press	148	1	4	153
1951 Betting, Lotteries and Gaming	27	24	17	68
1952 Scottish Affairs	27	30	8	65
1952 University Education in Dundee	3	17	2	22
1953 Civil Service	26	9	11	46
1953 East Africa	12	19	19	50
1955 Common Land	20	69	56	145
1955 Taxation of Profits and Income	93	19	26	138
1956 Marriage and Divorce	31	9	78	118
1957 Mental Illness and Deficiency	29	19	18	66
1960 Doctors' and Dentists' Pay	105	44	11	160
1960 Local Government in London	116	91	83	290
1961 The Press	144	1	5	150
1962 The Police	15	20	7	42
1965 Medical Education	102	130	21	253
1965 Trade Unions	223	37	21	281
1966 Tribunals of Inquiry	6	5	2	13
1969 Assizes and Quarter Sessions	52	34	3	89
1969 Local Government in England	111	133	113	357
1969 Local Government in Scotland	60	60	23	143
1969 The Constitution	16	86	22	124
1976 Standards of Conduct in Public Life	28	56	3	87
1977 The Press	66	25	18	109
1978 Civil Liability	175	63	57	295
1978 Gambling	84	35	24	143
1979 Legal Services	177	63	72	312
1979 NHS	344	748	132	1224
1981 Criminal Procedure	48	29	66	143
1993 Criminal Justice	69	62	64	195
Grand Total	**2,462**	**2,054**	**1,046**	**5,562**

Source: Royal Commission reports since 1944.

In certain instances Royal Commissions acquire 'standing' status and remain active. The Royal Commission on the Environment, created in 1970, has since produced 29 main reports plus a series of short interim reports. All together, it has taken evidence from 187 NGOs, though it was recently told that its activities will cease in 2011 due to the public sector cutbacks introduced by the Cameron coalition government. During its first decade those NGOs contributing tended to be a small number of 'establishment' environmental groups such as the CPRE and the RSPB; however, during the 1980s the number and breadth of NGO contributions expanded, as did the frequency of reports from 1990 (see Figures 8.21 and 8.22).

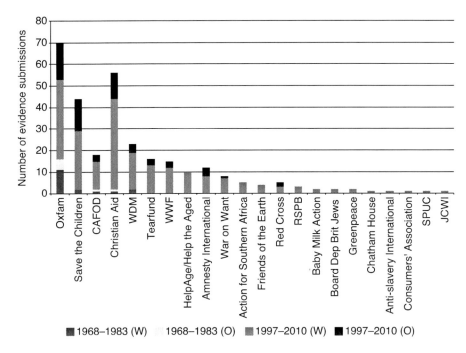

Figure 8.17: Evidence to select committee regarding international aid and development (by period – written (w) and oral (o))

Source: House of Commons Parliamentary Papers, http://parlipapers.chadwyck.co.uk.ezproxye.bham. ac.uk/home.do.

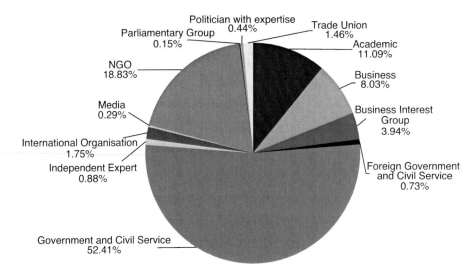

Figure 8.18: Submissions of evidence (written and oral) to the international development committees, 1968–83

Source: House of Commons Parliamentary Papers http://parlipapers.chadwyck.co.uk.ezproxye.bham.ac.uk/home.do.

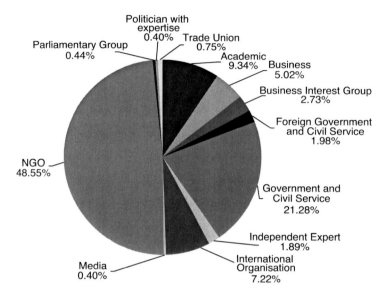

Figure 8.19: Submissions of evidence (written and oral) to the international development select committee, 1997–2010

Source: House of Commons Parliamentary Papers http://parlipapers.chadwyck.co.uk.ezproxye.bham.ac.uk/home.do.

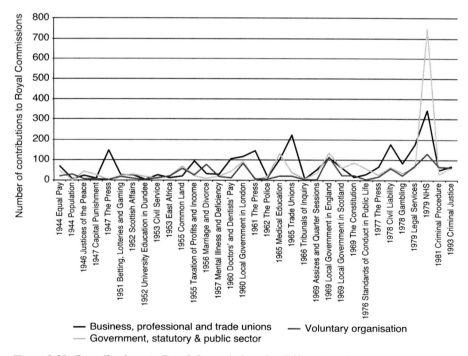

Figure 8.20: Contributions to Royal Commissions by different sectors

Source: Royal Commission reports since 1944.

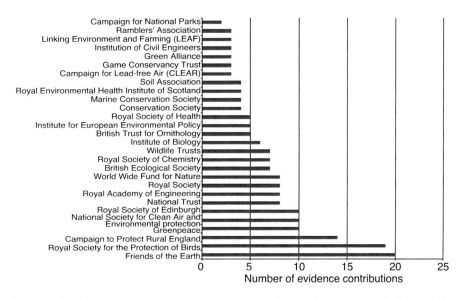

Figure 8.21: Number of evidence contributions to the Royal Commission on the Environment by NGOs, 1970–2010

Note: This excludes the first two reports as these do not list the evidence-givers.

Source: Royal Commission on the Environment website, www.rcep.org.uk/.

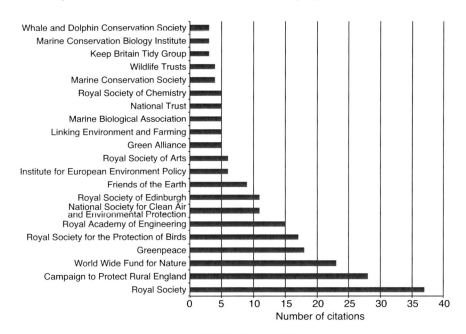

Figure 8.22: Number of mentions of NGOs in Royal Commission on the Environment reports, 1970–2010

Source: Royal Commission on the Environment website, www.rcep.org.uk.

Some NGOs have taken the conscious decision to eschew, or combine, a parliamentary strategy with one that establishes relations with Whitehall. Historically, a number of NGOs formed close 'insider' links with civil servants to the extent that they became synonymous with a particular Whitehall department. The Howard Defence League for Penal Reform was likened to being 'Her Majesty's Official Opposition' to the Home Office, whilst Whitehall officials have long traditions of relations with many of the established NGOs that work in the field of handicap, such as the RNIB and Scope, attending committee meetings and advising on policy changes. The relationships formed between civil servants and organisations can prove important because sympathetic civil servants can assist NGOs with policy documentation and advising on draft legislation, as well as seeking to mitigate the impact of legislation by the interpretation and advice they offer in their Codes of Guidance. Likewise, Whitehall will call upon NGOs to assist with committees of inquiry. In 1966 the National Assistance Board used the services of the Church Army, Salvation Army, Simon Community and Voluntary Hostels Conference to report on the changing nature of homelessness.

The relationship can also be strengthened by a trend likened to 'revolving doors' whereby individuals from the NGO sector move across to Whitehall and then return to the NGO sector, and vice versa. Initially confined to the most senior figures, this has become a much more commonplace career trajectory. Analysis of the careers of recent and current chief executives of our 63 NGOs suggests that a third have experienced both sectors during their careers. The trend began in the late 1960s when Brian Abel-Smith and Tony Lynes, both of CPAG, joined Wilson's government as special advisors. In 1990 Tom Burke of the Green Alliance became a special advisor to the Environment Secretary, Michael Heseltine; and more recently Louise Casey, formerly of Shelter and Centrepoint, became the Rough Sleeper Tsar and then headed up Tony Blair's Anti-Social Behaviour Unit. Former Oxfam employees who have worked for the Department of International Aid since the 1997 have been nick-named the 'ex-fams', whilst former Friends of the Earth staffers, who had begun their careers campaigning for carbon emission cuts, could be found working in government drafting the 2008 Climate Change Bill. The expectation is that these individuals bring a particular specialism to help inform government policy. Opinion divides over whether they are enhancing the NGO–Whitehall relationship or merely diluting the sector's ability to maintain the 'critical outsider' role. Some scepticism exists as to whether they become little more than the sounding board for Whitehall to test the potential reaction of NGOs to policy initiatives.

Beyond Westminster and Whitehall, recourse to the courts (whether national or European) has become an avenue that NGOs have increasingly begun to utilise, although much less so than in the United States. Since the 1970s, poverty groups such as CPAG and the Low Pay Unit have sought to test tribunal judgements to seek to establish the parameters of civil service guidance on issues such as welfare benefits. Environmental groups like Friends of the Earth used the Windscale, Sizewell and Hinkley Point planning inquiries as opportunities to raise wider issues about nuclear power and the social values associated with the risks of radiation from nuclear installations and the risks posed by an expansion of nuclear energy. Other environment groups, alongside women's groups, consumer groups and animal welfare organisations, realised from 1973 with Britain's accession to the European Union that the primacy of EU law over British offered alternative avenues for challenging national governments. Legal challenges and case actions are a frequent tactic of Greenpeace, which secured a 2007 High Court ruling that judged the 2006 Energy Review to be 'misleading' and 'seriously flawed'. In reality, these are procedural devices that do not confirm the rights of the cause but merely rule on the legality of the procedural operation.

Campaign case studies

'Stop the Seventy Tour' campaign, 1970

This was a campaign led by anti-apartheid activist Peter Hain aiming to prevent the 1970 cricket tour of the UK by the South Africans. Having earlier failed to halt a 25-match winter tour by the Springboks rugby team, despite disrupting games with pitch invasions, this small campaign represented part of a wider action against apartheid in South Africa. In sporting terms, the boycott was also linked to the threat from other African and Asian Commonwealth nations to boycott the July Edinburgh Commonwealth Games. The pressure from the Stop campaign led Prime Minister Harold Wilson to consider, in a secret committee, whether it would be possible to ban the South African team from entering the UK. Ultimately the government decided to request that the Cricket Council cancel the tour.

Friends of the Earth and the 'Big Ask' campaign, 2005–08

Friends of the Earth has been widely credited by the media (29 per cent of British newspaper articles on the Climate Change Bill mentioned Friends of the Earth) with encouraging the introduction of the Climate Change Act 2008 which made it legally binding for the government to reduce emissions of greenhouse gasses in the country by 80 per cent in 2050 and to introduce from 2009 'carbon budgets'. Friends of the Earth claimed that nearly 200,000 people had contacted their MP directly on the matter since the campaign was launched in May 2005 with a cinema advert and assisted by celebrity endorsement, meaning 'in three years people power has changed politics'. However, the role of scientists and other actors should not be excluded from explaining the success of this campaign in helping to frame the issues. In addition, the NGO was part of a broader coalition, 'Stop Climate Chaos', of over 70 environmental and development charities, trade unions, women's and faith groups who were also campaigning on the cause and helping to scrutinise the parliamentary legislation.

Joint Charities Group and the 1977 Housing (Homeless Persons) Act, 1973–77

Homelessness had been rediscovered in the mid 1960s and given a high profile with the launch of Shelter and with campaigns such as Crisis at Christmas. In 1973, five campaigning groups (Shelter, CPAG, Catholic Housing Aid Society, CHAR (Campaign for the Homeless and Rootless) and London Housing Aid Centre) came together to form the Joint Charities Group (JCG). Subsequently joined by the National Council for One Parent Families (NCOPF) and the Public Health Advisory Service, and with a similar coalition conceived in Scotland in 1975, the strategy adopted was to pressurise the civil service, to create a parliamentary lobby (initially comprising of 22 MPs and growing to 40) and to bring pressure to bear on the political parties by eliciting the support of activists. After an initial private member's bill was deemed unrealistic, the JCG secured ministerial pledges to introduce legislation. But Labour's 1976 Queen's Speech dropped the pledge. Stephen Ross agreed to introduce a JCG-drafted private member's bill, provided Scotland was included, but it was substituted with a more 'radical' civil service-drafted bill that secured cross-party support. Although significant amendments on intentional homelessness and locality reduced much of the radicalism of the bill, the code of guidance circulated by the Department of Environment appeared to mitigate these amendments. Whilst the Act defined the priority groups to be housed, and provided a statutory definition of homelessness for the first time, it gave priority to families with dependents over the single homeless and worked on a presumption that the problems were only 'temporary'. It marked the high point of state intervention in homelessness and moved it from being a matter of welfare to one of housing.

Campaign to ban hunting with animals, 1928 to date

This campaign was initially spearheaded by the National Society for the Abolition of Cruel Sports and the League Against Cruel Sports. In 1928 the National Society succeeded in persuading the Labour Party to confirm its opposition to hunting, but it was not until 1949, with the introduction of private members' bills, that MP-supporters of the anti-hunting lobby secured the opportunity to legislate. One bill was to ban the hunting of deer, otters and badgers as well as hare and rabbit coursing, whilst the second bill was to ban fox hunting. This separation was deliberate due to divisions within the animal rights movement and recognition of the public opposition to banning fox hunting. Neither of the bills succeeded, and instead the Labour government offered a departmental committee to examine the issues, which reported in 1951. Its recommendation was a bitter blow: namely, that whilst wild animals should be protected under the law, it should exempt those pursued by field sports because they provided healthy recreation. In 1969 the RSPCA balloted its 30,000 members on the issue, with a 10,000 majority opposed to hunting. Blood sports continued to remain a matter for individual conscience. During the 1970s the League Against Cruel Sports, despite support from some Labour parliamentarians, failed with private members' bills to ban hare coursing and otter hunting. In the late 1970s Tony Benn tried to persuade (unsuccessfully) Labour's National Executive Committee to make opposition to hunting a manifesto commitment, but electoral concerns about rural votes were strongly at play. Michael Foot did commit Labour's 1983 'longest suicide note' manifesto to banning fox hunting. Direct action was increasingly conducted by hunt saboteurs during the 1980s and 1990s, as they tried both to disrupt hunting and to collect evidence of illegal acts of animal cruelty and of hunt trespass. During the early 1990s various Labour MPs failed to secure private members' bills. Then in 1997 the Labour Party was elected with the manifesto promise of a free vote. Michael Foster, with administrative support and legal advice provided by the Campaign for the Protection of Hunted Animals, introduced a bill to ban hunting with dogs, but after a protracted and bitter campaign it was withdrawn in July 1998. Throughout the parliamentary process, the pro-hunt lobby was marshalled by the Countryside Alliance, mobilising at one point 250,000 to demonstrate on the streets of London. Eventually Blair's government introduced legislation on a free vote, but it met considerable opposition from the House of Lords. In November 2004 the speaker of the Commons invoked the Parliament Act to ensure that the bill to ban hunting was given royal assent. Bans were introduced in Scotland in 2002 (where separate legislation had gone through the Scottish Assembly in 2000–01) and then for England and Wales in 2005. Attempts by the Countryside Alliance to overturn the ban by legal appeal, in the High Court and European Court of Human Rights, failed. It remains to be seen whether the Cameron government will honour a pledge to revisit the ban.

Further reading

For organisational case studies, see Mike Ryan, *The Acceptable Pressure Group: Inequality in the Penal Lobby* (Farnborough, 1978), which compares the roles of the Howard League with Radical Alternatives to Prison; Tom Buchanan on Amnesty International's foundation '"The Truth Will Set You Free": The Making of Amnesty International', *Journal of Contemporary History*, 37:4 (2002), pp. 575–97, and Rob Skinner, *The Foundations of Anti-Apartheid: Liberal Humanitarians and Transnational Activists in Britain and the United States* (Basingstoke, 2010), which locates the anti-apartheid movement within a moral framework of political rights that can be traced back to earlier forms of humanitarianism. Frank Field, *Poverty and Politics: The Inside Story of the Child Poverty Action Group's Campaigns in the 1970s*, offers an insight into how CPAG devised new strategies for campaigning that inspired a new generation of groups, whilst some of the witness testimonies offered in Helene Curtis and Mimi Sanderson (eds), *The Unsung Sixties: Memoirs of Social Innovation* (London, 2004), give an insider perspective on working within a range of these groups.

More broadly, sector studies exist such as Paul Whiteley and Stephen Winyard, *Pressure for the Poor* (London, 1987), which evaluates the successes and limitations of the poverty lobby, considers the effectiveness of the strategies adopted by these NGOs and argues that they had influence but not power. Similarly, Grant Jordan and William Maloney, *The Protest Business? Mobilizing Campaign Groups* (Manchester, 1997), explores the campaigning roles of Amnesty International and Friends of the Earth. Also on the environmental movement, see John McCormick, *British Politics and the Environment* (London, 2009). The impact of the disability lobby, often campaigning from outside the system, and the way in which the disabled became disillusioned with their representation by middle-class non-disabled well-doers, is covered in Michael Oliver, *The Politics of Disablement* (Basingstoke, 1990).

For an understanding of the academic approach to the study of such groups, see Wyn Grant, *Pressure Groups and British Politics* (Basingstoke, 2000), which, written by the leading proponent of the insider/outsider thesis, introduces the reader to key characteristics of pressure groups and considers the environments in which they operate. Older case studies of pressure group activity written from the perspective of the commercial and professional lobbies demonstrate a club-like Establishment system, operating at the level of the executive and behind closed doors; see H. Hubert Wilson, *Pressure Group: The Campaign for Commercial Television in England* (London, 1961), and Harry Eckstein, *Pressure Group Politics: The Case of the British Medical Association* (Stanford, 1967).

Practical handbooks on lobbying include Charles Miller, *Lobbying Government: Understanding and Influencing the Corridors of Power* (Oxford, 1987), and Michael Burrell, *Lobbying and the Media: Working with Politicians and Journalists* (London, 2002).

9
Governance and Professionalism

When Margaret Thatcher addressed the Women's Royal Voluntary Service (WRVS) in January 1981, an organisation that was 100 per cent reliant on central government grants for its core funding, she observed that there was no way that Britain 'could produce statutory services to meet the needs which as volunteers you now satisfy'. Denying that she wanted to make such organisations the 'creatures of Government', she nevertheless saw 'our role' as being 'to help you do the administration and work of mobilising this enormous army of volunteers'. This concern of central government to invoke the skills of the NGO sector in the delivery of services was to have a profound impact on the evolution and landscape of this sector. Previous chapters have shown the complexities of the NGO sector and illustrated its expansion since 1945.

The purpose of this chapter is to explain how matters of governance and legal entity can explain both the challenges the sector has experienced and account for some of the organisational developments that have occurred. Chapter 1 addressed the issue of definition and this chapter will seek to explain in greater detail the legalistic, and sometimes multiple, entities that NGOs can, and sometimes have to, adopt. It is possible to broadly categorise the key developments that have occurred. What will become evident is that many NGOs have developed from amateur and voluntarist roots to becoming highly professionalised and even business-oriented organisations.

Foundation and 'charismatic leaders'

How an organisation came into existence is important. This is not something solely of interest to the historian, but can be integral to how that organisation both evolves and perceives itself. Sometimes these origins achieve a mythology of their own, which can subtly inform perceptions both for staff and supporters and the wider public. They are in effect little more than marketing. Many NGO accounts stress the voluntarist tendencies of their early years, or seek to recapture a time of hopefulness that embodies the contemporary zeitgeist. Timing and luck play their part too. Shelter, which came into being as a fundraising collaboration between several homeless/housing organisations, is often mistakenly perceived as having been inspired by the film *Cathy Come Home* (1966). In reality it was just coincidence and Shelter's launch from St Martin-in-the-Fields' Crypt was the culmination of a carefully and expertly planned six-month operation that drew upon Des Wilson's considerable specialism in journalism and public relations. Ultimately many of these foundation stories are just that, myths. The reality is that many NGOs were the product of professionalised middle classes who brought with them considerable social, cultural and intellectual capital.

Just as important to foundation myths are the legendary reputations of the founders. Save the Children was the inspiration of two sisters at the end of the First World War, single-parent group Gingerbread was due to Raga Woods, whilst Ann Pettifor was the inspiration for Jubilee 2000. Just as many of the nineteenth-century welfare charitable organisations discovered, as the lustre of founder legacy diminished in the early decades of the twentieth century, so similarly many newer organisations discovered that their creators could prove in the longer run to be hindrances. As the case studies in Boxes 9.1 and 9.2 suggest, the skills needed to

---

Box 9.1: Peter Benenson and Amnesty International

Peter Benenson supposedly hit upon the idea of founding Amnesty International after reading a *Daily Telegraph* report about two Portuguese political prisoners who had been jailed for toasting liberty in a Lisbon restaurant. No such article has ever been found. Amnesty was initially conceived as a short-term campaign, and launched by an article in the *Observer* in May 1961, but its membership, both in Britain and across Western Europe, grew rapidly, with its branches engaged in letter-writing campaigns on behalf of political prisoners. In the late 1960s it was rocked by a severe internal crisis as it became evident that Benenson was unable to provide adequate financial and bureaucratic oversight. A scandal, centring on allegations around the infiltration of Amnesty by the British security services, brought to light how far official oversight was lacking, and Benenson was forced to resign in 1967. He was replaced by Martin Ennals, previously of the National Council of Civil Liberties, who would place Amnesty on a new professional footing and who oversaw an expansion of its range of interests.

Box 9.2: Cecil Jackson-Cole, Oxfam and Help the Aged

Cecil Jackson-Cole was closely associated with the early years of Oxfam, an organisation he deemed his 'first love', and in 1961 he also founded Help the Aged. Using a charitable trust, the Voluntary Christian Service, he also launched Help Aged Refugees and Action in Distress (Action Aid). He brought innovation to the fundraising methods of Oxfam, arguing that such organisations needed to spend money on publicity in order to generate additional revenue, whilst with Help the Aged it was one of the first charities to use the press for advertising. With a reputation for being cantankerous, he was a philanthropist who combined entrepreneurialism with a strong Christian faith. He had an ability to recruit talented individuals to his organisations, but his idiosyncrasies and strong views could hinder developments, as Help the Aged discovered with his refusal to countenance the development of a chain of high street charity shops.

launch a campaign and nurture it in its early years are not always the same as those required to grow and develop a professionalised organisation.

The moves to professionalism

Since before the First World War there had been anxiety that the state and voluntary/ NGO sector could not coexist. Developments during the interwar years appeared to confirm the sense that the state was now responsible for the welfare of its citizens, even if in reality it was ad hoc and haphazard and the opportunities for the private citizen to dispense with voluntary help still existed. Indeed, the Second World War if anything reinforced the importance of groups in helping relieve the social deprivations and problems associated with war. But the creation of the welfare state in 1948 suggested that the state was ultimately taking responsibility for the citizen from the cradle to the grave.

Many observers predicted that this spelt the demise of the voluntary sector that had become so strongly prevalent in providing for the needs of the most vulnerable in society. The reality proved the opposite with an expansion in state welfare provision leading to a complementary expansion of the voluntary sector. Successive acts of legislation, such as the Children Act (1949) and the National Assistance Act (1949), extended the role of many organisations like the National Society for the Prevention of Cruelty to Children (NSPCC), as well as the areas of collaboration between the statutory authorities and the charitable welfare agencies. This led to calls for greater professionalism. The 1945 Nuffield Social Reconstruction Survey was one of the first to call for professional training to equip volunteers, especially in areas of social and welfare work, for the growing challenges of their role. It made the argument for casework to provide the link between the voluntary and state sectors. Over the next three decades training and qualifications for different aspects of the sector began to emerge. For example, the Children's Society nursery nurse training scheme became the template for training adopted by the Ministry of Education's National Nursery Examination Board. Universities also began to offer courses in social work and related areas as the social sciences developed as an academic discipline during the 1960s.

Changes to the funding regime began a process from the 1970s that heightened the degrees of accountability of these organisations which in turn led to a wave of professionalisation of their bureaucracies. The creation of the Voluntary Services Unit (VSU) within the Home Office in 1973 saw the state funding of the sector increase sharply. With this the language of the management structures of groups began to change: patrons became trustees and then boards of management, and chairmen became directors. Accountability within groups began to change – the notion of the founder leader gave way to boards of management that carried ultimate authority. Shelter by 1972 had become a charitable company, and the board of trustees a management committee, but the organisation was experiencing difficulties in leadership after Des Wilson's departure, and with the trustees who were considered unaccountable and alienated from staff members and those the organisation claimed to represent. When Wolfenden reported in 1978 he bemoaned the monopolistic bureaucracy of much of the sector and highlighted the problems of diminished accountability to users of services. The 1970s also saw a new breed of NGO emerge, especially in the area of disability, which were being run by the stakeholders themselves, representing themselves and offering solutions to their difficulties rather than being 'represented' by others.

The 1980s marked a significant sea change, as the Thatcher government sought to attack excessive public sector funding. It looked instead to the charitable sector to take up the slack as it cut back on public services. Using money, particularly through the Manpower Services Commission, it sought to bring the ethos of business to welfare provision. But alongside this came the insistence that groups in receipt of public money had to increase their accountability. The role of the audit commission was expanded with the explicit intention of improving the standards of management. By the 1990s it was the language of business and the age of the contract culture. This could be seen in a new wave of professionalism (which was different to that of the casework skills of the 1950s and 1960s) in which a new managerialism and corporate culture infected the NGO sector.

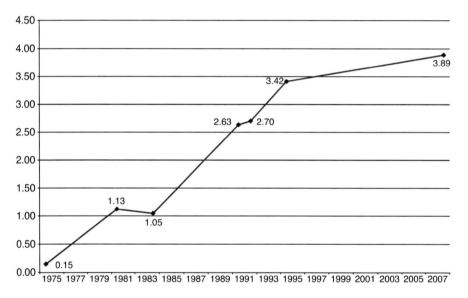

Figure 9.1: Average number of staff per registered charity, 1975–2008

Note: Figure created by dividing the number of staff working for all charities in Britain by the total number of charities in the same year.

Sources: (a) For the total number of charities: Jeremy Kendall and Martin Knapp, *The Voluntary Sector in the United Kingdom, Johns Hopkins Nonprofit Sector Series* (Manchester, 1996), p. 5; *Wolfenden 1978*, p. 34; Charity Statistics (various years); NCVO Almanac (various years); *Charity Commission Annual Report 2009/10*, p. 22, available at: www.charity-commission.gov.uk/Library/about_us/Charity_Commission_Annual_ Report_09_10.pdf; Charity Commission, www.charity-commission.gov.uk/About_us/About_charities/ factfigures.aspx. (b) For the total number of staff working for charities in Britain: *Charity Commission Annual Report 2009/10*, p. 22; Commission on the Future of the Voluntary Sector, *Meeting the Challenge of Change: Voluntary Action into the 21st Century: The Report of the Commission on the Future of the Voluntary Sector* (London, 1996) (Deakin Report), p. 31; *Charity Statistics*, 1996, pp. 6–8; 1995, p. 38; 14 (1991), p. 8; 7 (1983), p. 8; 8 (1984), p. 76; *Wolfenden 1978*, p. 36.

The trend was spearheaded by the rise of the CEO. Mind was led by a general secretary until 1972, then a director until 1996 and thereafter a chief executive. These new public management ideals were encouraged by the involvement of business in the funding of management development training, and the recruitment of senior businessmen as advisors and leaders of NGOs. The example of Reg Bailey who heads the Mothers' Union in 2011, having formerly been CEO of the Danish Bacon Company and Del Monte Foods, perfectly captures this trend. By the 1990s the new culture could be seen in the rebranding that organisations began to undergo, a trend which has multiplied during the first decade of the twenty-first century, as mission statements, logos and brands were developed, often followed by organisational renaming.

Evidence for this expanding professionalism can be seen in the growing staffing levels of many organisations. As Figure 9.1 shows, the average number of staff per registered charity has grown significantly since the 1970s, with the total numbers employed rising from 157,000 in 1981 to 700,000 in 2008 (equivalent to 2.3 per cent of the UK workforce). Not all NGOs were able or willing to accept this new managerialism, but these were often organisations operating on the small community scale, often representing ethnic or minority interests, or were deliberately excluded because they were campaigning pressure groups, but even many within this latter element have since felt it necessary to develop their brand. Others are wary of professionalisation. As the 1996 Deakin Report warned, the sector had to learn to manage professionally but not allow professionalism to dominate its agenda.

Main administrative structures

The following section outlines the main 'legal' entities that NGOs may adopt. Most will have begun life as unincorporated organisations and then, as income has grown, will have adopted the dual additional identity of being a charity. Then when a realisation is made about the potential liabilities facing the organisation, it may decide to become a company limited by guarantee which in turn obligates it to re-register as a charity. Sometimes this means that the same organisation has two charity identities, forgetting about the need to wind up the original charity or intentionally keeping it because of the limitations imposed on the amount of trading a charity may undertake in a given financial year. Consequently, it is not unheard of for an organisation to have two or three different legal entities, even though usually only the accountants know about this. The example in Figure 9.2 shows how Liberty has three identities: association, company and charitable. Liberty 'the company' took incorporated status in October 1996 and is the operational entity of the organisation. 'The association' is the unincorporated element of the organisation and is governed by a constitution and elected Privy Council which in turns appoints the Executive Committee. Finally, Liberty works closely with the Civil Liberties Trust, a charity that works to promote human rights and civil liberties through research, policy work, litigation and education.

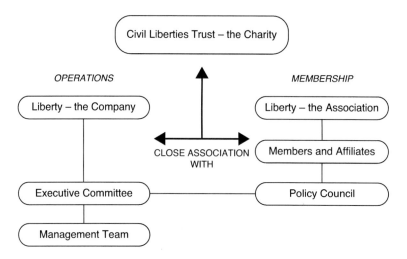

Figure 9.2: National Council for Civil Liberties (Liberty) organisational structure

Source: National Council for Civil Liberties (Liberty) *Report and Financial Statement Year Ending 31 December 2009*, p. 3.

Unincorporated organisations with no legal structure

Some organisations have chosen to be unincorporated associations. This essentially means that any group of people can come together and agree to adopt a constitution which provides the rules under which they operate. Any assets of the organisation are effectively held in trust by the individual members of the committee – meaning that in the event of legal action against the organisation, the members (in reality the officers/committee members) will be personally liable. There is no onus on unincorporated organisations to register their status. If they wish to open a bank account then they are required to have a constitution, but are not obligated to declare any donations to the HM Revenue & Customs (HMRC) unless they are trading as a company. Organisations like Abortion Rights or Action for Southern Africa (formerly the Anti-Apartheid Movement) appear to have chosen this route, as have many more community-based associations such as playgroups and sports clubs. There is no prevention from employing staff, provided the organisation registers with HMRC as an employer.

Companies

Most organisations (including the vast majority of charities) are companies limited by guarantee. The main reason for organisations to be incorporated as companies is to limit their liabilities in case of judiciary action against them. With trading activity, the organisation has to register with HMRC for tax purposes, which explains why some of these organisations have been vociferous in their complaints about value added tax (VAT), often encouraging sympathetic MPs to raise the issue in the House of Commons or to table Early Day Motions on the matter.

Charities

It has been estimated that of the 500,000 organisations in Britain that could be potentially labelled as NGOs, roughly 200,000 of them have adopted charitable status. Of the 63 NGOs profiled in Chapter 4 of this volume, only twelve are not charities (less than 20 per cent). In order to be recognised as a charity, an organisation must register with the Charity Commission, and since 1996 has been obliged to file annual accounts with them. Now all charities with an income over £25,000 will have their reports published on the Commission's website, whilst paper copies are retained at the Commission headquarters for those with a lesser income.

As Chapter 1 demonstrated, the first charity law was introduced in 1601 just before the death of Queen Elizabeth I, and in reality the basic premise of charity law has changed little since. It determines that charities should be concerned with the advancement of education and or religion, the relief of poverty, and intend to provide benefit to the community. It is the ability to fulfil one or more of these key criteria that has determined whether or not an NGO may adopt charitable status, but it has also thrown up considerable difficulties and confusion for the wider public. It means that organisations as diverse as public schools like Eton, or cultural establishments such as the Royal Opera House, can be legally defined as charities alongside groups that are clearly perceived by the public as fulfilling good deeds for the less fortunate of society.

As Chapter 8 showed, the public perception of charities and what constitutes charitable activity is blurred, with much of the public clearly resentful of charities that adopt campaigning strategies and anxious that charity should be about caring for the deprived elements of society. Public opinion clearly believes that it is important that charity should be independent of both government and business,

---

Box 9.3: Key legislative changes affecting charity

1958   Recreational Charities Act enables recreational and leisure-time facilities used in the interests of social welfare to be deemed charitable

1960   Charities Act obligates better methods of administration and revises the role of the Charity Commissioners, enhancing their powers of oversight

1972   Local Government Act transfers the licensing of charitable collection from the police to local authorities

1986   Chancellor Lawson introduces a payroll deduction scheme for charitable giving

1992   Charities Act sought to regulate fundraising activities

1993   Charities Act brings in reforms relating to the role of Trustees and introduces the requirement of annual accounts being placed with the Charity Commissioners

1993   National Lottery Act introduces the National Lottery and determines that a proportion of the revenues should be given to 'Good Causes' and also the 'Heritage Lottery Fund'

2000   Trustee Act provides for the remuneration of trustees for professional/specialist services

2006   Charity Act revises the 1601 definition of what constitutes charitable purposes and takes a more permissive view of political and campaigning

2011   Cameron government introduces Charities Bill with aim of consolidating existing charity legislation

and is clearly unaware of the close intertwining of the three. This is also symptomatic of the media outcries over the expenditure of charities on administration, education and campaigning, as both the NSPCC and the Diana, Princes of Wales, Memorial Fund have discovered to their cost. It is this latter element, campaigning, that is the most restrictive element of charitable law: namely, that a charity may not engage in party political action. It is acceptable to seek to educate civil servants or politicians on a particular cause, but the moment that campaign appears to be party political then an organisation can leave itself open to investigation by the Charity Commissioners. This has led to some high-profile organisations such as Oxfam, Shelter and War On Want coming under scrutiny.

Membership versus elite organisations

Aside from the legalistic styles of organisation that can exist, other models are in operation within these frameworks. This is about whether an organisation seeks to have a membership or whether it is more elite-oriented, perhaps only seeking financial donations from sympathisers; and if it does choose to have a membership base, what is the role of these members? The contrast in approaches can be seen in two different environmental groups: the Conservation Society and Greenpeace. The Conservation Society, formed in 1966, was concerned about the rate of population growth. It was a membership organisation, with only a very small full-time staff, and its membership peaked in 1973 with around 900 members. It regarded its activist base as the intellectual and campaigning heart of its organisation, who would engage in letter writing, publicity campaigning and serving on working parties. In reality only 10 per cent of members were active, and the membership was in rapid decline from the mid 1970s, with branches being reduced to only 31 by 1981. The organisation folded a few years later. In contrast, Greenpeace had ignored the issue of members until it decided in the mid 1980s that it would begin to recruit to form a network of supporters' groups and to fundraise. Crucially, these members were to be seen as supporters not campaigners. Campaigning was to be left to national headquarters and the professional elites of the organisation.

Membership can for some organisations provide a significant source of revenue – as is the case, for example, with Amnesty International. Within the membership profile, some organisations will seek to have a centralised membership, while others will have branch affiliations and open memberships. As the Wolfenden Report observed in 1978, tensions can also arise between the professional staffers at national head office and the volunteer members spread around the country, because the staffers often want and need to move on issues more quickly than the members, who do not have time to spend looking at issues (refer to the individual NGO profiles in Chapter 4 for further details). All of these models raise questions about the internal democracy of an NGO.

Accountability and decision making within NGOs

The diversity of models for decision making within NGOs is considerable. By the 1970s the Wolfenden Report noted that federal structures with executive committees were the most common pattern, but that variations in the degree of democratic accountability existed. Liberty (then the National Council of Civil Liberties) chose its executive members by 'one member, one vote' postal ballots, whilst the Royal National Lifeboat Institution's Committee of Management was determined by donors. Other organisations had much more open committee memberships, or included representatives of local authorities such as the Citizens' Advice Bureaux. As Box 9.4 shows, the moves towards greater public accountability have meant that significant changes occurred from the 1980s onwards as 'accountability' and 'governance' became buzz-words. Importantly, it also suggests that momentum for change has come from government and Whitehall rather than from within the organisations themselves.

Box 9.4: The Alzheimer's Society

Founded in 1979 by a small group of carers to provide support and information on dementia, the Alzheimer's Society received a £130,000 Department of Health grant in 1985. Following a routine audit in 1987, the Department of Health said that it would not continue funding unless the organisation either merged with Age Concern or significantly reformed its management structures. With a new chairman and treasurer appointed, and the selection of new committee members, the organisation's financial and legal controls were centralised, satisfying civil service concerns. Since then, income has doubled in size every two years, and by the late 1990s it employed 470 staff, 413 of whom provided care services for dementia patients.

Source: John Plummer *How Are Charities Accountable?* (London, 1996), pp. 16–17.

The state and the NGO sector

The notion that somehow NGOs (in whatever legal guise they may exist) are entirely independent of government is very much a misnomer. Whether it is through funding or regulation, the activities of government have had considerable impact on the shaping of the sector. By the end of the twentieth century it was reported that many organisations were reliant upon government grants for one-third of their income.

Box 9.5: The Deakin Report

The Deakin Report took the view that

'Government and voluntary organisations have many interests in common. They often can, and should, collaborate to achieve shared policy goals. Such collaboration has increased in recent years; the scale of activities of many voluntary organisations has been determined by the continuing provision of government funding. In itself this is desirable and effective.'

Commission on the Future of the Voluntary Sector, *Meeting the Challenge of Change: Voluntary Action into the 21st Century: The Report of the Commission on the Future of the Voluntary Sector* (Deakin Report) (London, 1996), p. 49.

Indeed, funding initiatives, such as the Department of Health and Social Security's 'Opportunities for Volunteering Scheme', launched in May 1982 with a budget of £3.3 million, and policy initiatives such as *Next Steps* (the 1988 reform of the civil service which devolved considerable amounts of executive responsibilities from the civil service to agencies focused on operational delivery), have often skewed the priorities of the NGO sector as organisations chase grants. Whilst many different departments of government (such as the Departments of Health and the Environment, and the Foreign Office) have made grants to NGOs since the 1970s, there have been a number of government units that have had very specific responsibility for the sector:

1. The *Voluntary Services Unit* was established in 1973 within the Home Office as a result of the 1969 Aves Report, with the initial aim of mounting rescue operations for worthwhile organisations and supporting the development and expansion of services. By 1998 it was giving grants totalling £11 million. Critics suggested that the VSU carried little political weight within Whitehall and was unable to influence the political agenda.
2. The *Manpower Services Commission* (MSC) provided 20 per cent of funding for the voluntary sector during the 1980s, of which 72 per cent was channelled through its Community Programme. By the time this programme finished in 1988, over half of its projects were delivered by voluntary organisations. Many contemporaries were sceptical at the time, believing that its initiatives were little more than attempts to massage the unemployment figures, and a number of organisations which became reliant upon its funding found themselves in difficulties when the money was withdrawn.
3. The *Audit Commission* was formed in April 1983 and, at the time of writing, is to be disbanded in December 2012. Its interest in the voluntary sector stems from its initial remit to scrutinise the expenditure of local government. Over the decades its area of coverage was expanded, and under provisions in the 1993 Charities Act it began to audit charities working in the National Health Service sector, as well as collaborating with the voluntary sector from 1996 over the National Fraud Initiative. It has produced a series of reports into the sector such as *Working with the Third Sector* (2005).
4. The *Office for the Third Sector* (Office for Civil Society from 2010), created in May 2006, coordinates the work of government in its support for what New Labour had identified as the third sector (voluntary and community groups, social enterprises, charities, co-operatives and mutuals). With the Cameron government's emphasis on Big Society, the office was renamed in May 2010.

With the growth of public funds being offered to the NGO sector came greater Whitehall anxiety about ensuring that the monies being used were delivering value for money and that the organisations in receipt were sufficiently accountable. In the 1970s there had been anxiety that some streams of funding were being used by organisations to then campaign against government. For example, the Campaign for the Homeless and Rootless (CHAR) received an emergency grant to continue its operation on the understanding that it would continue as a coordinating body for homeless groups rather than adopt a role as a pressure group. As the ethos of new public management ideals took hold within government, so came repeated government initiatives aimed at improving the accountability and management of the voluntary and charitable sector.

In this sense, it is clear that the Big Society is but the latest manifestation of a long-term relationship between the state and what has been variously called the voluntary sector, civil society, charity, NGOs and the third sector. This is not the place to draw extended lessons from the past, but two points do stand out. Firstly, to make a clear distinction between the governmental and the non-governmental is to ignore the reality of a far more complicated set of interactions. Secondly, the two have not been, and are unlikely to be, substitutes for one another. Indeed, states and NGOs have grown in parallel, with developments in one often triggering responses and expansions in the other.

Further reading

Contemporary reports on the state of the sector can offer useful insights into the nature and condition of the sector at a given point. See particularly John Wolfenden, *The Future of Voluntary Organisations: Report of the Wolfenden Committee* (London, 1978); Commission on the Future of the Voluntary Sector, *Meeting the Challenge of Change: Voluntary Action into the 21st Century: The Report of the Commission on the Future of the Voluntary Sector* (London, 1996), which is commonly referred to as the Deakin Report, and the NCVO and Centre for Civil Society, *Next Steps in Voluntary Action* (London, 2001).

For a series of case studies concerning the governance of charities, see John Plummer, *How Are Charities Accountable?* (London, 1996). Also, for the debates surrounding internal accountability and democracy, see Darren Halpin, 'NGOs and Democratisation: Assessing Variation in the Internal Democratic Practices of NGOs', in Nick Crowson, Matthew Hilton and James McKay (eds), *NGOs in Contemporary Britain: Non-State Actors in Society and Politics since 1945* (Basingstoke, 2009), pp. 261–80.

For a good overview of the development of the relationship between the state and the voluntary sector, see Nicholas Deakin, 'The Perils of Partnership', in Justin Davis Smith et al. (eds), *An Introduction to the Voluntary Sector* (London, 1995), pp. 40–65.

For a study of the impact of membership on organisational and campaign development, see Grant Jordan and William A. Maloney, *The Protest Business? Mobilizing Campaign Groups* (Manchester, 1997). This study uses Amnesty International and Friends of the Earth as case studies. For a retrospective sense of the experiences of volunteers and staffers who joined groups that emerged in the 1960s, see Helene Curtis and Mimi Sanderson (eds), *The Unsung Sixties: Memoirs of Social Innovation* (London, 2004).

10
International Comparisons

The trends outlined in this book can hardly be said to be specific to the United Kingdom. Clearly volunteering and philanthropy takes place all around the world. The types of new social movement associated with the 1960s emerged throughout Europe and North America. The spread of economic globalisation and the expanding infrastructure of global governance (that is, the United Nations and its myriad offshoots) gave rise to numerous transnational activist networks and international NGOs. And in more recent decades, NGOs have become more than just a Western or Northern phenomenon. Social movements, NGOs and advocacy groups have appeared in huge numbers across Africa, Asia and Latin America: following the end of the Cold War too and the creation of a civil society in the former Soviet bloc, the growth has been seemingly exponential.

Numerous scholars and officials have sought to capture this flourishing of non-profit activity (the term usually employed in the US). Yet so far, comparative data have not included trends over time. A true historical, international comparison of the NGO sector is therefore not possible. What is offered in the following pages is therefore largely a series of snapshots, as well as some pointers as to where such data are currently being generated. What is clear, though, is that Britain is by no means atypical and much future research is likely to be directed at capturing the dynamics and contours of what is frequently referred to as 'global civil society'.

Transnational actors

It is at the United Nations where the term 'NGO' was first commonly used, though it has also been attributed earlier to President Herbert Hoover. It is also the UN that has been the centre of gravity for international NGOs ever since. NGOs played a role in the very origins of the UN. At the San Francisco conference held in 1945 to set out its the UN's Charter, a number of NGOs were also in attendance. Forty-two NGOs worked with the official US delegation alone in advising on the economic and social aspects of international relations, while a total of 1,200 voluntary groups had some form of presence in San Francisco. Although the creation of the UN was undoubtedly the product of the diplomacy of the great powers, it is often argued that the outcome of the conference provides an early example of the global impact of NGOs. The opening words of the UN Charter – 'We, the peoples of the United Nations …' – have been attributed to the presence of NGOs, as has the inclusion of Article 71 which enabled the Economic and Social Council (ECOSOC) to communicate with NGOs.

The UN has built up an incredible bureaucracy for dealing with NGOs, which itself has further stimulated the creation of international NGOs. ECOSOC granted 'consultative status' to a number of NGOs, especially those dealing with social, economic and humanitarian issues. It also used a broad-ranging definition of NGO (see Chapter 1), such that while it included the sorts of large-scale member organisations included in this book (for example, Rotary International), it also included economic interest groups such as the International Conference of Free Trade Unions and the International Chamber of Commerce. In subsequent years, they have been joined by a whole range of NGO actors, participating in both ECOSOC and UN-sponsored conferences. By 1990, there were more than 90 UN offices handling NGO relations and, to cite just one example, 4,000 NGOs participated in the Beijing Women's Conference of 1995.

Figure 10.1 shows the number of NGOs formally recognised by the UN. The nature of 'consultative status' at ECOSOC has been periodically revised, but if we include all types of organisation (see Figure 10.1) the figure has increased from 41 in 1948, to 377 in 1968, to 1,350 in 1998 and over 2,500 from 2005. British NGOs have not

---

Box 10.1: NGO consultative status at the United Nations

Article 71 of the UN Charter enabled ECOSOC to enter into special consultation arrangements with NGOs. Today, NGOs are granted consultative status according to three categories, as set out in ECOSOC Resolution 1996/31 (available at http://esango. un.org/paperless/reports/1996_31_E.pdf). The three categories are:

General
'Organizations that are concerned with most of the activities of the Council and its subsidiary bodies and can demonstrate to the satisfaction of the Council that they have substantive and sustained contributions to make to the achievement of the objectives of the United Nations … and are closely involved with the economic and social life of the peoples of the areas they represent and whose membership, which should be considerable, is broadly representative of major segments of society in a large number of countries in different regions of the world.'

Special
'Organizations that have a special competence in, and are concerned specifically with, only a few of the fields of activity covered by the Council and its subsidiary bodies, and that are known within the fields for which they have or seek consultative status.'

Roster
'Other organizations that do not have general or special consultative status but that the Council, or the Secretary-General of the United Nations in consultation with the Council or its Committee on Non-Governmental Organizations, considers can make occasional and useful contributions to the work of the Council or its subsidiary bodies or other United Nations bodies within their competence.'

been an inconsiderable presence at the UN. Figure 10.2 shows that today around 180 British-based NGOs have consultative status at the UN which, as a proportion, has been around 5 per cent and 10 per cent of the total (see Figure 10.3).

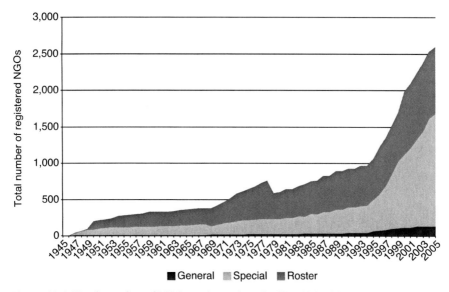

Figure 10.1: Total number of NGOs registered at the UN, 1945–2005

Sources: *Global Civil Society 2005–6* (London, 2006), p. 421 (chapter available online at www.lse.ac.uk/Depts/global/Publications/Yearbooks/2005/recordsection05.pdf); UN website, www.un.org/esa/coordination/ngo/.

The UN, though, just represents the pinnacle of international NGO activity. The actual number is likely to be much higher, though definitions vary. One study, conducted by John Boli and George Thomas,[1] estimated that there were 200 active organisations in 1900. By 1930 there were around 300 international NGOs, a figure which increased to 2,000 in 1960 and 4,000 by 1980. In 2000, the figure was estimated to be 13,000. However, the *Yearbook of International Organisations*, published by the Union of International Association, lists 63,993 such organisations in 2010. Here, though, the definition is much looser, incorporating any national-based NGO that nevertheless tackles global issues. The boundaries of such a definition can then become very wide indeed, and the figure could run into many hundreds of thousands.

If counting is difficult, measuring effectiveness verges on the impossible and at least goes beyond the scope of this volume. However, some attempts have been made. To cite just one example, Harold Jacobson, a political scientist, in the early 1980s counted the number of formal consultative arrangements international NGOs had with various intergovernmental agencies: not just that of ECOSOC but the less precisely worded arrangements set out by the likes of the Food and Agriculture

1   John Boli and George M. Thomas, 'INGOs and the Organisation of World Culture', in John Boli and George M. Thomas, *Constructing World Culture: International Nongovernmental Organisations since 1875* (Stanford CA, 1999), pp. 13–49.

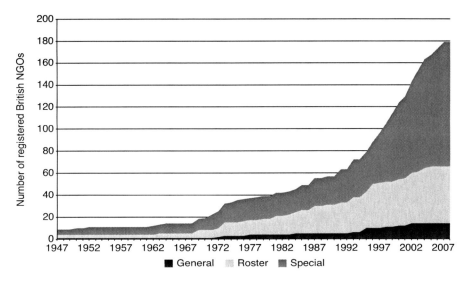

Figure 10.2: Growth in the number of British NGOs registered at the UN in various categories, 1947–2007

Note: The data for British NGOs have been extracted from the UN NGO database using advanced search with country 'United Kingdom', available at: http://esa.un.org/coordination/ngo/new/index. asp?page=advSearchPage.

Sources: *Global Civil Society 2005–6* (London, 2006), p. 421 (chapter available online at www.lse.ac.uk/Depts/ global/Publications/Yearbooks/2005/recordsection05.pdf); UN website, www.un.org/esa/coordination/ngo/.

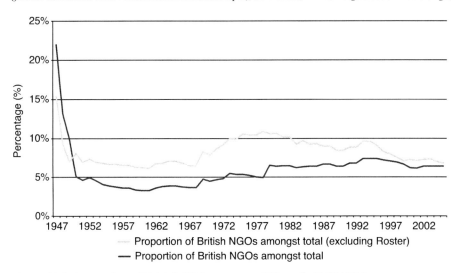

Figure 10.3: Proportion of British NGOs amongst UN total, 1947–2005

Note: The data for British NGOs have been extracted from the UN NGO database using advanced search with country 'United Kingdom', available at: http://esa.un.org/coordination/ngo/new/index. asp?page=advSearchPage.

Sources: *Global Civil Society 2005–6* (London, 2006), p. 421 (chapter available online at www.lse.ac.uk/Depts/ global/Publications/Yearbooks/2005/recordsection05.pdf); UN website, www.un.org/esa/coordination/ngo/.

Organisation, the World Health Organisation, and the International Labour Office. He awarded points (out of a maximum of 60) based on the number and strength of these associations (for example, 3 points for 'general' status at ECOSOC, 2 for 'special', 1 for 'roster'). Table 10.1 shows the top-ranking organisations. It includes

Table 10.1: International NGOs ranked by extent of consultative relationships with intergovernmental organisations

NGO	Points
International Organisation for Standardisation	37
International Chamber of Commerce	33
International Council of Voluntary Agencies	26
World Confederation of Labour	26
International Federation of Agricultural Producers	25
International Confederation of Free Trade Unions	24
World Confederation of Organisations of the Teaching Profession	23
International Co-operative Alliance	20
International Union for Conservation of Nature and Natural Resources	20
League of Red Cross Societies	20
Co-operative for American Relief Everywhere	19
International Council of Women	19
International Council on Social Welfare	19
International Electrotechnical Commission	18
International Organisation of Consumers Unions	18
World Federation of Trade Unions	18
World Federation of United Nations Associations	18
International Union of Architects	17
European Confederation of Agriculture	16
International Planned Parenthood Federation	16
World Veterans' Federation	16
International Commission on Irrigation and Drainage	15
International Commission on Radiological Protection	15
International Council of Scientific Unions	15
International Council on Jewish Social and Welfare Services	15
International Federation for Home Economics	15
Commission of the Churches on International Affairs	14
International Chamber of Shipping	14
International Social Service	14
International Union for Child Welfare	14
International Union of Family Organisations	14
International Cargo Handling Coordination Association	13
International Union of Socialist Youth	13
Rehabilitation International	13
Catholic International Union for Social Service	12
International Union of Local Authorities	12
Soroptimist International Association	12
World Crafts Council	12
World Jewish Congress	12
World Union of Catholic Women's Organisations	12
World Young Women's Christian Association	12

Source: Harold K. Jacobson, *Networks of Interdependence: International Organisations and the Global Political System*, 2nd edn (New York, 1984), pp. 411–12.

the sorts of economic interest group defined as NGOs by the UN but excluded from our own definition (see Chapter 1). As with the evidence for Britain, the more prominent NGOs are not necessarily those that have obtained the highest media profile. According to this, admittedly limited, measure of effectiveness, the top-ranking NGOs include the International Council of Voluntary Agencies, the International Union for Conservation of Nature and Natural Resources and the League of Red Cross Societies, the International Organisation of Consumers Unions and the World Federation of United Nations Associations.

What such measures do not do is capture the sheer breadth of operations of many of today's more prominent international NGOs. They have become global brands operating in dozens of different countries around the world. Those working in the sphere of international aid and development, for instance, have entered into formal relationships with governments around the world. Figure 10.4 shows just how much the presence of NGOs has increased through their officially recognised work.

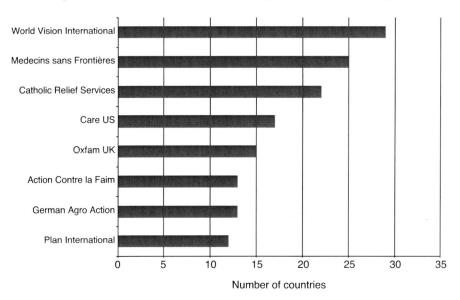

Figure 10.4: Number of countries with which main international NGO partners collaborate with the United Nations World Food Programme

Source: *Global Civil Society 2009* (London, 2009), pp. 298–9.

Comparative data

If the historical data on international NGOs is limited, this is also the case when one wants to make meaningful comparisons over time between NGOs in Britain and those in other countries. What can only be offered at this stage of research is a series of snapshots that relate to some of the issues that have been tracked in the previous chapters. For instance, we can get a sense of the relative importance of NGO activity in different countries through the proportion of the workforce either being paid or volunteering for the organisation. Data collected from or around 1995 are presented in Figure 10.5, showing that while Britain's non-profit sector's share of total employment was much higher than the average, it still fell short of a number of countries, especially the Netherlands where getting on for one-fifth of the population was either paid to work or volunteered for NGOs.

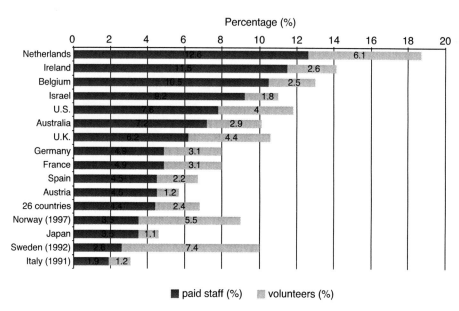

■ paid staff (%)   volunteers (%)

Figure 10.5: Non-profit share of total employment, with and without volunteers, by country, c. 1995

Source: Johns Hopkins Comparative Nonprofit Sector Project, *Global Civil Society At-a-Glance* (Johns Hopkins University, 2001), p. 5.

One of the more interesting measures to facilitate international comparison is the Global Civil Society Index developed at the London School of Economics' Centre for Civil Society and Centre for the Study of Global Governance. This generates a single figure based on a basket of measures including levels of political participation, membership of civil society groups and the membership density of international NGOs in any one country. However, it also includes the more normative criteria of levels of tolerance towards immigrants and the extent to which toleration is encouraged in children. A similar Global Civil Society Index has been generated by researchers at the Centre for Civil Society Studies at the Johns Hopkins Institute for Policy Studies. This creates a score based on three criteria: 'capacity', which measures the size of the sector through its levels of employment, number of volunteers, the amount of charitable contributions (as a proportion of GDP) and the diversity of the sector; 'sustainability' which measures NGOs' generation of their own income, the amount of government funding, overall volunteering rates in a country, and the legal environment that regulates the voluntary sector; and 'impact', as measured by the overall economic contribution to the economy, the share of total employment in the country, the funds dedicated to advocacy and lobbying, the proportion of adults being a member of an organisation, plus an assessment of NGO operations as judged by examination of case studies. The results covering the first few years of the new millennium show Britain's relatively high performance according to this index, with only the Netherlands, Australia and the US obtaining higher overall scores (see Figure 10.6).

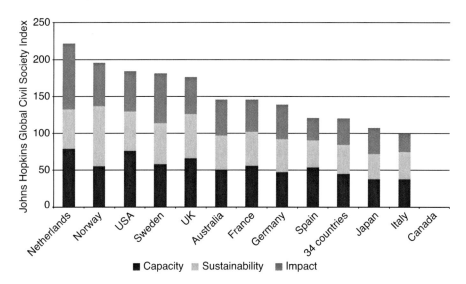

Figure 10.6: Johns Hopkins Global Civil Society Index

Source: Lester M. Salamon and S. Wojciech Sokolowski, 'Measuring Civil Society: The Johns Hopkins Global Civil Society Index', in Lester M. Salamon, S. Wojciech Sokolowski and Associates, *Global Civil Society: Dimensions of the Non-Profit Sector*, Vol. 2 (Bloomfield, CT, 2004), p. 78.

Indeed, if we look at snapshots of any of these figures, Britain stands well in comparison with other countries. Volunteering rates and levels of private giving were high over the period 1995–2002 (see Figure 10.7), while levels of government funding for the NGO sector have been generally high (see Figure 10.8). Likewise, government support of NGOs, especially of international NGOs, has also increased in recent years, a trend which has been commonplace across the developed world (see Figure 10.9).

Social capital

Some of the most useful comparative data has been generated by the World Values Survey. Although this has only intermittently been conducted since the early 1980s, and originally had a strong European bias, it nevertheless captures many of the social and political values of societies in ways that relate to the expansion of NGOs and their impact. For instance, one of the key debates in recent years has been about the

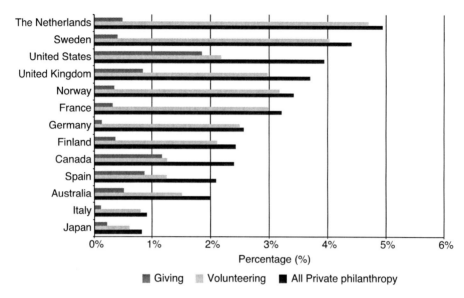

Figure 10.7: Volunteering and giving as a share of GDP by country, including gifts to religious worship organisations where available, c. 1995–2002

Source: Johns Hopkins Comparative Nonprofit Sector Project, 'Private Philanthropy Across the World', available at: www.ccss.jhu.edu/pdfs/CNP/CNP_comptable5_dec05.pdf.

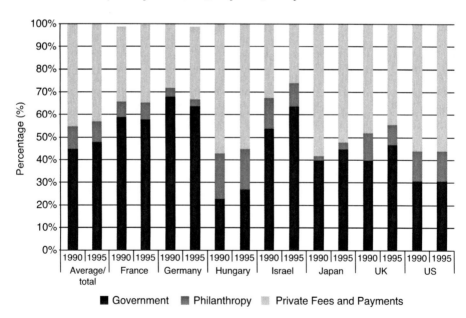

Figure 10.8: Changes in share of non-profit revenue (adjusted for inflation, 2009), by source and country, 1990–95

Source: Johns Hopkins Comparative Nonprofit Sector Project, 'Changes in Nonprofit Revenue (Inflation Adjusted), by Source and Country, 1990–95', available at www.ccss.jhu.edu/pdfs/CNP/ct11.pdf.

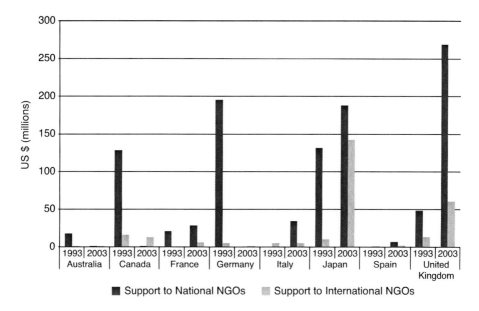

Figure 10.9: Government support for NGOs, national and international, 1993–2003

Source: *Global Civil Society 2005/6*, p. 425, available at: www2.lse.ac.uk/internationalDevelopment/research/CSHS/civilSociety/yearBook/contentsPages/2005-2006.aspx.

extent to which affluent societies have become more politically apathetic, especially in the UK and the US. One of the reasons given is that people are less willing to 'join in' and less likely to trust one another. Yet the comparative data, based on people's own statements as to whether they are members of different types of organisation, suggest that the British are broadly in line with those in equivalent countries (see Figure 10.10) and, on certain issues such as international aid and humanitarianism, show a strong tendency to get involved. Figures 10.11–10.14 present a number of case studies of sectors to show comparative rates of volunteering, including both active and inactive forms of membership.

Likewise, when it comes to issues of trust, the evidence for the British public's unwillingness to trust strangers or people from different backgrounds is also patchy. Indeed, Figures 10.15–10.17 suggest that in some circumstances the British are more trusting. But since such evidence is highly subjective, one cannot read too much into it. The most significant point, as with surveys conducted within the UK, is that it is difficult to make highly confident assertions either way about the rates of social trust.

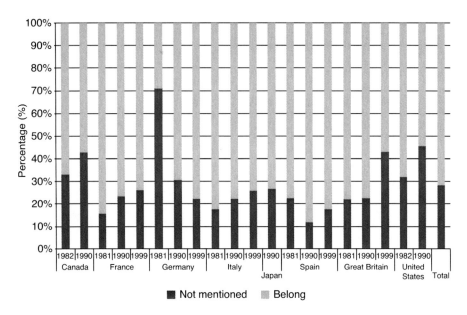

Figure 10.10: Proportion of public who did not mention any form of volunteering, selected years

Source: World Values Survey.

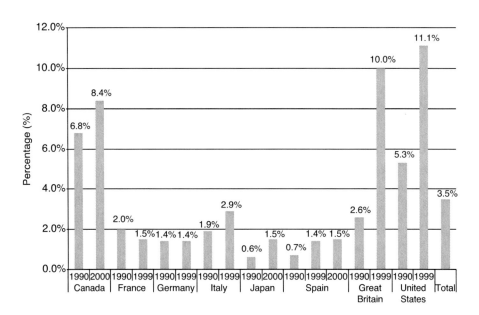

Figure 10.11: Proportion of population who engage in unpaid work for organisations concerned with health issues, selected years

Source: World Values Survey.

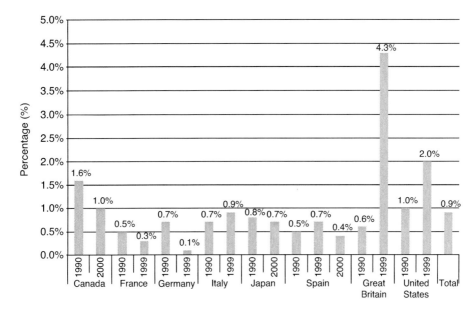

Figure 10.12: Proportion of population who engage in unpaid work for organisations concerned with peace, selected years

Source: World Values Survey.

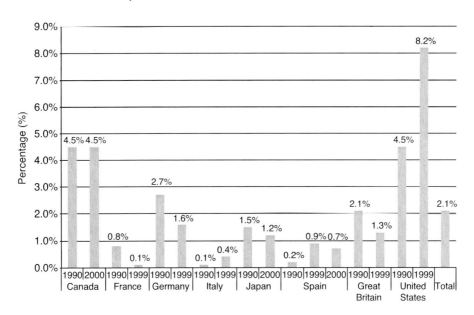

Figure 10.13: Proportion of population who engage in unpaid work for women's organisations, selected years

Source: World Values Survey.

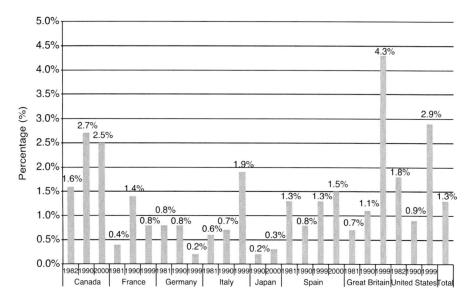

Figure 10.14: Proportion of population who engage in unpaid work for organisations concerned with human rights, selected years

Source: World Values Survey.

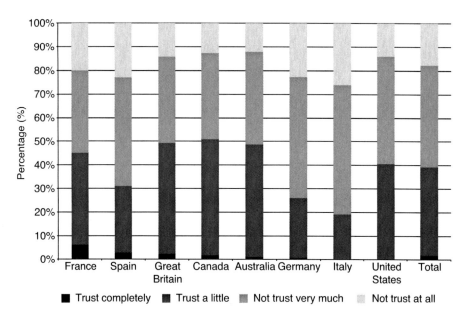

Figure 10.15: Trust in strangers, c. 2006

Source: World Values Survey.

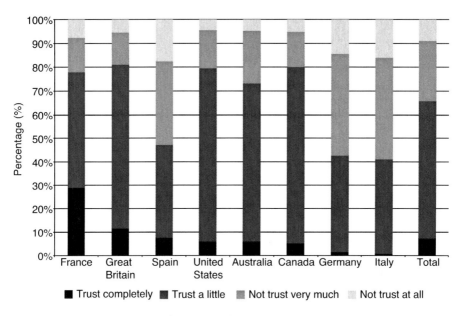

Figure 10.16: Trust in people of another religion, c. 2006

Source: *World Values Survey.*

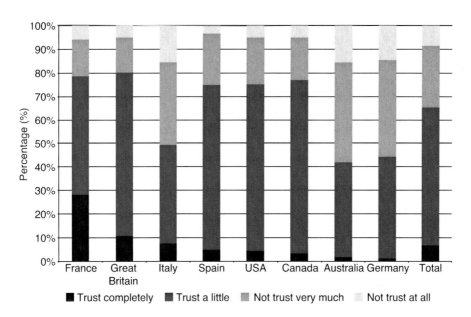

Figure 10.17: Trust in people of another nationality, c. 2006

Source: World Values Survey.

Political participation

Similarly, when it comes to issues of political apathy, the comparative data also suggest that Britain is in line with many other affluent Western countries and that interest in politics remains high. Figure 10.18 shows that the stated interest in politics by the British public is roughly the same as in equivalent countries.

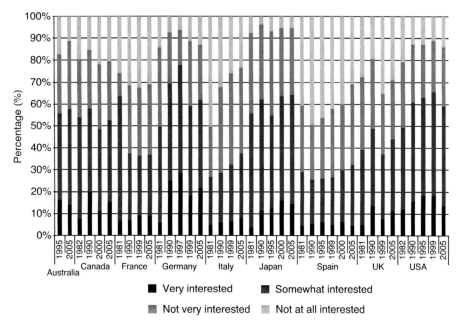

Figure 10.18: Interest in politics, selected years

Source: World Values Survey.

Given the evidence that has been presented for the UK in earlier chapters, it may well be that such interest does not manifest itself in high membership rates of mainstream political parties or voter turnout rates at elections. An interesting index used in this regard is that developed by Ronald Inglehart. As a major figure in the creation and work of the World Values Survey, Inglehart has encouraged the testing of whether people are interested in politics for materialist or post-materialist reasons. That is, are people more concerned about defending their material needs (wages, economic growth, job security, and so on) or their post-materialist values (for example, concern for civil and human rights, the environment, international aid). The former have been more usually associated with the agendas of political parties and the latter with the campaigns of new socio-political actors such as NGOs, charities and voluntary associations. The World Values Survey has attempted to trace the respective motivations for people's interest in politics, and Figure 10.19 shows some simplified results. Although only slight, the trend since the early 1980s is for the increasing importance of post-materialist political concerns, with Britain being roughly in line with other affluent Western states.

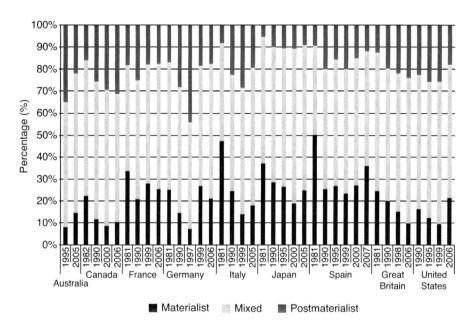

Figure 10.19: Inglehart's indicators of material and post-material motivations, selected years

Source: World Values Survey.

If post-materialism is a factor, we might also expect citizens to behave in alternative forms of political action. The Survey has attempted to assess the public's willingness to engage in various tactics, as well as their stated expressions of having done so. What the comparative data suggest here is that the British public are less willing to engage in more extreme or radical forms of political action: their willingness to occupy buildings (Figure 10.20), undertake unofficial strikes (Figure 10.21) or attend a demonstration (Figure 10.22) tends to be at the average or slightly lower. Yet the public are slightly more likely to sign a petition (Figure 10.23) or boycott a product (Figure 10.24): that is, precisely those tactics associated with modern NGOs. Again, though, considerable care needs to be taken in dealing with such evidence. The divergences from the mean may be too insignificant to make any assessment of typicality, and the subjective nature of the questions and responses remains a factor. Despite the evidence of Figures 10.20–10.22, one similar survey of people's stated claim to have engaged in physical damage to property as a political tactic showed that Britain ranked highest among Western European and North American states.

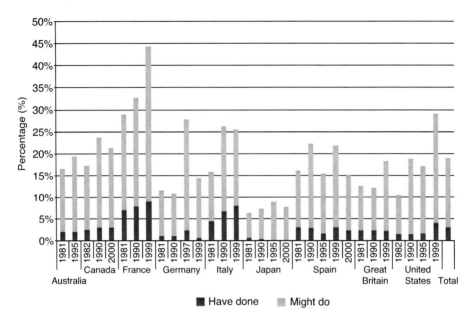

Figure 10.20: Political action: occupying buildings or factories, selected years

Source: World Values Survey.

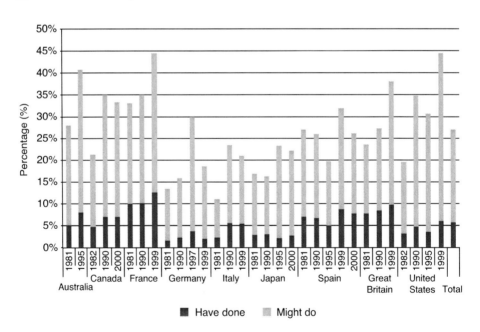

Figure 10.21: Political action: joining unofficial strikes, selected years

Source: World Values Survey.

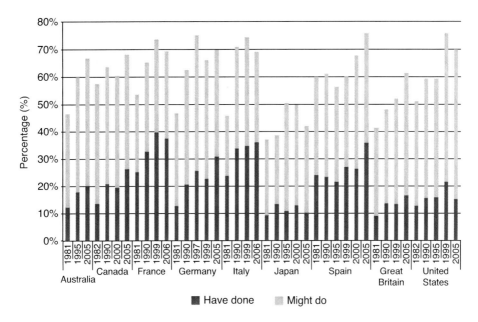

Figure 10.22: Political action: attending lawful demonstrations, selected years

Source: World Values Survey.

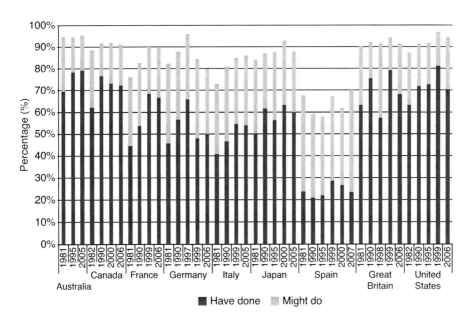

Figure 10.23: Political action: signing a petition, selected years

Source: World Values Survey.

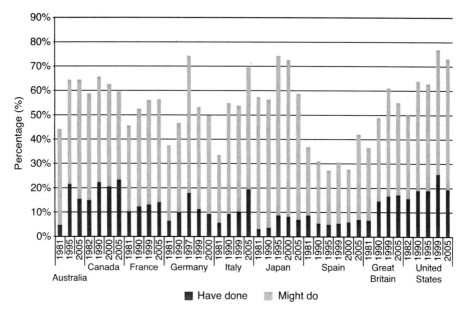

Figure 10.24: Political action: joining a boycott, selected years

Source: World Values Survey.

Impact of NGOs

Measuring the impact of NGOs, voluntary associations and charities is clearly one of the most difficult forms of research to undertake. The World Values Survey, though, does provide certain forms of evidence that go some way to assessing this from country to country. One question it has regularly fielded is whether respondents approve of particular social movements. Although the evidence presented in Figures 10.25–10.30 is confined to those with more radical or controversial wings (as opposed to, say, international aid and development), it does give a sense of how organisations have come to be regarded in each country. What stands out is that, despite the comparatively high levels of volunteering, membership and support for NGOs observed in other indices, here the evidence suggests that socio-political organisations have not won over the general British public to quite the same extent as they have in other countries.

Yet again, though, care must be taken when using such international data. Against the trends recorded in the previous figures, the British public have shown a strong affinity with aid and development causes. When asked if they would be willing to pay higher taxes in order to increase foreign aid, British citizens approved at levels slightly above the average (see Figure 10.31), suggesting that in this sphere at least, aid and development NGOs have had some impact on the general public.

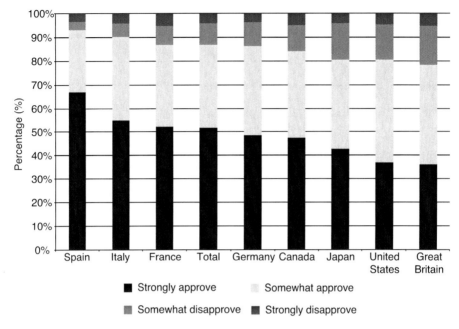

Figure 10.25: Approval of movements: anti-apartheid, 1990

Source: World Values Survey.

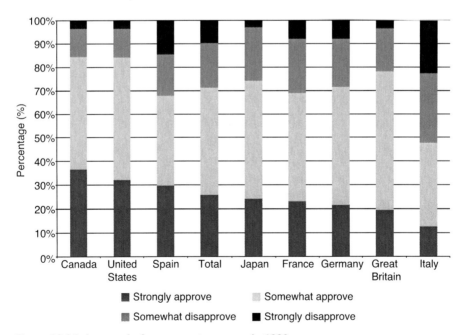

Figure 10.26: Approval of movements: women's, 1990

Source: World Values Survey.

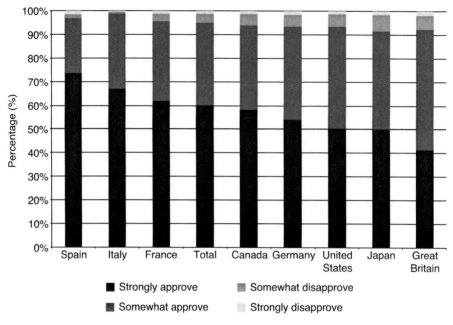

Figure 10.27: Approval of movements: human rights, 1990

Source: World Values Survey.

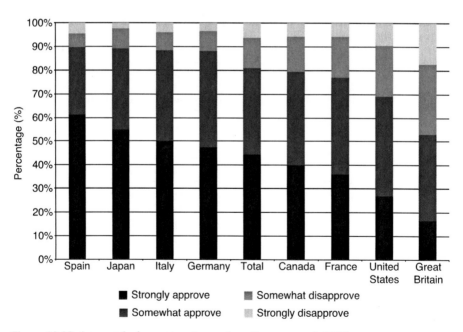

Figure 10.28: Approval of movements: nuclear disarmament, 1990

Source: World Values Survey.

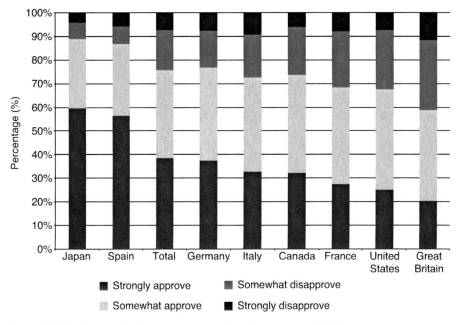

Figure 10.29: Approval of movements: anti-nuclear energy, 1990

Source: World Values Survey.

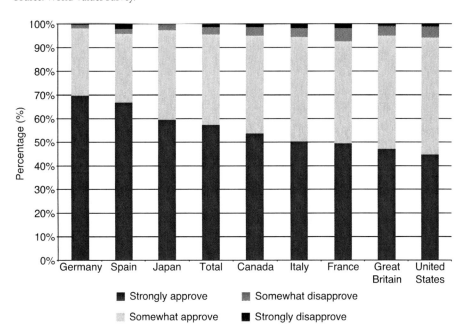

Figure 10.30: Approval of movements: ecology or nature protection, 1990

Source: World Values Survey.

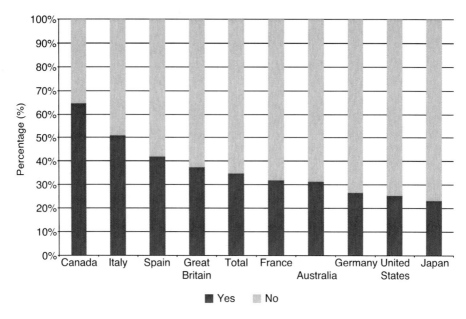

Figure 10.31: Willingness to pay higher taxes in order to increase foreign aid, c. 2006

Source: World Values Survey.

However, the higher approval ratings for other social movements in different countries ought not to be used as the basis for making too exaggerated claims. There are limits placed on the trust invested in these institutions. When it comes to deciding who should make the final judgements about issues such as human rights or international aid, publics around the world invariably place more faith in government and intergovernmental institutions. Survey data invariably find in all countries that the high authority in which NGO opinion is held ought not to be translated into an executive function. Ultimately, it is felt that elected bodies should decide, the support for NGO decision making often being negligible.

Further reading and guide to further information

There are a number of official sources of data collection as well as academic research projects that have been attempting to compile international and comparative data. Some of the most important include:

- Eurobarometer (http://ec.europa.eu/public_opinion/index_en.htm)
- Johns Hopkins Center for Civil Society Studies (www.ccss.jhu.edu/)
- London School of Economics (LSE) Centre for the Study of Global Governance (www.lse.ac.uk/Depts/global/researchgcsresearch.htm)
- Union of International Associations (UIA) (www.uia.be)
- United Nations NGO resources (www.un.org/esa/coordination/ngo/)
- World Values Survey (www.worldvaluessurvey.org)

Some of the most useful publications coming out of this include the UIA's Yearbook of International Associations, available at: www.uia.be/yearbook; the LSE's Global Civil Society Yearbook, of which the most recent is Martin Albrow and Hakan Seckinelgin, *Global Civil Society 2011: Globality and Absence of Justice* (London, 2010); and the overviews provided by Johns Hopkins University: Lester M. Salamon, S. Wojciech Sokolowski and Associates, *Global Civil Society: Dimensions of the Non-Profit Sector* (Baltimore, MD, 1999), and *Global Civil Society: Dimensions of the Non-Profit Sector, Vol. 2* (Bloomfield, CT, 2004).

For work on NGOs and the UN, see William Korey, *NGOs and the Universal Declaration of Human Rights: 'A Curious Grapevine'* (Basingstoke, 1998), pp. 29–50; Chadwick Alger, 'The Emerging Roles of NGOs in the UN System: From Article 71 to a People's Millennium Assembly', *Global Governance*, 8 (2002), pp. 93–117; Peter Willets (ed.), *'The Conscience of the World': The Influence of Non-Governmental Organisations in the UN System* (London, 1996); Harold K. Jacobson, *Networks of Interdependence: International Organisations and the Global Political System*, 2nd edn (New York, 1984), and Kerstin Martens, *NGOs and the United Nations: Institutionalisation, Professionalisation and Adaptation* (Basingstoke, 2005).

More generally, there is a historical literature emerging that acknowledges the role of NGOs on the global politics stage: Akira Iriye, *Global Community: The Role of International Organisations in the Making of the Contemporary World* (Berkeley, CA, 2002); John Boli and George M. Thomas, 'INGOs and the Organisation of World Culture', in John Boli and George M. Thomas, *Constructing World Culture: International Nongovernmental Organisations since 1875* (Stanford, CA, 1999), pp. 13–49; Helmut Anheier, Marlies Glasius and Mary Kaldor (eds), *Global Civil Society 2001* (Oxford, 2001); Bruce Mazlish, *The New Global History* (New York, 2006); Bruce Mazlish and Akira Iriye (eds), *The Global History Reader* (New York, 2005); Paul M. Kennedy, *The Parliament of Man: The United Nations and the Quest for World Government* (London, 2006), and John Bayliss, Steve Smith and Patricia Owens, *The Globalization of World Politics: An Introduction to International Relations*, 4th edn (Oxford, 2007).

For a literature on transnational activism, see Margaret E. Keck and Kathryn Sikkink, *Activists beyond Borders: Advocacy Networks in International Politics* (Ithaca, NY, 1998); John Clark (ed.), *Globalising Civic Engagement: Civil Society and Transnational Action* (London: Earthscan, 2003); John Keane, *Global Civil Society* (Cambridge, 2003); Mary Kaldor, *Global Civil Society: An Answer to War* (Cambridge, 2003); John Clark, *Worlds Apart: Civil Society and the Battle for Ethical Globalisation* (London, 2003), and Manuel Castells, *The Information Age: Economy, Society and Culture: Vol. I. The Rise of the Network Society*, 2nd edn (Oxford, 2000).

For work on international social movements, see David A. Snow, Sarah A. Soule and Hanspeter Kriesi (eds), *The Blackwell Companion to Social Movements* (Oxford, 2004); Sydney Tarrow, *Power in Movement: Social Movements and Contentious Politics*, 2nd edn (Cambridge, 1998); Donatella Della Porta and Mario Diani, *Social Movements: An Introduction* (Oxford, 1998), and Steven M. Buechler, *Social Movements in Advanced Capitalism: The Political Economy and Cultural Construction of Social Activism* (Oxford, 2000).

And for an introduction to Ingelhart's post-materialism, see Ronald Inglehart, *The Silent Revolution: Changing Values and Political Styles among Western Publics* (Princeton, NJ, 1977). But see also Frank Parkin *Middle-Class Radicalism: The Social Bases of the British Campaign for Nuclear Disarmament* (Manchester, 1968); Alain Touraine, *The Voice and the Eye* (Cambridge, 1981); Alberto Melucci *Nomads of the Present* (London, 1988), and Alberto Melucci, *Challenging Codes: Collective Action in the Information Age* (Cambridge, 1996).

Index

To be used in conjunction with the lists of tables and figures